Oh My Goddess!

ああ女神さま

QUEEN SAYOKO

Oh My Goddess!

ああっ女神さまっ

QUEEN SAYOKO

v.14

STORY AND ART BY

Kosuke Fujishima

TRANSLATION BY

Dana Lewis & Toren Smith

LETTERING AND TOUCH-UP BY

Susie Lee & PC Orz

DARK HORSE COMICS®

PUBLISHER
Mike Richardson

SERIES EDITOR
Mike Hansen

COLLECTION EDITOR
Chris Warner

COLLECTION DESIGNER
Amy Arendts

ART DIRECTOR
Mark Cox

English-language version produced by Studio Proteus
for Dark Horse Comics, Inc.

OH MY GODDESS! Vol. XIV: Queen Sayoko

This volume collects issues one through seven of the Dark Horse comic book series *Oh My Goddess! Part IX.*

Published by
Dark Horse Comics, Inc.
10956 SE Main Street
Milwaukie, OR 97222

www.darkhorse.com

To find a comics shop in your area, call the Comic Shop
Locator Service toll-free at 1-888-266-4226

First edition: November 2002
ISBN: 1-56971-766-4

1 3 5 7 9 10 8 6 4 2
Printed in Canada

Pretty in Scarlet

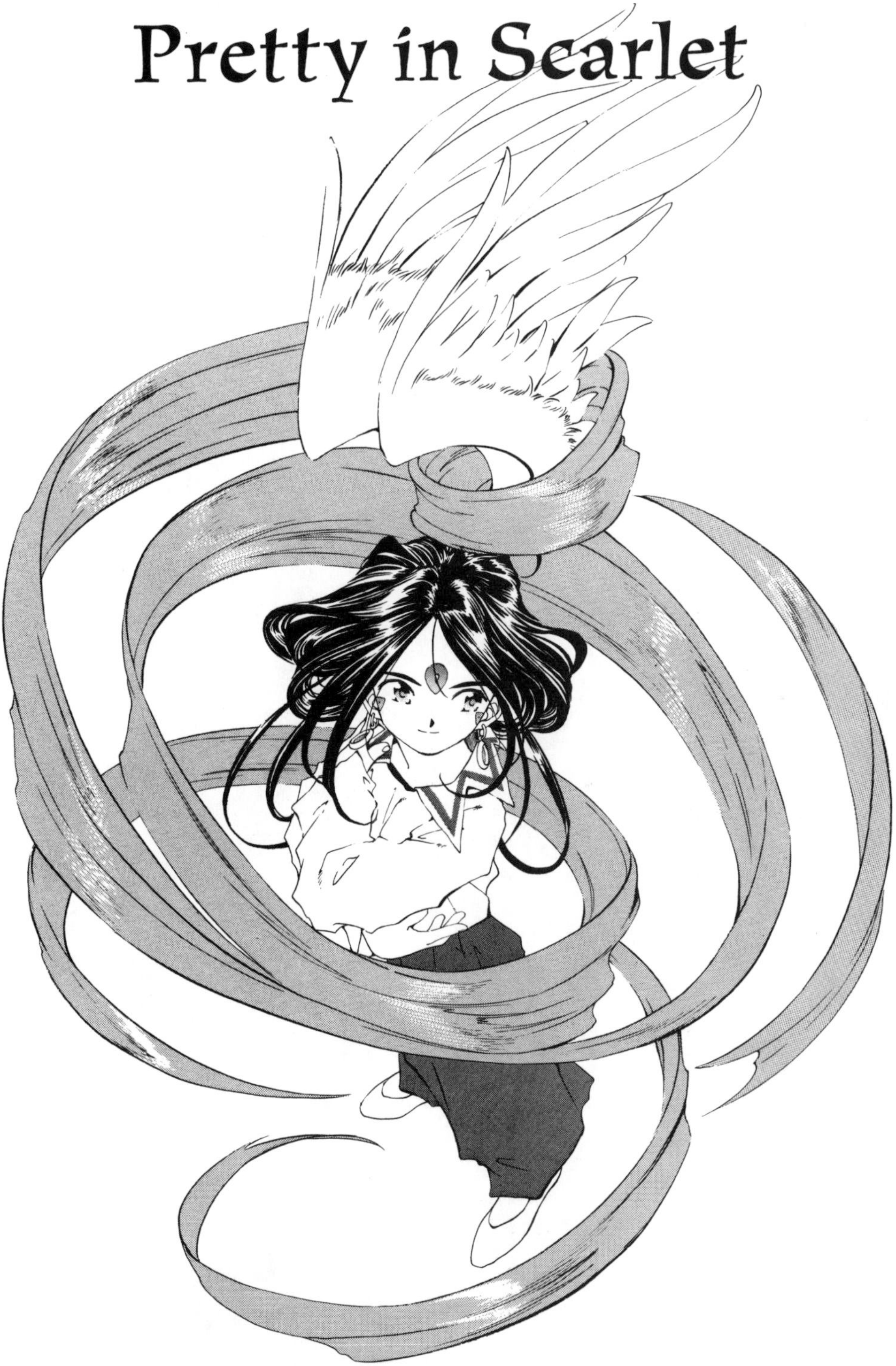

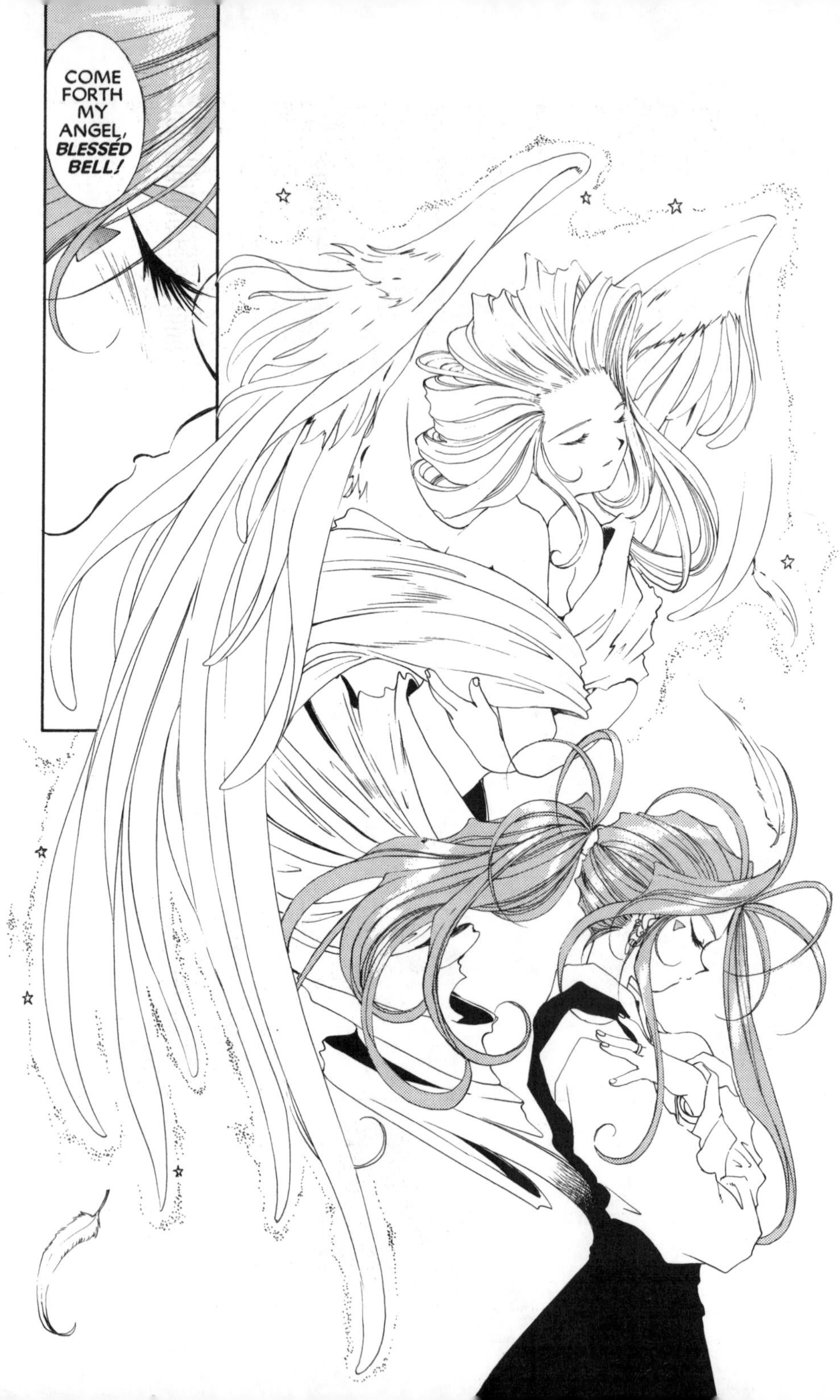
COME FORTH MY ANGEL, BLESSED BELL!

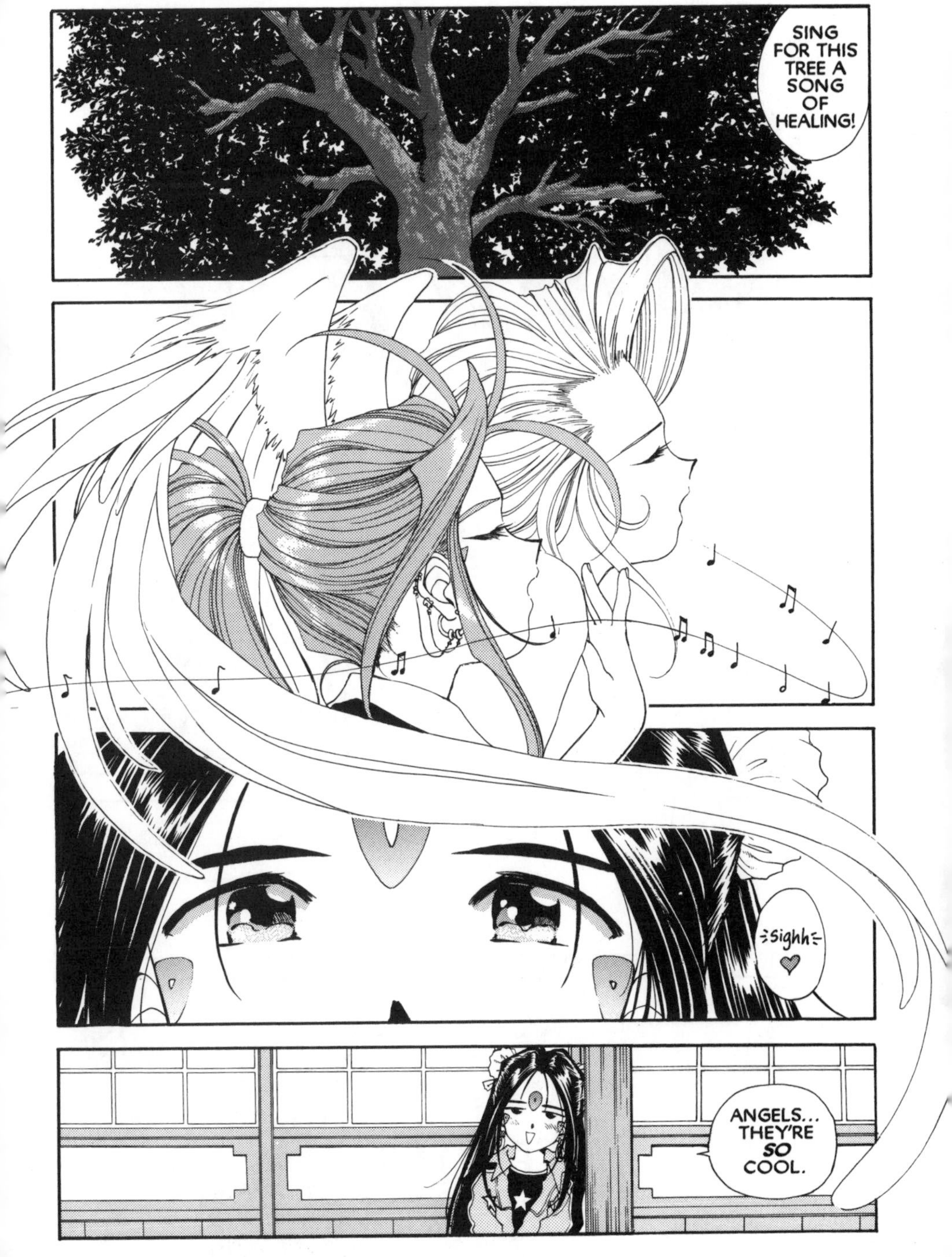
SING FOR THIS TREE A SONG OF HEALING!
Sighh
ANGELS... THEY'RE SO COOL.

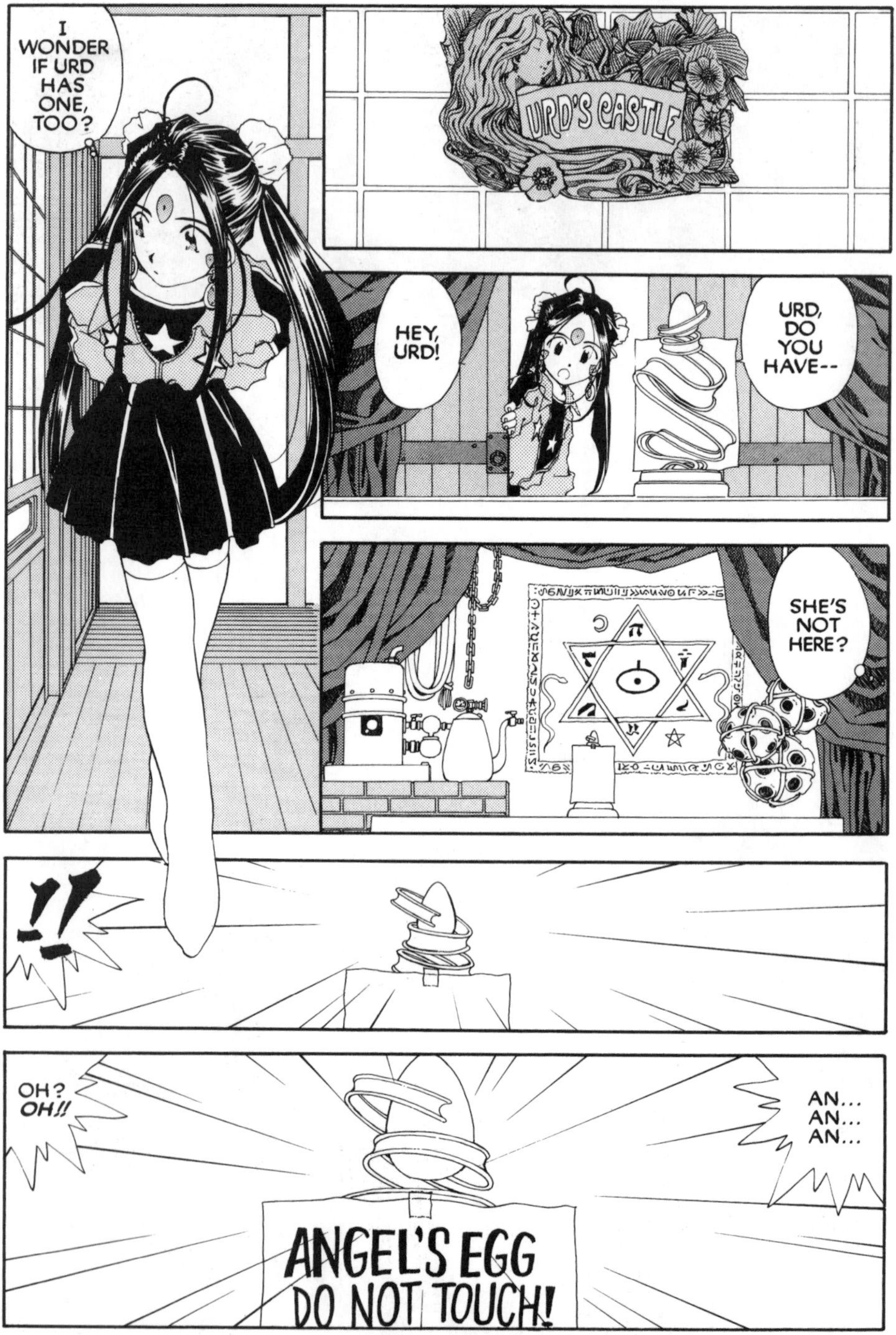
I WONDER IF URD HAS ONE, TOO?
URD'S CASTLE
HEY, URD!
URD, DO YOU HAVE--
SHE'S NOT HERE?
!!
OH? OH!!
AN... AN... AN...
ANGEL'S EGG
DO NOT TOUCH!

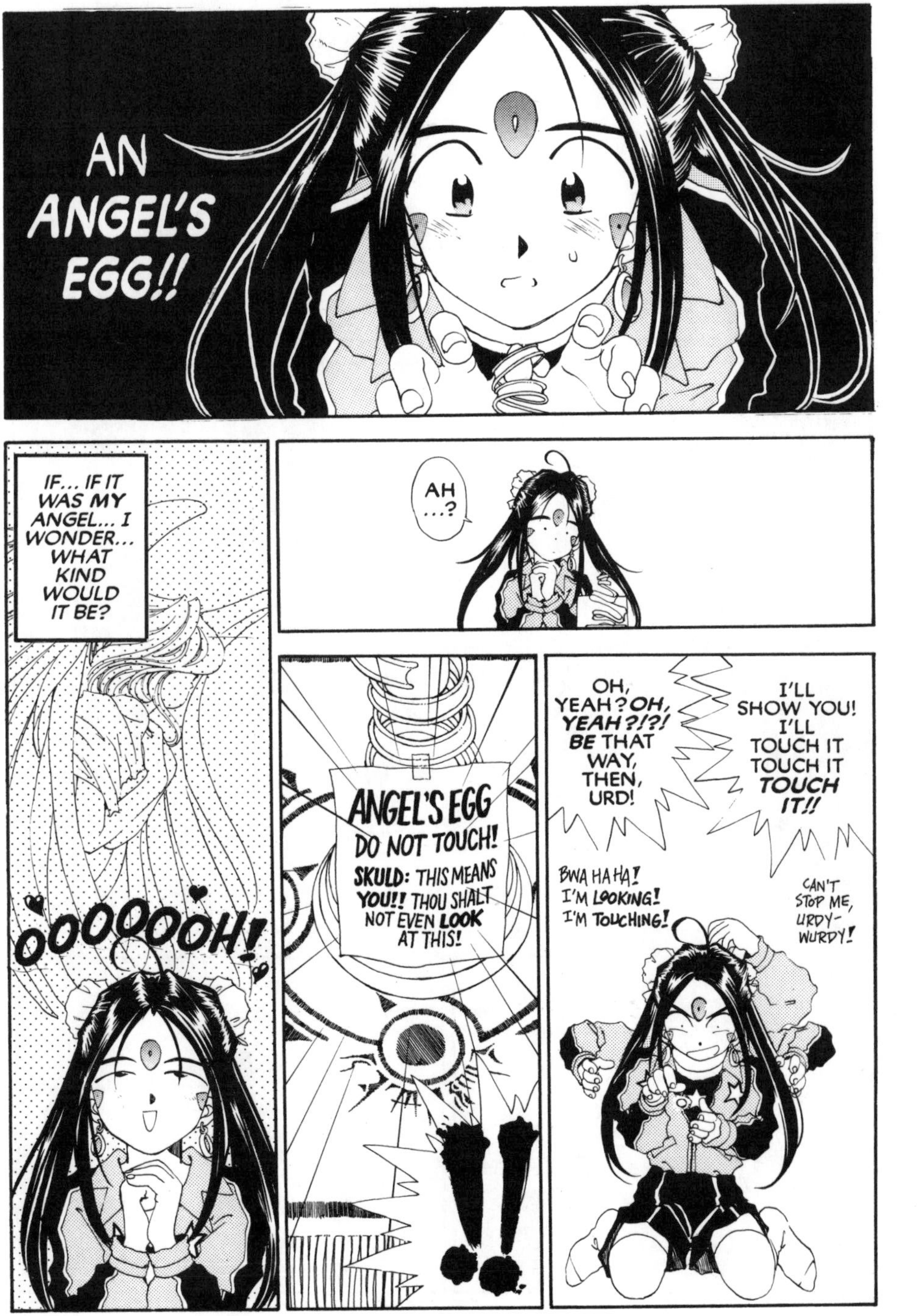
AN ANGEL'S EGG!!
IF... IF IT WAS MY ANGEL... I WONDER... WHAT KIND WOULD IT BE?
AH ...?
OOOOOOH!
ANGEL'S EGG DO NOT TOUCH! SKULD: THIS MEANS YOU!! THOU SHALT NOT EVEN LOOK AT THIS!
OH, YEAH? OH, YEAH?!?! BE THAT WAY, THEN, URD!
I'LL SHOW YOU! I'LL TOUCH IT TOUCH IT TOUCH IT!!
BWA HA HA! I'M LOOKING! I'M TOUCHING!
CAN'T STOP ME, URDY-WURDY!

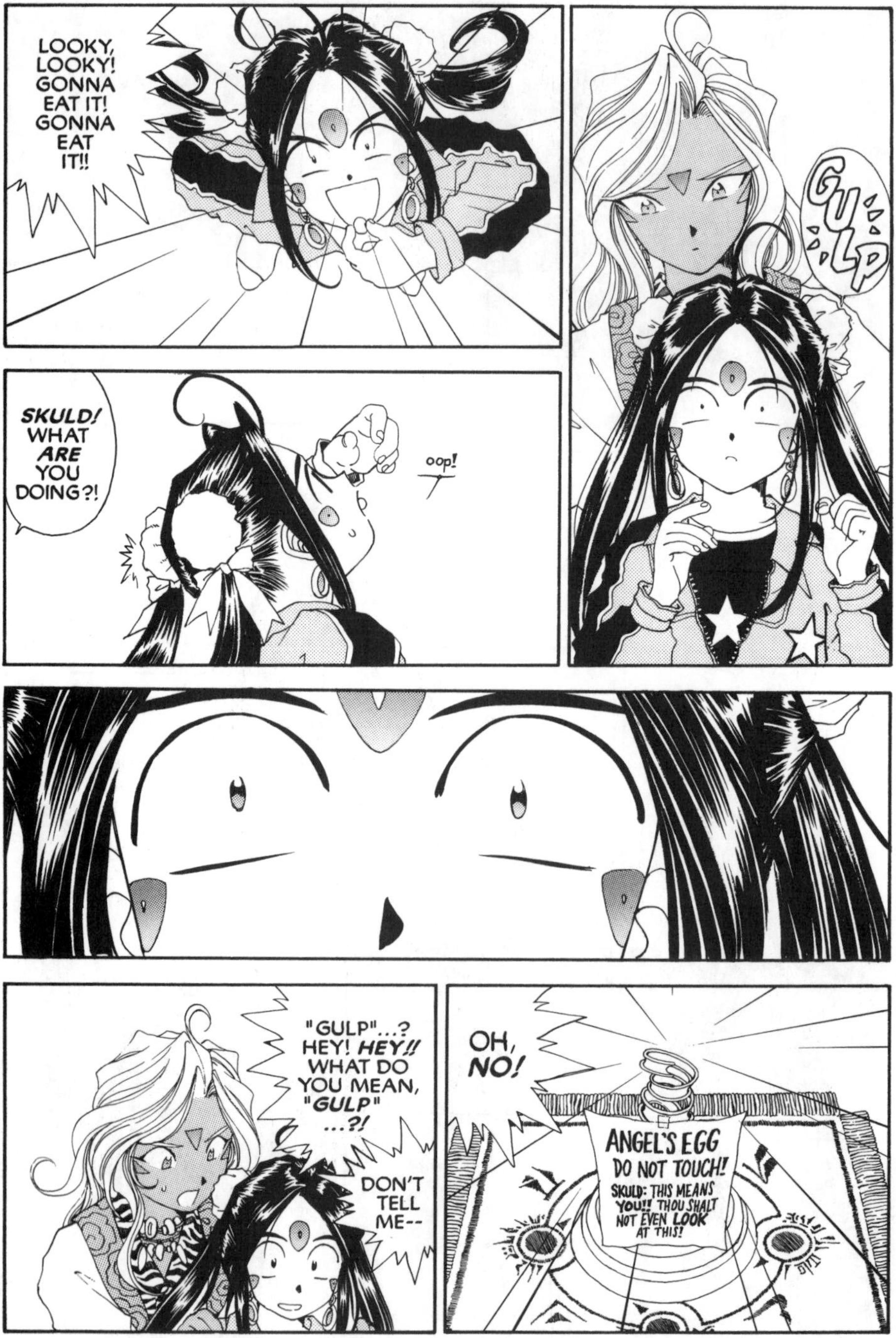
LOOKY, LOOKY! GONNA EAT IT! GONNA EAT IT!!
GULP
SKULD! WHAT ARE YOU DOING?!
oop!
"GULP"...? HEY! HEY!! WHAT DO YOU MEAN, "GULP" ...?!
DON'T TELL ME--
OH, NO!
ANGEL'S EGG
DO NOT TOUCH!
SKULD: THIS MEANS YOU!! THOU SHALT NOT EVEN LOOK AT THIS!

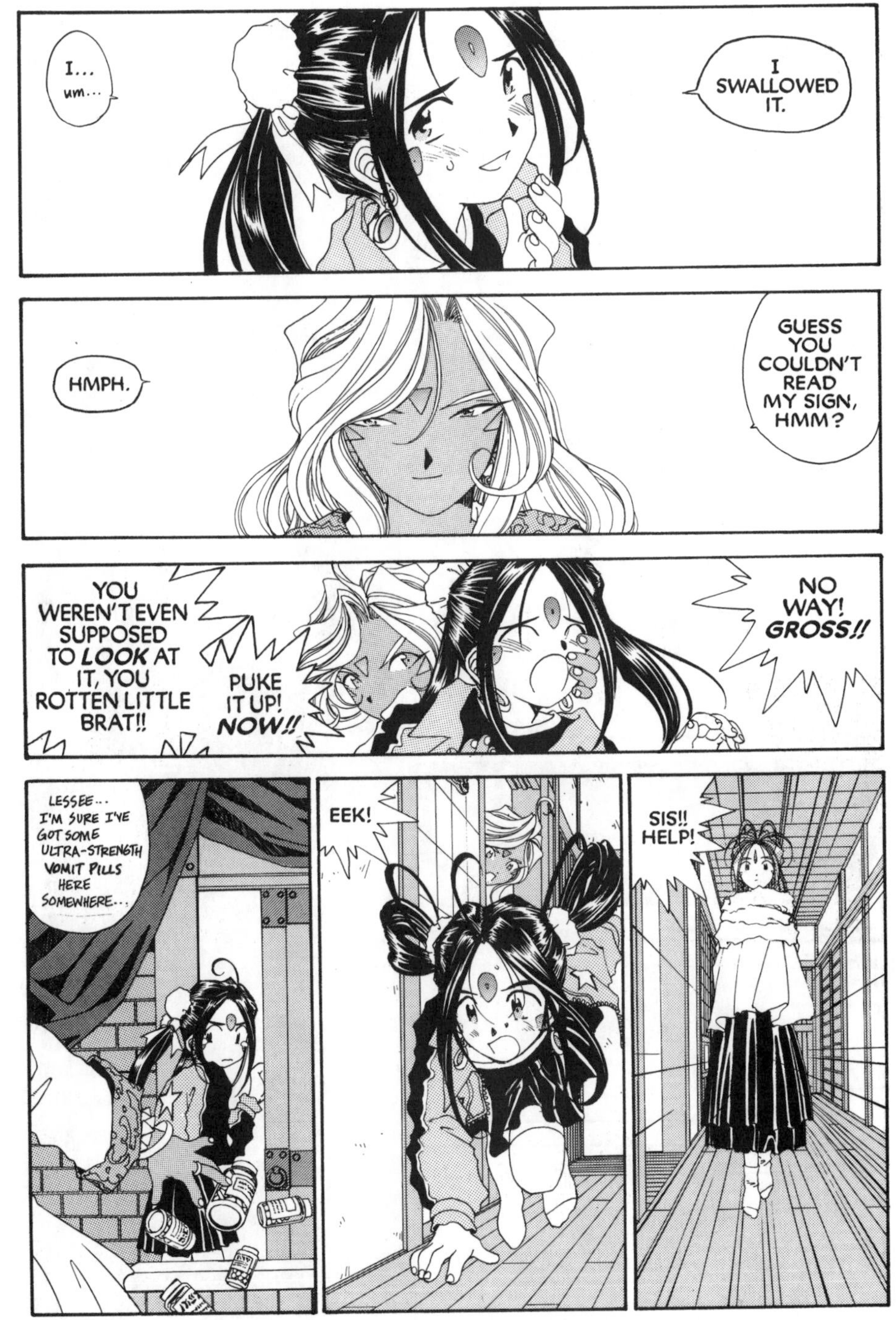
I... um...
I SWALLOWED IT.
HMPH.
GUESS YOU COULDN'T READ MY SIGN, HMM?
YOU WEREN'T EVEN SUPPOSED TO LOOK AT IT, YOU ROTTEN LITTLE BRAT!!
PUKE IT UP! NOW!!
NO WAY! GROSS!!
LESSEE... I'M SURE I'VE GOT SOME ULTRA-STRENGTH VOMIT PILLS HERE SOMEWHERE...
EEK!
SIS!! HELP!

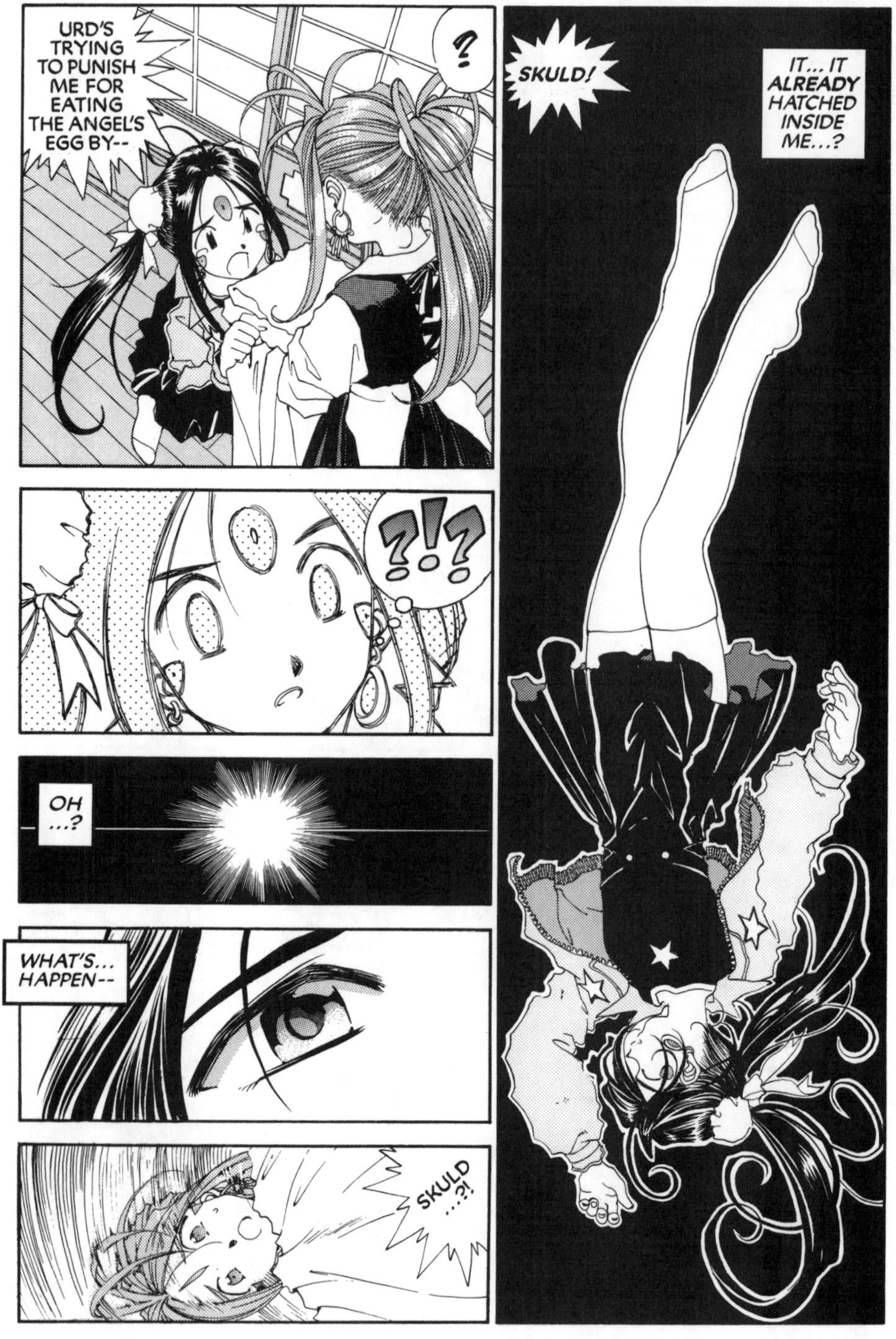
URD'S TRYING TO PUNISH ME FOR EATING THE ANGEL'S EGG BY--
?
?!?
OH ...?
WHAT'S... HAPPEN--
SKULD ...?!
SKULD!
IT... IT ALREADY HATCHED INSIDE ME...?

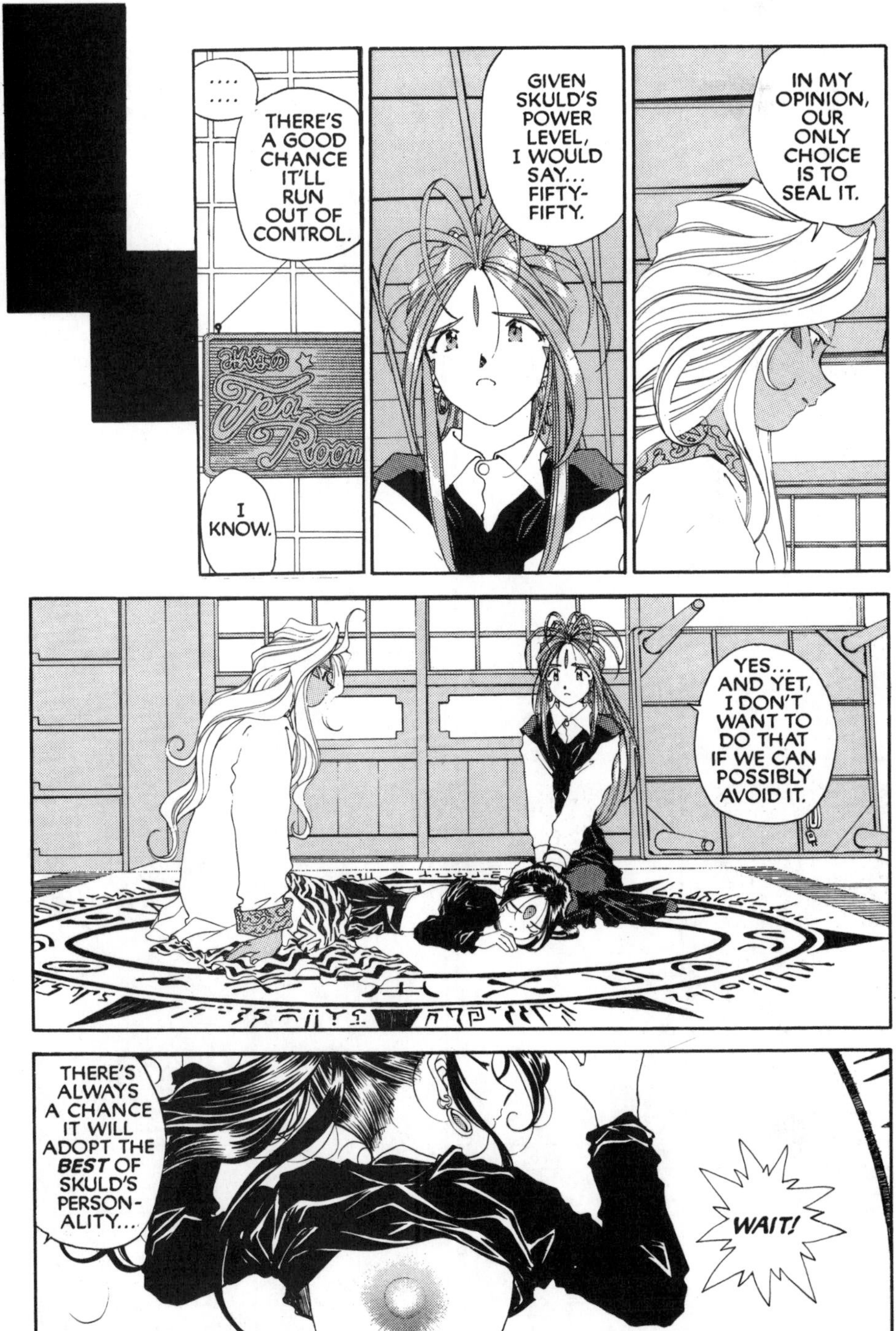

....
....
THERE'S A GOOD CHANCE IT'LL RUN OUT OF CONTROL.
I KNOW.
GIVEN SKULD'S POWER LEVEL, I WOULD SAY... FIFTY-FIFTY.
IN MY OPINION, OUR ONLY CHOICE IS TO SEAL IT.
YES... AND YET, I DON'T WANT TO DO THAT IF WE CAN POSSIBLY AVOID IT.
THERE'S ALWAYS A CHANCE IT WILL ADOPT THE *BEST* OF SKULD'S PERSON-ALITY...
WAIT!

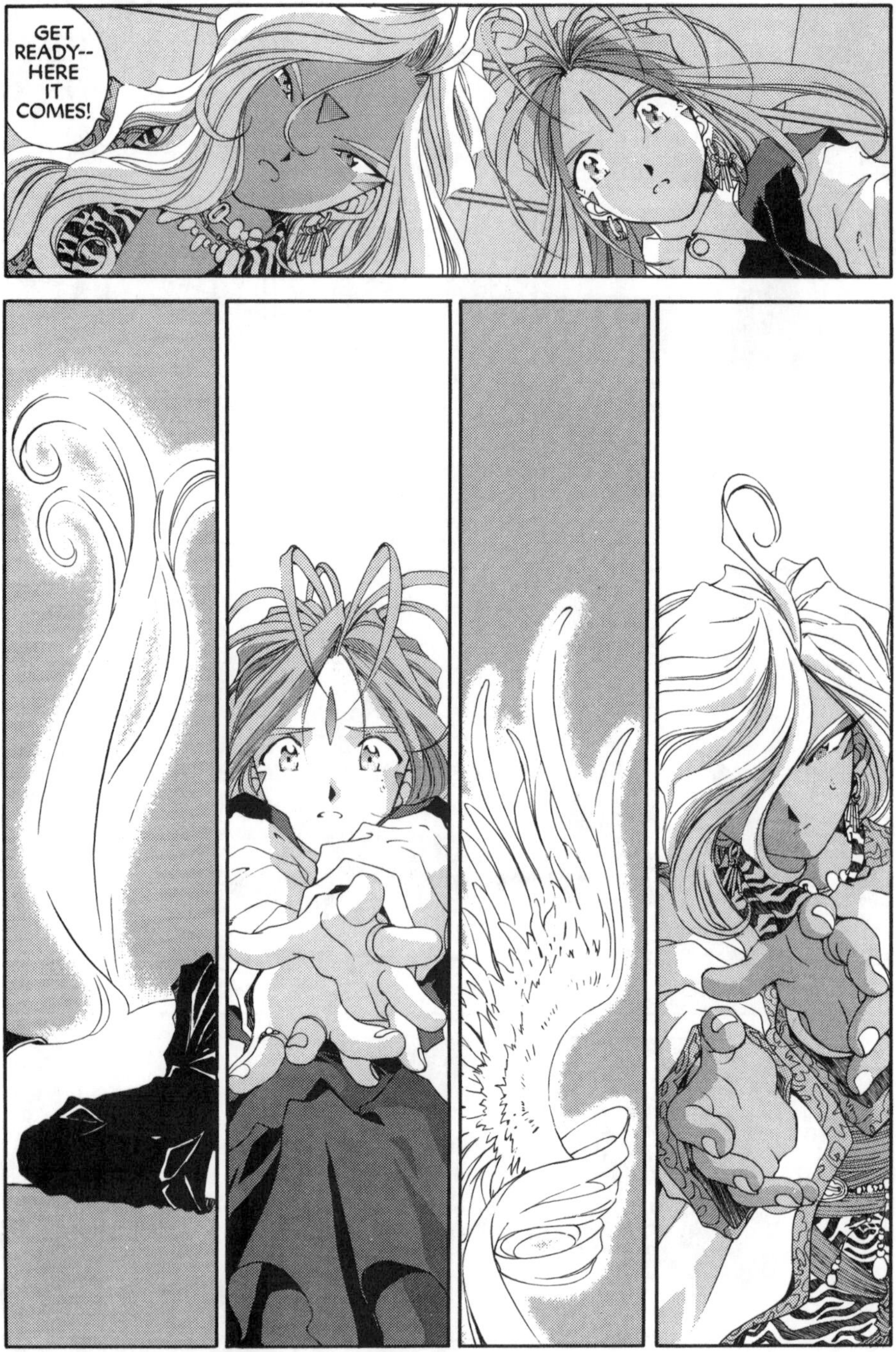
GET READY-- HERE IT COMES!

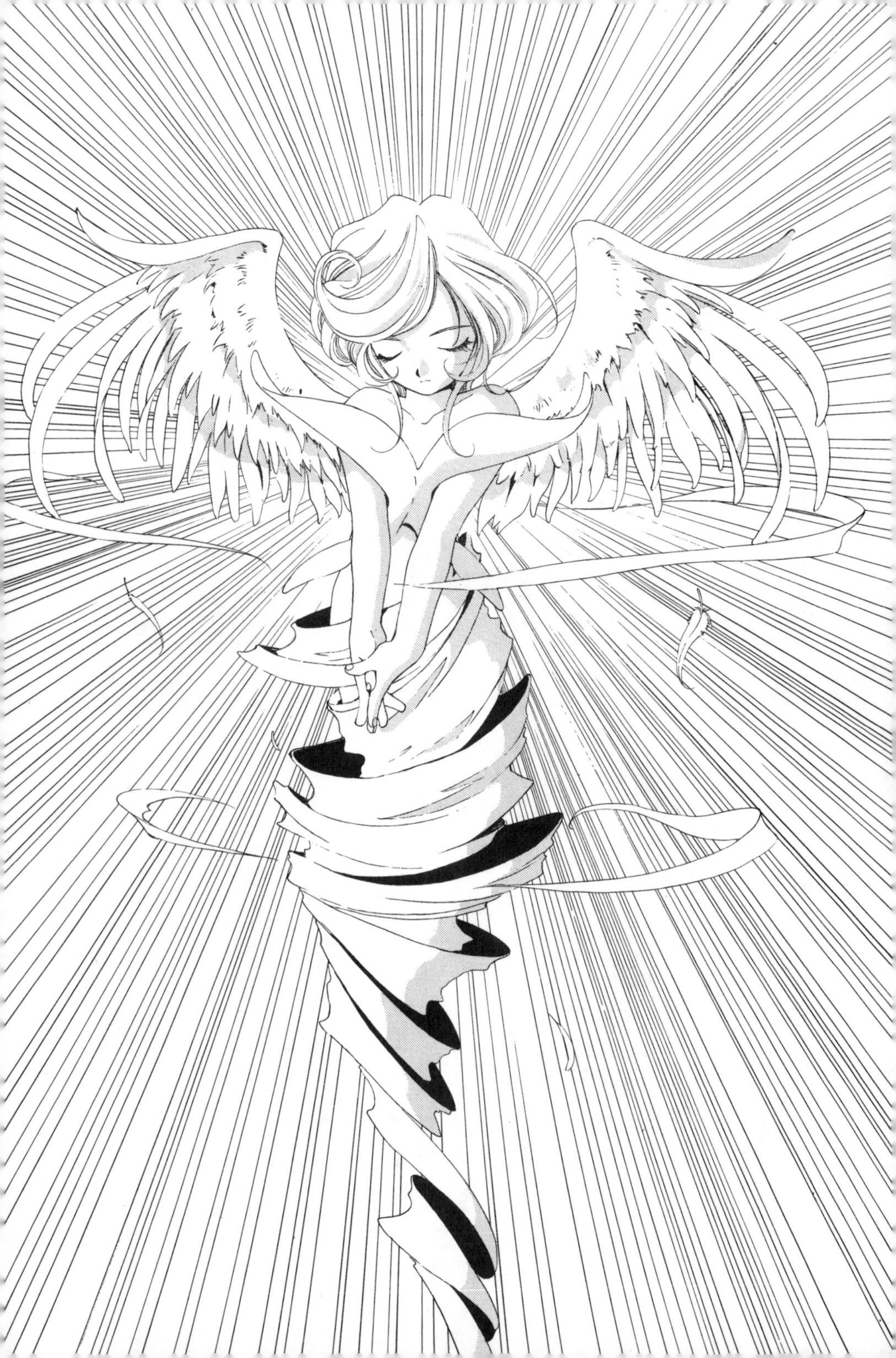

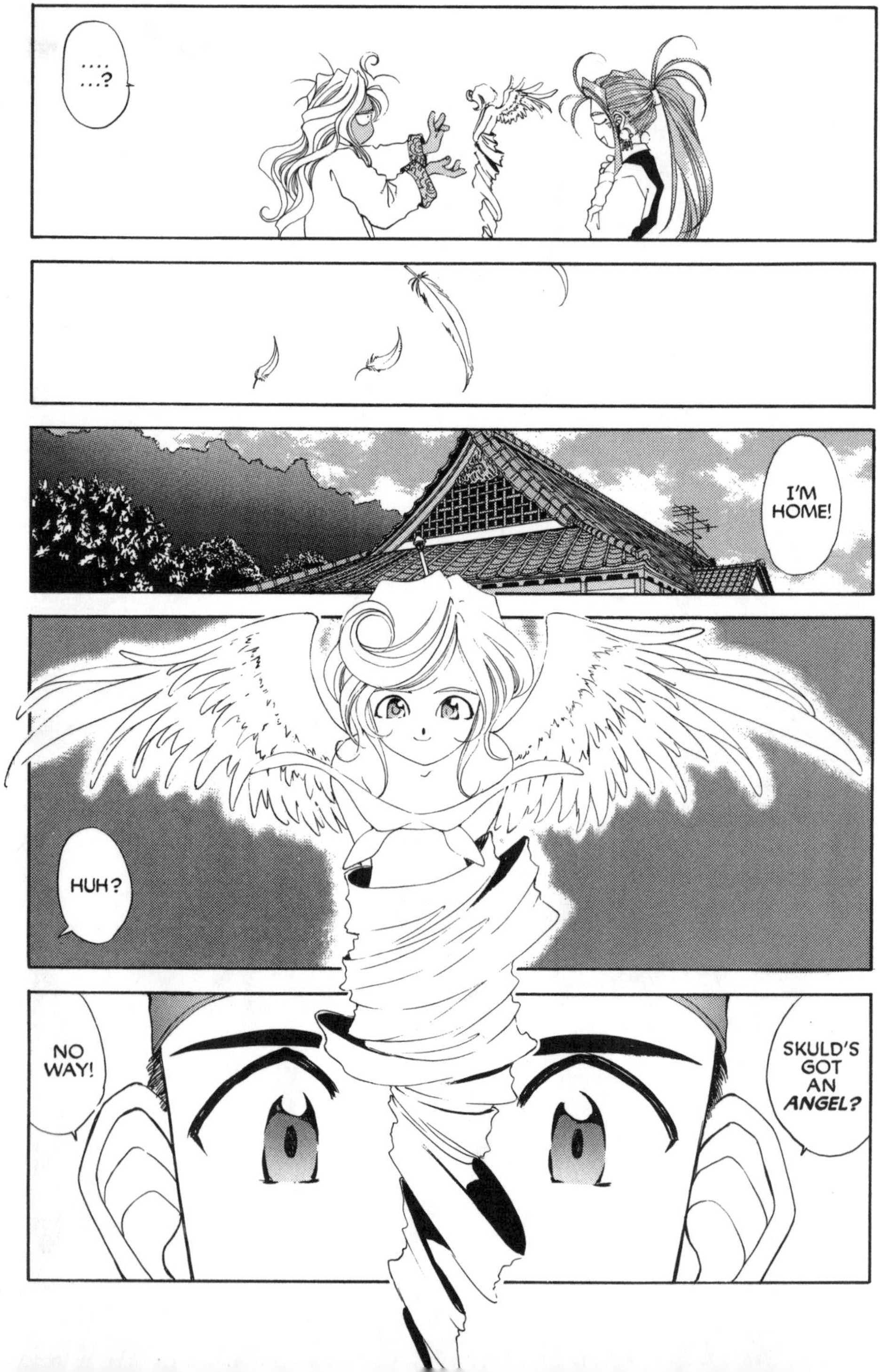
....?
I'M HOME!
HUH?
NO WAY!
SKULD'S GOT AN *ANGEL?*

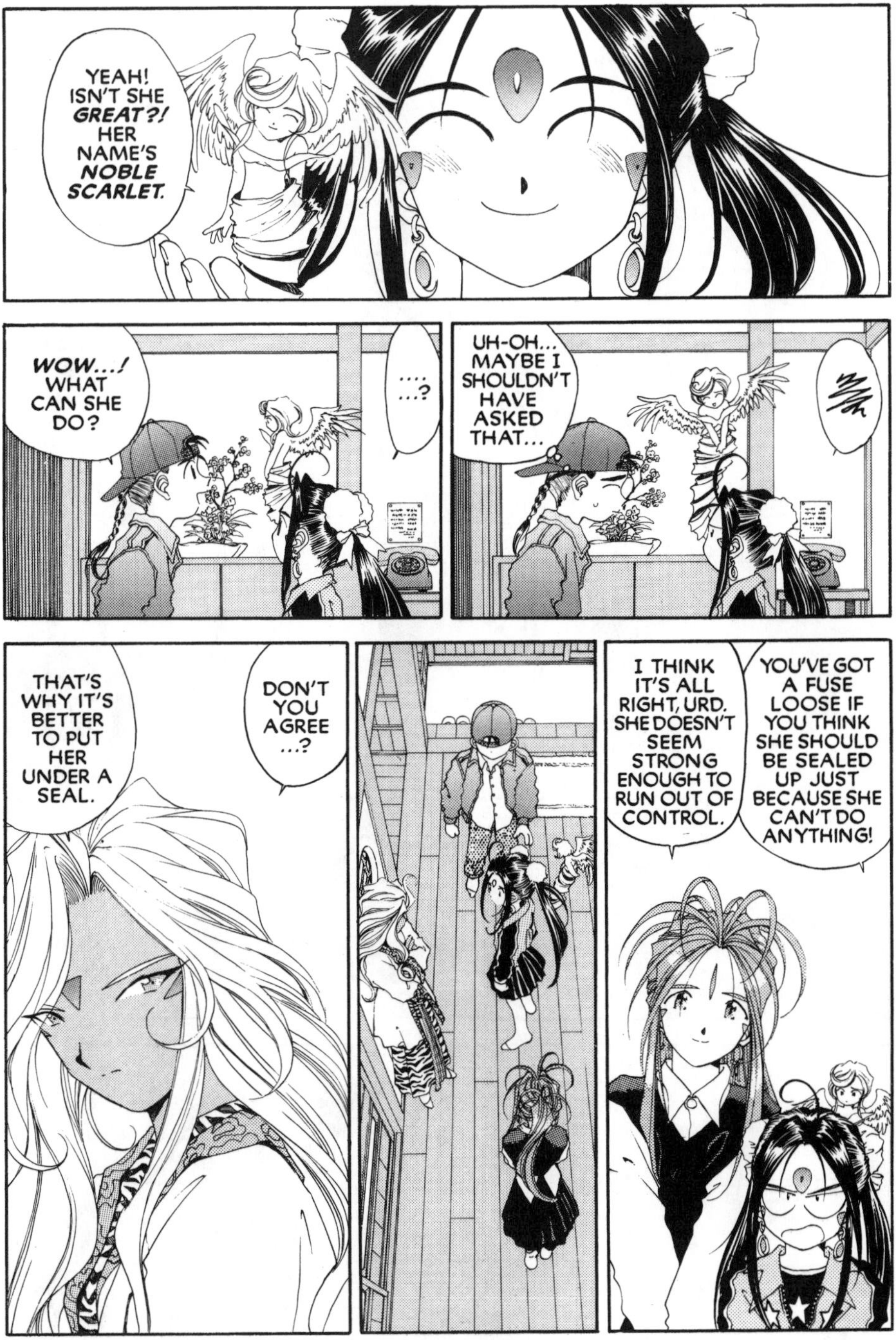

YEAH! ISN'T SHE GREAT?! HER NAME'S NOBLE SCARLET.
WOW...! WHAT CAN SHE DO?
... ...?
UH-OH... MAYBE I SHOULDN'T HAVE ASKED THAT...
THAT'S WHY IT'S BETTER TO PUT HER UNDER A SEAL.
DON'T YOU AGREE ...?
I THINK IT'S ALL RIGHT, URD. SHE DOESN'T SEEM STRONG ENOUGH TO RUN OUT OF CONTROL.
YOU'VE GOT A FUSE LOOSE IF YOU THINK SHE SHOULD BE SEALED UP JUST BECAUSE SHE CAN'T DO ANYTHING!

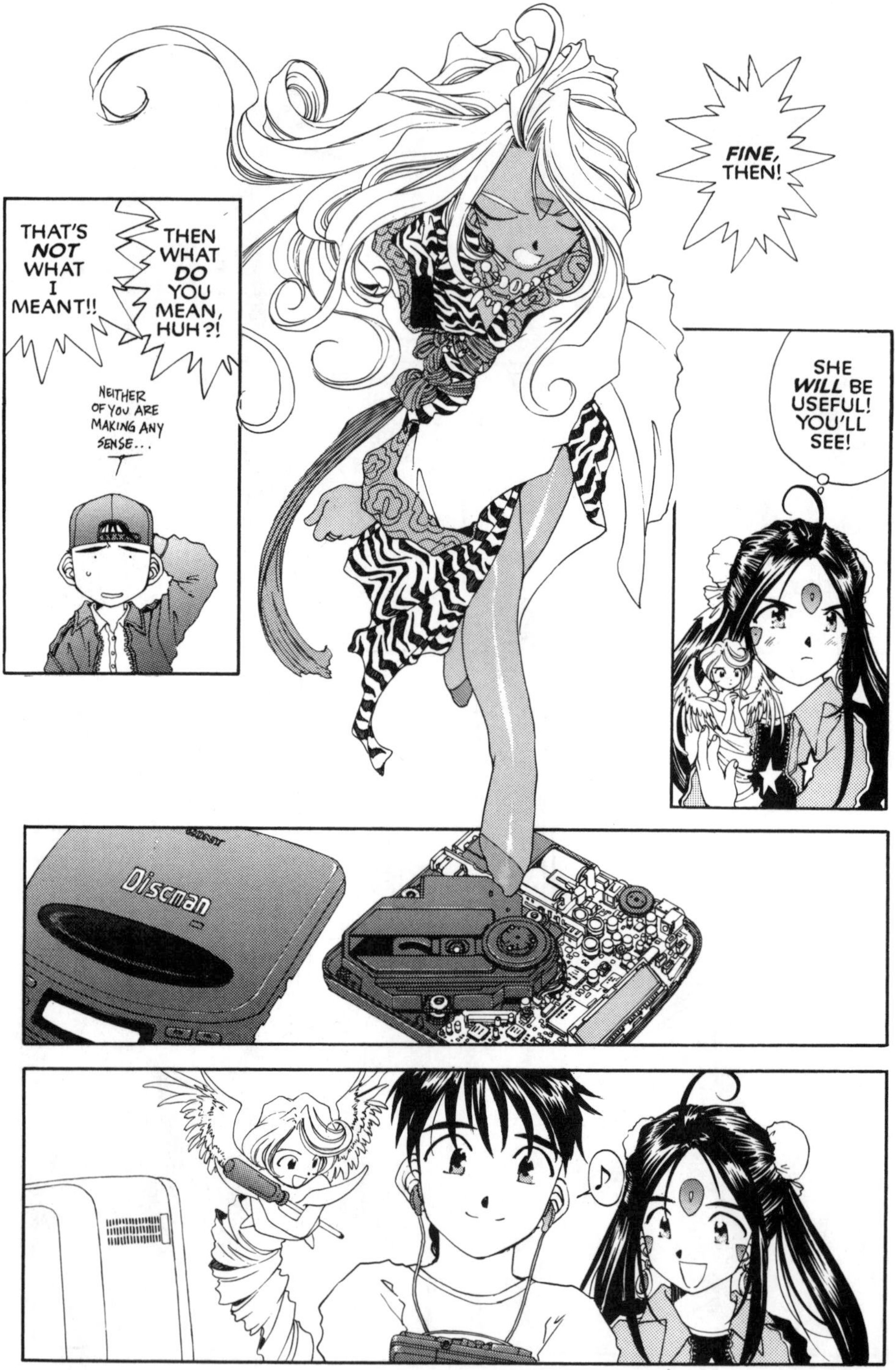
THAT'S NOT WHAT I MEANT!!
THEN WHAT DO YOU MEAN, HUH?!
NEITHER OF YOU ARE MAKING ANY SENSE...
FINE, THEN!
SHE WILL BE USEFUL! YOU'LL SEE!
Discman

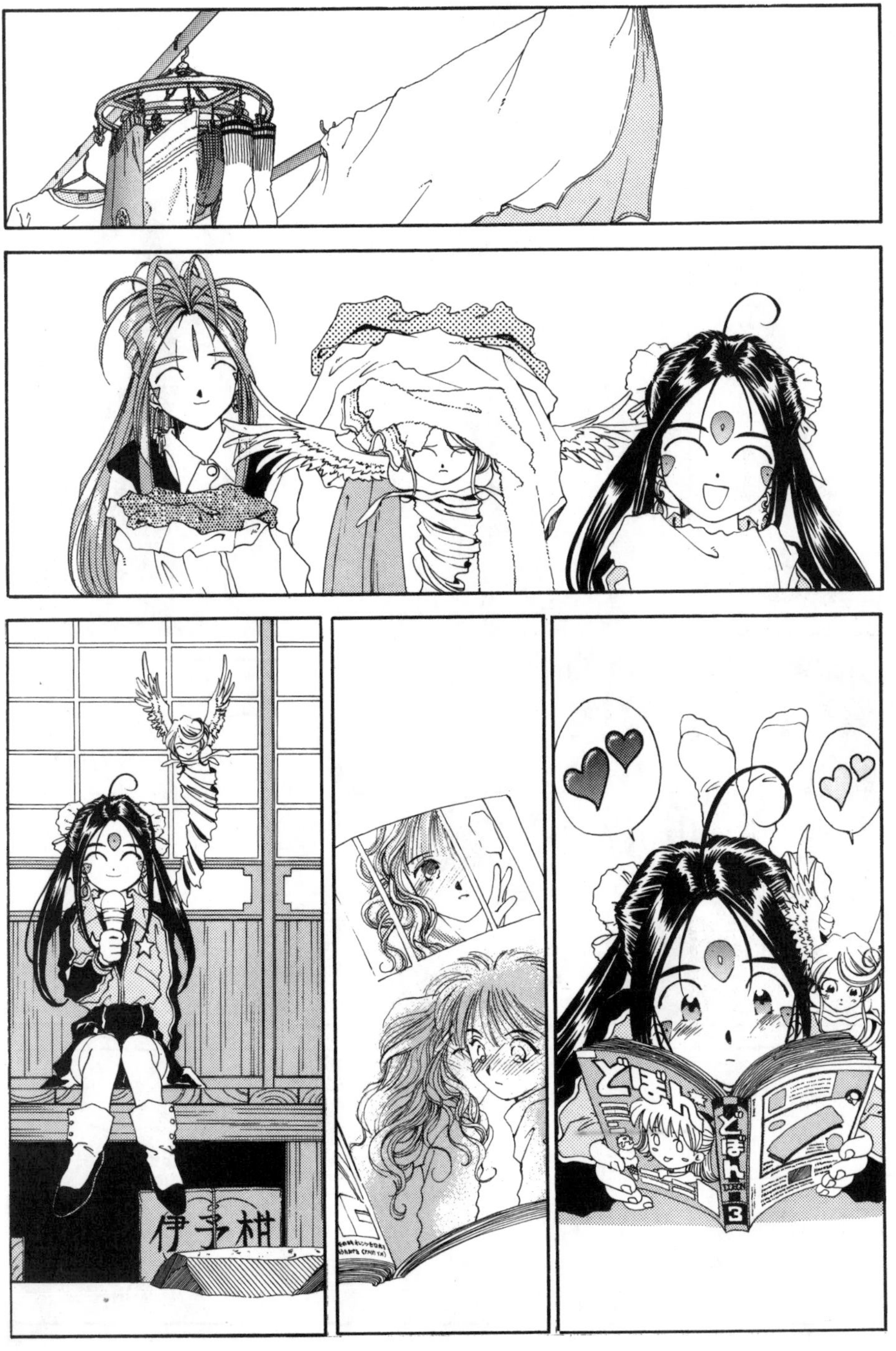
伊予柑
どぼん
どぼん
3

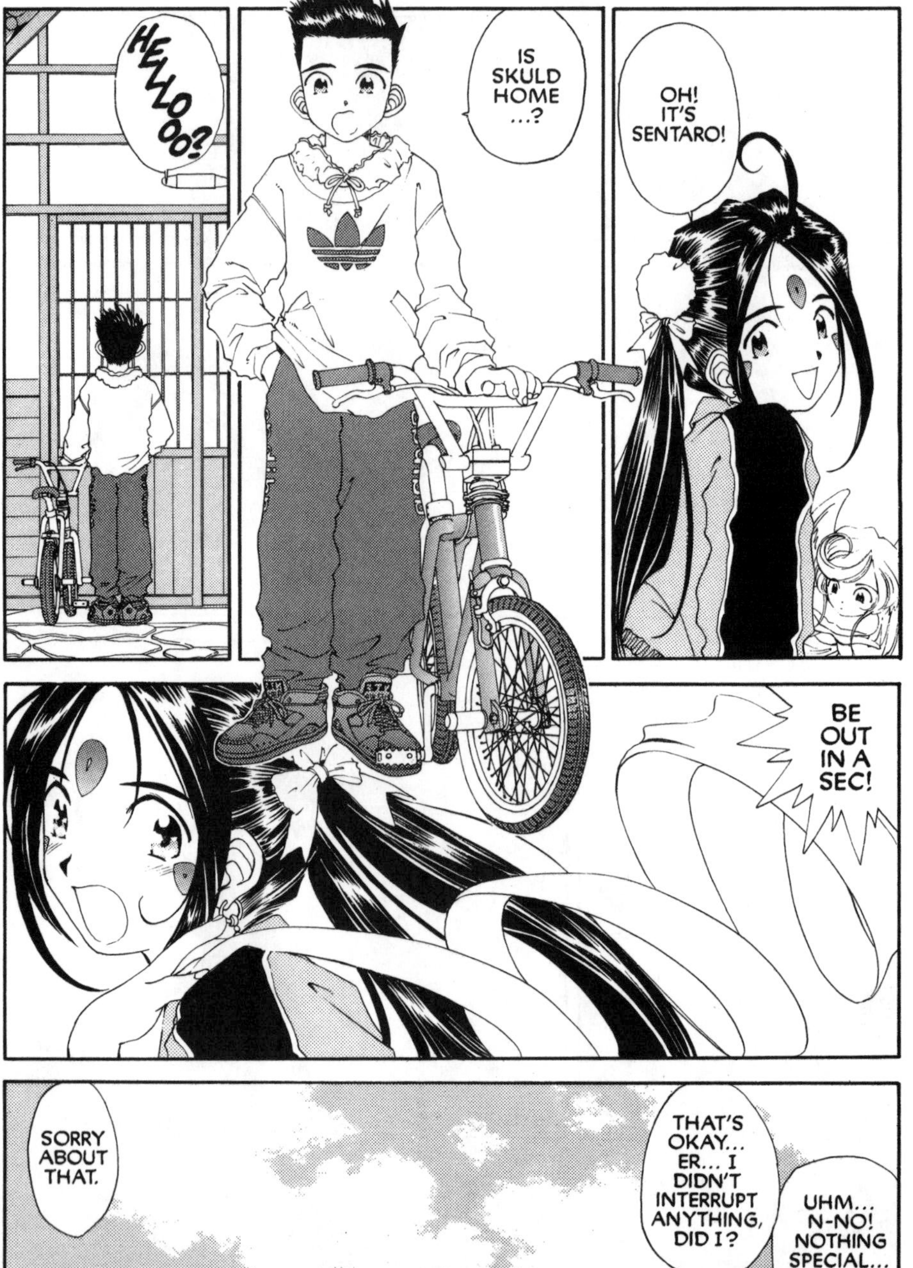
HELLOOO?
IS SKULD HOME ...?
OH! IT'S SENTARO!
BE OUT IN A SEC!
SORRY ABOUT THAT.
THAT'S OKAY... ER... I DIDN'T INTERRUPT ANYTHING, DID I?
UHM... N-NO! NOTHING SPECIAL... I WAS JUST...

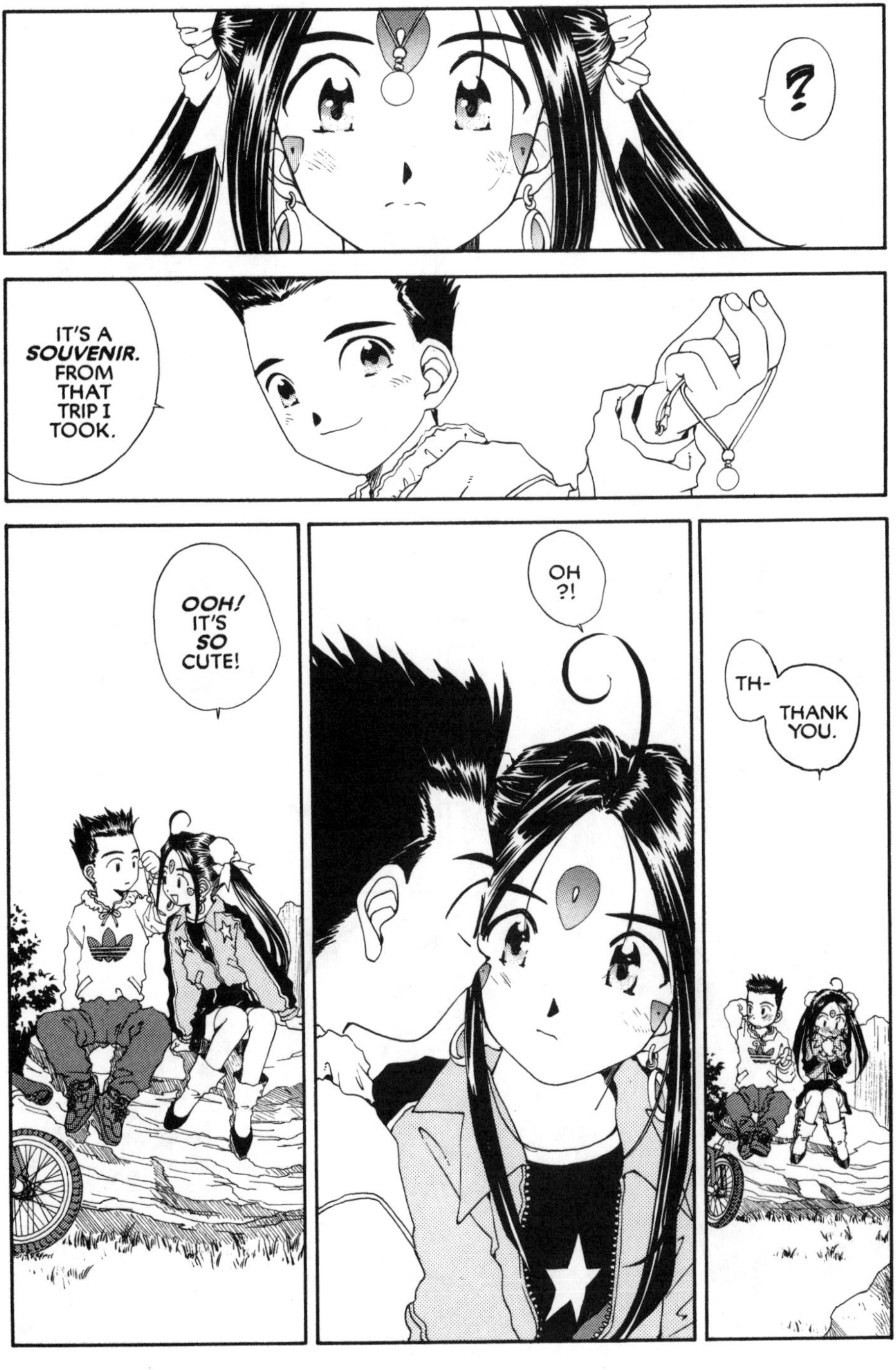
?
IT'S A SOUVENIR. FROM THAT TRIP I TOOK.
OOH! IT'S SO CUTE!
OH ?!
TH- THANK YOU.

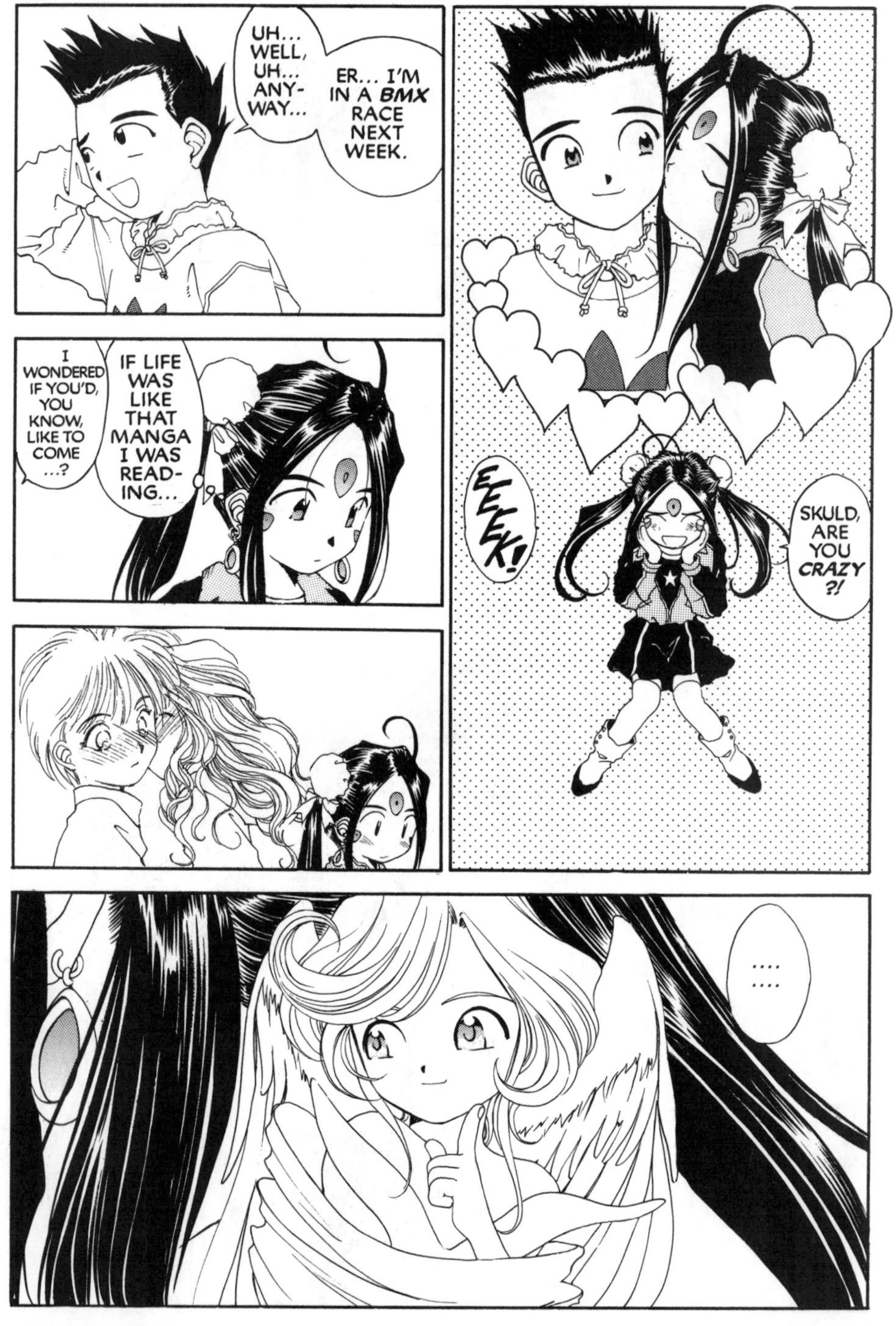

UH... WELL, UH... ANY-WAY...
ER... I'M IN A *BMX* RACE NEXT WEEK.
I WONDERED IF YOU'D, YOU KNOW, LIKE TO COME ...?
IF LIFE WAS LIKE THAT MANGA I WAS READ-ING...
EEEEK!
SKULD, ARE YOU *CRAZY* ?!
....
....

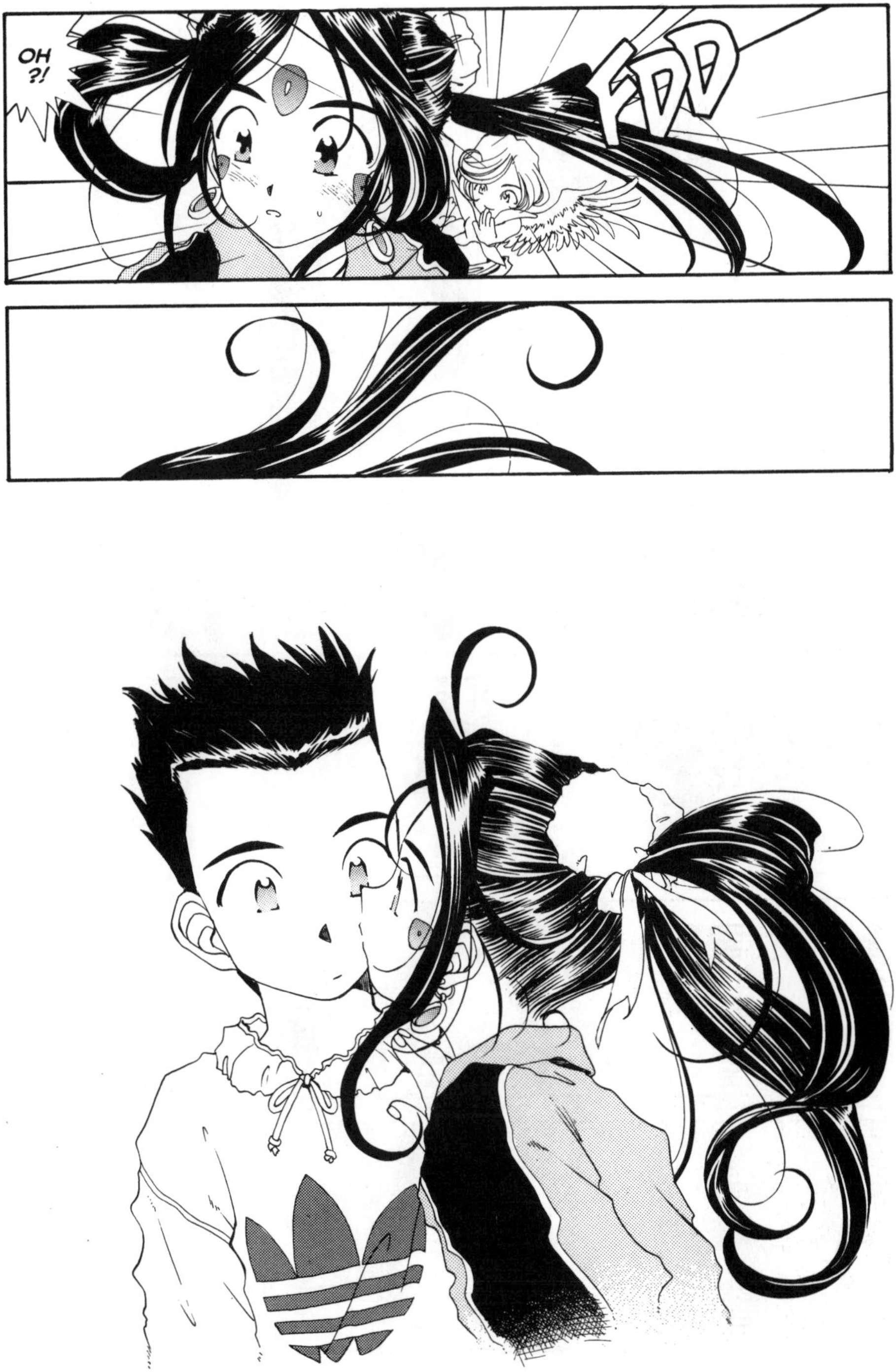
OH ?!
FDD

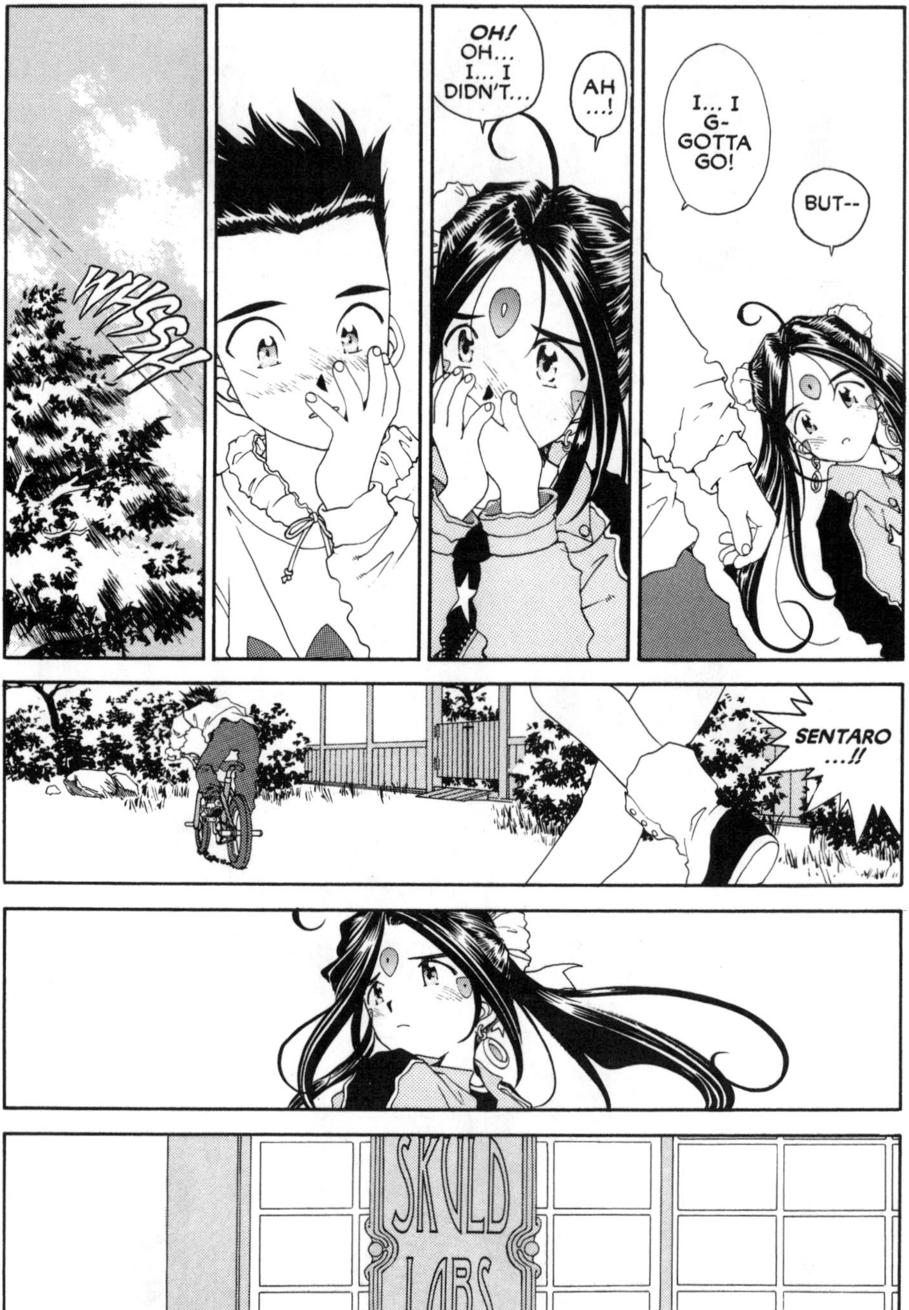
WHSSH
OH! OH... I... I DIDN'T...
AH ...!
I... I G-GOTTA GO!
BUT--
SENTARO ...!!
SKULD LABS

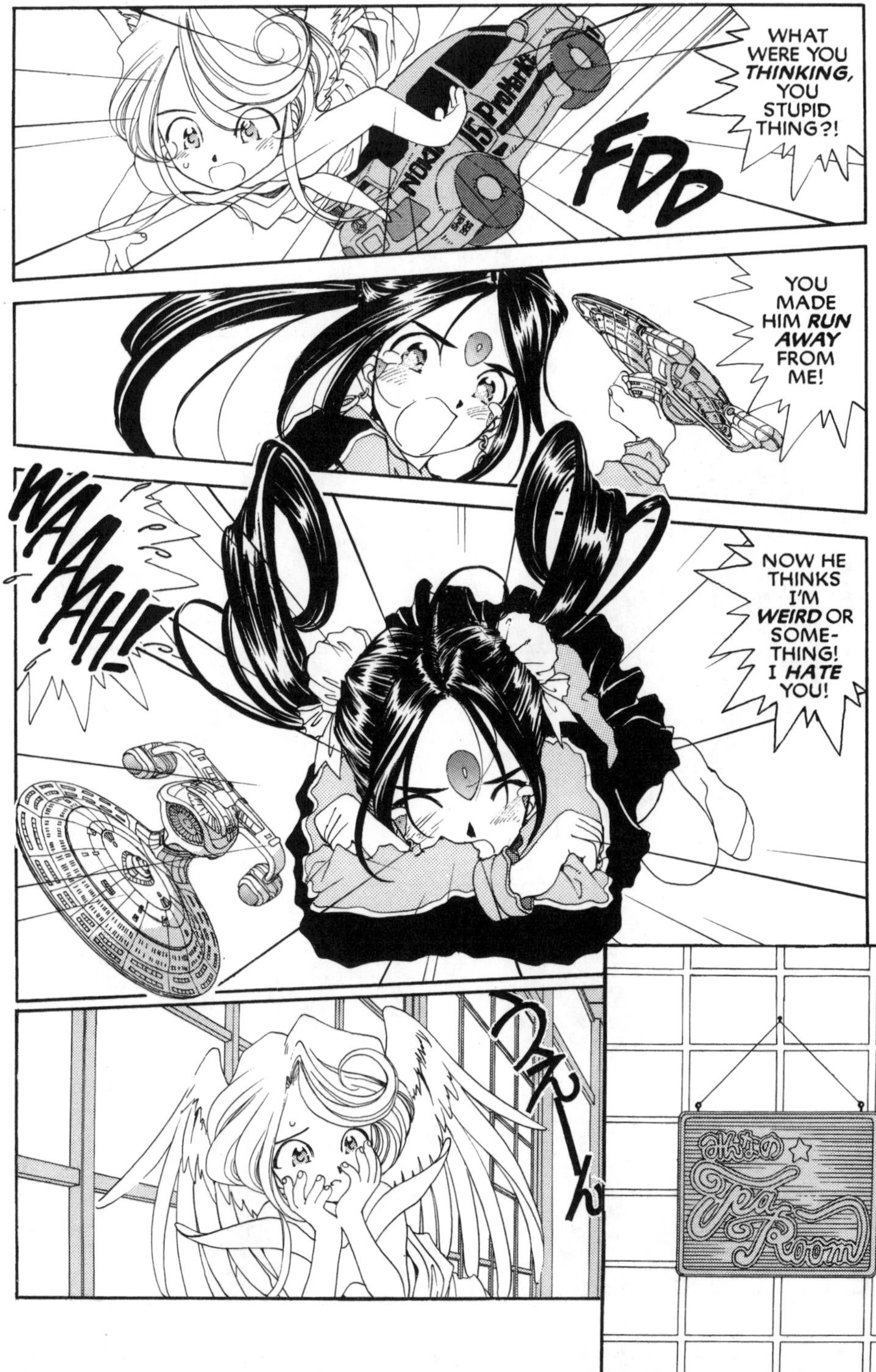
WHAT WERE YOU THINKING, YOU STUPID THING?!
FDD
YOU MADE HIM RUN AWAY FROM ME!
WAAAH!
NOW HE THINKS I'M WEIRD OR SOME-THING! I HATE YOU!
みんなの☆
Tea Room

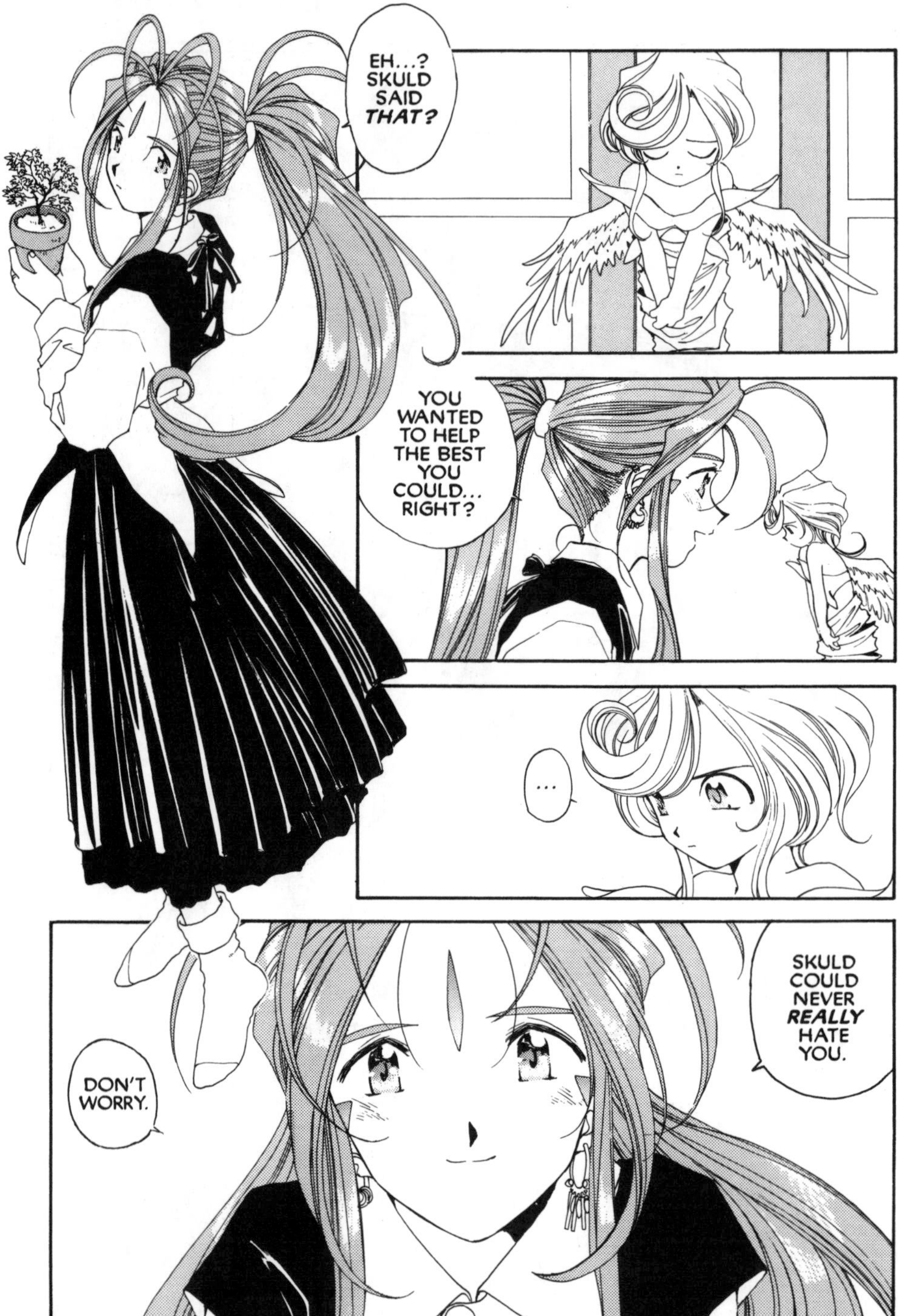
EH...? SKULD SAID *THAT?*
YOU WANTED TO HELP THE BEST YOU COULD... RIGHT?
...
SKULD COULD NEVER ***REALLY*** HATE YOU.
DON'T WORRY.

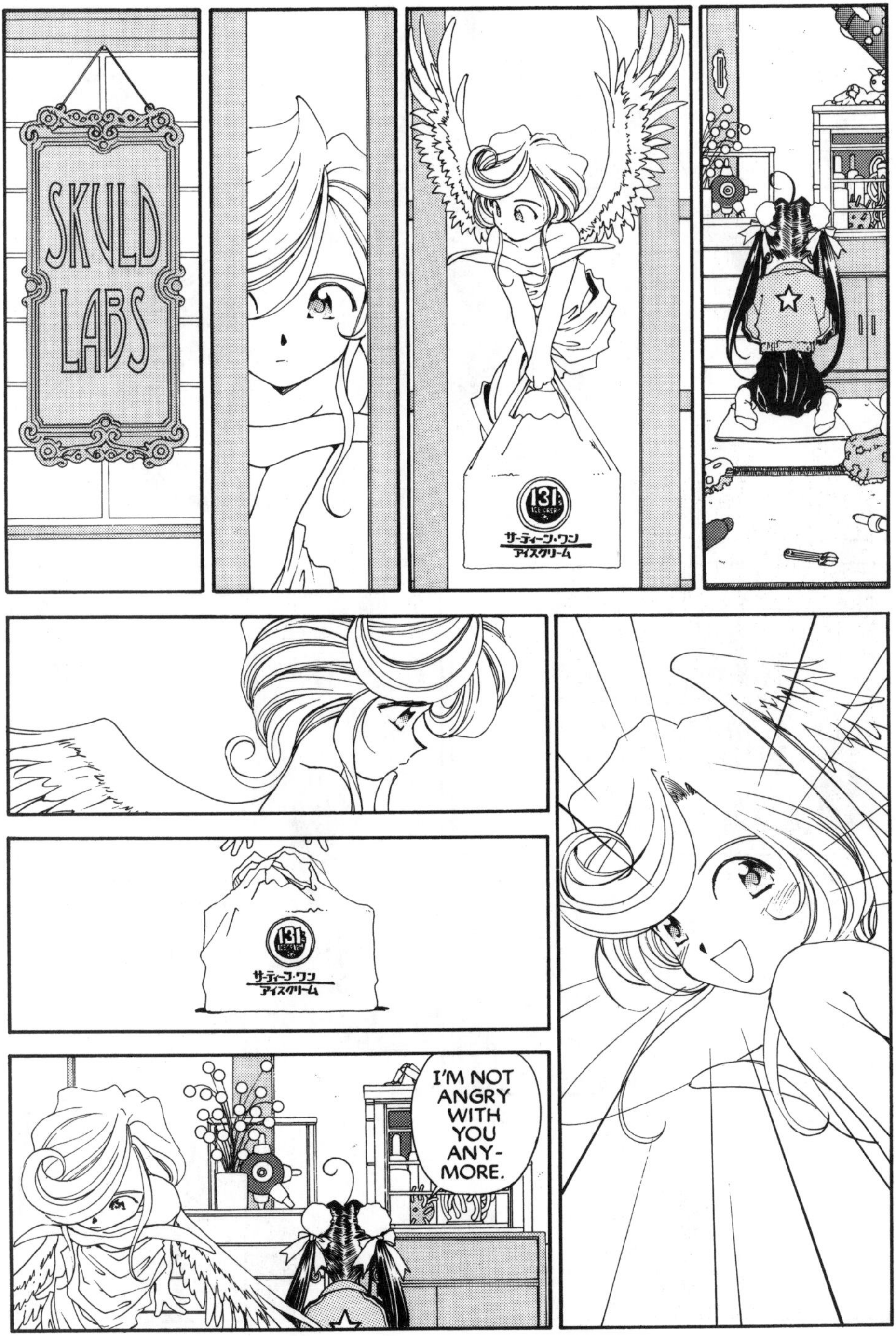
SKULD
LABS
131
サーティーン・ワン
アイスクリーム
131
サーティーン・ワン
アイスクリーム
I'M NOT ANGRY WITH YOU ANY-MORE.

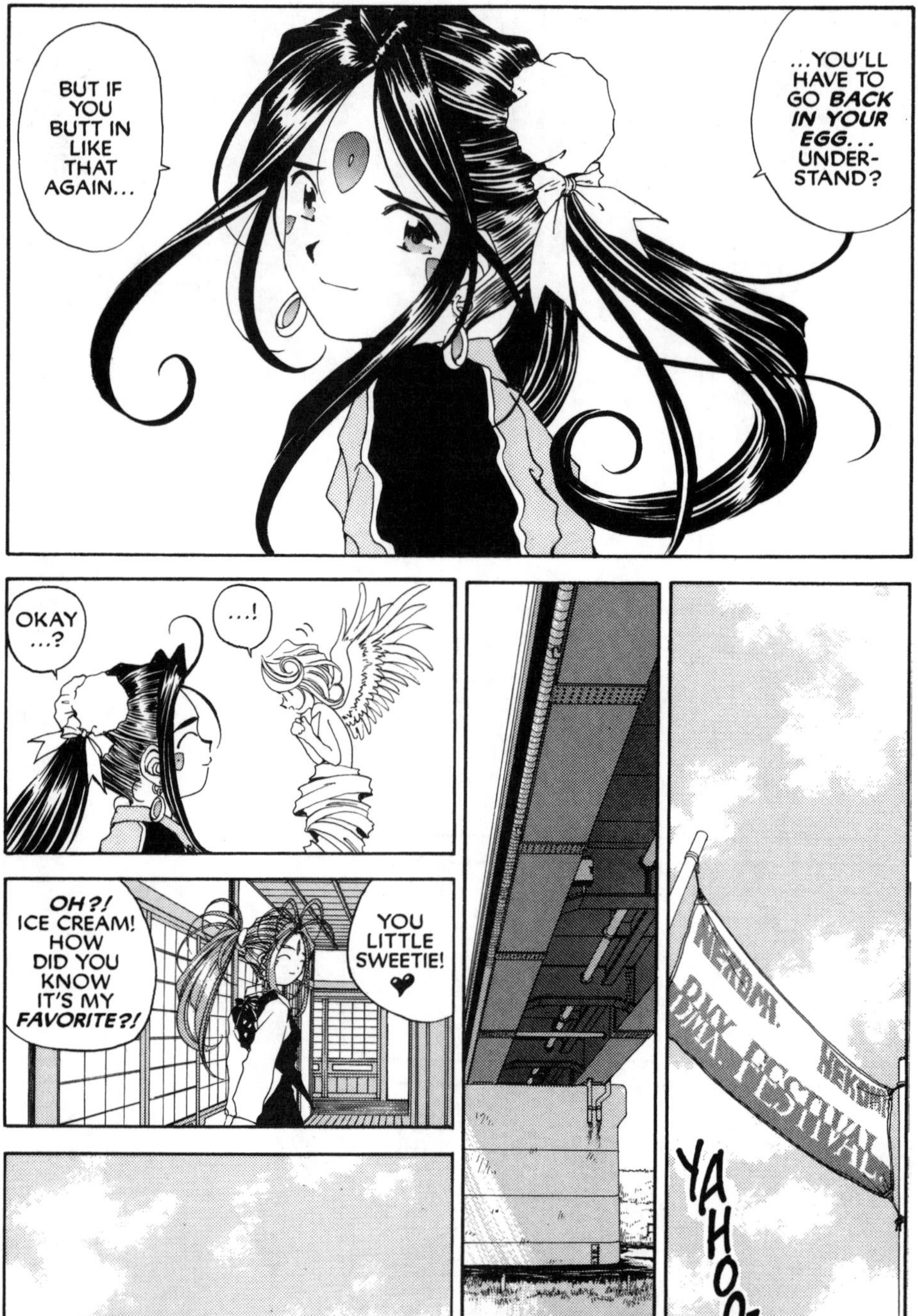
BUT IF YOU BUTT IN LIKE THAT AGAIN...
...YOU'LL HAVE TO GO *BACK IN YOUR EGG*... UNDERSTAND?
OKAY ...?
...!
OH?! ICE CREAM! HOW DID YOU KNOW IT'S MY *FAVORITE?!*
YOU LITTLE SWEETIE! ❤
NEKOMI. BMX. FESTIVAL
YAHOO!

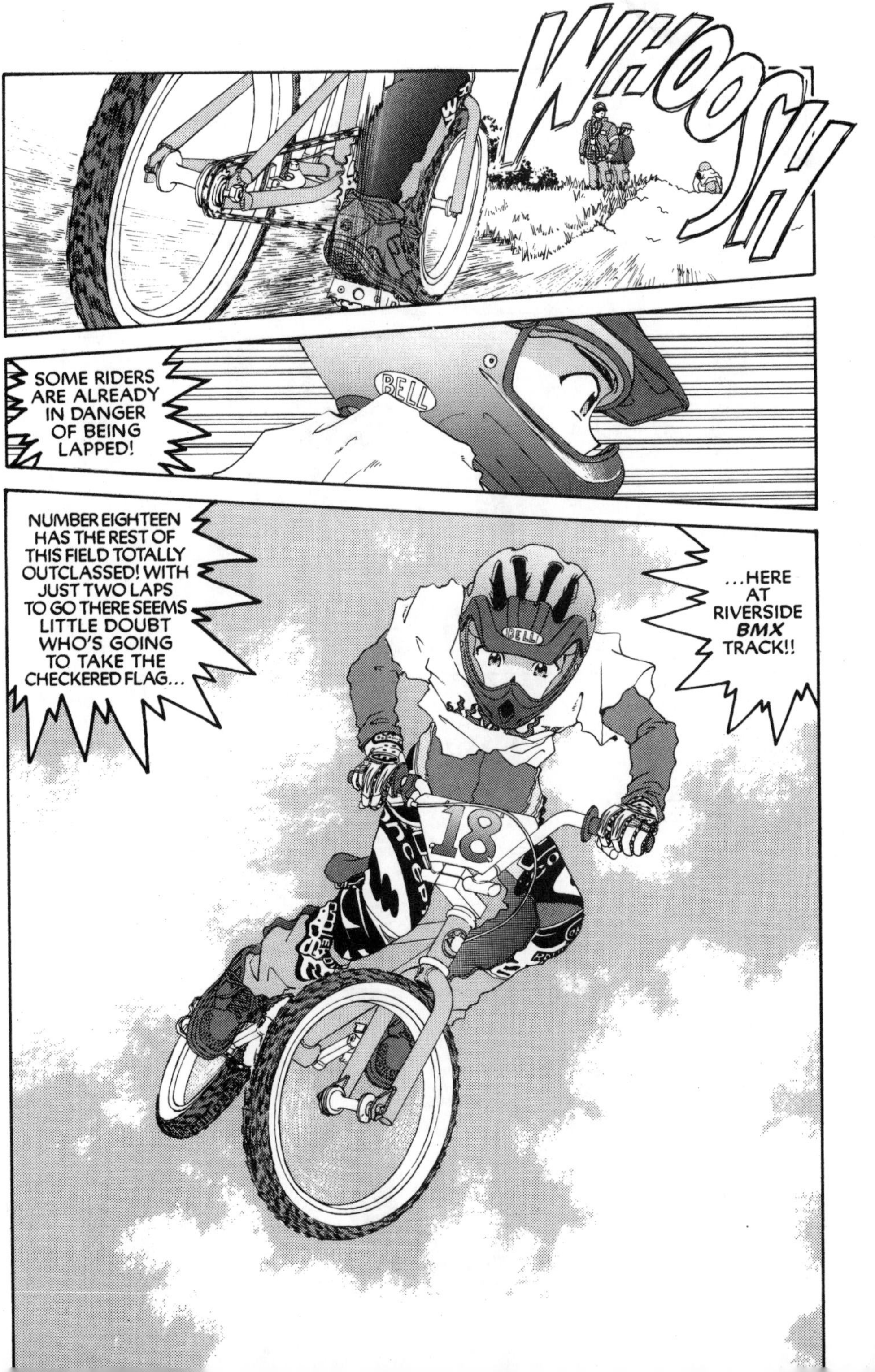
WHOOSH
SOME RIDERS ARE ALREADY IN DANGER OF BEING LAPPED!
BELL
NUMBER EIGHTEEN HAS THE REST OF THIS FIELD TOTALLY OUTCLASSED! WITH JUST TWO LAPS TO GO THERE SEEMS LITTLE DOUBT WHO'S GOING TO TAKE THE CHECKERED FLAG...
...HERE AT RIVERSIDE BMX TRACK!!
BELL
18

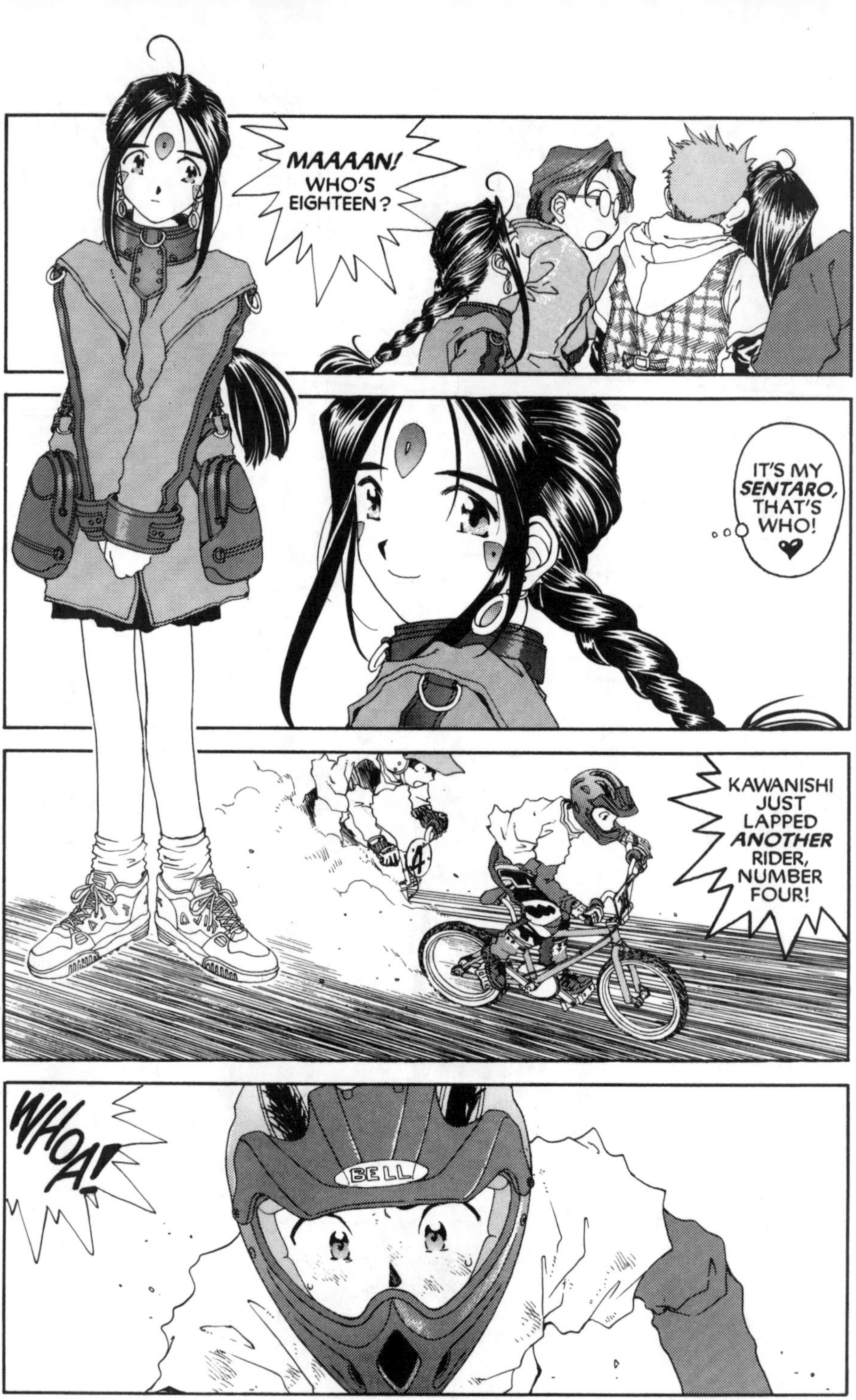
MAAAAN! WHO'S EIGHTEEN?
IT'S MY SENTARO, THAT'S WHO!
KAWANISHI JUST LAPPED ANOTHER RIDER, NUMBER FOUR!
WHOA!
BELL

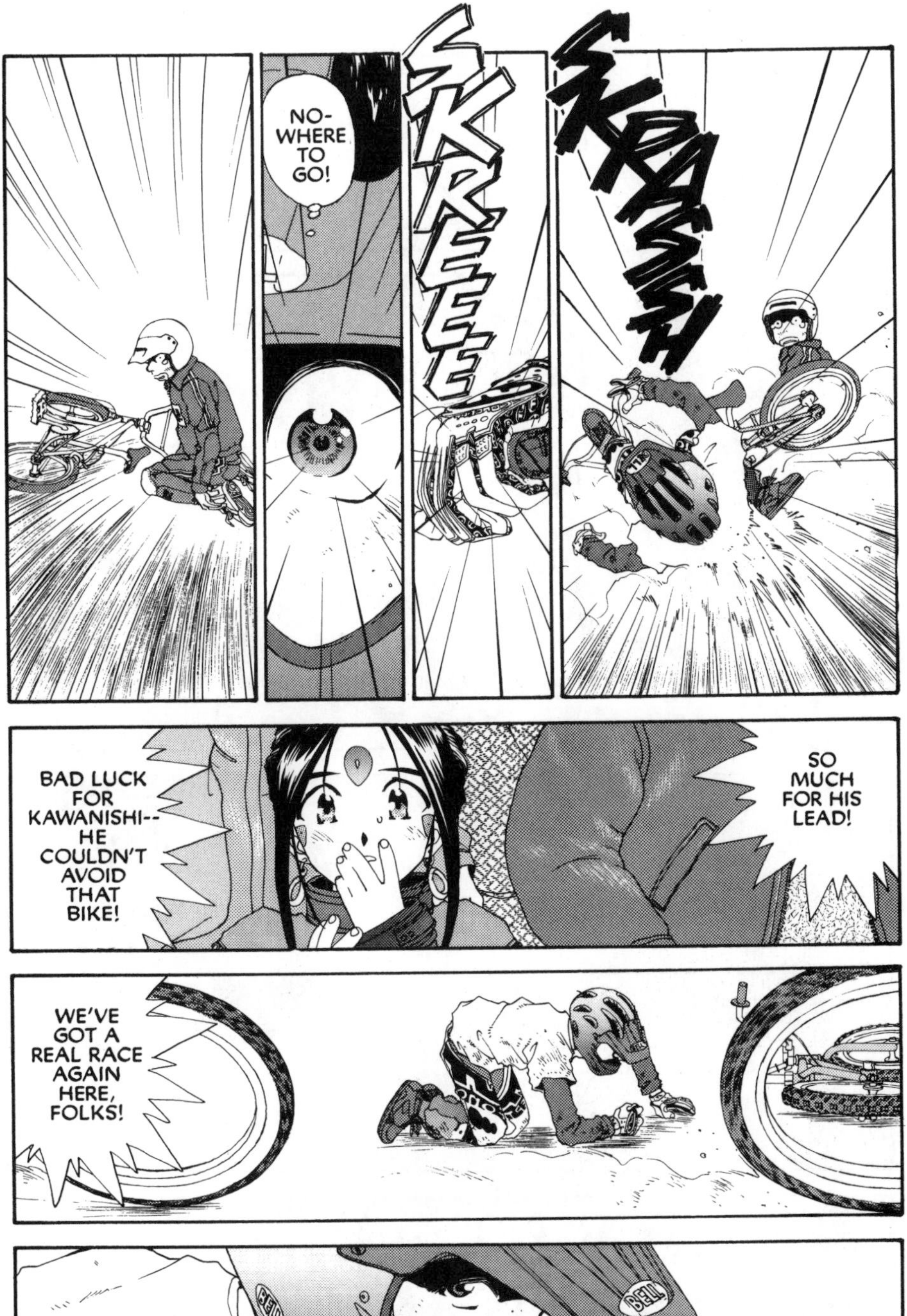
NO-WHERE TO GO!
SKREEEE
SKRASSSH
BAD LUCK FOR KAWANISHI--HE COULDN'T AVOID THAT BIKE!
SO MUCH FOR HIS LEAD!
WE'VE GOT A REAL RACE AGAIN HERE, FOLKS!

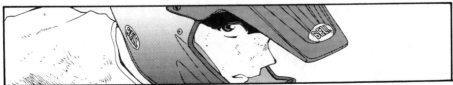

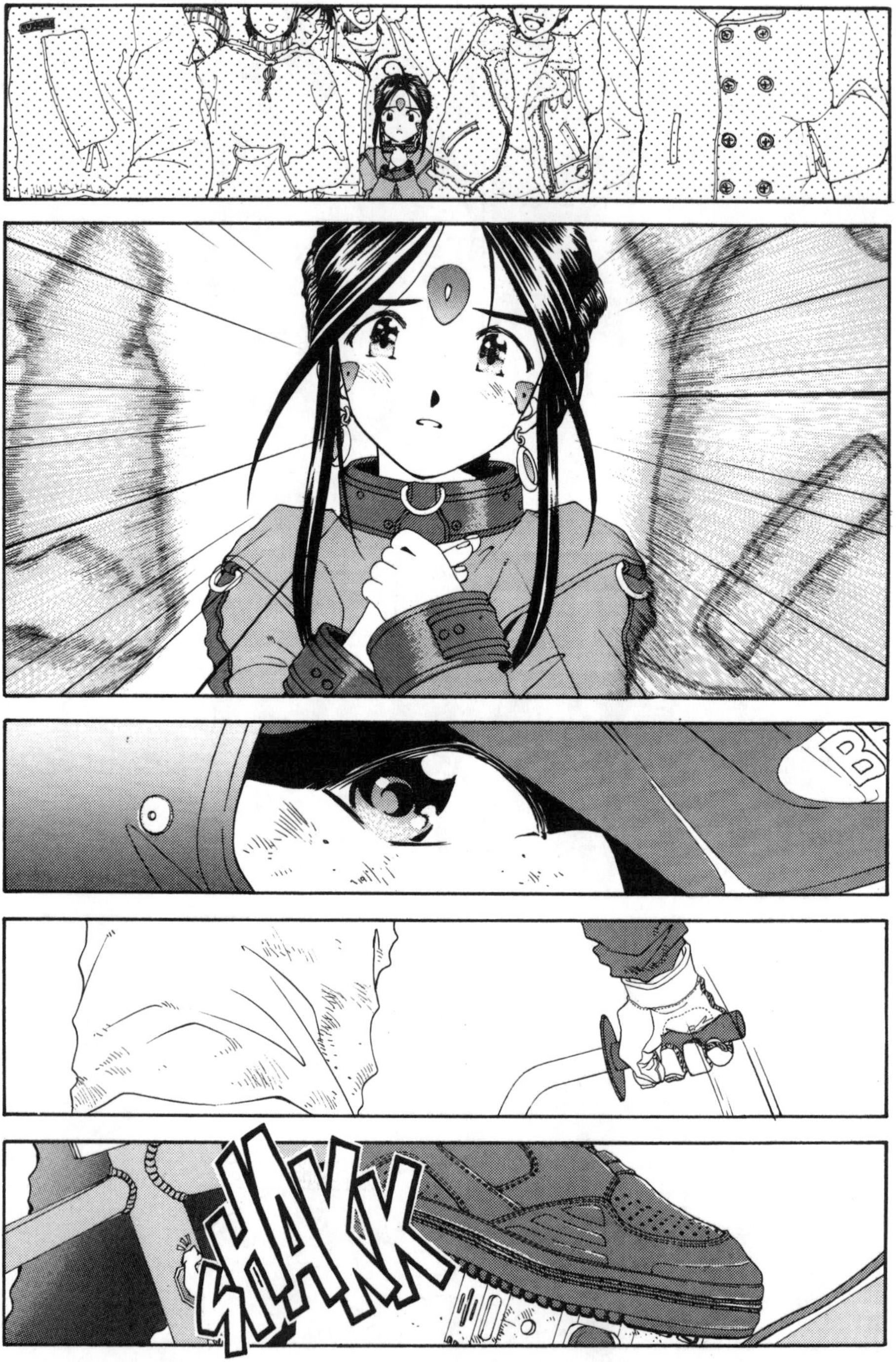
SHAKK

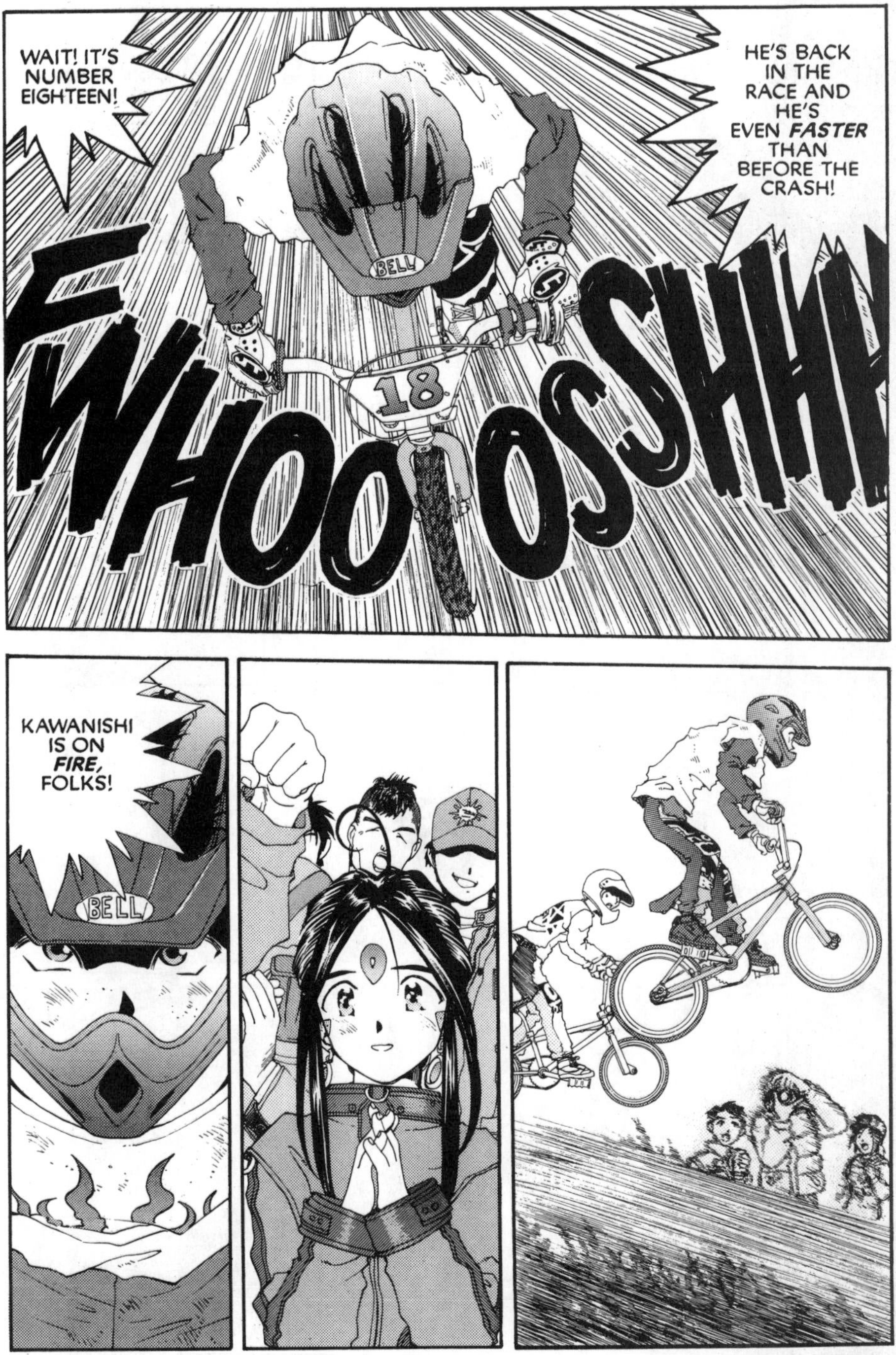
WAIT! IT'S NUMBER EIGHTEEN!
HE'S BACK IN THE RACE AND HE'S EVEN *FASTER* THAN BEFORE THE CRASH!
WHOOOSSHHH
KAWANISHI IS ON *FIRE,* FOLKS!

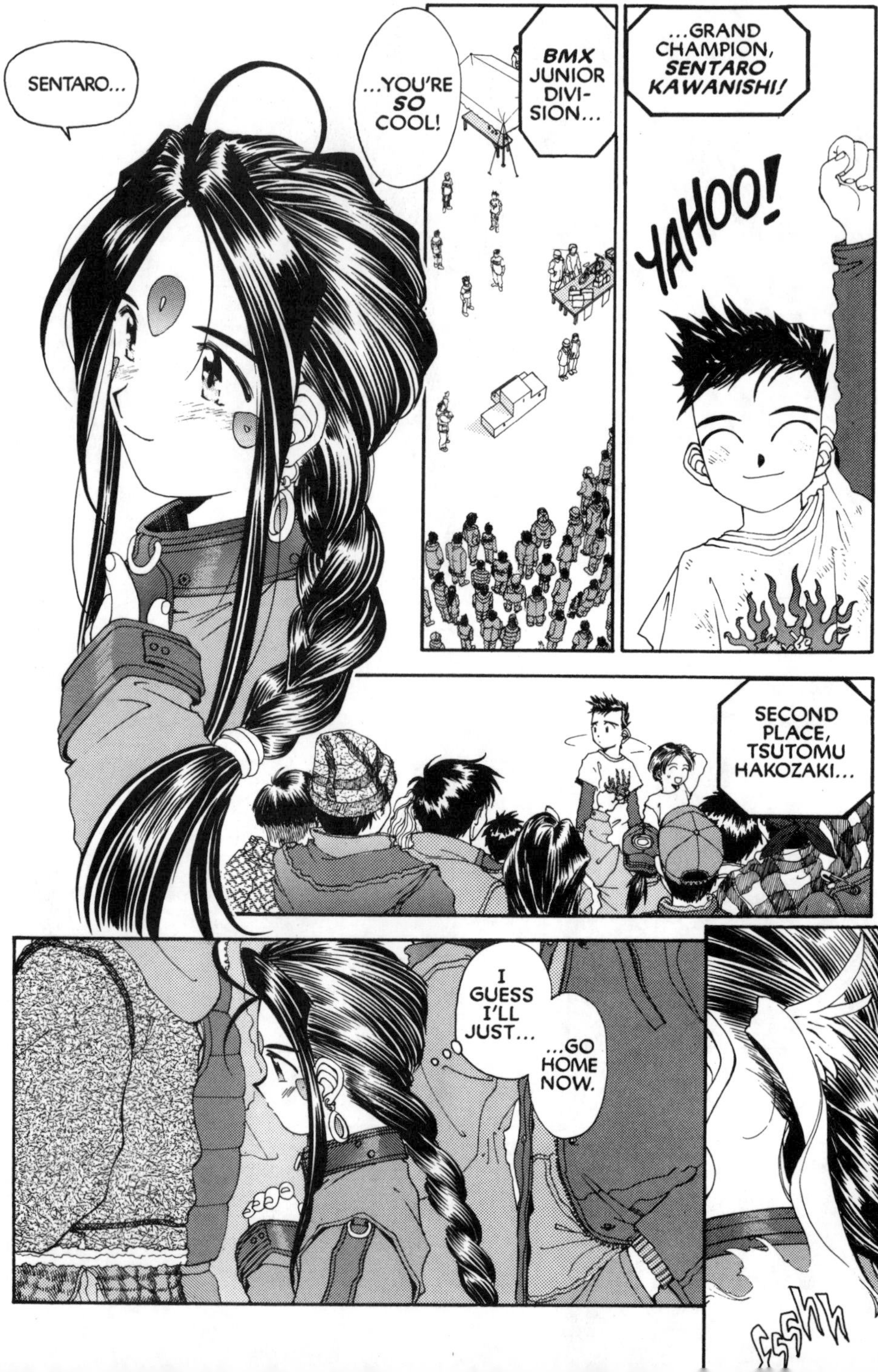
SENTARO...
...YOU'RE *SO* COOL!
BMX JUNIOR DIVI-SION...
...GRAND CHAMPION, *SENTARO KAWANISHI!*
YAHOO!
SECOND PLACE, TSUTOMU HAKOZAKI...
I GUESS I'LL JUST...
...GO HOME NOW.
ssshh

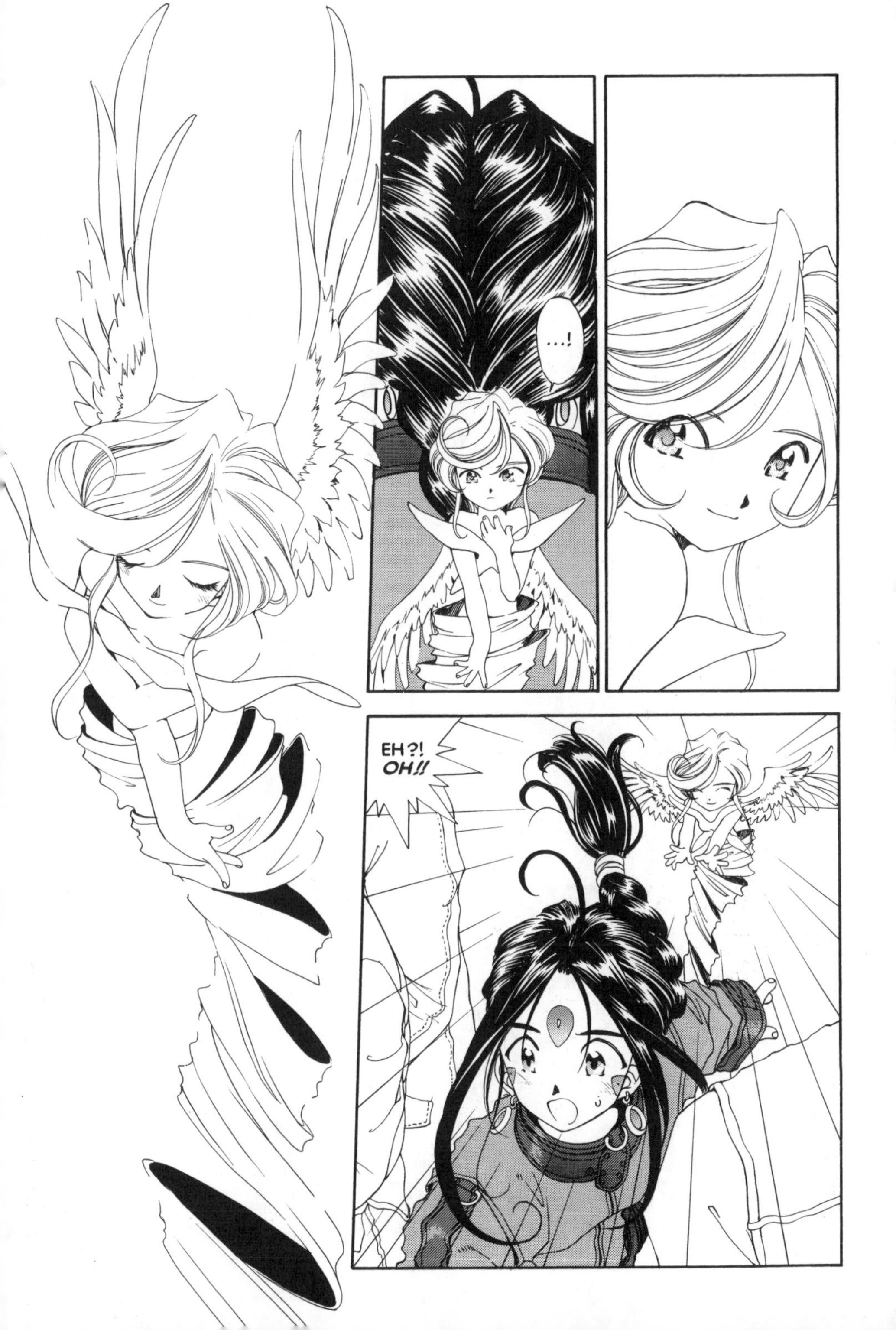
...!
EH?!
OH!!

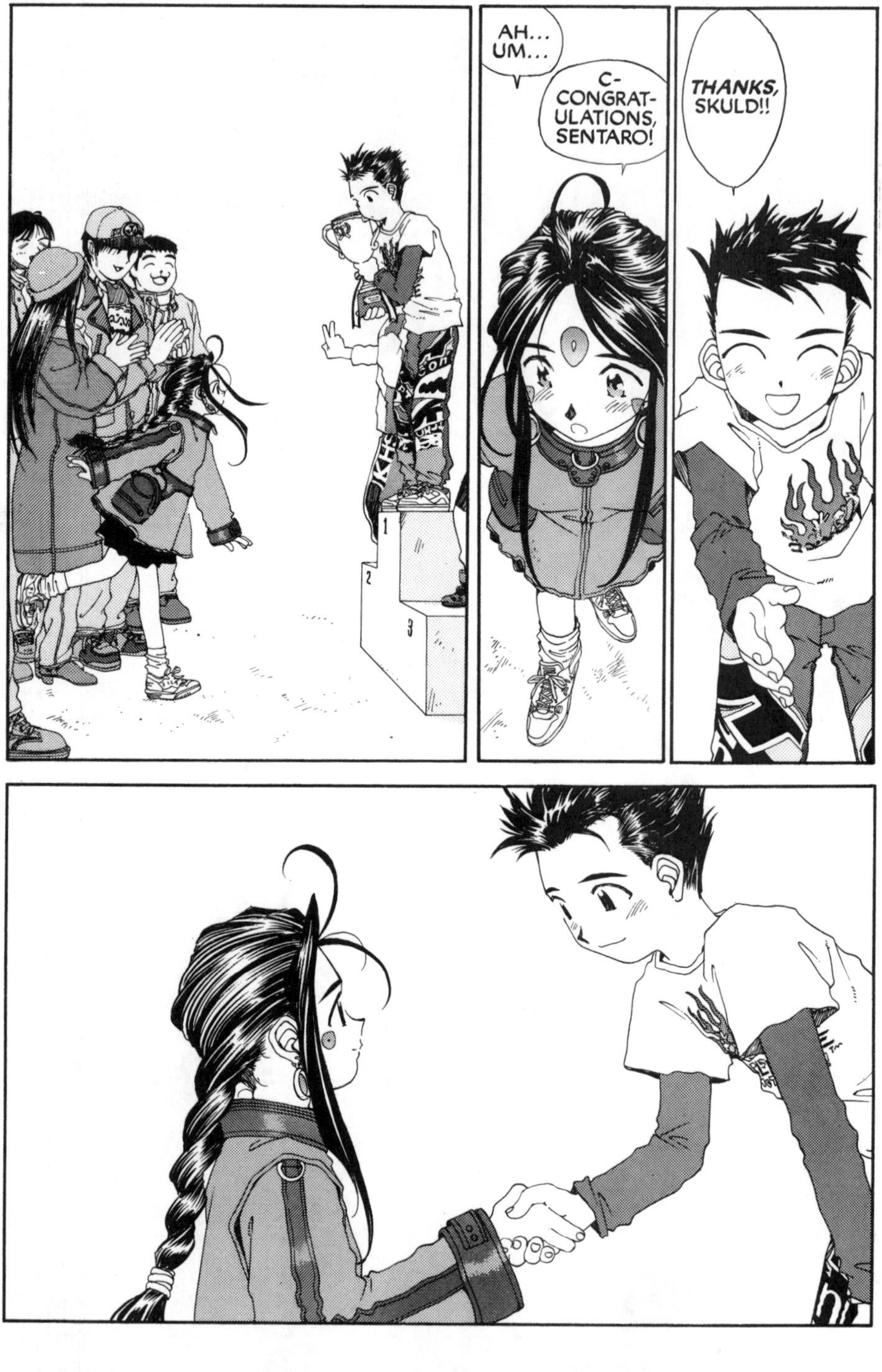
AH... UM...
C-CONGRAT-ULATIONS, SENTARO!
THANKS, SKULD!!

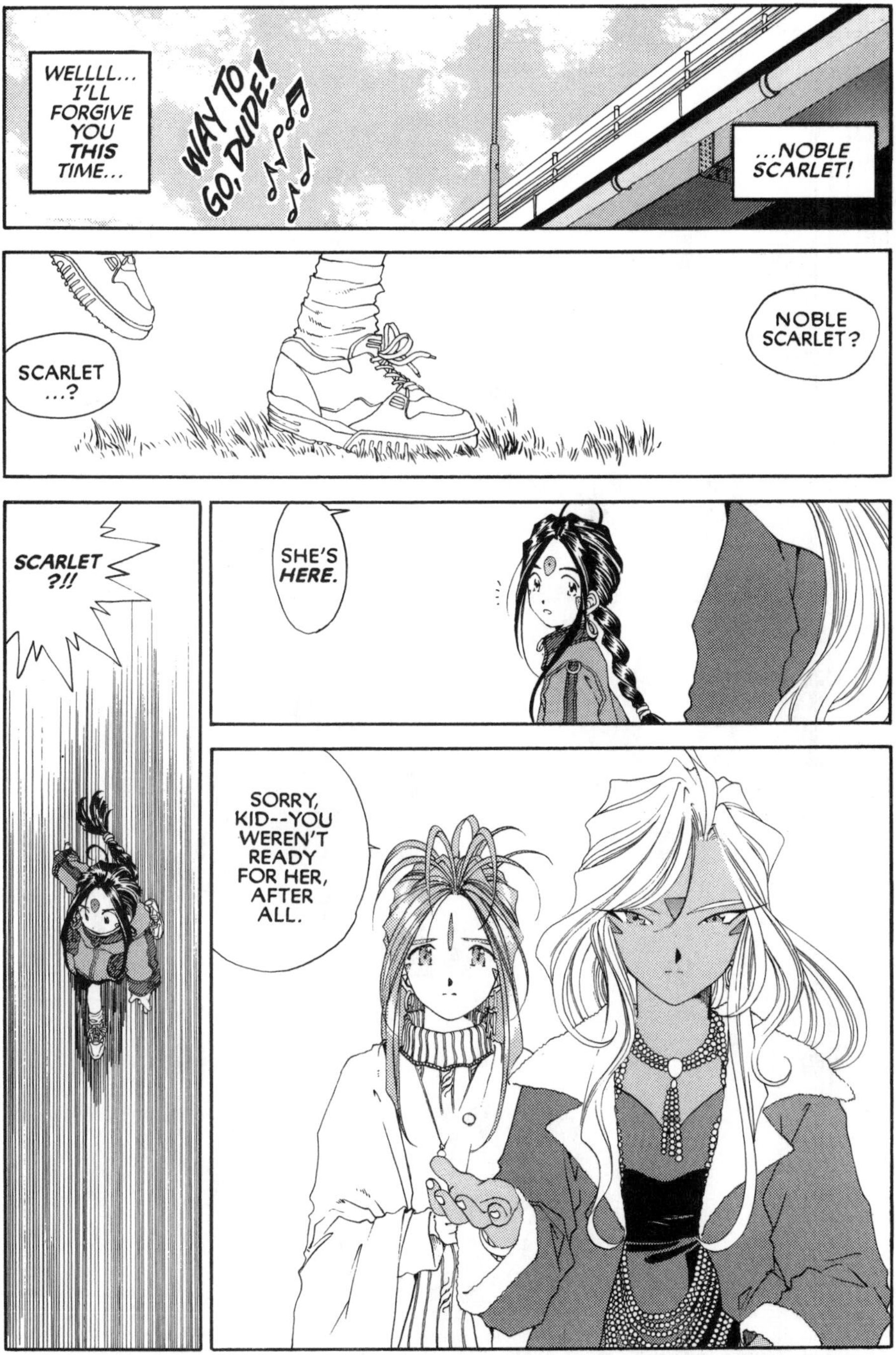
WELLLL... I'LL FORGIVE YOU THIS TIME...
WAY TO GO, DUDE!
...NOBLE SCARLET!
SCARLET ...?
NOBLE SCARLET?
SCARLET ?!!
SHE'S HERE.
SORRY, KID--YOU WEREN'T READY FOR HER, AFTER ALL.

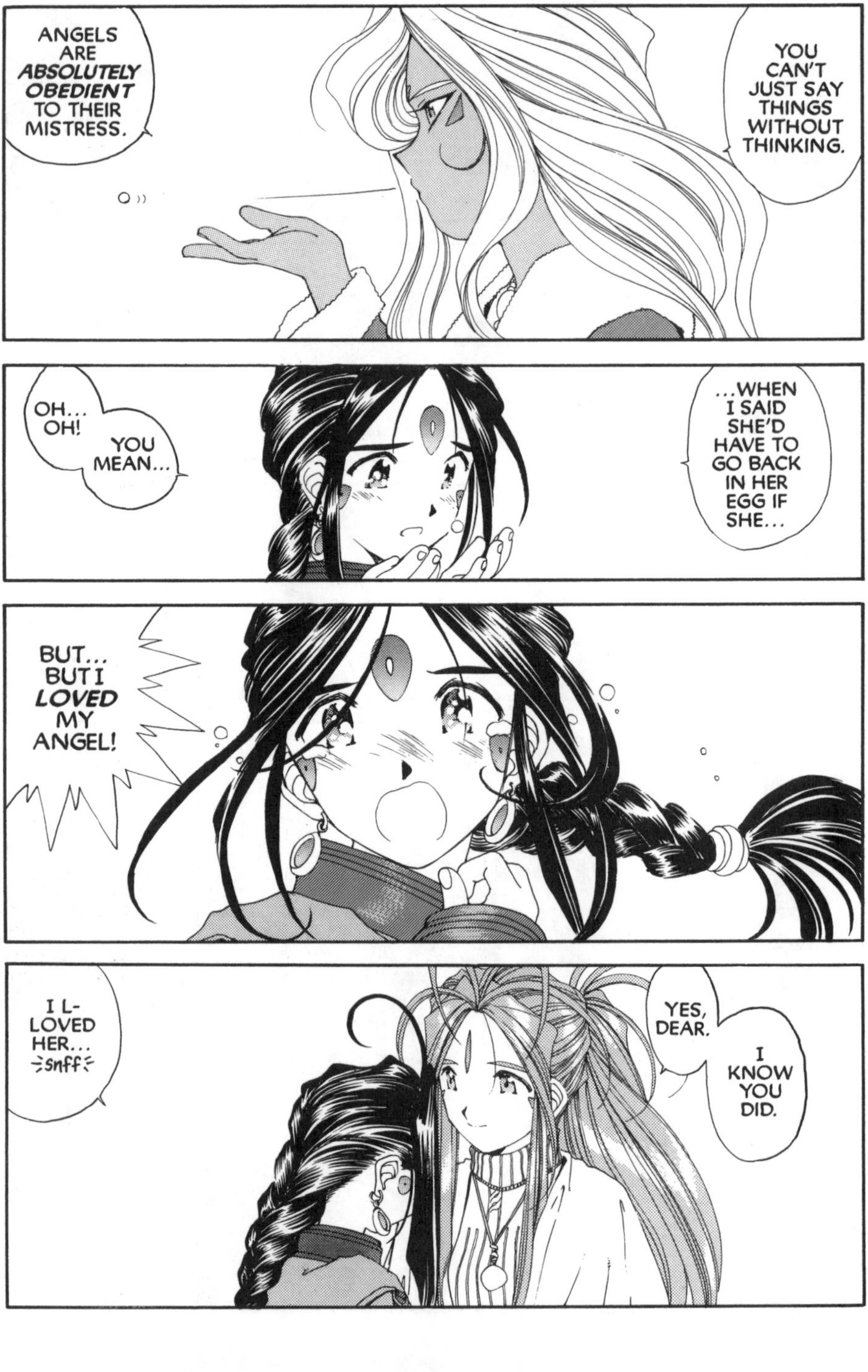
ANGELS ARE *ABSOLUTELY OBEDIENT* TO THEIR MISTRESS.
YOU CAN'T JUST SAY THINGS WITHOUT THINKING.
OH... OH!
YOU MEAN...
...WHEN I SAID SHE'D HAVE TO GO BACK IN HER EGG IF SHE...
BUT... BUT I *LOVED* MY ANGEL!
I L-LOVED HER... snff
YES, DEAR.
I KNOW YOU DID.

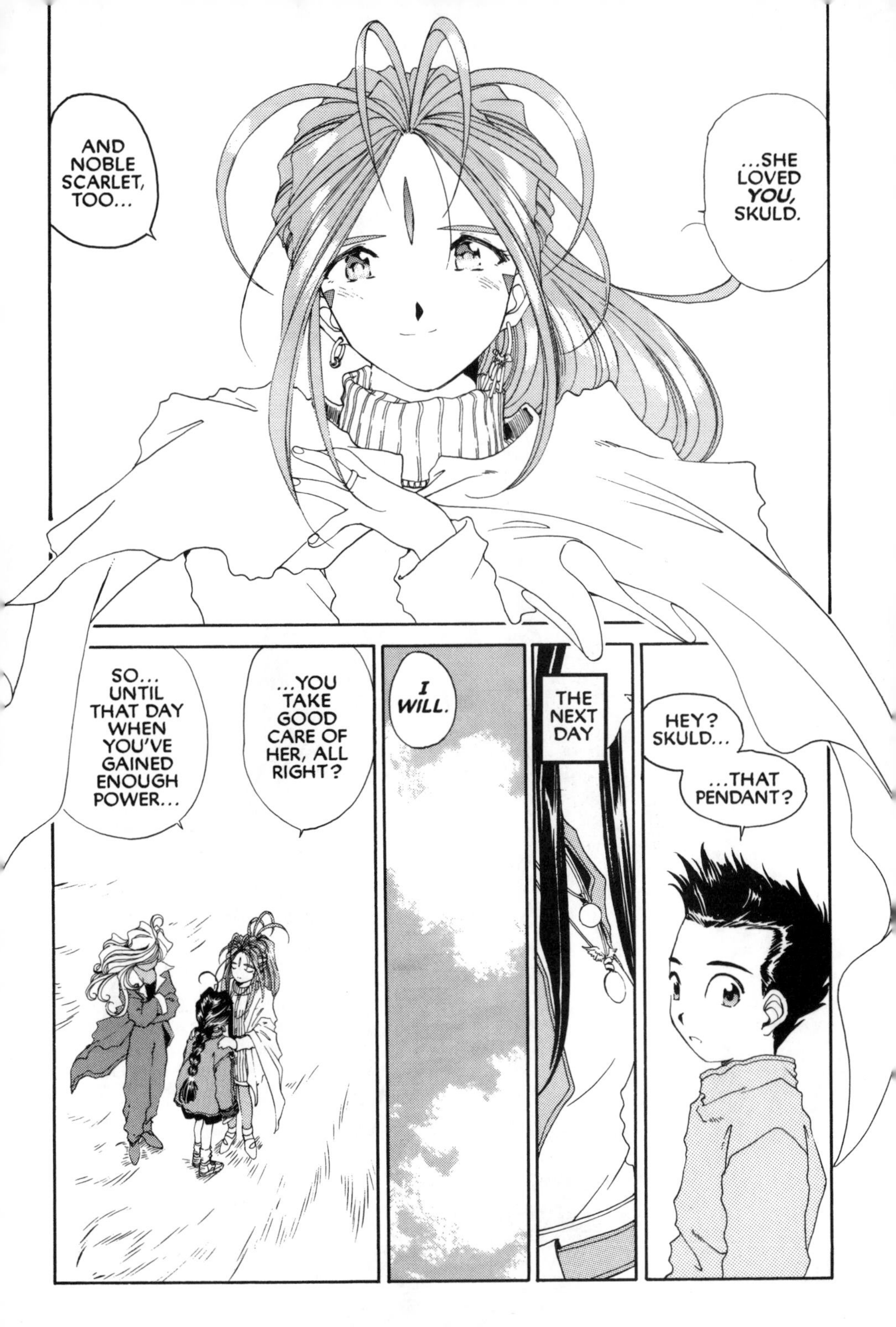
AND NOBLE SCARLET, TOO...
...SHE LOVED ***YOU,*** SKULD.
SO... UNTIL THAT DAY WHEN YOU'VE GAINED ENOUGH POWER...
...YOU TAKE GOOD CARE OF HER, ALL RIGHT?
I WILL.
THE NEXT DAY
HEY? SKULD...
...THAT PENDANT?

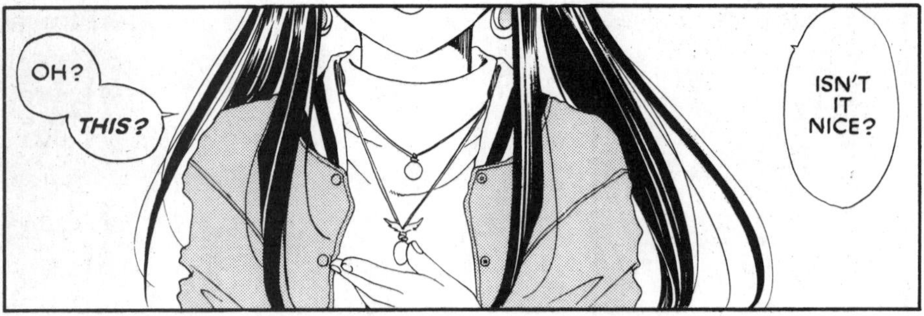
OH? THIS?
ISN'T IT NICE?

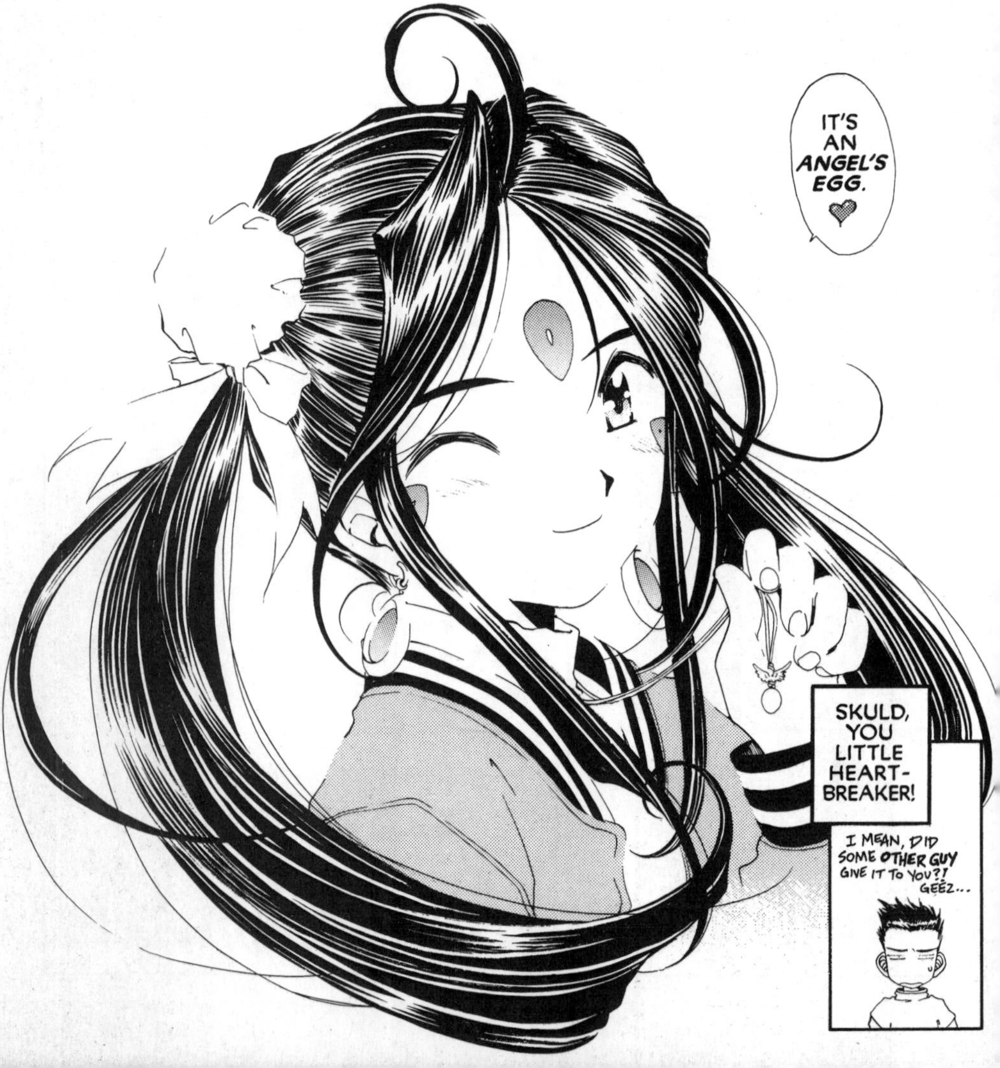
IT'S AN ANGEL'S EGG. ♥
SKULD, YOU LITTLE HEART-BREAKER!
I MEAN, DID SOME OTHER GUY GIVE IT TO YOU?! GEEZ...

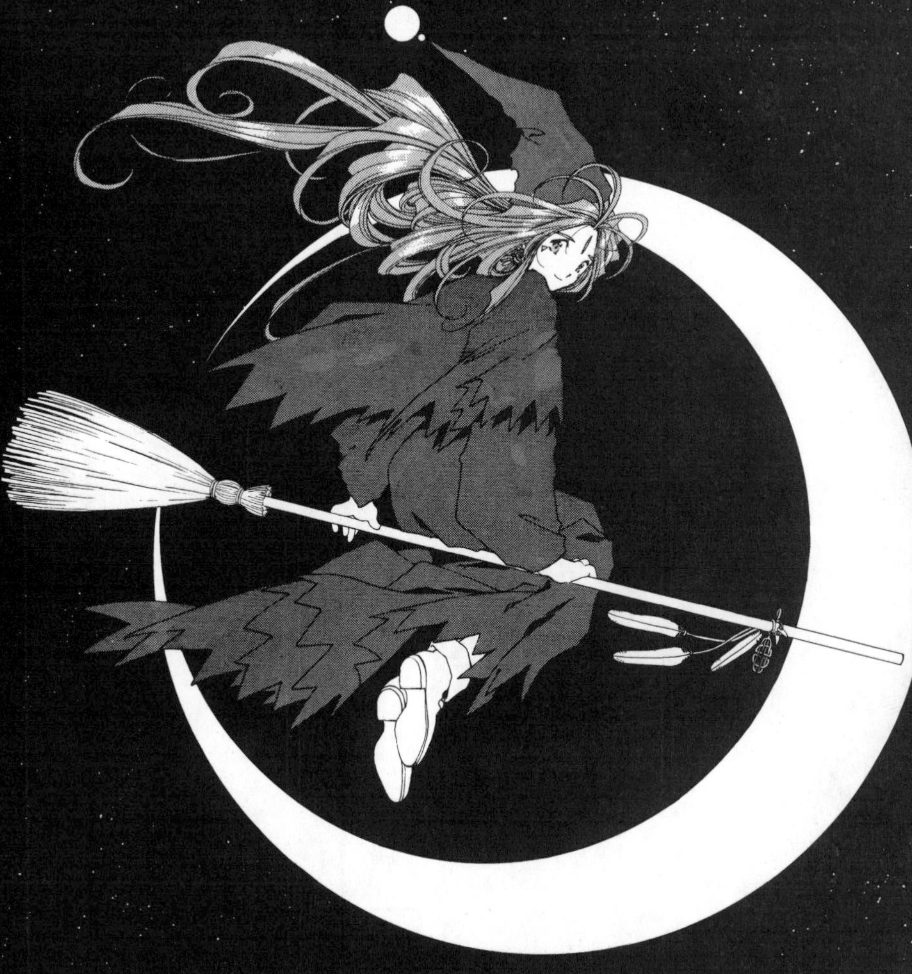

The Goddess's Apprentice

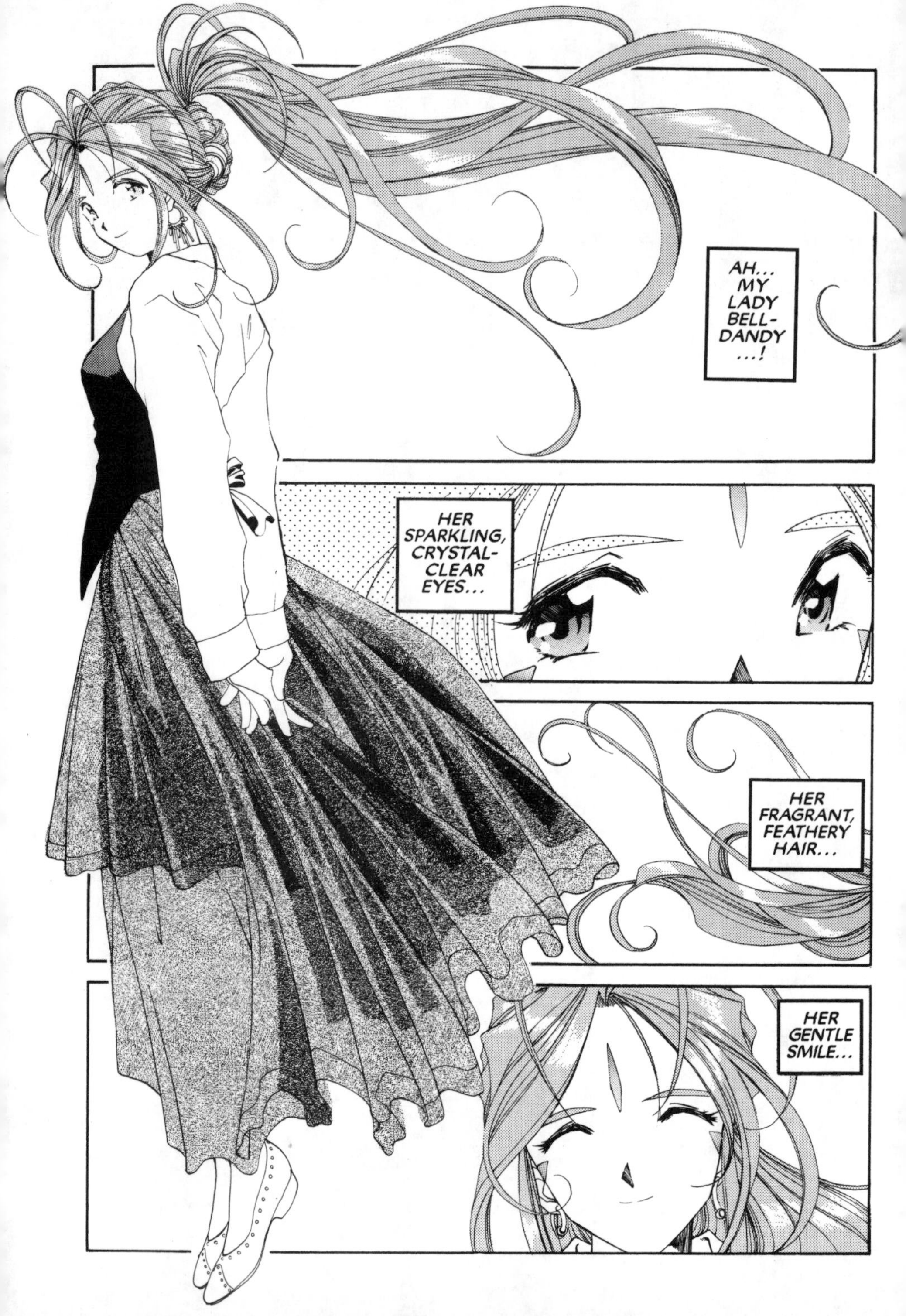
AH... MY LADY BELL-DANDY ...!
HER SPARKLING, CRYSTAL-CLEAR EYES...
HER FRAGRANT, FEATHERY HAIR...
HER GENTLE SMILE...

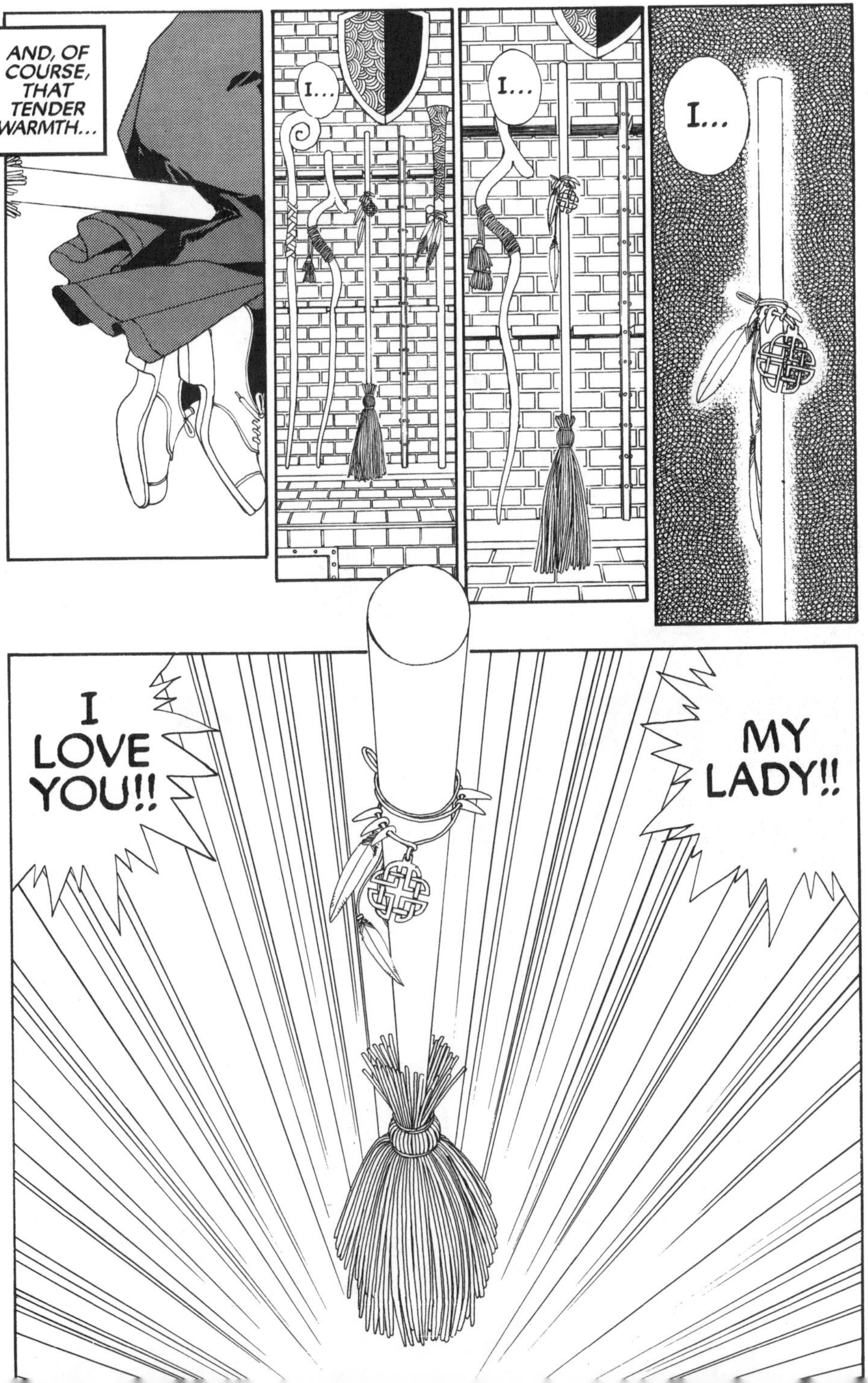
AND, OF COURSE, THAT TENDER WARMTH...
I...
I...
I...
I LOVE YOU!!
MY LADY!!

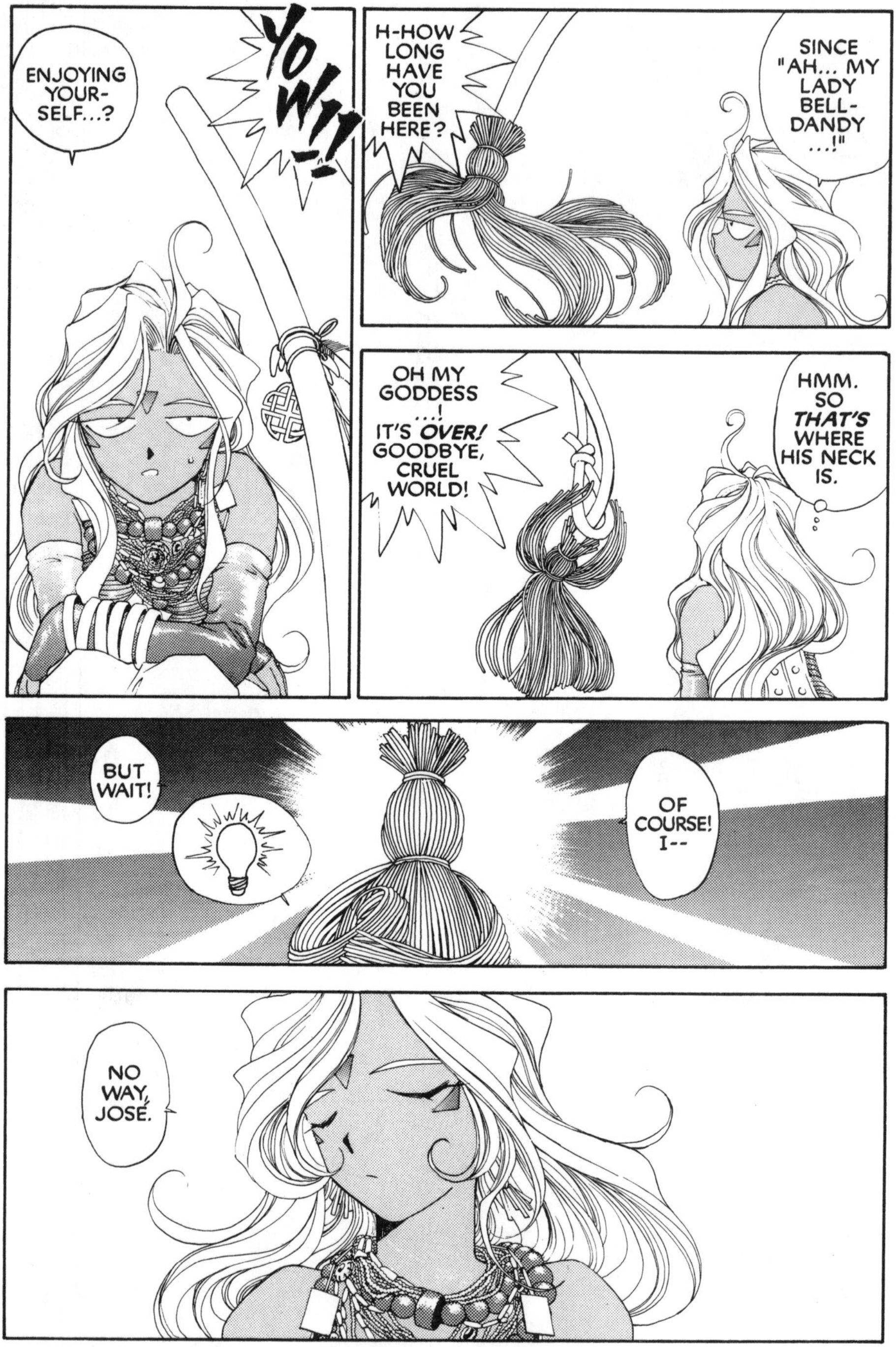
ENJOYING YOURSELF...?
YOWL!!
H-HOW LONG HAVE YOU BEEN HERE?
SINCE "AH... MY LADY BELLDANDY...!"
OH MY GODDESS...! IT'S *OVER!* GOODBYE, CRUEL WORLD!
HMM. SO *THAT'S* WHERE HIS NECK IS.
BUT WAIT!
OF COURSE! I--
NO WAY, JOSÉ.

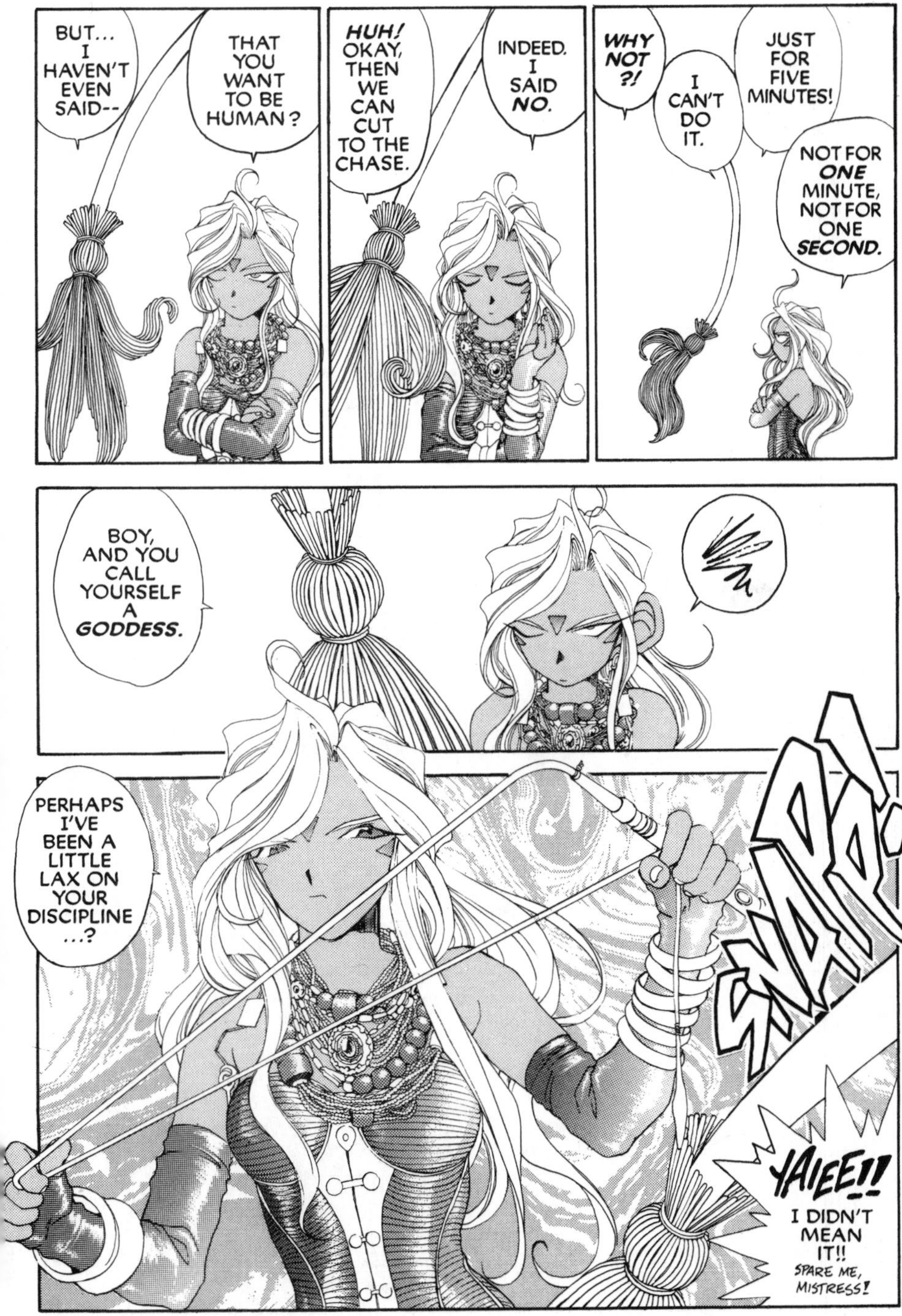
BUT... I HAVEN'T EVEN SAID--
THAT YOU WANT TO BE HUMAN?
HUH! OKAY, THEN WE CAN CUT TO THE CHASE.
INDEED. I SAID NO.
WHY NOT?!
JUST FOR FIVE MINUTES!
I CAN'T DO IT.
NOT FOR ONE MINUTE, NOT FOR ONE SECOND.
BOY, AND YOU CALL YOURSELF A GODDESS.
PERHAPS I'VE BEEN A LITTLE LAX ON YOUR DISCIPLINE ...?
SNAP!
YAIEE!! I DIDN'T MEAN IT!! SPARE ME, MISTRESS!

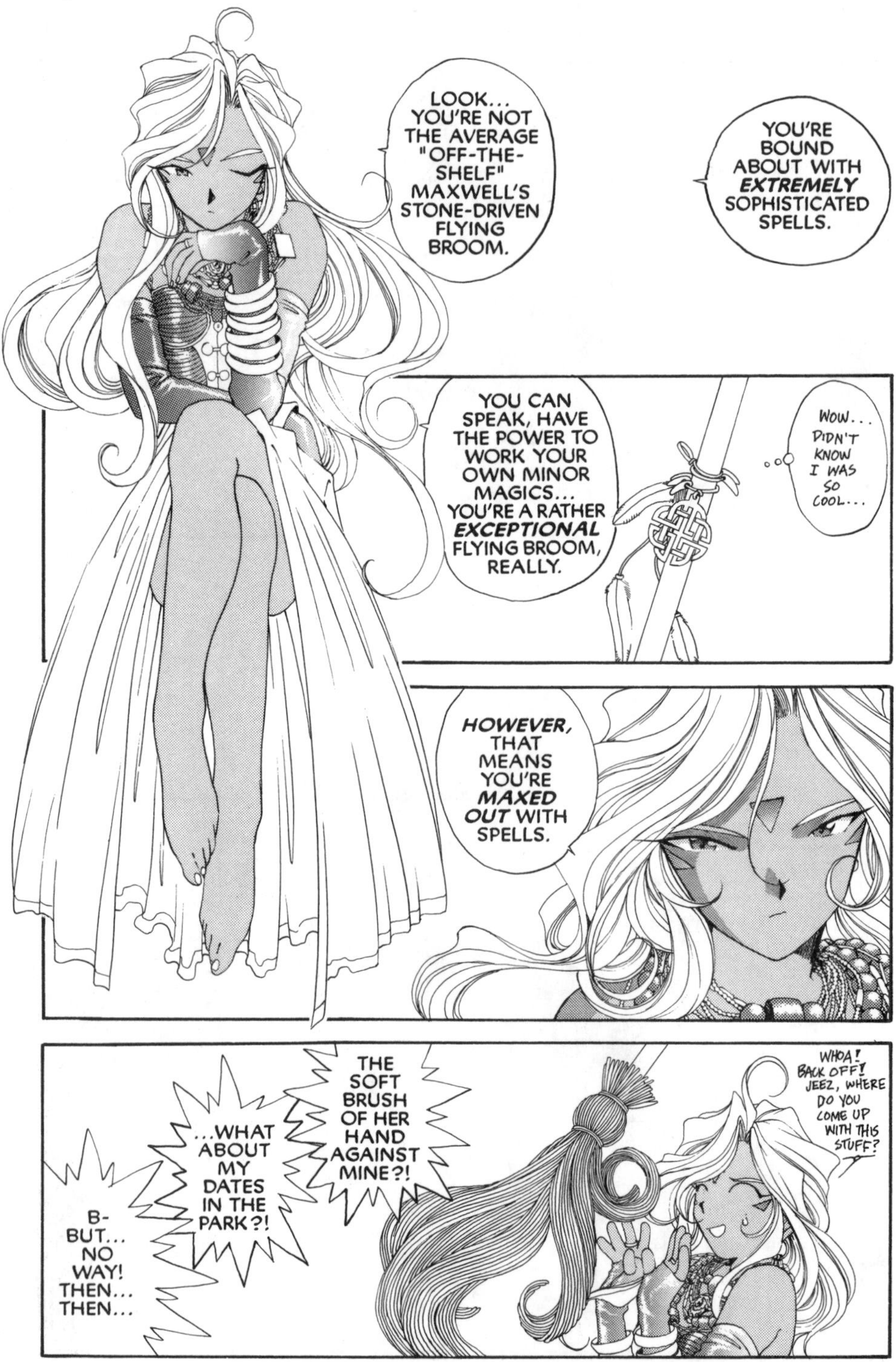
LOOK... YOU'RE NOT THE AVERAGE "OFF-THE-SHELF" MAXWELL'S STONE-DRIVEN FLYING BROOM.
YOU'RE BOUND ABOUT WITH *EXTREMELY* SOPHISTICATED SPELLS.
YOU CAN SPEAK, HAVE THE POWER TO WORK YOUR OWN MINOR MAGICS... YOU'RE A RATHER *EXCEPTIONAL* FLYING BROOM, REALLY.
WOW... DIDN'T KNOW I WAS SO COOL...
HOWEVER, THAT MEANS YOU'RE *MAXED OUT* WITH SPELLS.
B-BUT... NO WAY! THEN... THEN...
...WHAT ABOUT MY DATES IN THE PARK?!
THE SOFT BRUSH OF HER HAND AGAINST MINE?!
WHOA! BACK OFF! JEEZ, WHERE DO YOU COME UP WITH THIS STUFF?

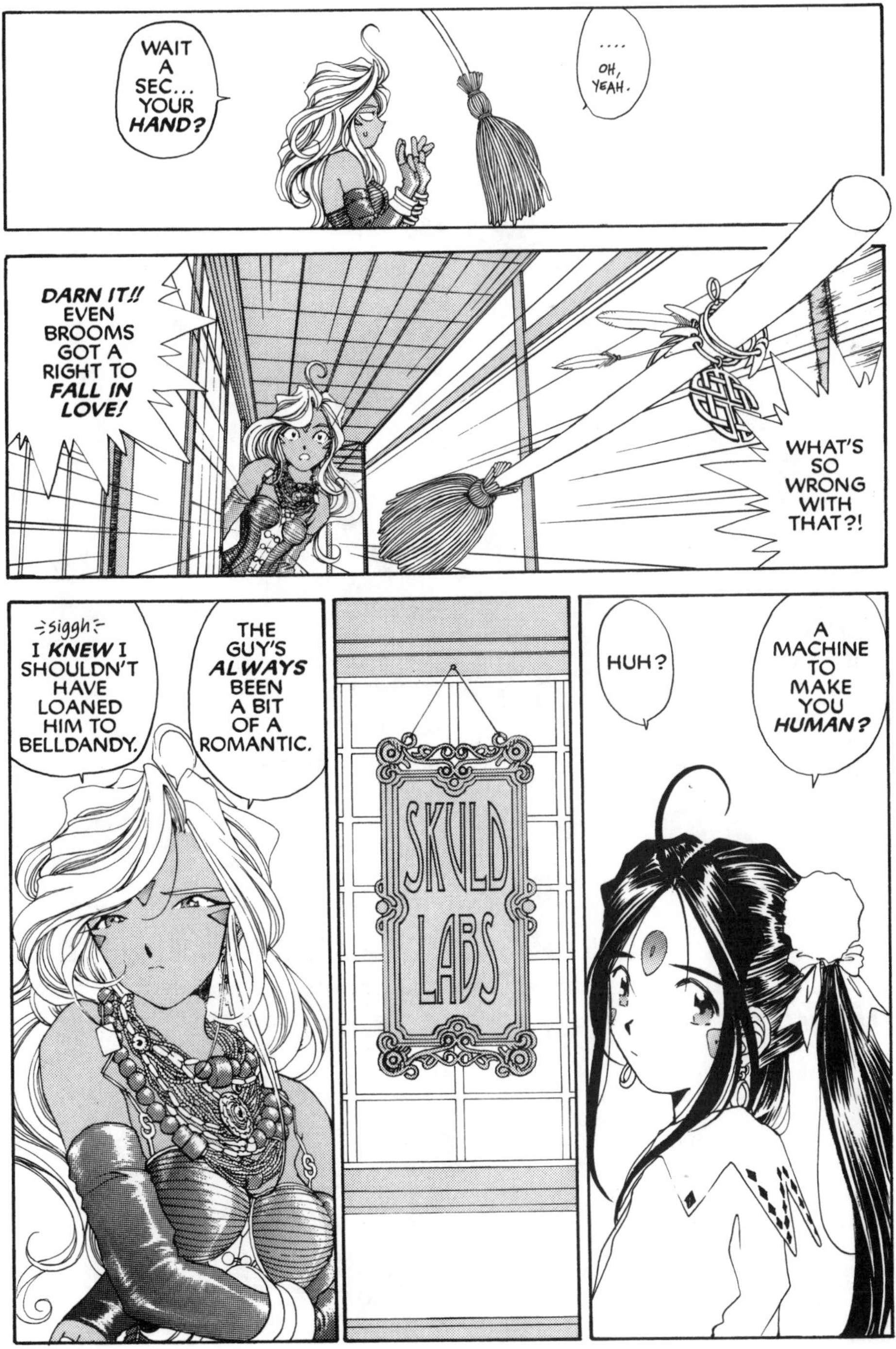
WAIT A SEC... YOUR HAND?
.... OH, YEAH.
DARN IT!! EVEN BROOMS GOT A RIGHT TO FALL IN LOVE!
WHAT'S SO WRONG WITH THAT?!
≈sighh≈ I KNEW I SHOULDN'T HAVE LOANED HIM TO BELLDANDY.
THE GUY'S ALWAYS BEEN A BIT OF A ROMANTIC.
SKULD LABS
HUH?
A MACHINE TO MAKE YOU HUMAN?

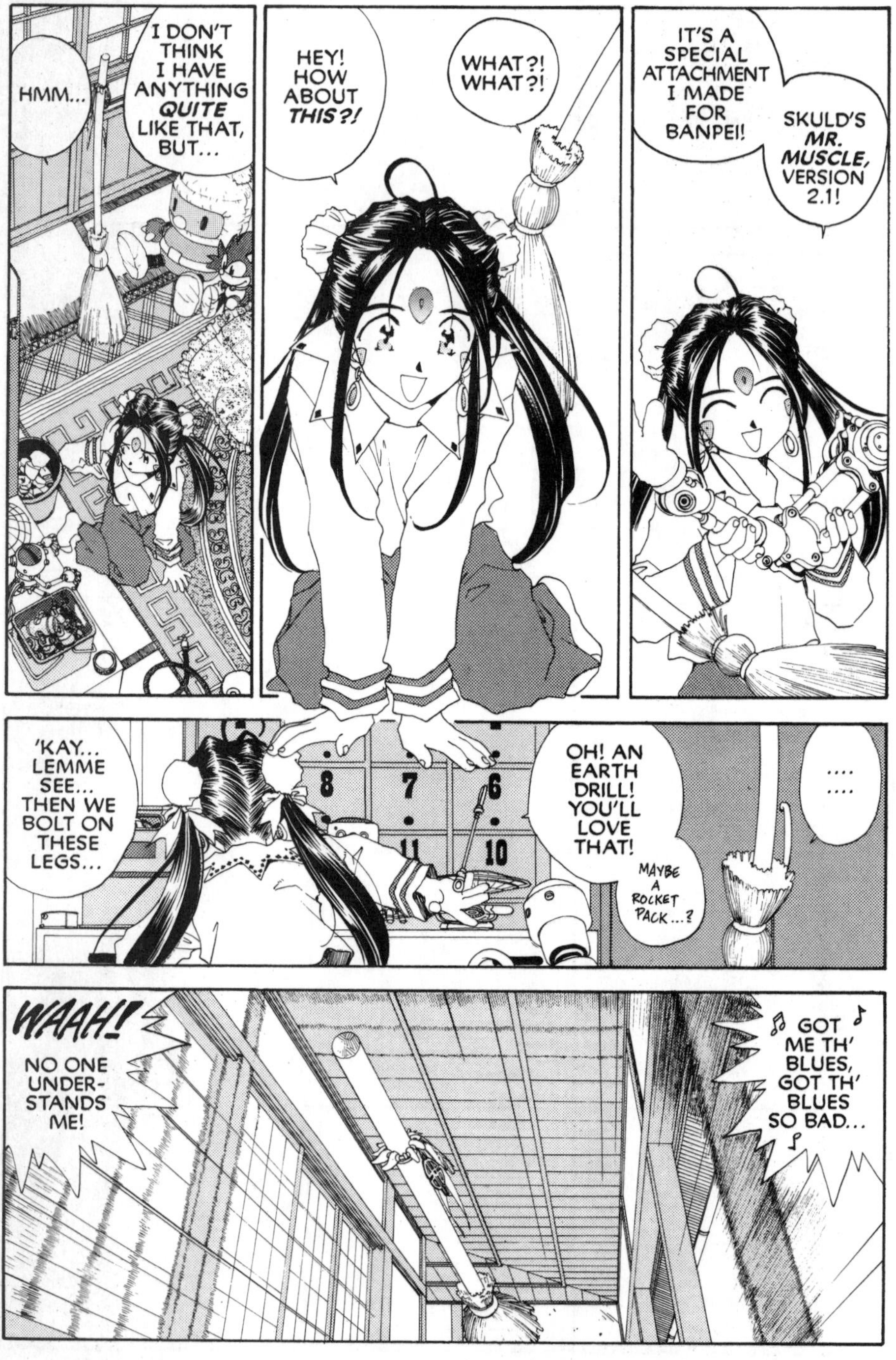
HMM...
I DON'T THINK I HAVE ANYTHING QUITE LIKE THAT, BUT...
HEY! HOW ABOUT THIS?!
WHAT?! WHAT?!
IT'S A SPECIAL ATTACHMENT I MADE FOR BANPEI!
SKULD'S MR. MUSCLE, VERSION 2.1!
'KAY... LEMME SEE... THEN WE BOLT ON THESE LEGS...
OH! AN EARTH DRILL! YOU'LL LOVE THAT!
MAYBE A ROCKET PACK...?
....
....
WAAH!
NO ONE UNDER-STANDS ME!
♪ GOT ME TH' BLUES, GOT TH' BLUES SO BAD... ♪

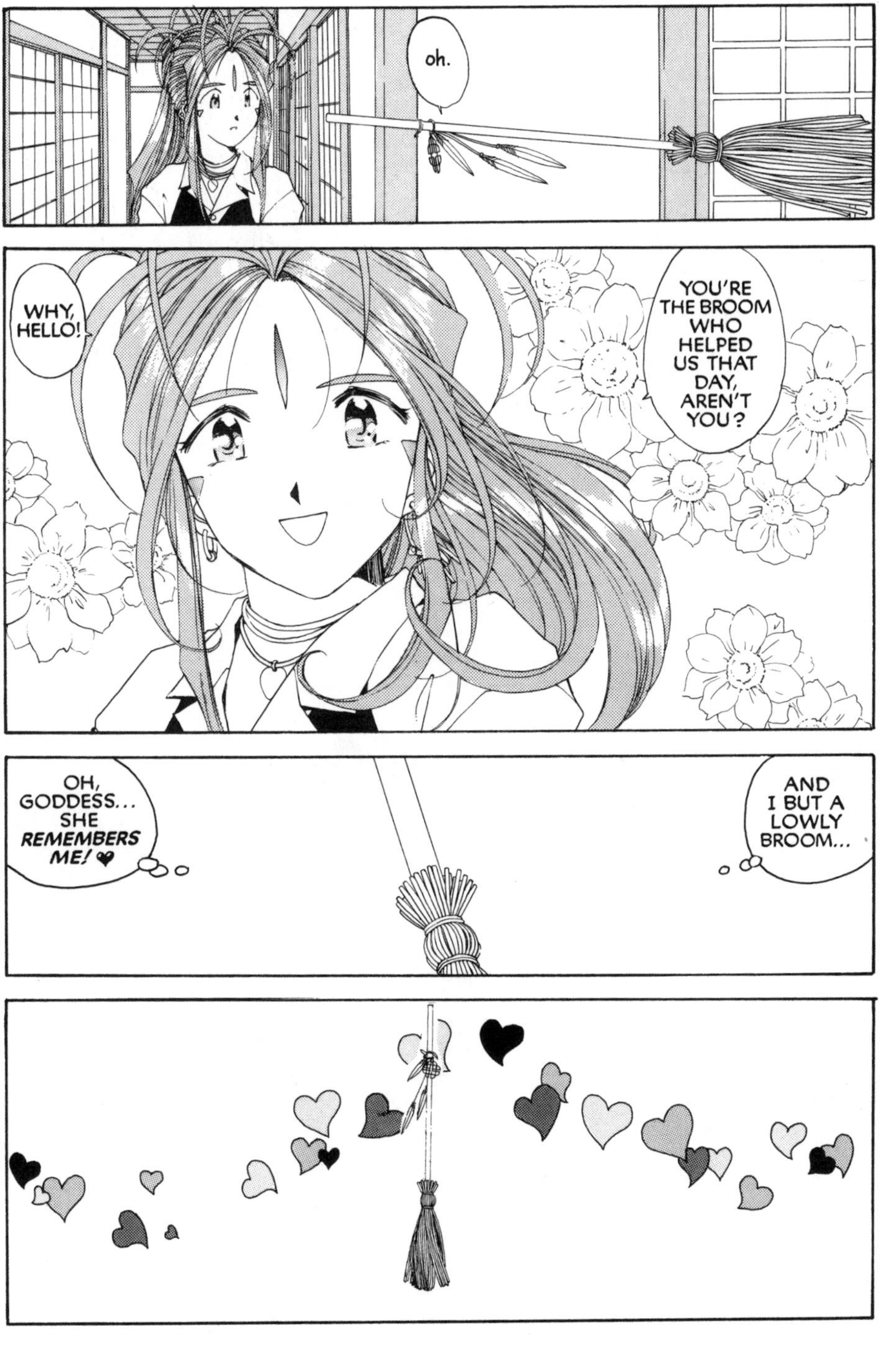
oh.
WHY, HELLO!
YOU'RE THE BROOM WHO HELPED US THAT DAY, AREN'T YOU?
OH, GODDESS... SHE *REMEMBERS ME!* ❤
AND I BUT A LOWLY BROOM...

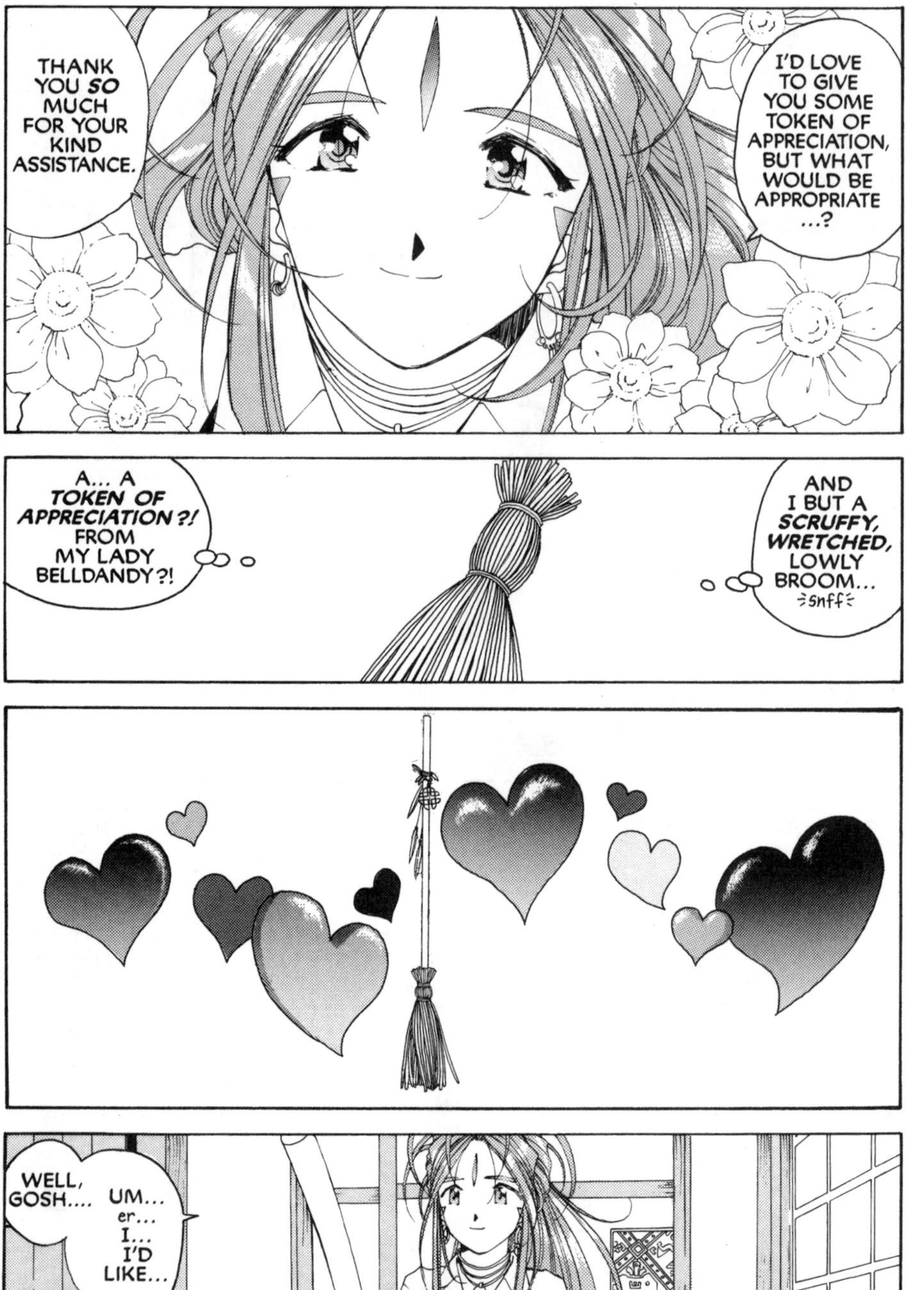
THANK YOU SO MUCH FOR YOUR KIND ASSISTANCE.
I'D LOVE TO GIVE YOU SOME TOKEN OF APPRECIATION, BUT WHAT WOULD BE APPROPRIATE ...?
A... A TOKEN OF APPRECIATION?! FROM MY LADY BELLDANDY?!
AND I BUT A SCRUFFY, WRETCHED, LOWLY BROOM...
snff
WELL, GOSH.... UM... er... I... I'D LIKE...

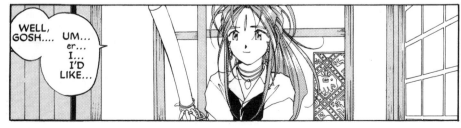

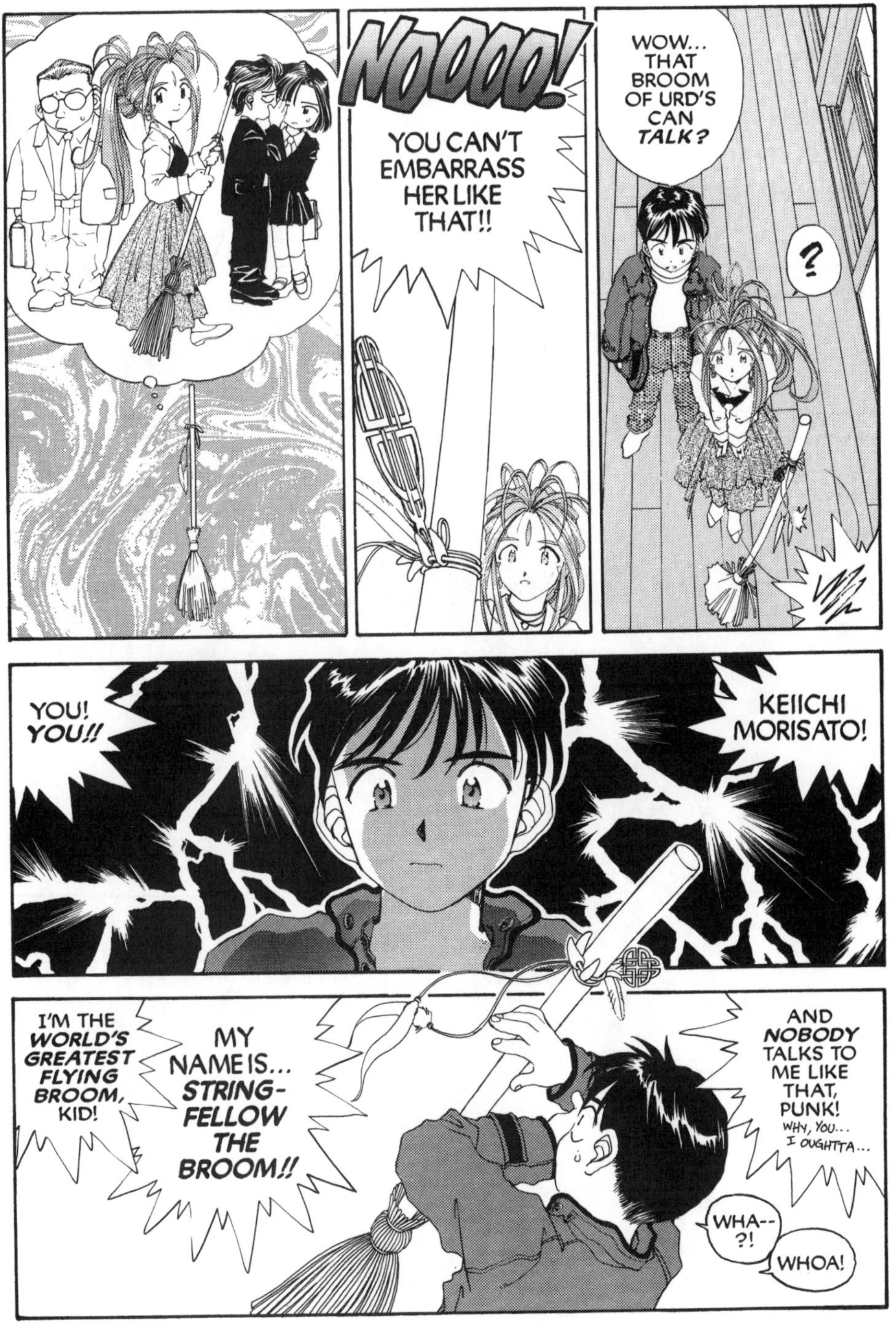
NOOOO!
YOU CAN'T EMBARRASS HER LIKE THAT!!
WOW... THAT BROOM OF URD'S CAN *TALK?*
?
YOU! *YOU!!*
KEIICHI MORISATO!
I'M THE *WORLD'S GREATEST FLYING BROOM,* KID!
MY NAME IS... *STRING-FELLOW THE BROOM!!*
AND *NOBODY* TALKS TO ME LIKE THAT, PUNK!
WHY, YOU... I OUGHTTA...
WHA-- ?!
WHOA!

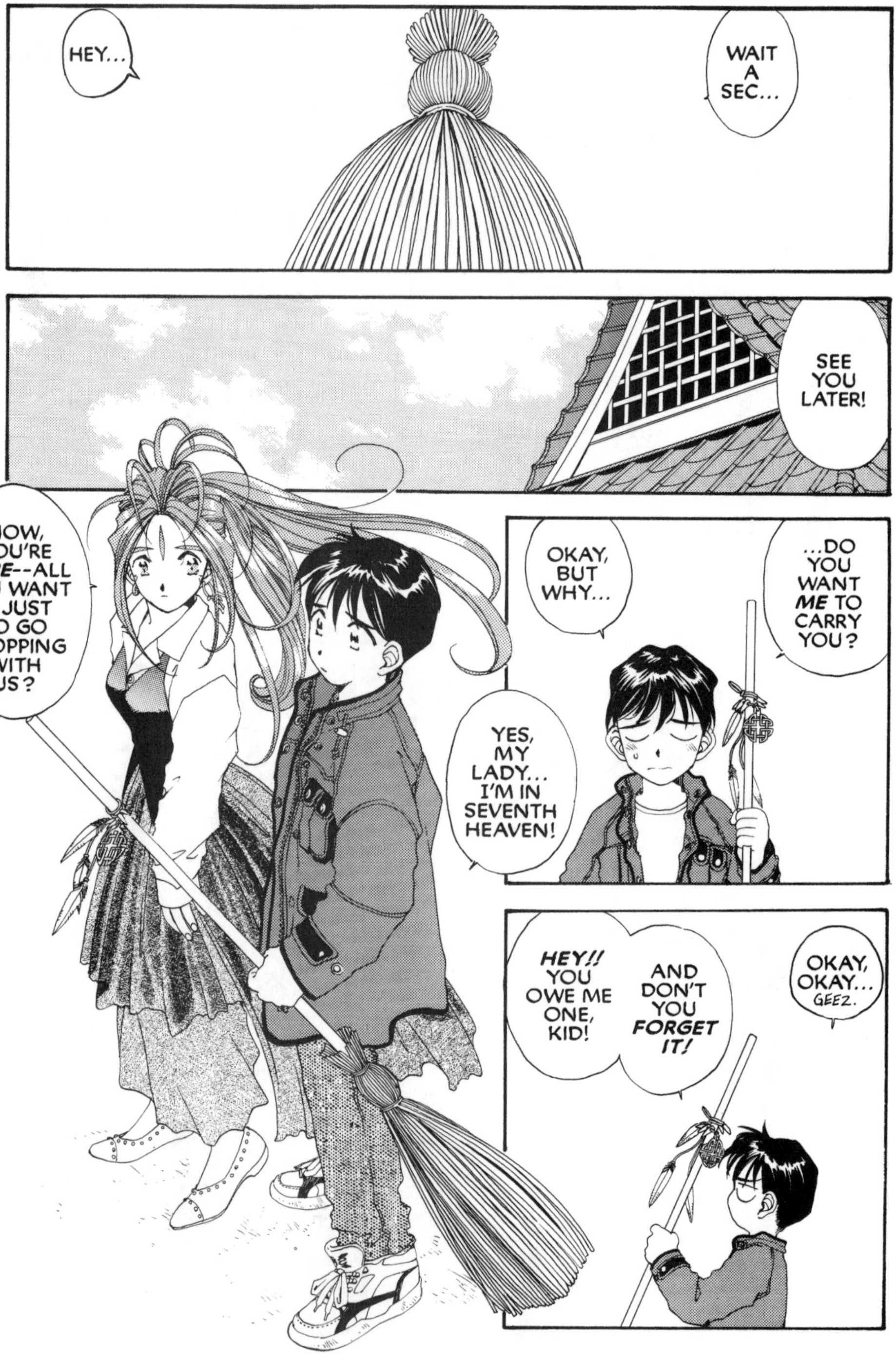
HEY...
WAIT A SEC...
SEE YOU LATER!
NOW, YOU'RE *SURE*--ALL YOU WANT IS JUST TO GO SHOPPING WITH US?
YES, MY LADY... I'M IN SEVENTH HEAVEN!
OKAY, BUT WHY...
...DO YOU WANT *ME* TO CARRY YOU?
HEY!! YOU OWE ME ONE, KID!
AND DON'T YOU *FORGET IT!*
OKAY, OKAY... GEEZ.

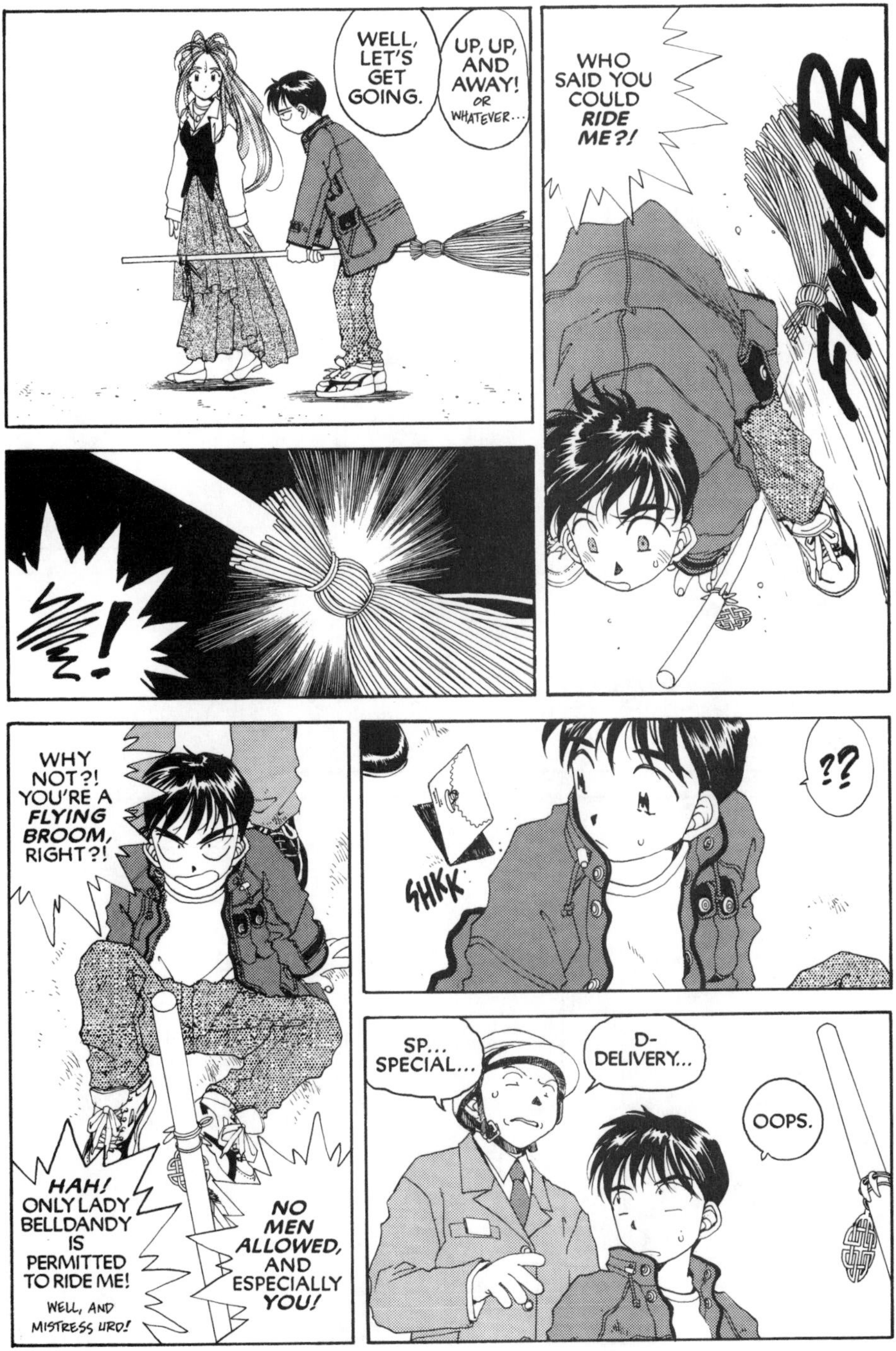
WELL, LET'S GET GOING.
UP, UP, AND AWAY! OR WHATEVER...
WHO SAID YOU COULD RIDE ME?!
SWAP
WHY NOT?! YOU'RE A FLYING BROOM, RIGHT?!
HAH! ONLY LADY BELLDANDY IS PERMITTED TO RIDE ME!
WELL, AND MISTRESS URD!
NO MEN ALLOWED, AND ESPECIALLY YOU!
??
SHKK
SP... SPECIAL...
D- DELIVERY...
OOPS.

ARE YOU... uh... A *MAGICIAN?*

THAT'S AN AMAZING TRICK.

OH, YEAH! JUST PRACTICING!

HA HA HA HA heh

HOW *RUDE!* I AM *NOT* A "TRICK"...! I'M THE WORLD'S GREATEST...

ETCETERA, ETCETERA...

ALWAYS SOMETHING INTERESTING AT THIS PLACE.

THANK HEAVENS IT'S A TRICK. A MAGIC TRICK.

SORRY ABOUT THAT... HEH, HEH...

ARE YOU TALKIN' TO *ME,* PAL?!

WELL, I GUESS WE'D REALLY STICK OUT IF WE FLEW, ANYWAY.

I'M GONNA GO *POSTAL* ON YOU, POSTMAN! HEY! *HEY!!*

BUT THIS ISN'T MUCH BETTER. YEESH.

DUMB BROOM...

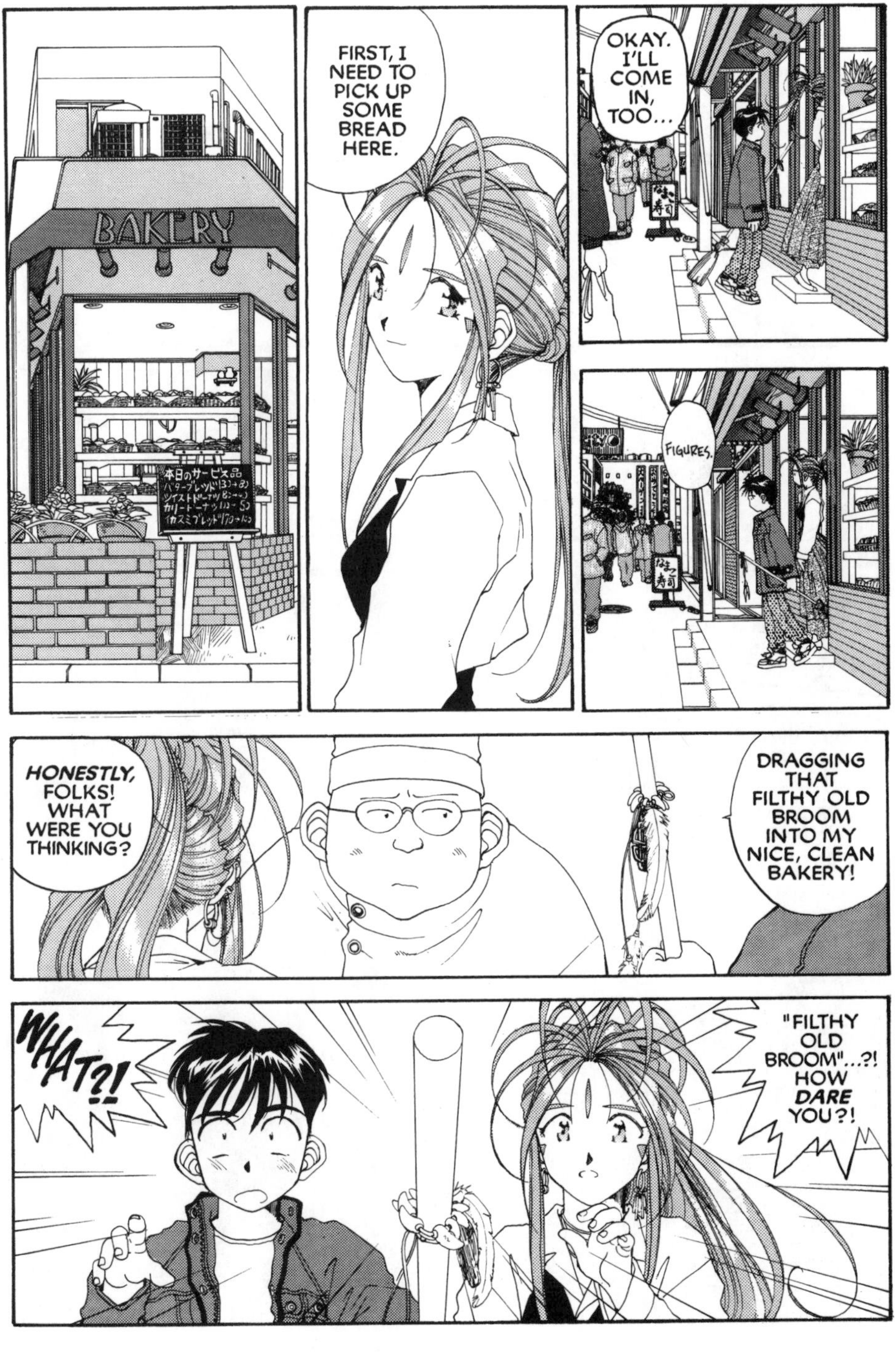
BAKERY
本日のサービス品
FIRST, I NEED TO PICK UP SOME BREAD HERE.
OKAY. I'LL COME IN, TOO...
FIGURES.
HONESTLY, FOLKS! WHAT WERE YOU THINKING?
DRAGGING THAT FILTHY OLD BROOM INTO MY NICE, CLEAN BAKERY!
WHAT?!
"FILTHY OLD BROOM"...?! HOW *DARE* YOU?!

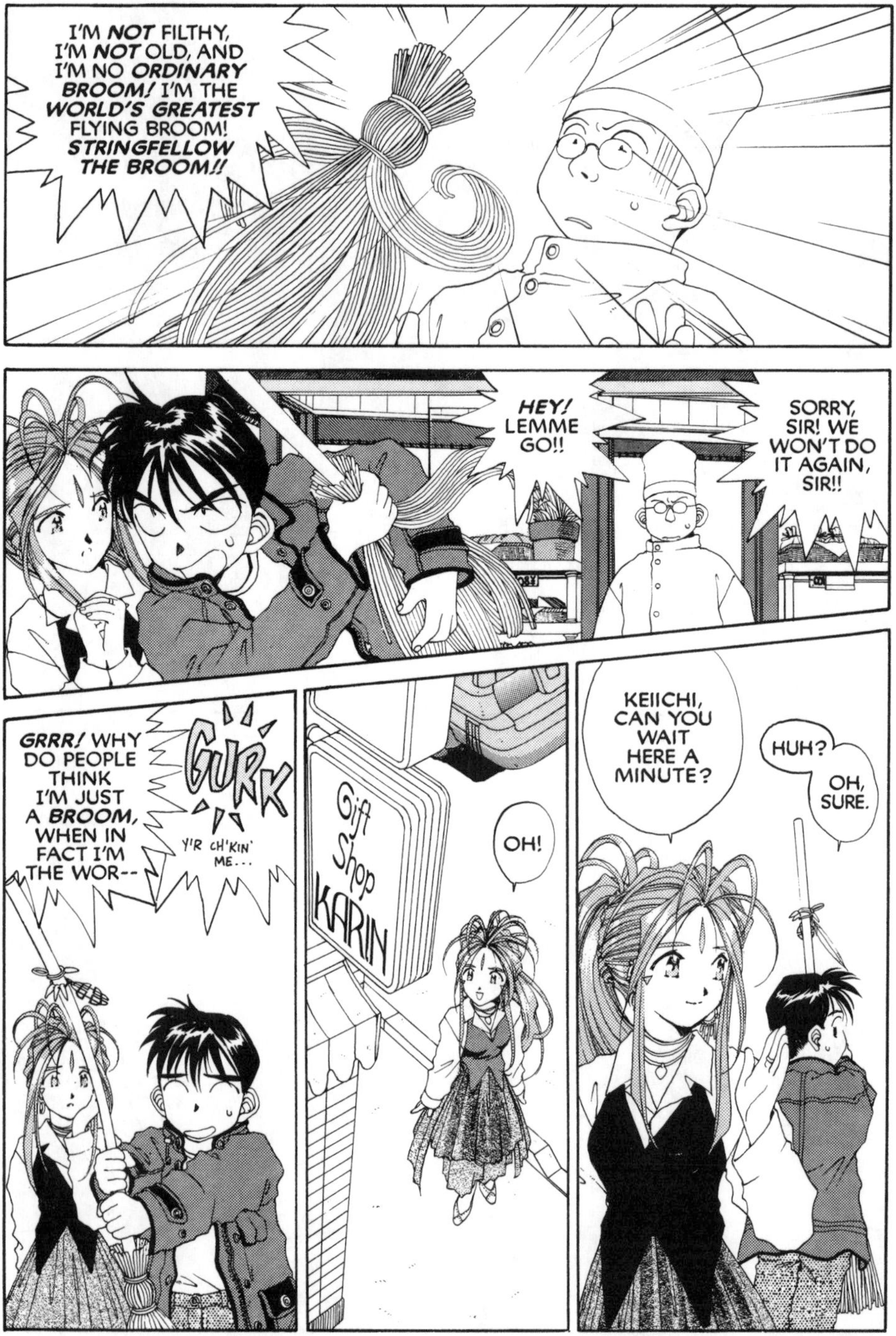

I'M ***NOT*** FILTHY, I'M ***NOT*** OLD, AND I'M NO ***ORDINARY BROOM!*** I'M THE ***WORLD'S GREATEST*** FLYING BROOM! ***STRINGFELLOW THE BROOM!!***
HEY! LEMME GO!!
SORRY, SIR! WE WON'T DO IT AGAIN, SIR!!
GRRR! WHY DO PEOPLE THINK I'M JUST A ***BROOM,*** WHEN IN FACT I'M THE WOR--
GURK
Y'R CH'KIN' ME...
Gift Shop KARIN
OH!
KEIICHI, CAN YOU WAIT HERE A MINUTE?
HUH?
OH, SURE.

SEE YOU LATER, HONEY! ♥
HEY, HEY!
NOW I GET IT.
GET WHAT?
YOU'RE IN LOVE WITH BELL-DANDY... RIGHT?
YEAH? SO?!
OKAY, I KNOW I'M JUST A BROOM!
BUT BROOMS GOT A RIGHT TO FALL IN LOVE, TOO!
I WANT TO TOUCH THAT BEAUTIFUL, SILKEN HAIR...
I WANT TO HOLD THOSE SOFT, SWEET HANDS...

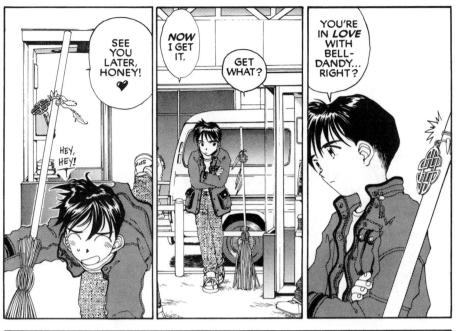

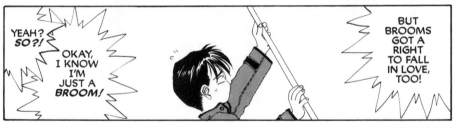

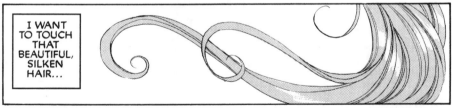

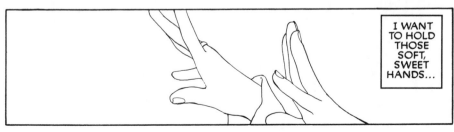

LOOK-- I'M NOT DUMB. I KNOW I'M A BROOM, AND SHE'S A GODDESS.

I KNOW I CAN'T HOPE FOR MUCH, BUT...

I SEE.

HMM... HE'S THE SAME AS ME, REALLY.

I DON'T KNOW IF A MERE HUMAN AND A GODDESS CAN REALLY--

AARGHH!

AT THE *VERY* LEAST, I WANT HER TO PICK ME UP... HOLD ME TIGHT...

AND THEN...

...I WANT HER TO TAKE HER HANDS AND--

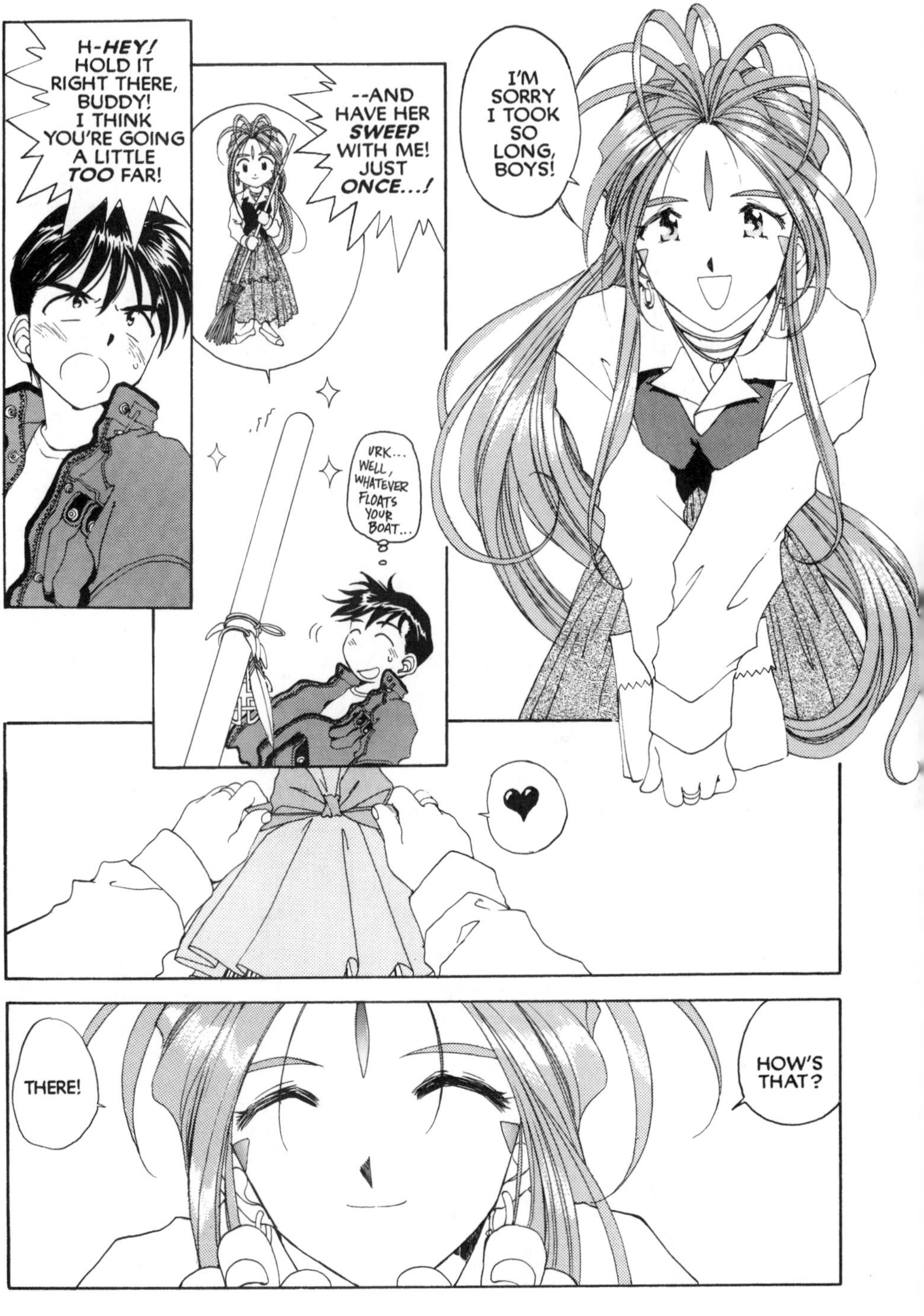
H-HEY! HOLD IT RIGHT THERE, BUDDY! I THINK YOU'RE GOING A LITTLE TOO FAR!
--AND HAVE HER SWEEP WITH ME! JUST ONCE...!
URK... WELL, WHATEVER FLOATS YOUR BOAT...
I'M SORRY I TOOK SO LONG, BOYS!
THERE!
HOW'S THAT?

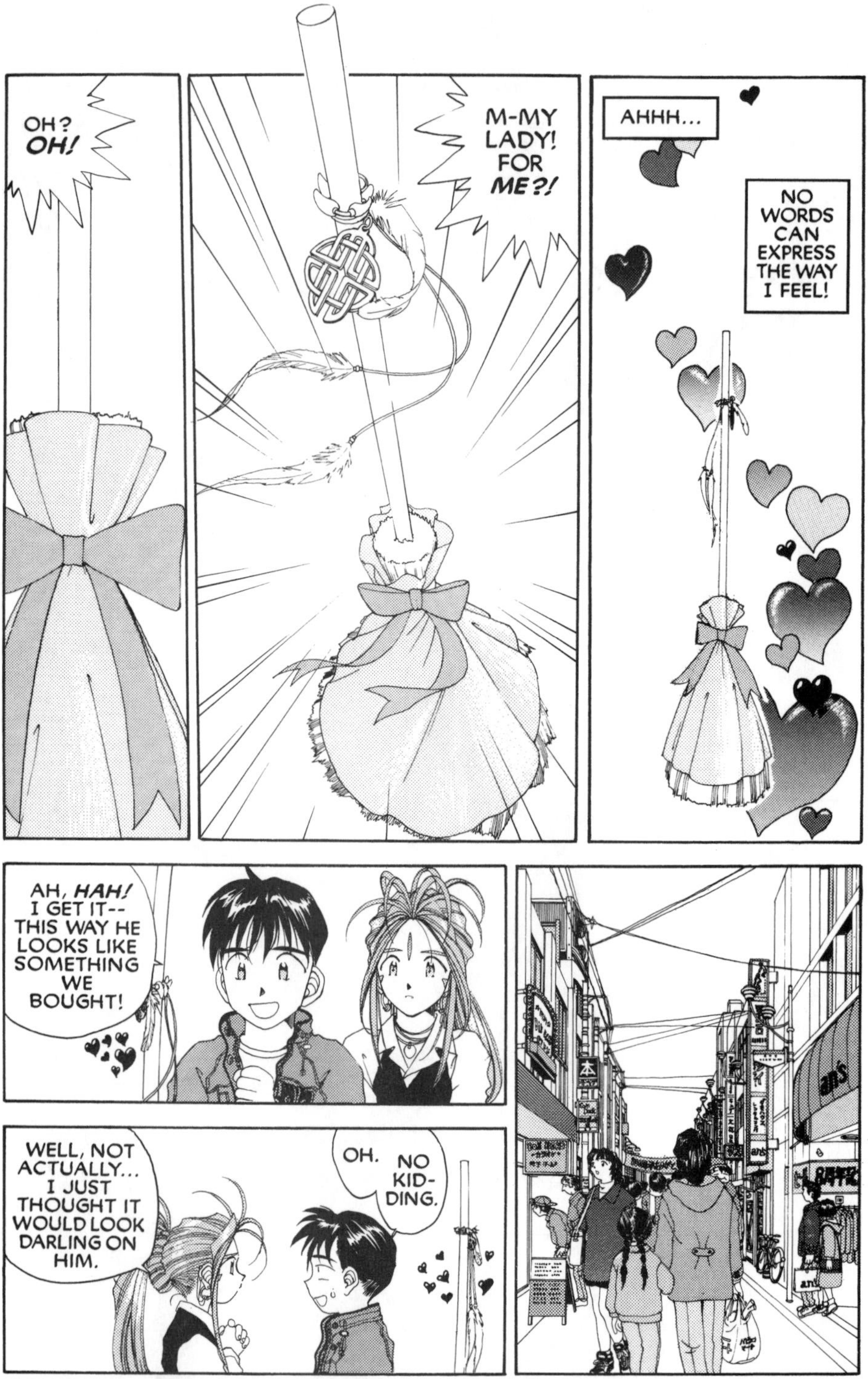
OH? *OH!*
M-MY LADY! FOR *ME?!*
AHHH...
NO WORDS CAN EXPRESS THE WAY I FEEL!
AH, *HAH!* I GET IT-- THIS WAY HE LOOKS LIKE SOMETHING WE BOUGHT!
WELL, NOT ACTUALLY... I JUST THOUGHT IT WOULD LOOK DARLING ON HIM.
OH.
NO KID-DING.
an's

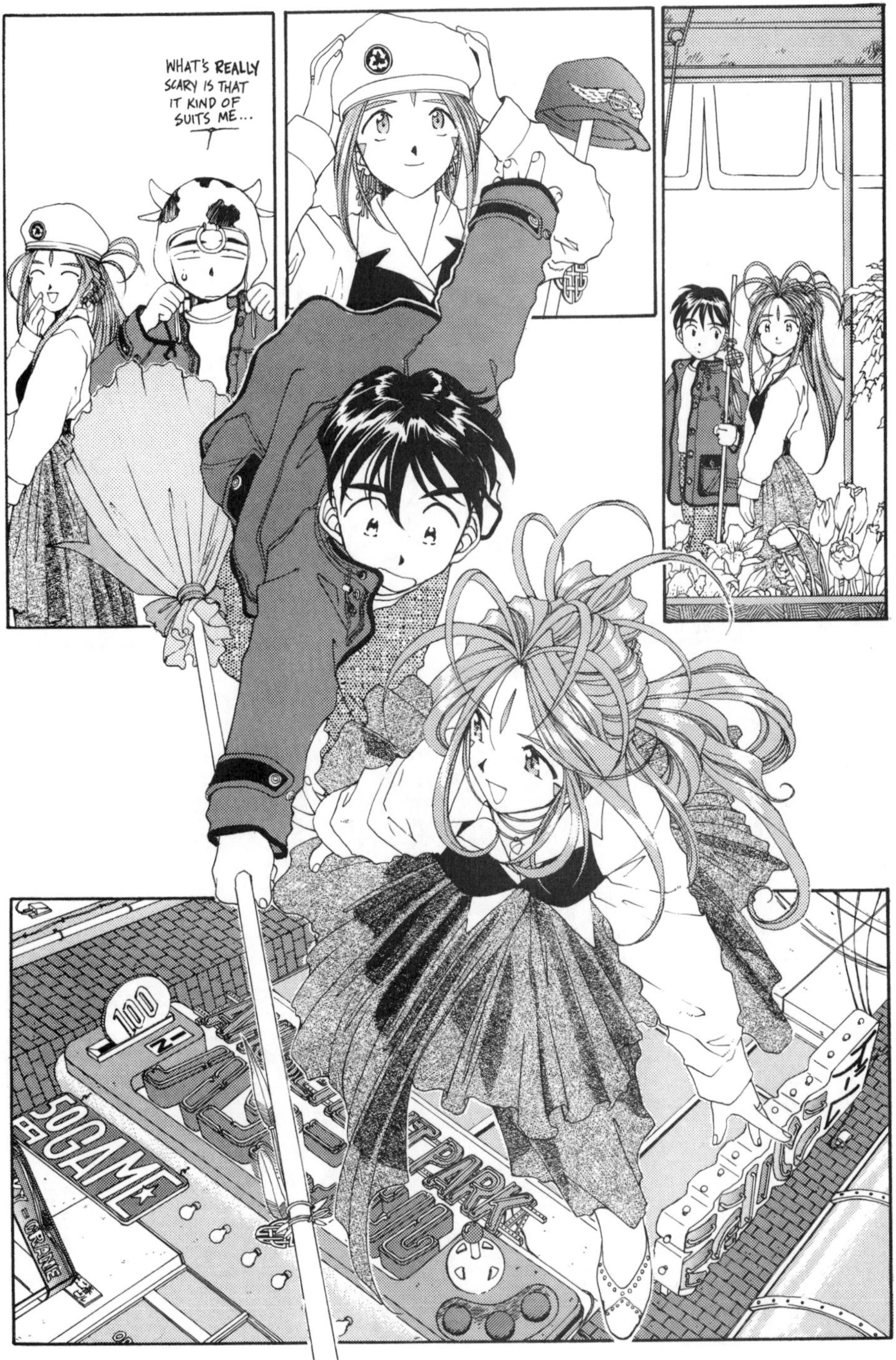
WHAT'S REALLY SCARY IS THAT IT KIND OF SUITS ME...
100
SOGAME
CRANE

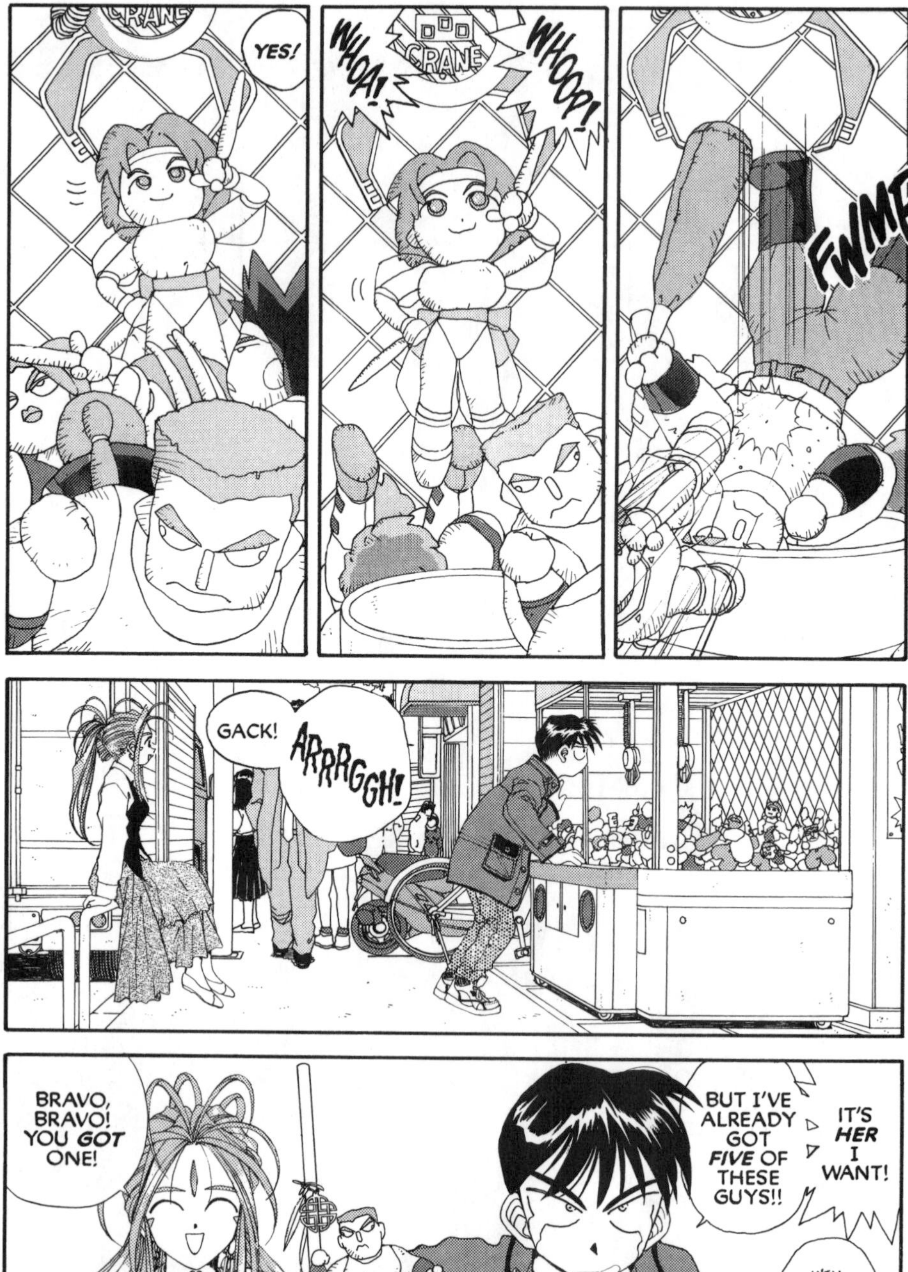
CRANE
YES!
WHOA!
CRANE
WHOOP!
FWMP
GACK!
ARRRGGH!
BRAVO, BRAVO! YOU *GOT* ONE!
BUT I'VE ALREADY GOT *FIVE* OF THESE GUYS!!
IT'S *HER* I WANT!
WELL, TRY, TRY AGAIN...

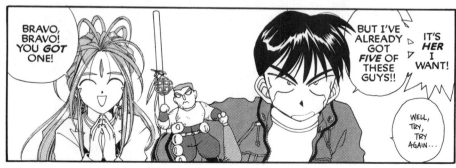

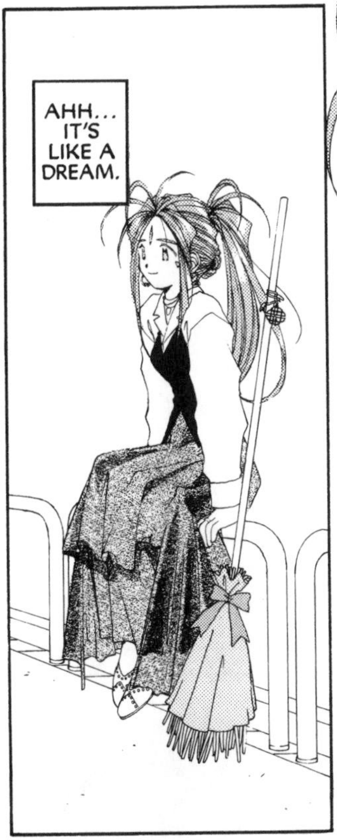
AHH... IT'S LIKE A DREAM.

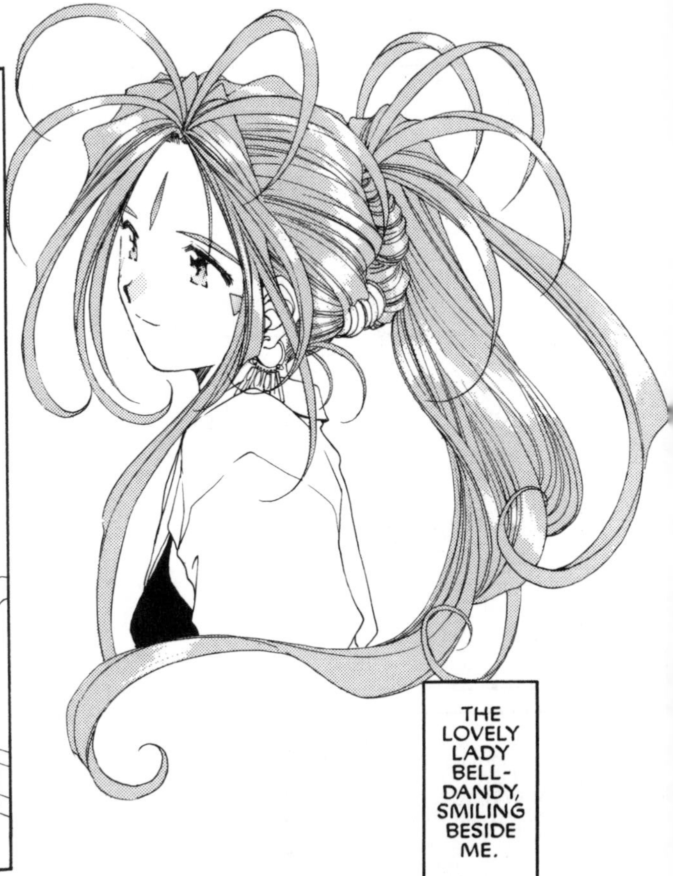
THE LOVELY LADY BELL-DANDY, SMILING BESIDE ME.

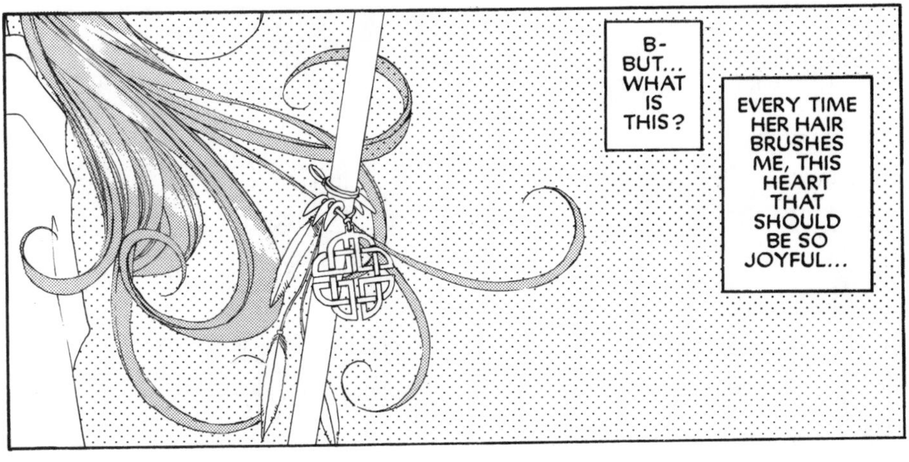
B-BUT... WHAT IS THIS?
EVERY TIME HER HAIR BRUSHES ME, THIS HEART THAT SHOULD BE SO JOYFUL...

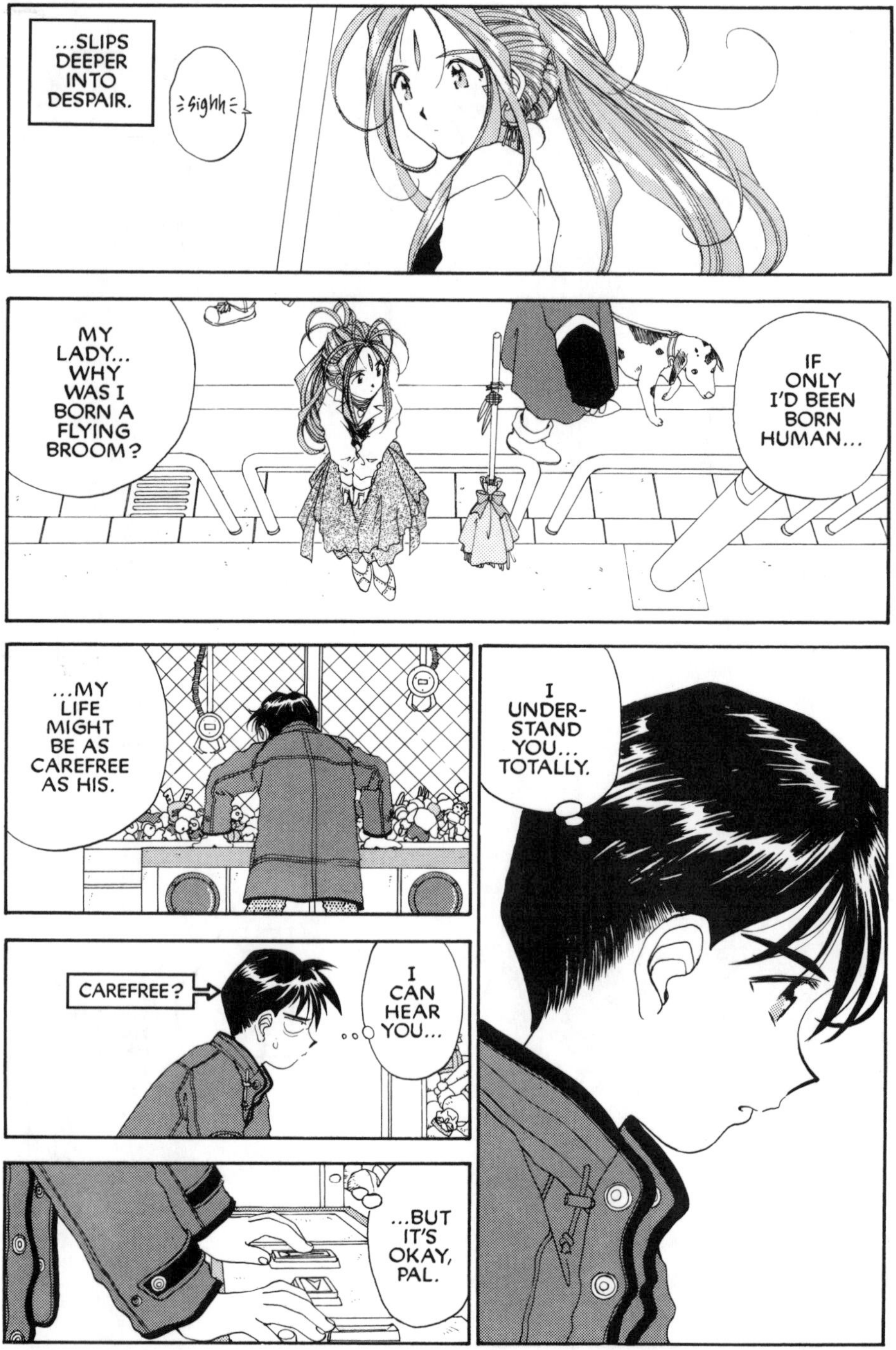
...SLIPS DEEPER INTO DESPAIR.
sighh
MY LADY... WHY WAS I BORN A FLYING BROOM?
IF ONLY I'D BEEN BORN HUMAN...
...MY LIFE MIGHT BE AS CAREFREE AS HIS.
CAREFREE?
I CAN HEAR YOU...
...BUT IT'S OKAY, PAL.
I UNDER-STAND YOU... TOTALLY.

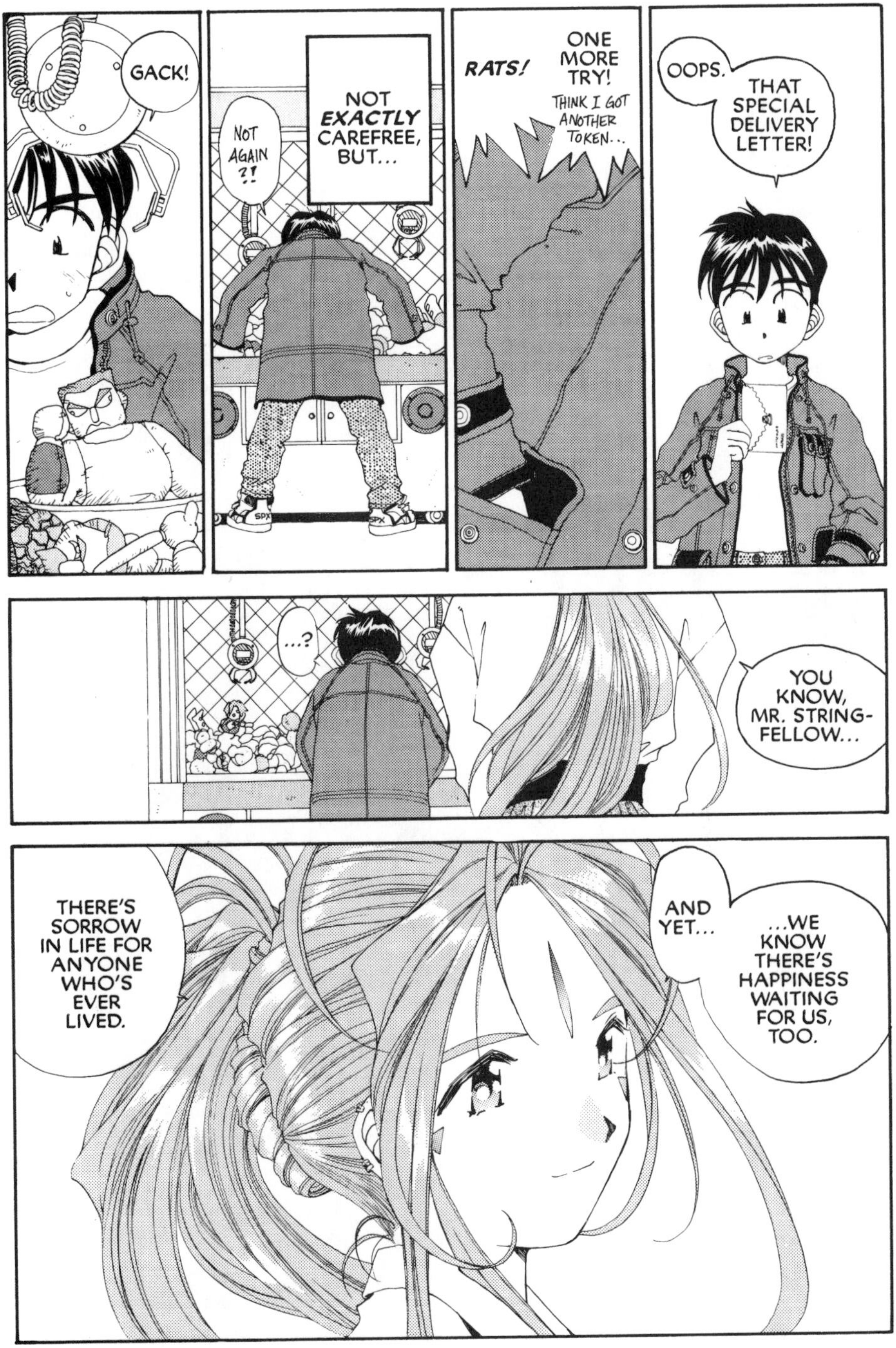
GACK!
NOT AGAIN ?!
NOT *EXACTLY* CAREFREE, BUT...
RATS!
ONE MORE TRY!
THINK I GOT ANOTHER TOKEN...
OOPS.
THAT SPECIAL DELIVERY LETTER!
...?
YOU KNOW, MR. STRING-FELLOW...
THERE'S SORROW IN LIFE FOR ANYONE WHO'S EVER LIVED.
AND YET...
...WE KNOW THERE'S HAPPINESS WAITING FOR US, TOO.

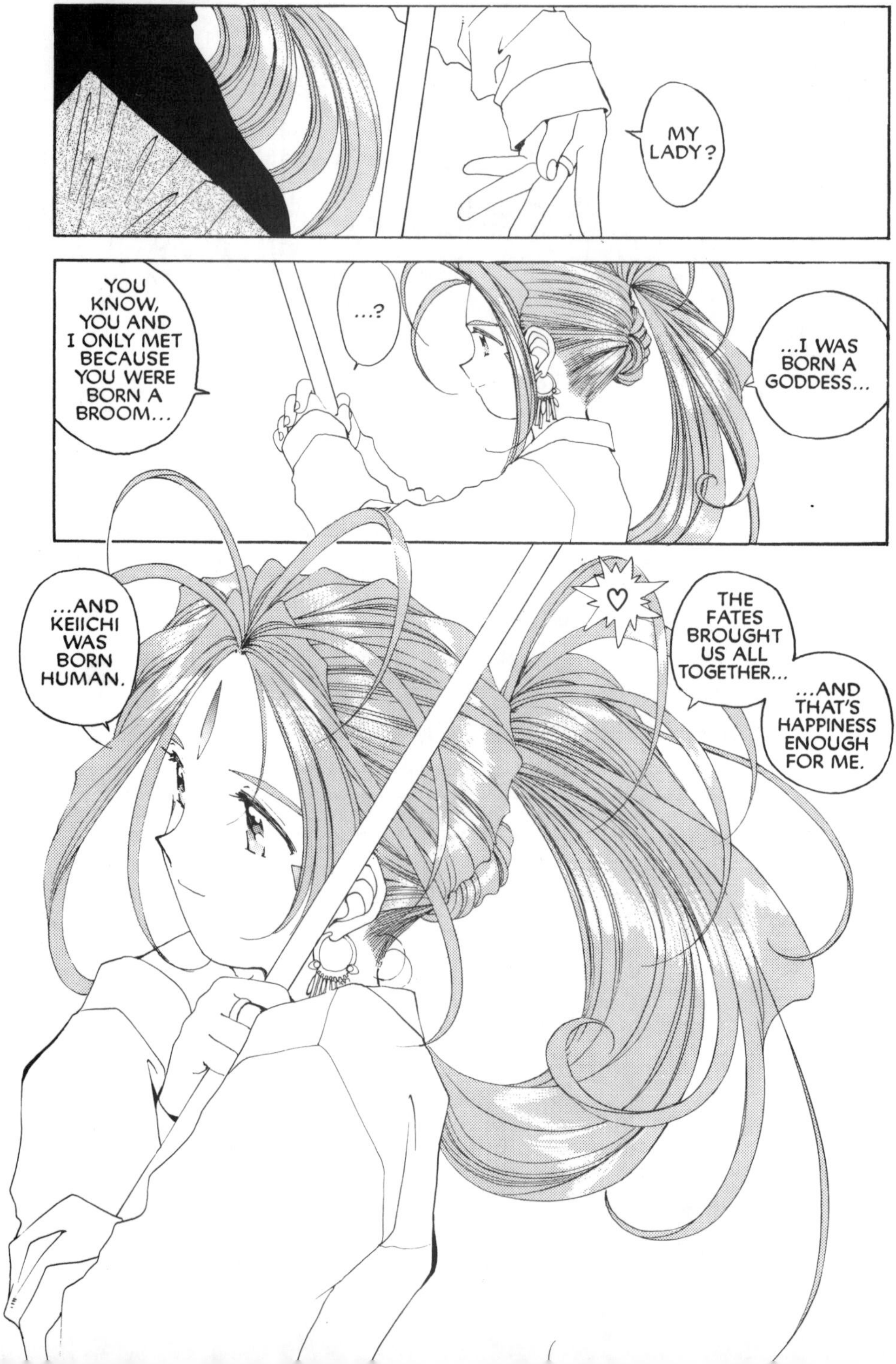
MY LADY?
YOU KNOW, YOU AND I ONLY MET BECAUSE YOU WERE BORN A BROOM...
...?
...I WAS BORN A GODDESS...
...AND KEIICHI WAS BORN HUMAN.
THE FATES BROUGHT US ALL TOGETHER...
...AND THAT'S HAPPINESS ENOUGH FOR ME.

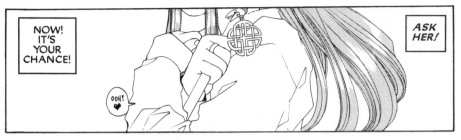

NOW! IT'S YOUR CHANCE!

OOH! ♥

ASK HER!

MY LADY B-BELL-DANDY!

PLEASE--

SORRY!

SORRY TO INTERRUPT, BUT WE GOTTA GO!

HAH! YOU DIRTY RAT!

CAN'T TAKE IT, HUH? JEALOUS, HUH?!

GIMME A BREAK!

WHAT HAPPENED, KEIICHI?

THIS LETTER-- IT'S FROM CHIHIRO.

OH! THE SPECIAL DELIVERY!

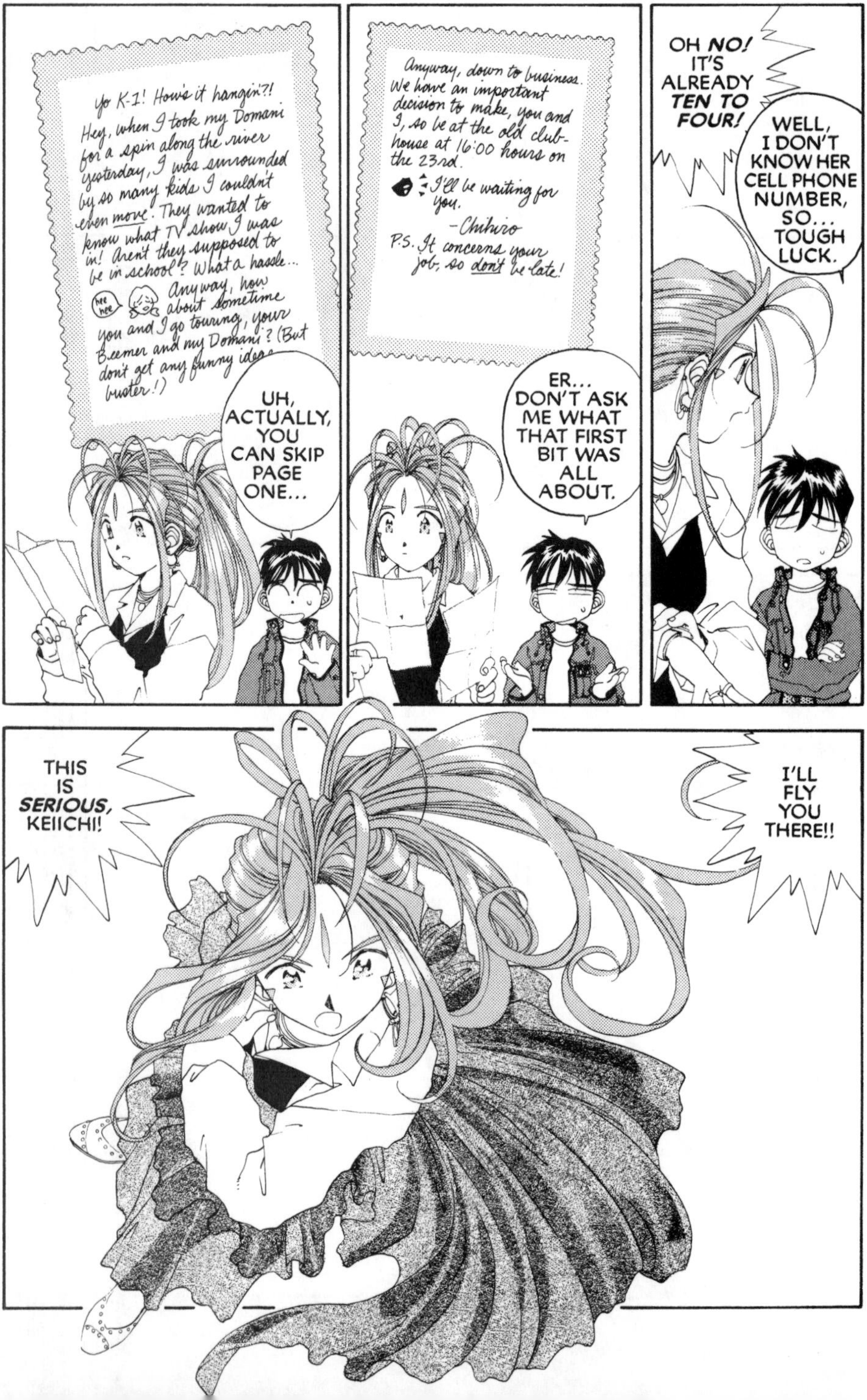
Yo K-1! How's it hangin'?!
Hey, when I took my Domani for a spin along the river yesterday, I was surrounded by so many kids I couldn't even move. They wanted to know what TV show I was in! Aren't they supposed to be in school? What a hassle...
hee hee
Anyway, how about sometime you and I go touring, your Beemer and my Domani? (But don't get any funny idea
buster!)
UH, ACTUALLY, YOU CAN SKIP PAGE ONE...
Anyway, down to business. We have an important decision to make, you and I, so be at the old club-house at 16:00 hours on the 23rd.
I'll be waiting for you.
-Chihiro
P.S. It concerns your job, so don't be late!
ER... DON'T ASK ME WHAT THAT FIRST BIT WAS ALL ABOUT.
OH NO! IT'S ALREADY TEN TO FOUR!
WELL, I DON'T KNOW HER CELL PHONE NUMBER, SO... TOUGH LUCK.
THIS IS SERIOUS, KEIICHI!
I'LL FLY YOU THERE!!

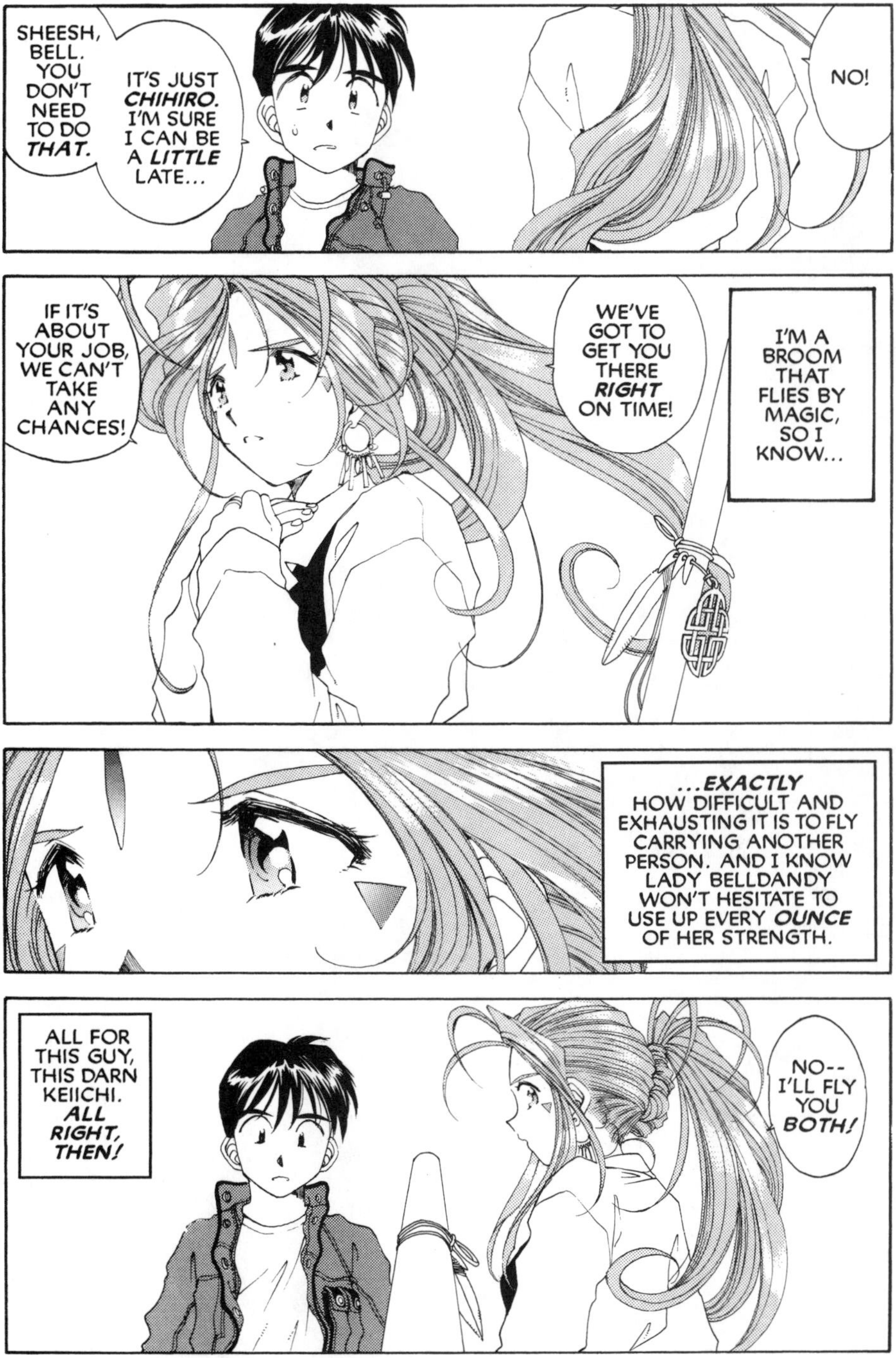
SHEESH, BELL. YOU DON'T NEED TO DO *THAT.*
IT'S JUST *CHIHIRO.* I'M SURE I CAN BE A *LITTLE* LATE...
NO!
IF IT'S ABOUT YOUR JOB, WE CAN'T TAKE ANY CHANCES!
WE'VE GOT TO GET YOU THERE *RIGHT* ON TIME!
I'M A BROOM THAT FLIES BY MAGIC, SO I KNOW...
...EXACTLY HOW DIFFICULT AND EXHAUSTING IT IS TO FLY CARRYING ANOTHER PERSON. AND I KNOW LADY BELLDANDY WON'T HESITATE TO USE UP EVERY *OUNCE* OF HER STRENGTH.
ALL FOR THIS GUY, THIS DARN KEIICHI. *ALL RIGHT, THEN!*
NO-- I'LL FLY YOU *BOTH!*

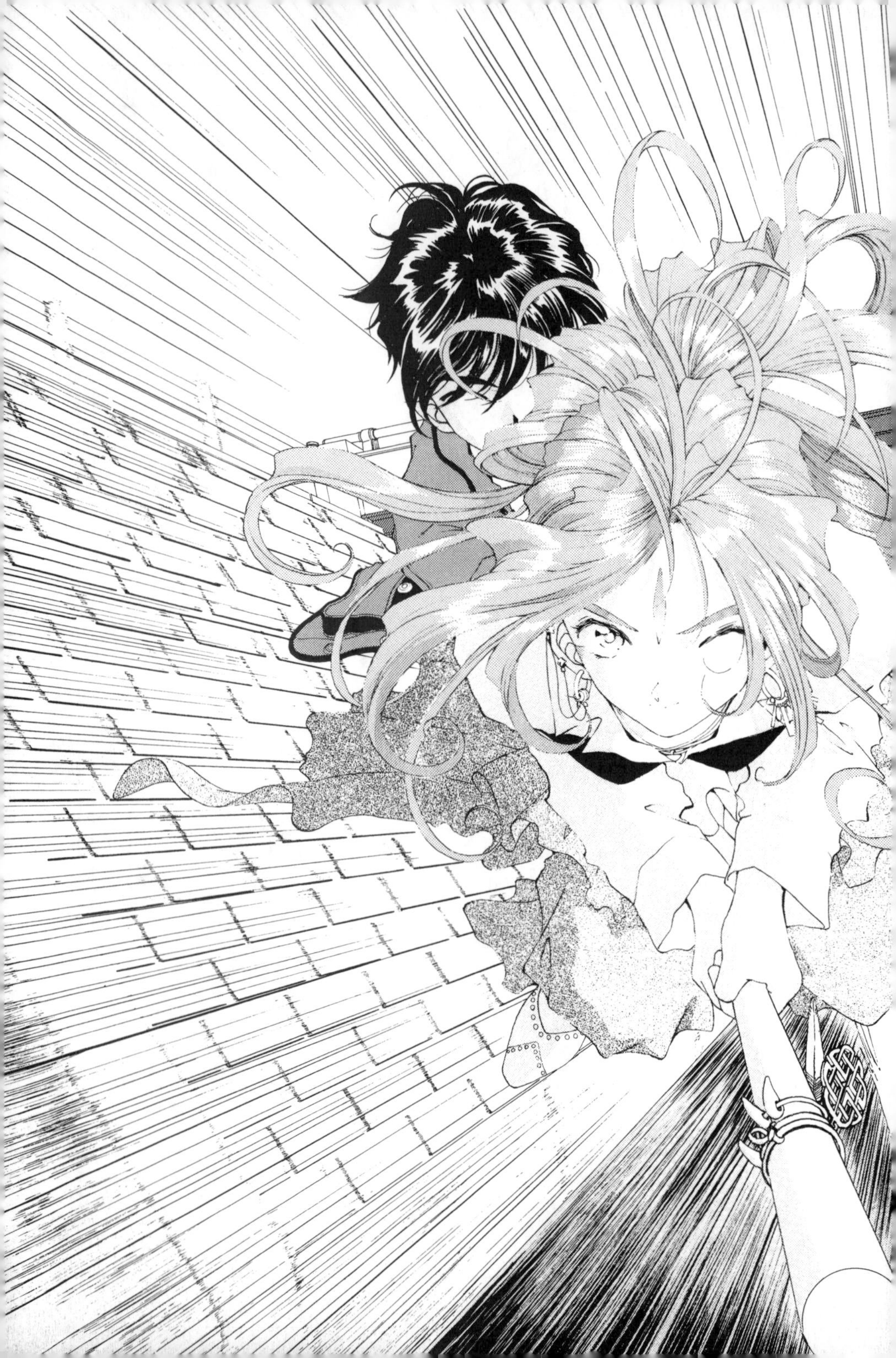

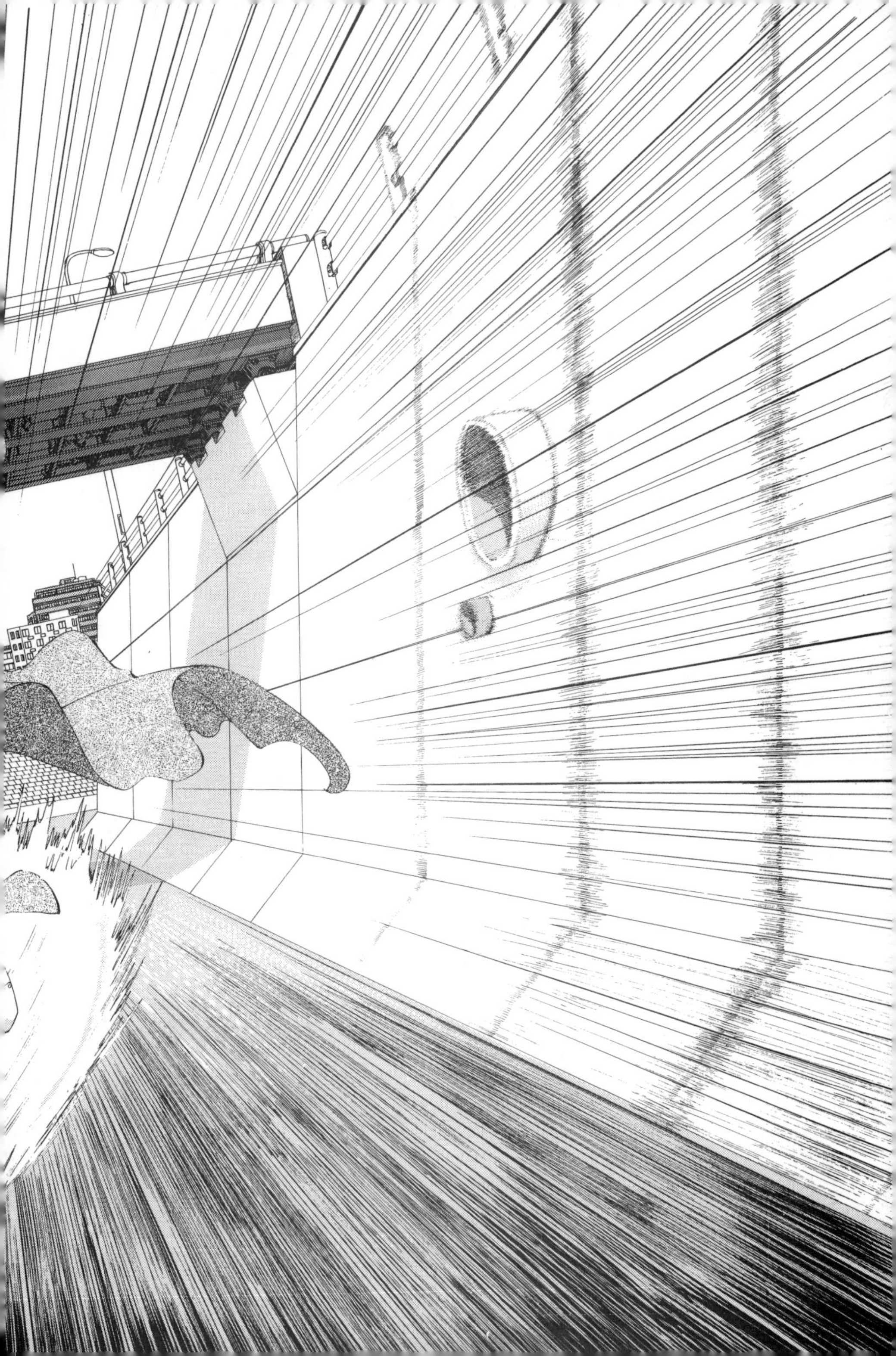

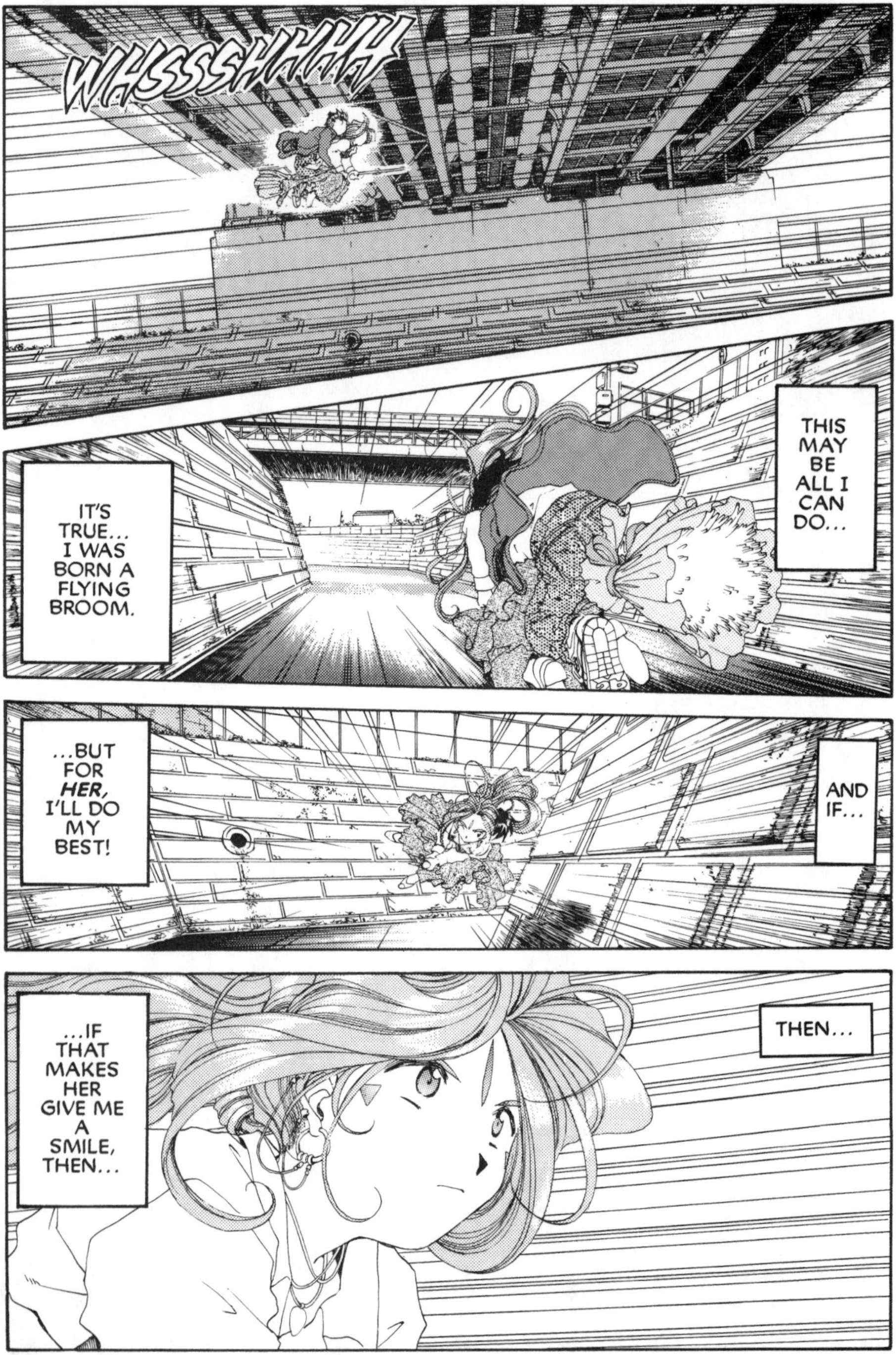
WHSSSSHHHHH
IT'S TRUE... I WAS BORN A FLYING BROOM.
THIS MAY BE ALL I CAN DO...
...BUT FOR HER, I'LL DO MY BEST!
AND IF...
...IF THAT MAKES HER GIVE ME A SMILE, THEN...
THEN...

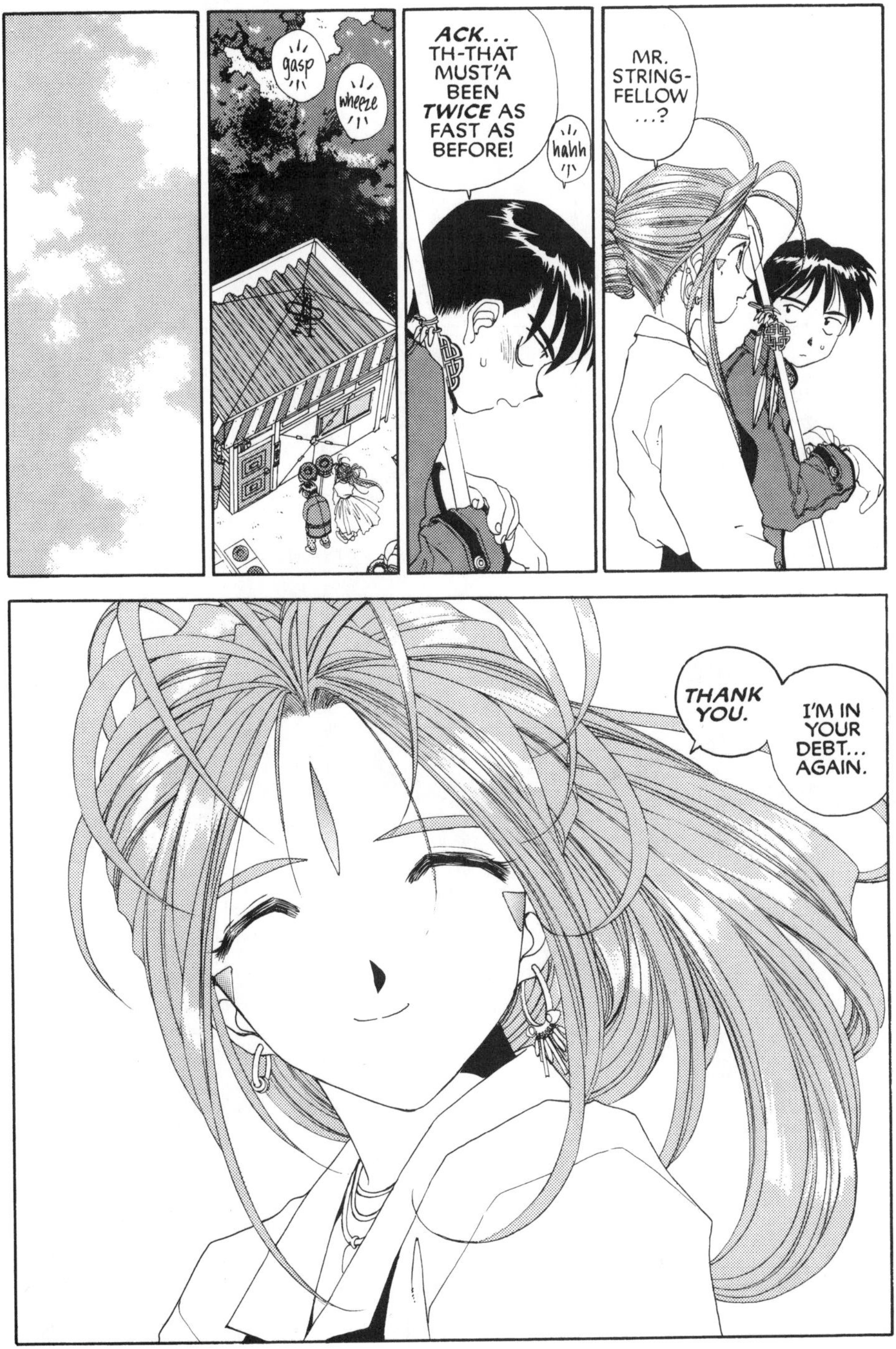
gasp
wheeze
ACK... TH-THAT MUST'A BEEN TWICE AS FAST AS BEFORE!
hahh
MR. STRING-FELLOW ...?
THANK YOU.
I'M IN YOUR DEBT... AGAIN.

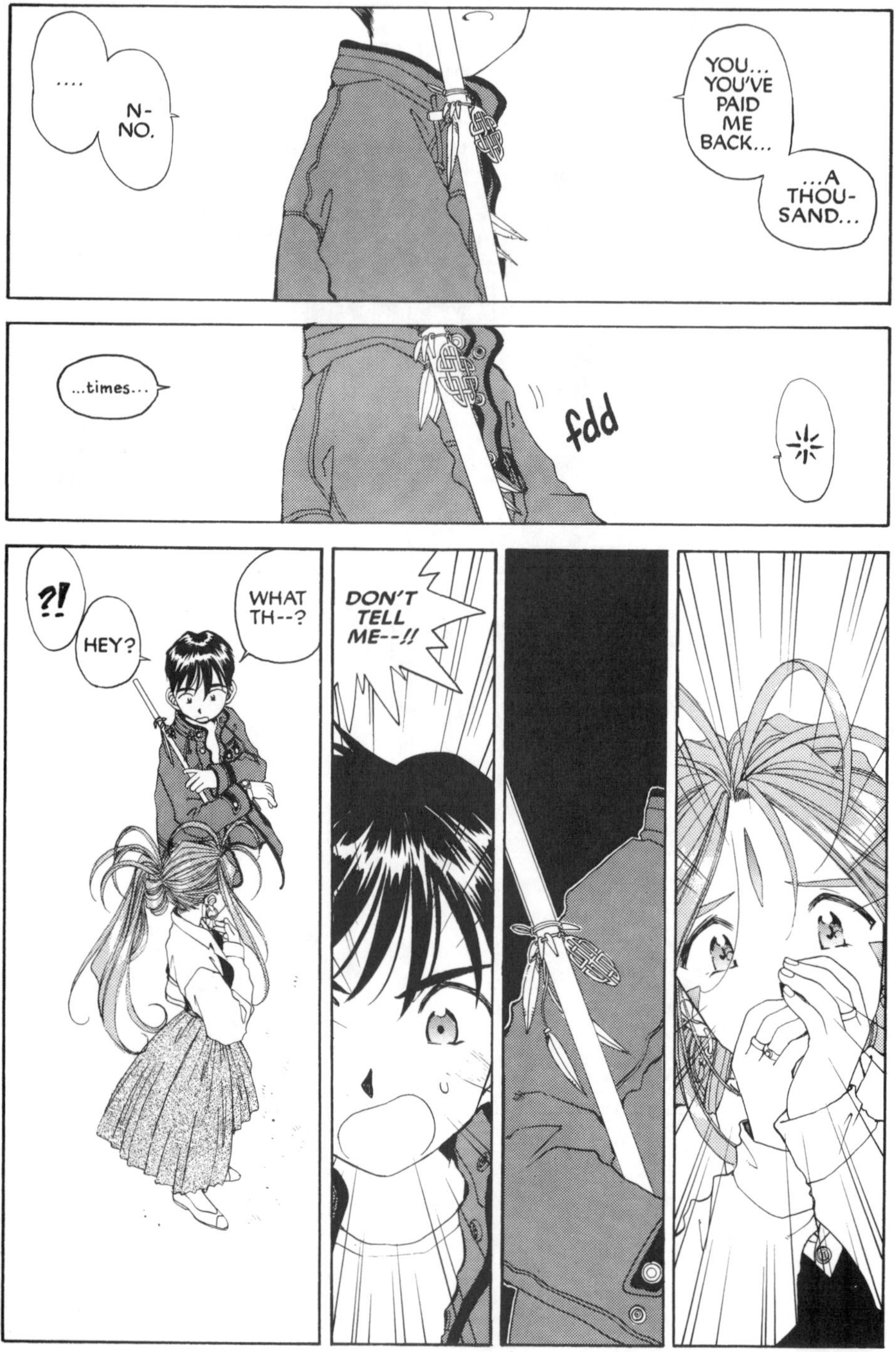
....
N-
NO.
YOU... YOU'VE PAID ME BACK...
...A THOU-SAND...
...times...
fdd
?!
HEY?
WHAT TH--?
DON'T TELL ME--!!

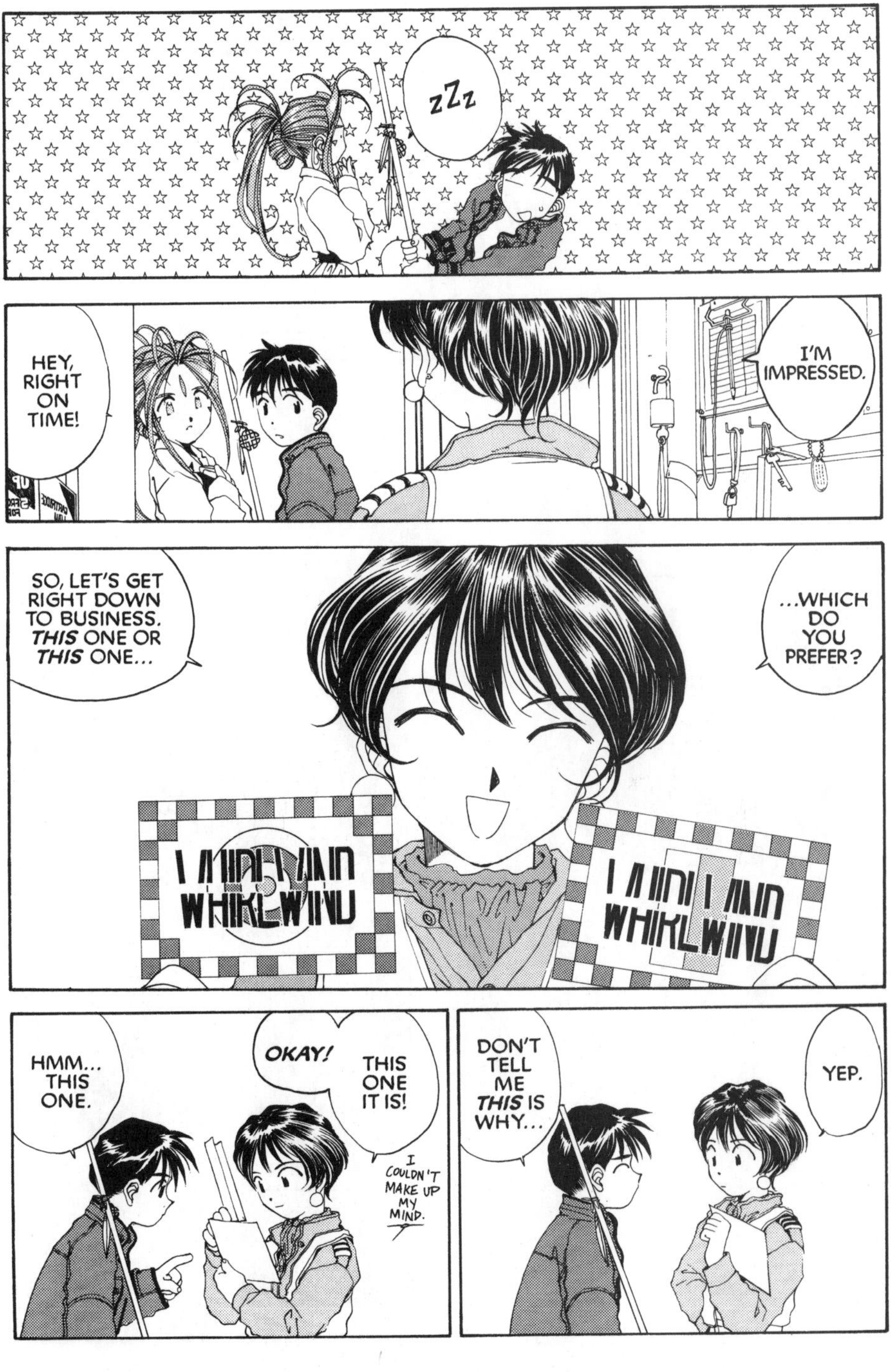
zZz
HEY, RIGHT ON TIME!
I'M IMPRESSED.
SO, LET'S GET RIGHT DOWN TO BUSINESS. *THIS* ONE OR *THIS* ONE...
...WHICH DO YOU PREFER?
WHIRLWIND
WHIRLWIND
HMM... THIS ONE.
OKAY!
THIS ONE IT IS!
I COULDN'T MAKE UP MY MIND.
DON'T TELL ME *THIS* IS WHY...
YEP.

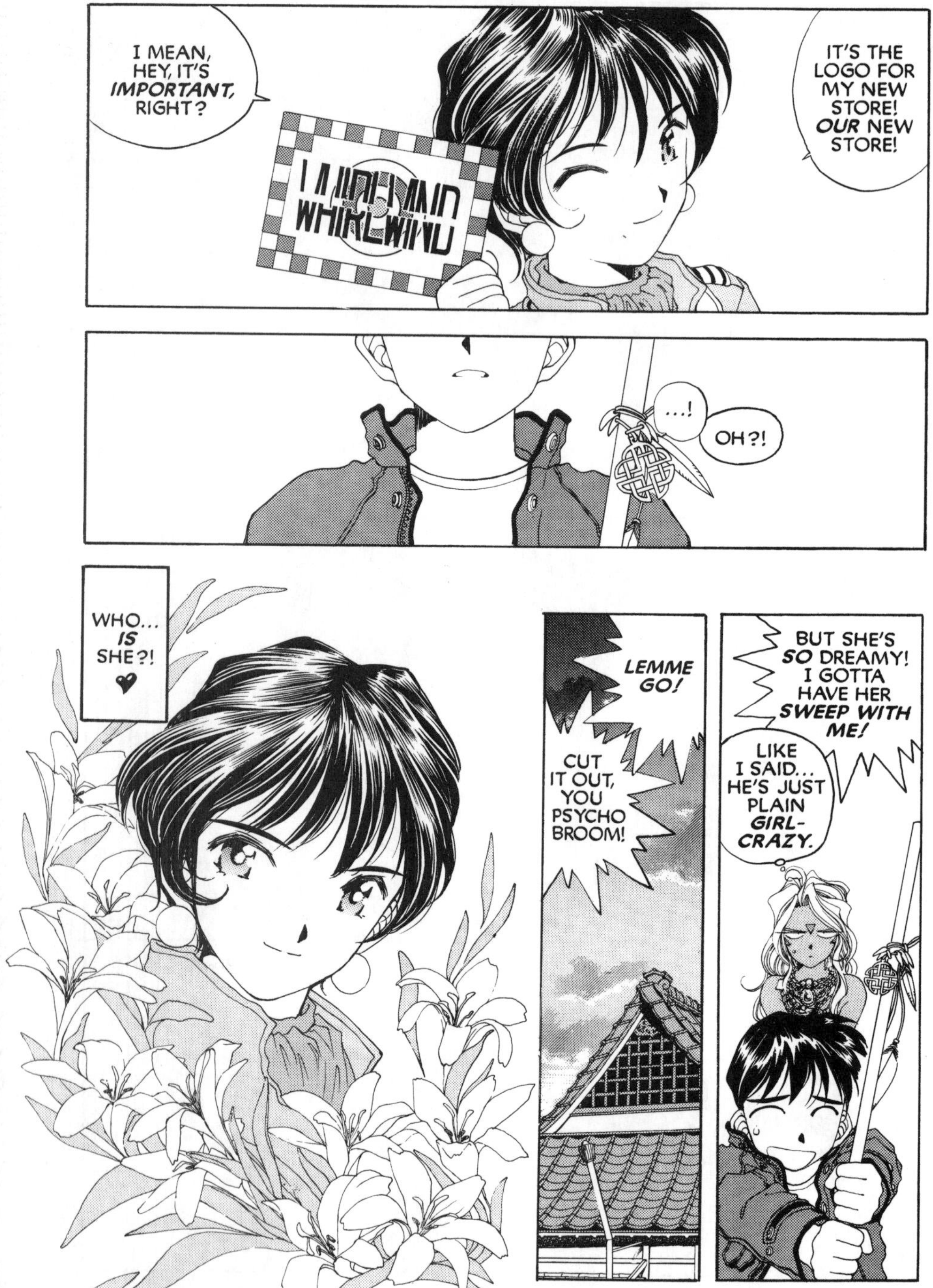
I MEAN, HEY, IT'S *IMPORTANT,* RIGHT?
IT'S THE LOGO FOR MY NEW STORE! *OUR* NEW STORE!
WHIRLWIND
...!
OH?!
WHO... *IS* SHE?! ♥
LEMME GO!
CUT IT OUT, YOU PSYCHO BROOM!
BUT SHE'S *SO* DREAMY! I GOTTA HAVE HER *SWEEP WITH ME!*
LIKE I SAID... HE'S JUST PLAIN *GIRL-CRAZY.*

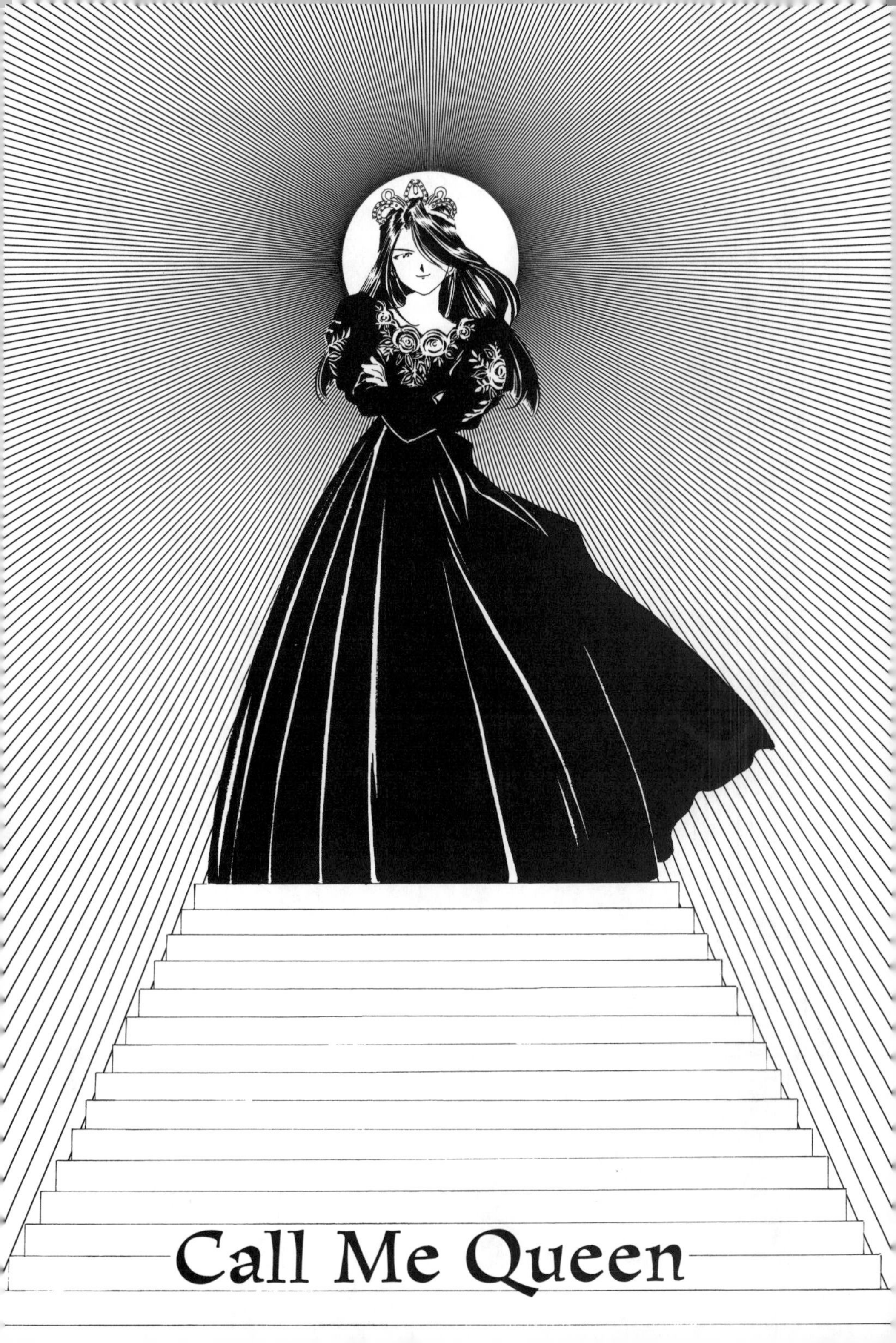
Call Me Queen

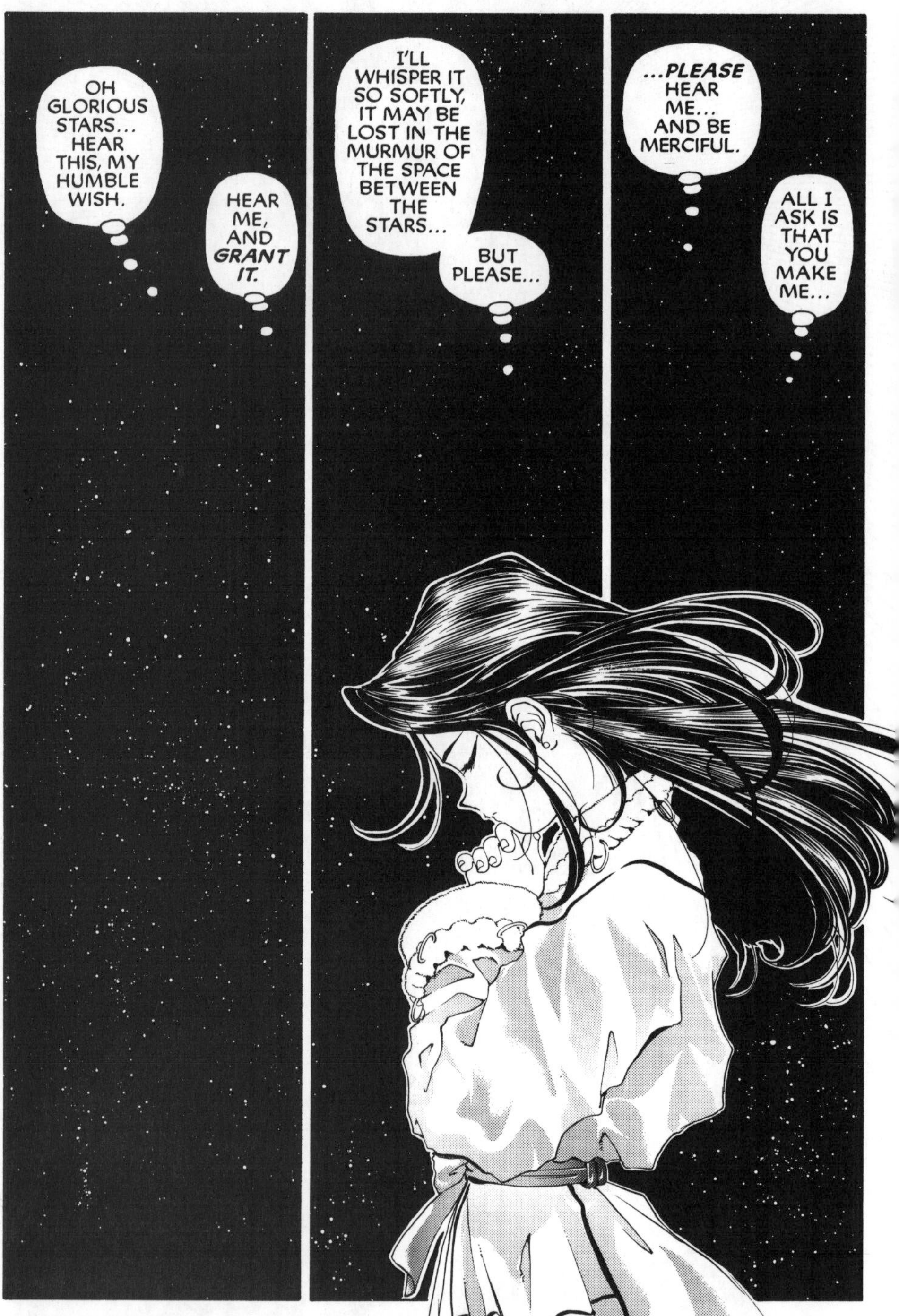
OH GLORIOUS STARS... HEAR THIS, MY HUMBLE WISH.
HEAR ME, AND *GRANT IT.*
I'LL WHISPER IT SO SOFTLY, IT MAY BE LOST IN THE MURMUR OF THE SPACE BETWEEN THE STARS...
BUT PLEASE...
...*PLEASE* HEAR ME... AND BE MERCIFUL.
ALL I ASK IS THAT YOU MAKE ME...

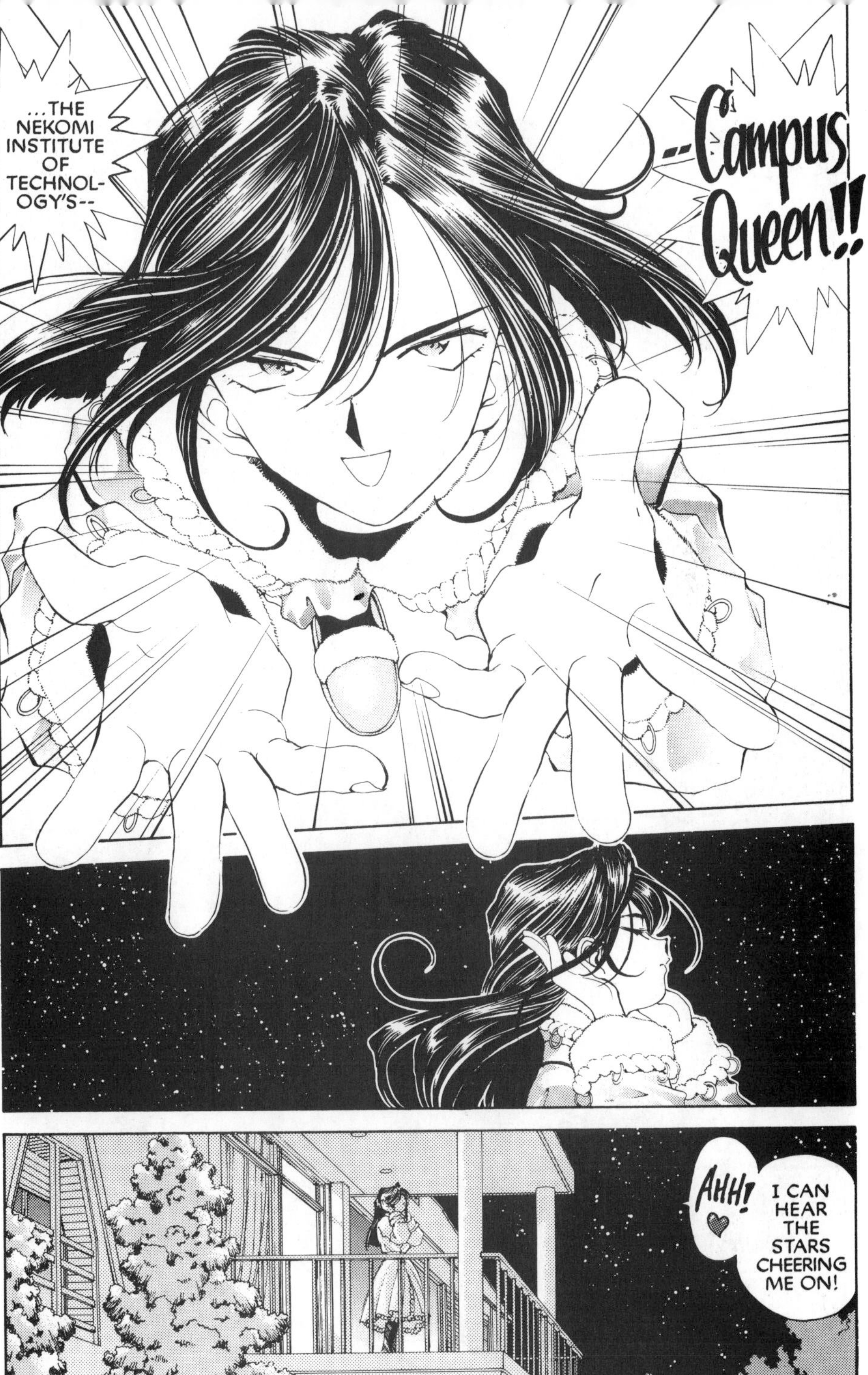
...THE NEKOMI INSTITUTE OF TECHNOL-OGY'S--
--Campus Queen!!
AHH! ♥
I CAN HEAR THE STARS CHEERING ME ON!

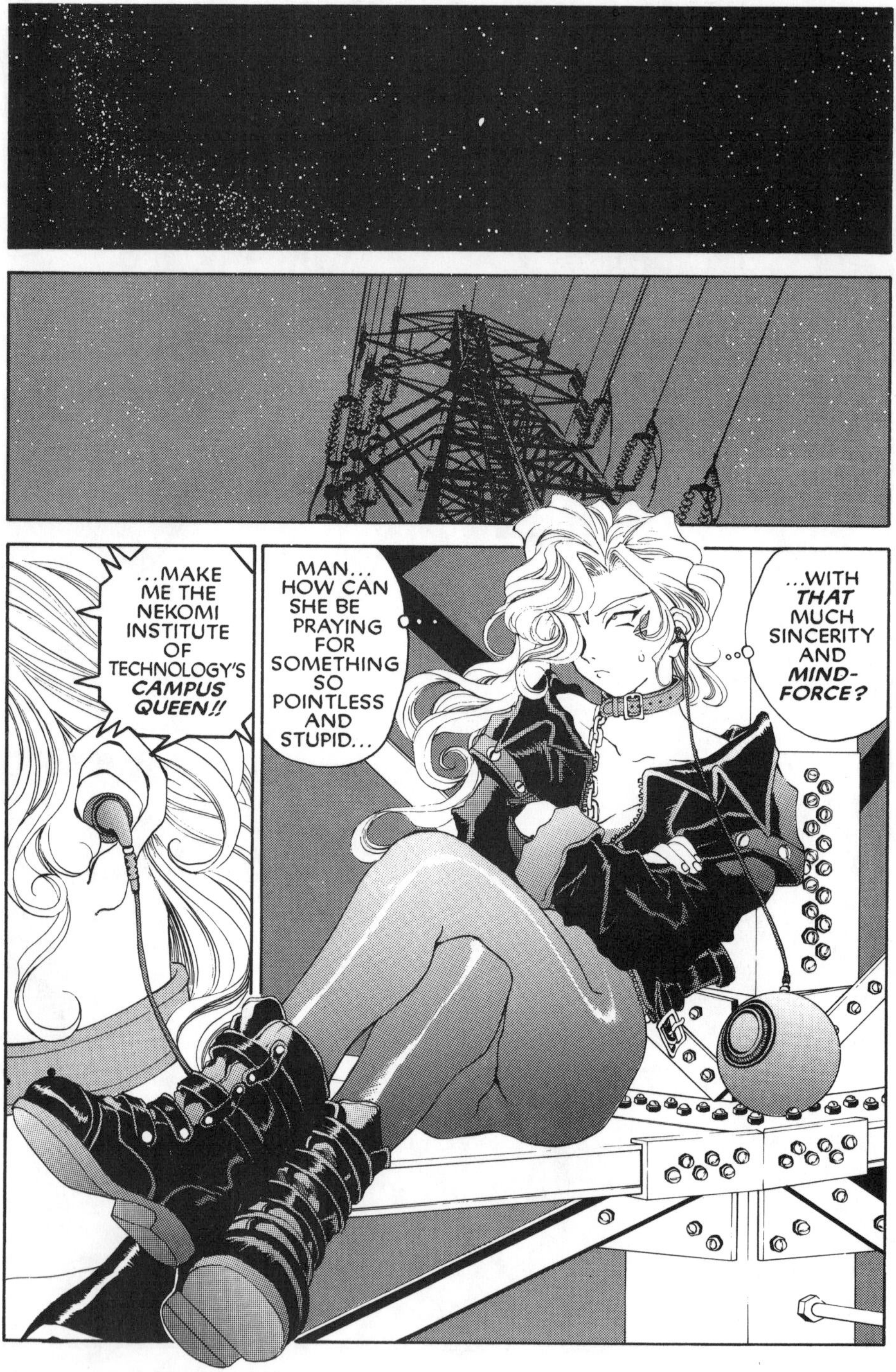
...MAKE ME THE NEKOMI INSTITUTE OF TECHNOLOGY'S *CAMPUS QUEEN!!*
MAN... HOW CAN SHE BE PRAYING FOR SOMETHING SO POINTLESS AND STUPID...
...WITH *THAT* MUCH SINCERITY AND *MIND-FORCE?*

OH, WELL, WHAT-EVER.

ASK AND YE SHALL *RECEIVE*, MY DEAR!

AND BESIDES, THIS IS JUST *PERFECT*, ISN'T IT?

BWA HA HA!!

THE NEXT DAY

JEEN: BELLDA

QUEI

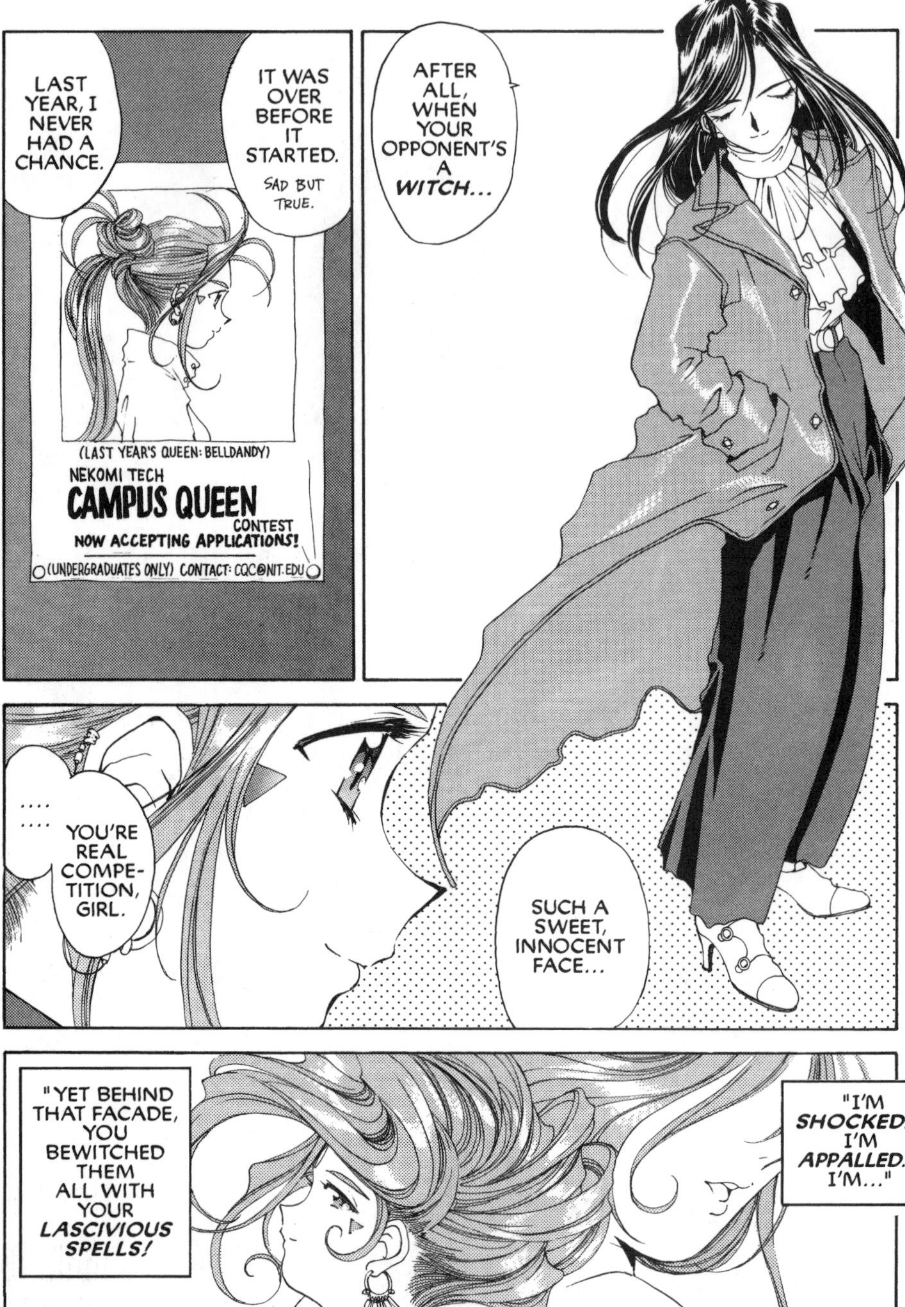

LAST YEAR, I NEVER HAD A CHANCE.
IT WAS OVER BEFORE IT STARTED.
SAD BUT TRUE.
(LAST YEAR'S QUEEN: BELLDANDY)
NEKOMI TECH
CAMPUS QUEEN
CONTEST
NOW ACCEPTING APPLICATIONS!
(UNDERGRADUATES ONLY) CONTACT: CQC@NIT.EDU
AFTER ALL, WHEN YOUR OPPONENT'S A *WITCH...*
....
YOU'RE REAL COMPETITION, GIRL.
SUCH A SWEET, INNOCENT FACE...
"YET BEHIND THAT FACADE, YOU BEWITCHED THEM ALL WITH YOUR ***LASCIVIOUS SPELLS!***
"I'M ***SHOCKED...*** I'M ***APPALLED...*** I'M..."

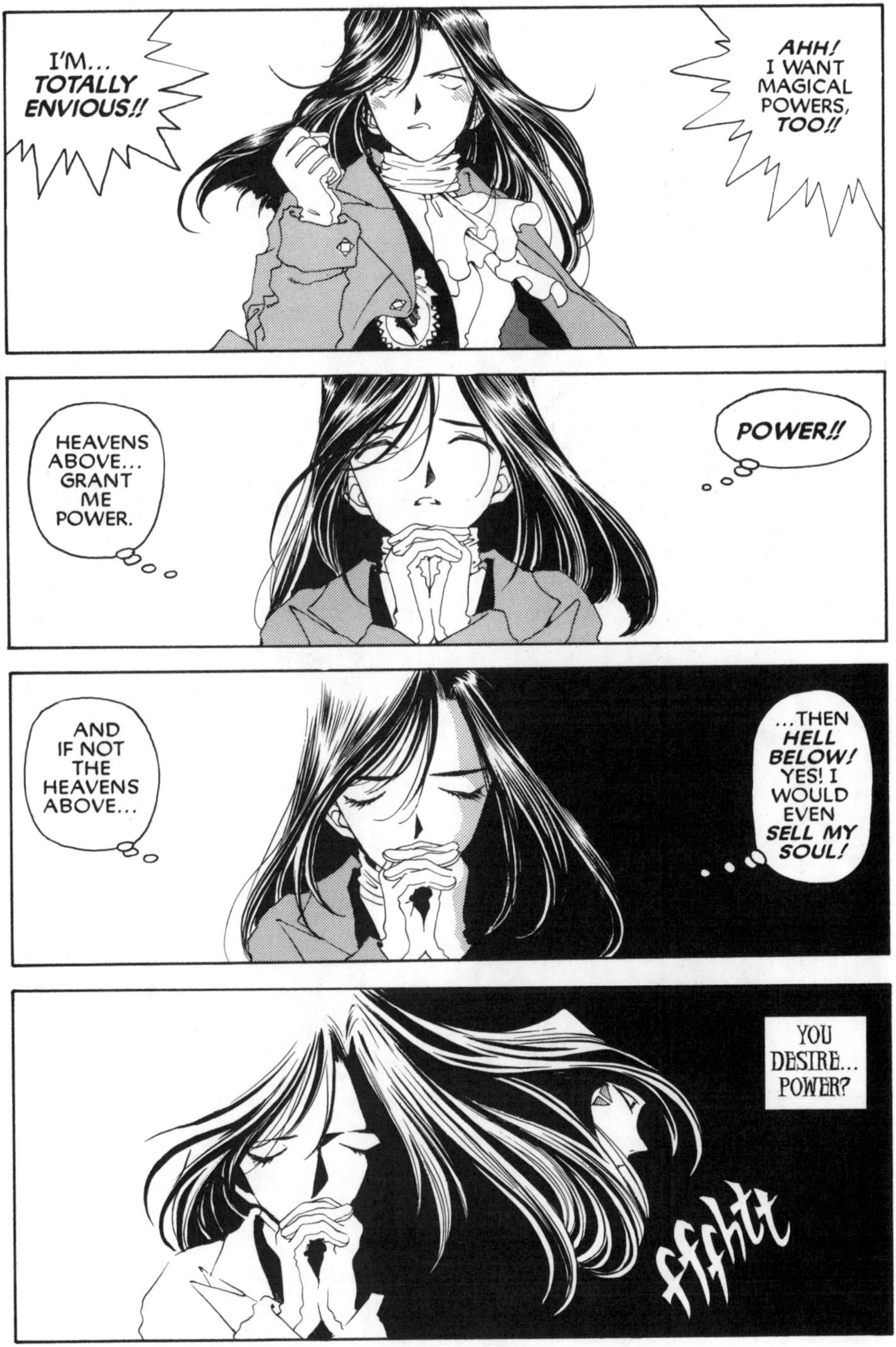
I'M... TOTALLY ENVIOUS!!
AHH! I WANT MAGICAL POWERS, TOO!!
HEAVENS ABOVE... GRANT ME POWER.
POWER!!
AND IF NOT THE HEAVENS ABOVE...
...THEN HELL BELOW! YES! I WOULD EVEN SELL MY SOUL!
YOU DESIRE... POWER?
ffshtt

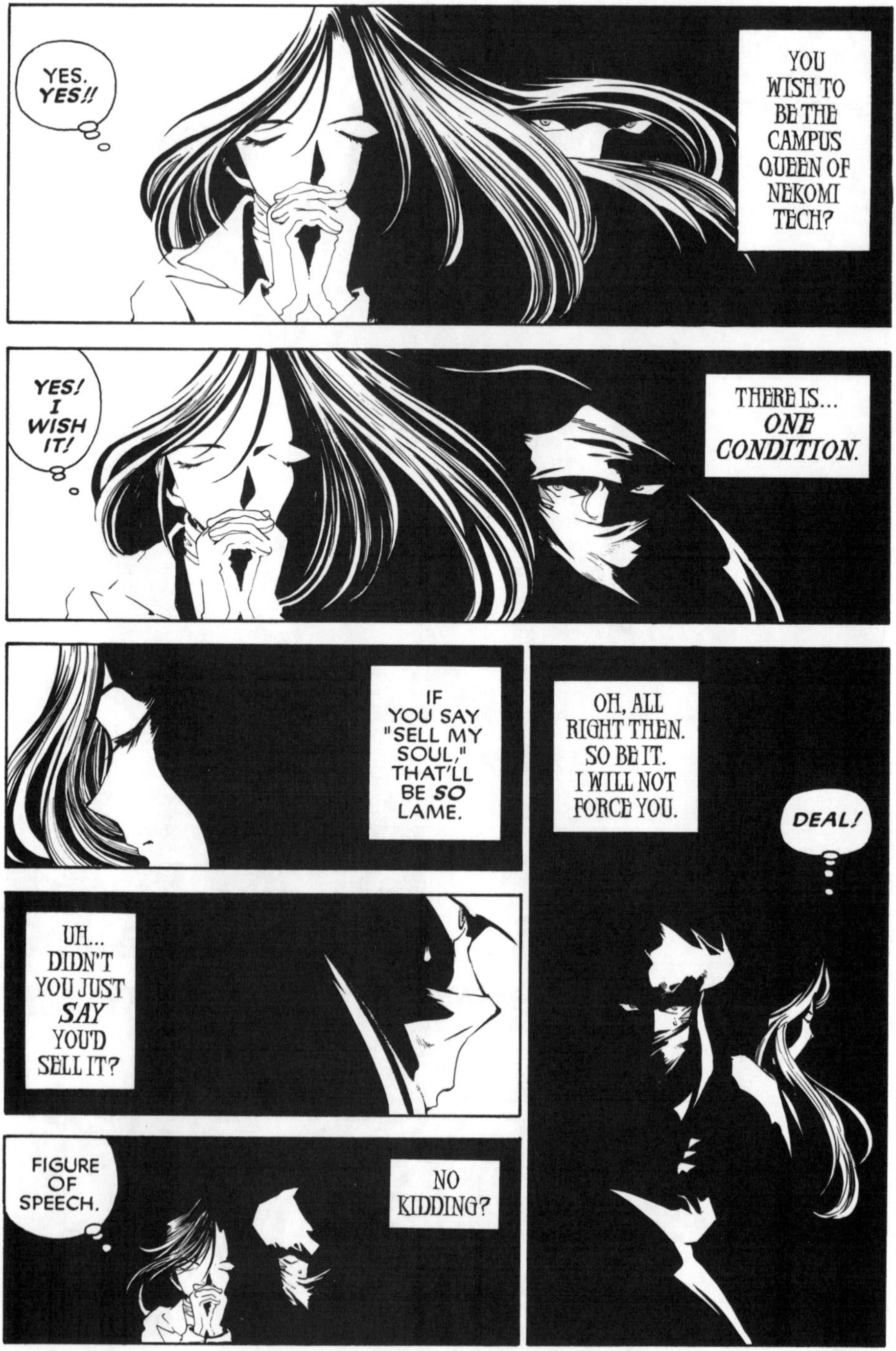
YES. YES!!
YOU WISH TO BE THE CAMPUS QUEEN OF NEKOMI TECH?
YES! I WISH IT!
THERE IS... ONE CONDITION.
IF YOU SAY "SELL MY SOUL," THAT'LL BE SO LAME.
UH... DIDN'T YOU JUST SAY YOU'D SELL IT?
FIGURE OF SPEECH.
NO KIDDING?
OH, ALL RIGHT THEN. SO BE IT. I WILL NOT FORCE YOU.
DEAL!

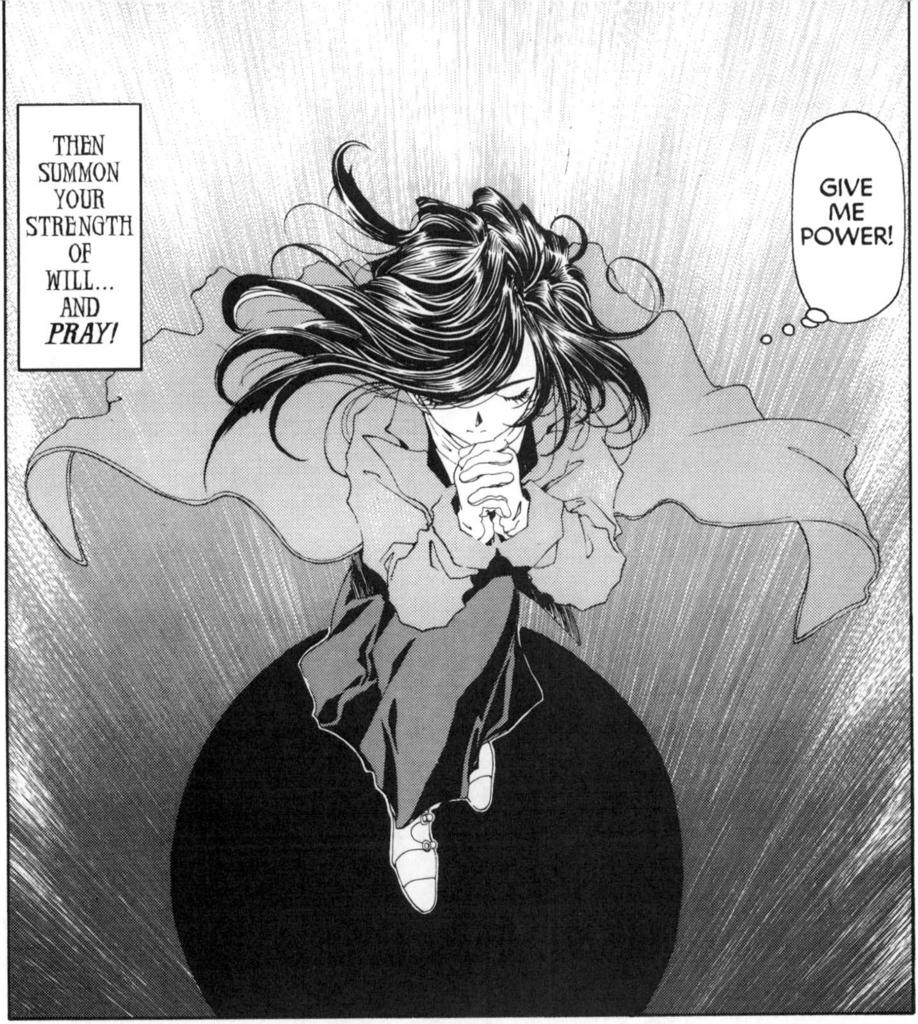
THEN SUMMON YOUR STRENGTH OF WILL... AND *PRAY!*
GIVE ME POWER!
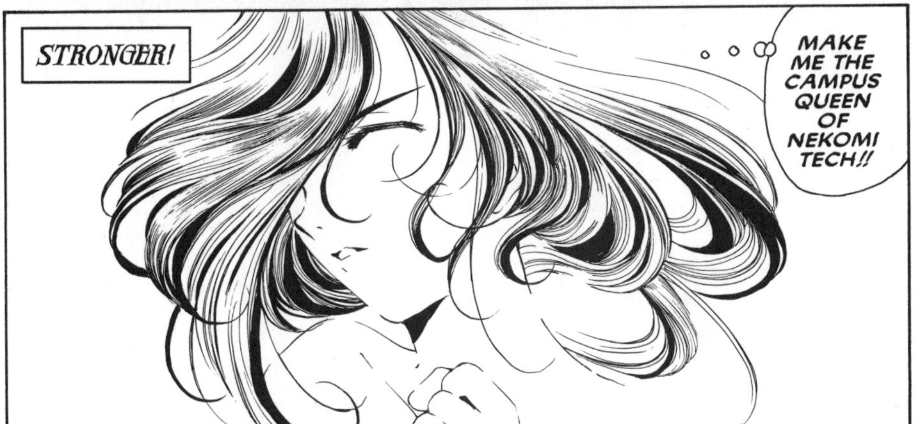
STRONGER!
MAKE ME THE CAMPUS QUEEN OF NEKOMI TECH!!

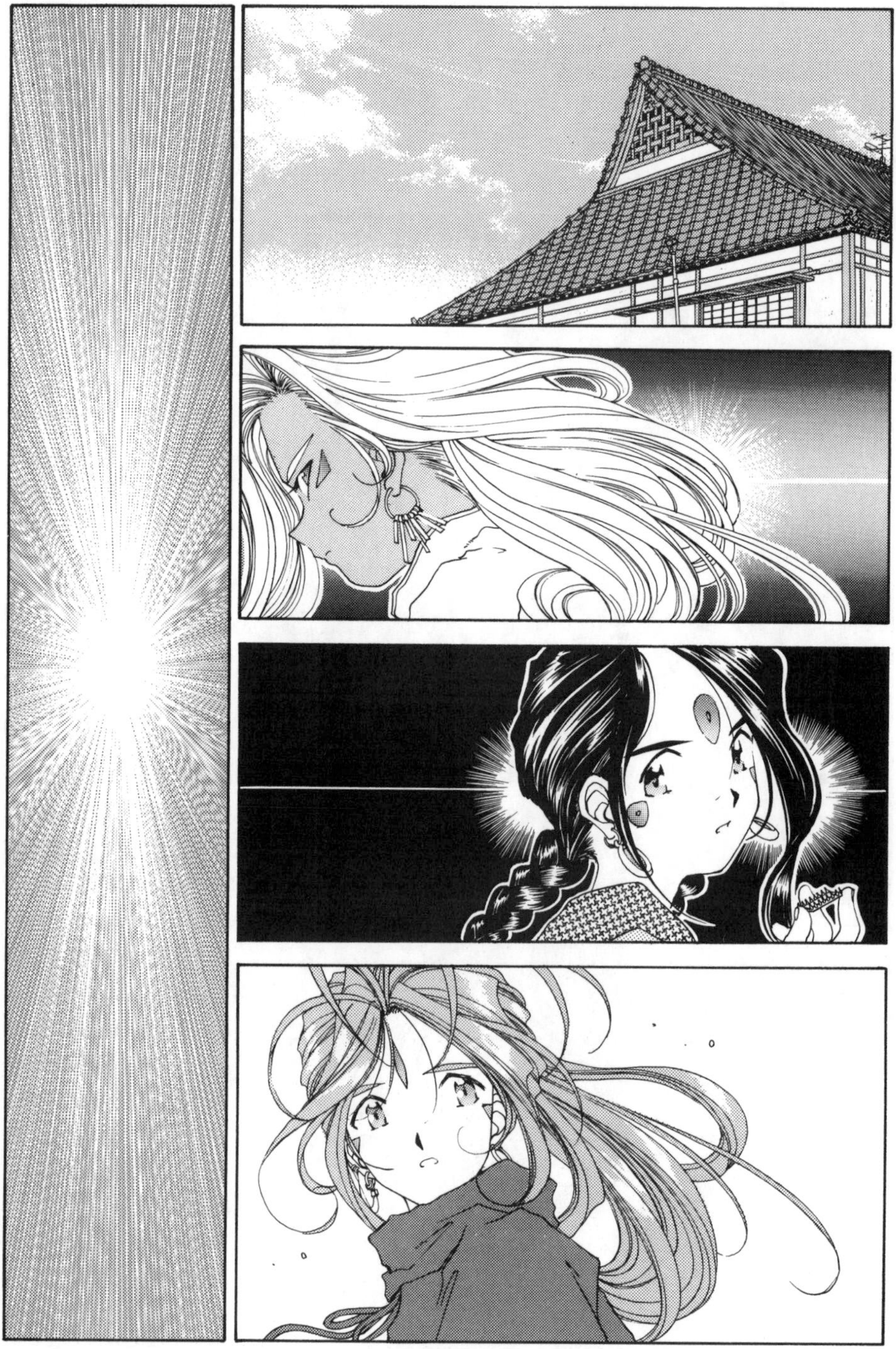

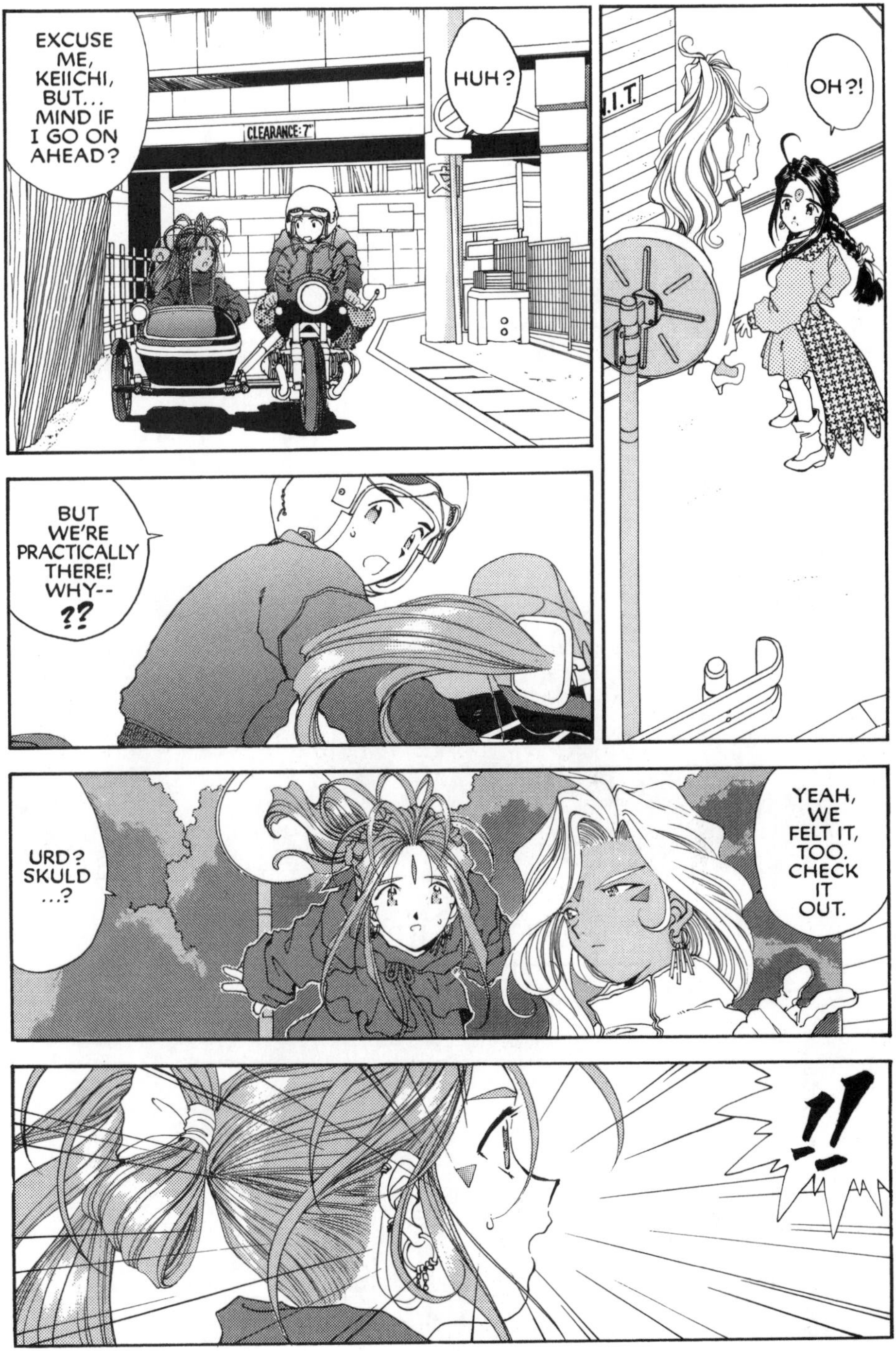
EXCUSE ME, KEIICHI, BUT... MIND IF I GO ON AHEAD?
CLEARANCE: 7'
HUH?
BUT WE'RE PRACTICALLY THERE! WHY-- ??
N.I.T.
OH?!
URD? SKULD ...?
YEAH, WE FELT IT, TOO. CHECK IT OUT.
!!

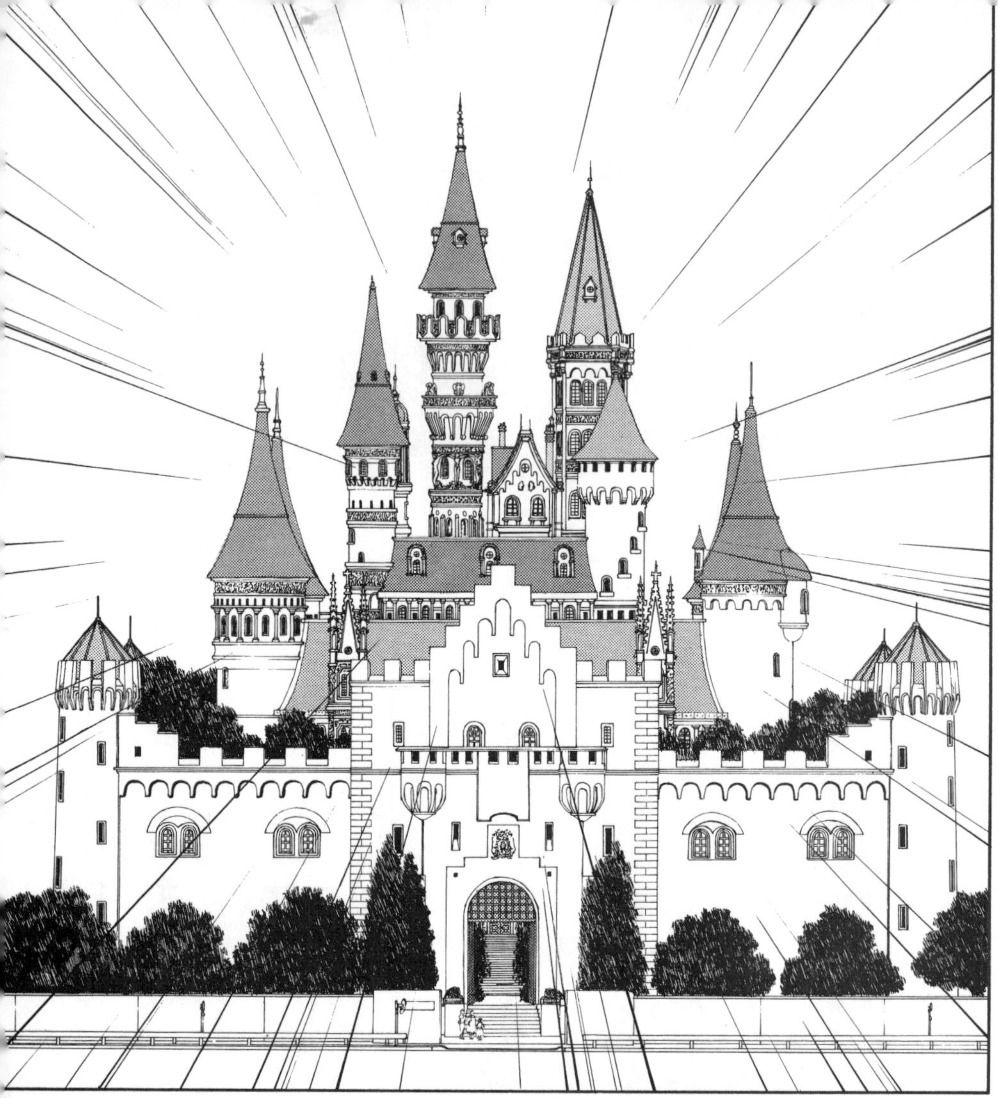

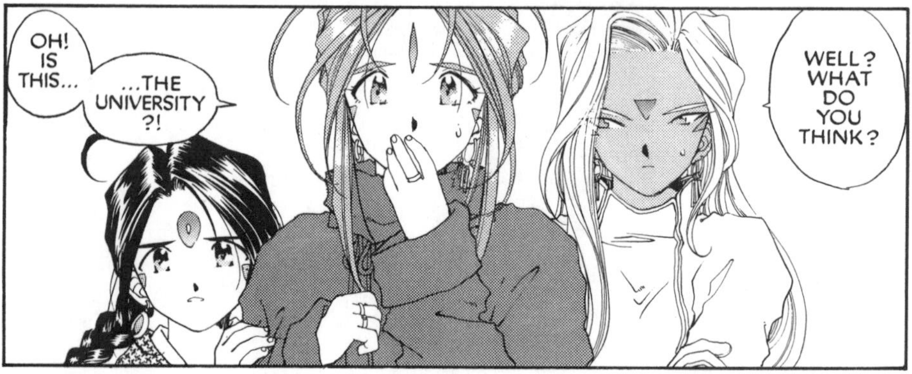
OH! IS THIS...
...THE UNIVERSITY ?!
WELL? WHAT DO YOU THINK?

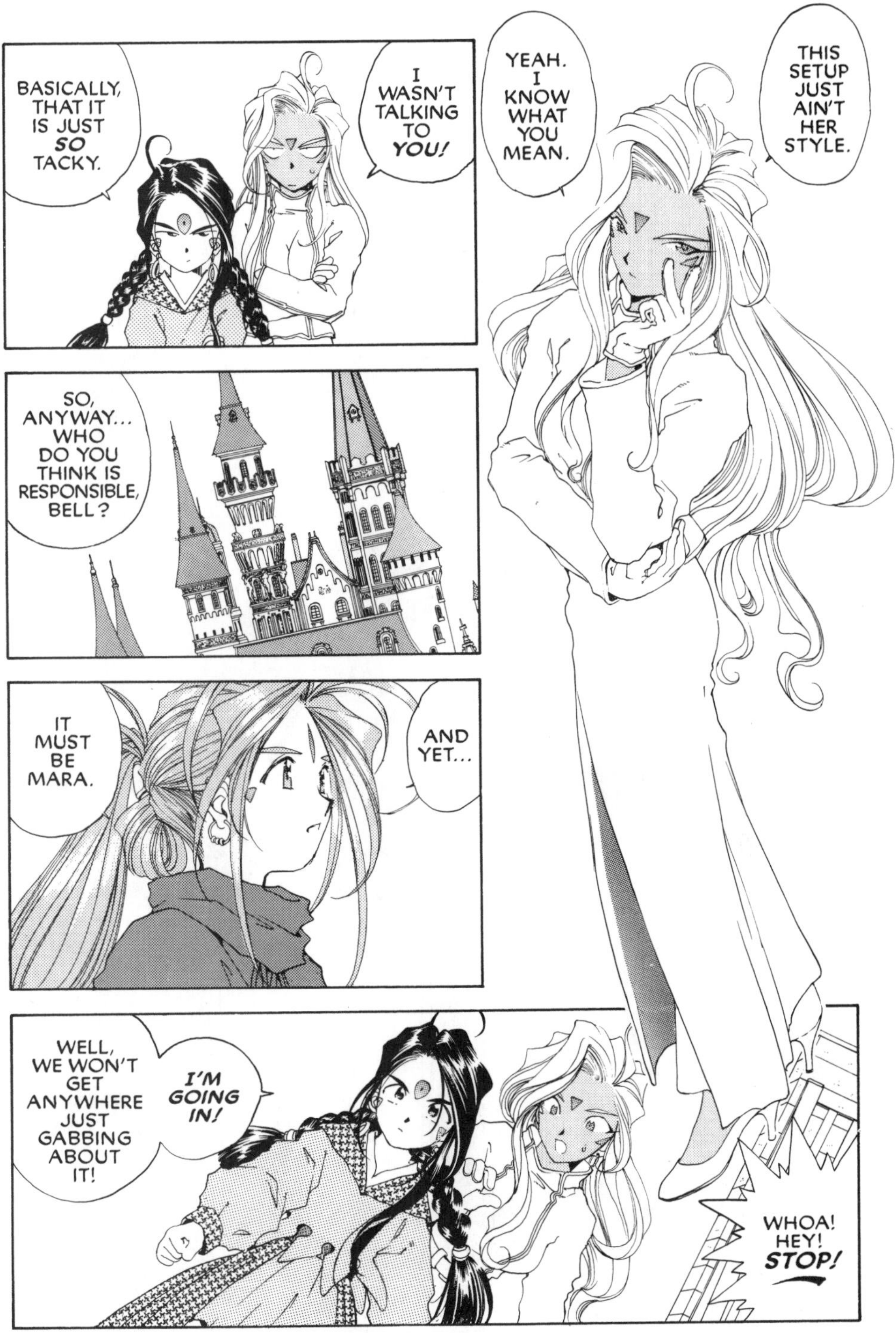
BASICALLY, THAT IT IS JUST *SO* TACKY.
I WASN'T TALKING TO ***YOU!***
SO, ANYWAY... WHO DO YOU THINK IS RESPONSIBLE, BELL?
IT MUST BE MARA.
AND YET...
YEAH. I KNOW WHAT YOU MEAN.
THIS SETUP JUST AIN'T HER STYLE.
WELL, WE WON'T GET ANYWHERE JUST GABBING ABOUT IT!
I'M GOING IN!
WHOA! HEY! ***STOP!***

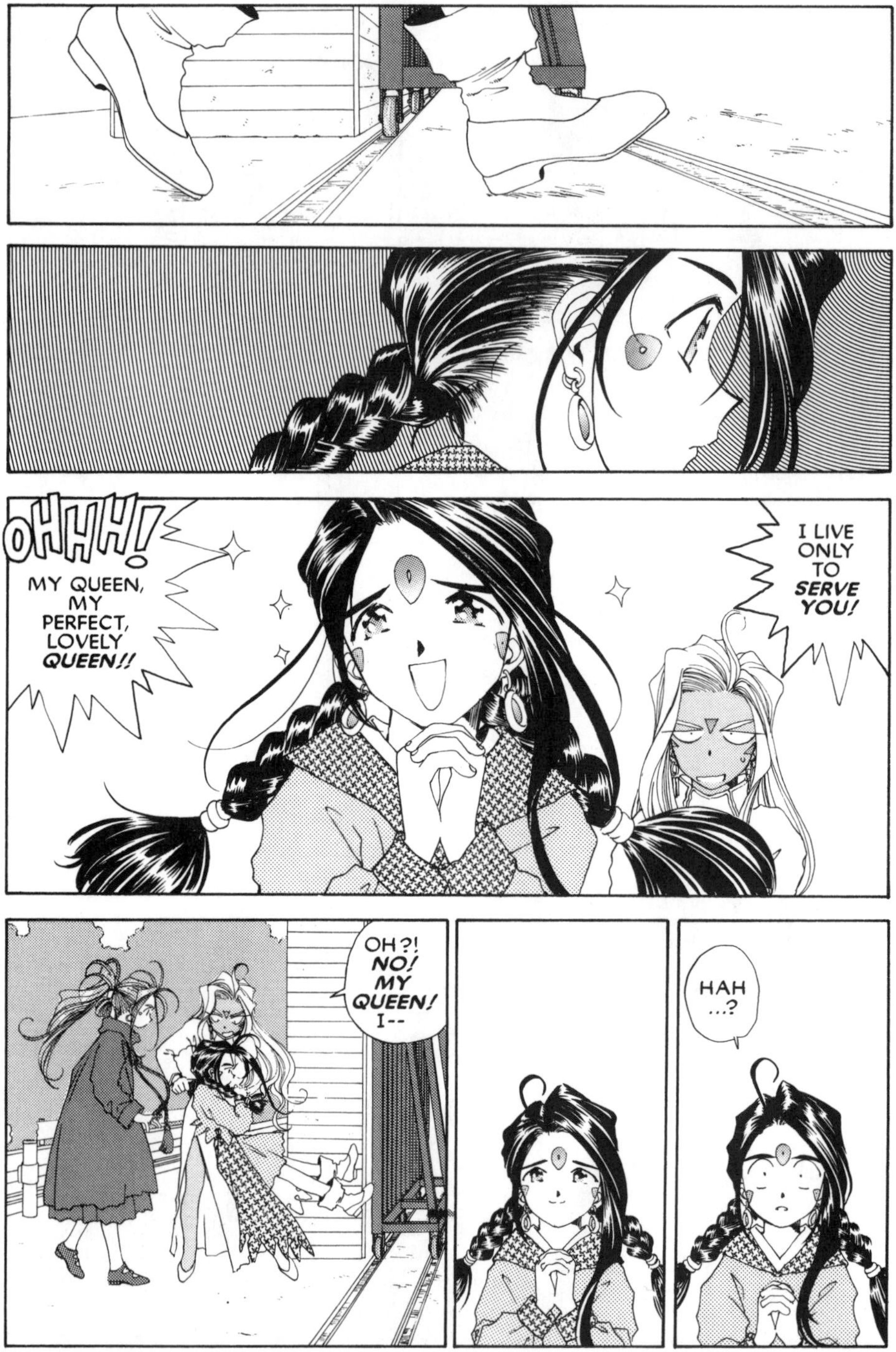
OHHH!
MY QUEEN, MY PERFECT, LOVELY QUEEN!!
I LIVE ONLY TO SERVE YOU!
OH?! NO! MY QUEEN! I--
HAH ...?

IT'S A **MIND-FORCE** FIELD!! THE BIGGEST AND STRONGEST I'VE EVER SEEN!

N-NO KIDDING! EVEN *I* COULDN'T RESIST IT!

WHAT DO YOU MEAN, "EVEN *I*"...?

≥whewf≥ CLOSE CALL...

HEY!

N.I.T

OH!

HUH?

WHAT THE HECK WAS THAT ABOUT?

SUDDENLY YOU JUST VANISHED, AND--

≥hff≥

≥hff≥

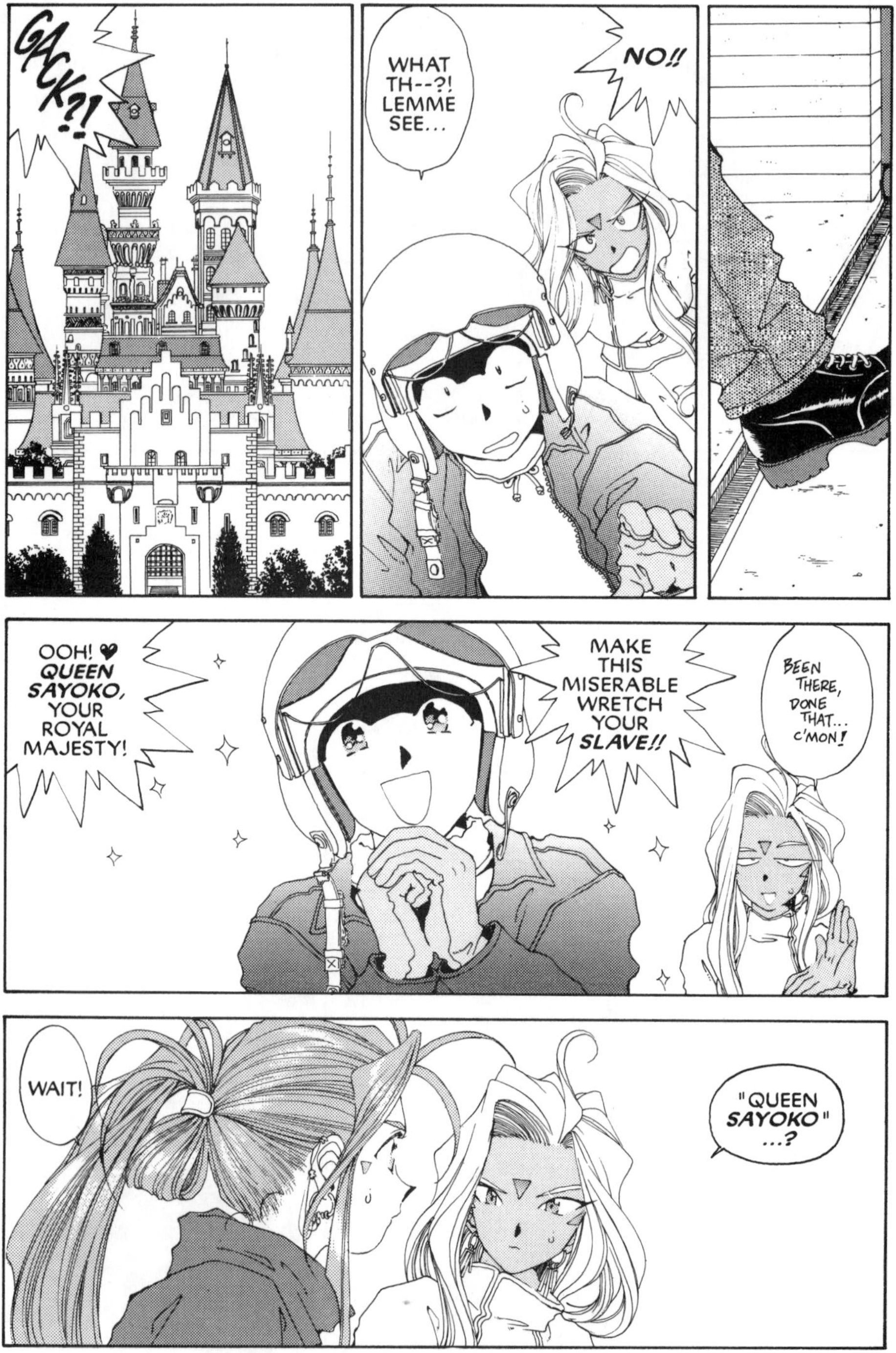
GACK?!
WHAT TH--?! LEMME SEE...
NO!!
OOH! ❤ QUEEN SAYOKO, YOUR ROYAL MAJESTY!
MAKE THIS MISERABLE WRETCH YOUR SLAVE!!
BEEN THERE, DONE THAT... C'MON!
WAIT!
"QUEEN SAYOKO" ...?

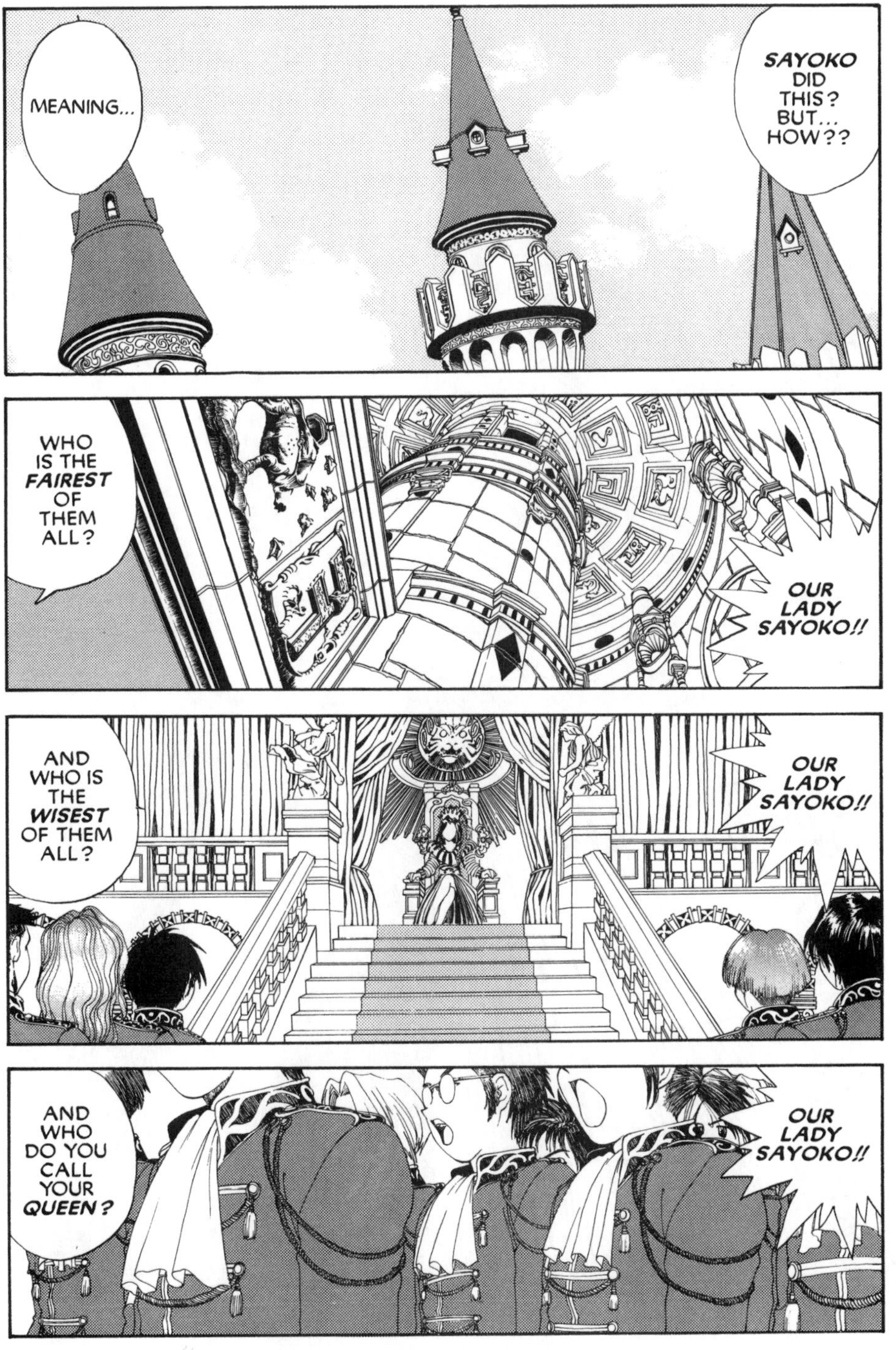
MEANING...
SAYOKO DID THIS? BUT... HOW??
WHO IS THE *FAIREST* OF THEM ALL?
OUR LADY SAYOKO!!
AND WHO IS THE *WISEST* OF THEM ALL?
OUR LADY SAYOKO!!
AND WHO DO YOU CALL YOUR ***QUEEN?***
OUR LADY SAYOKO!!

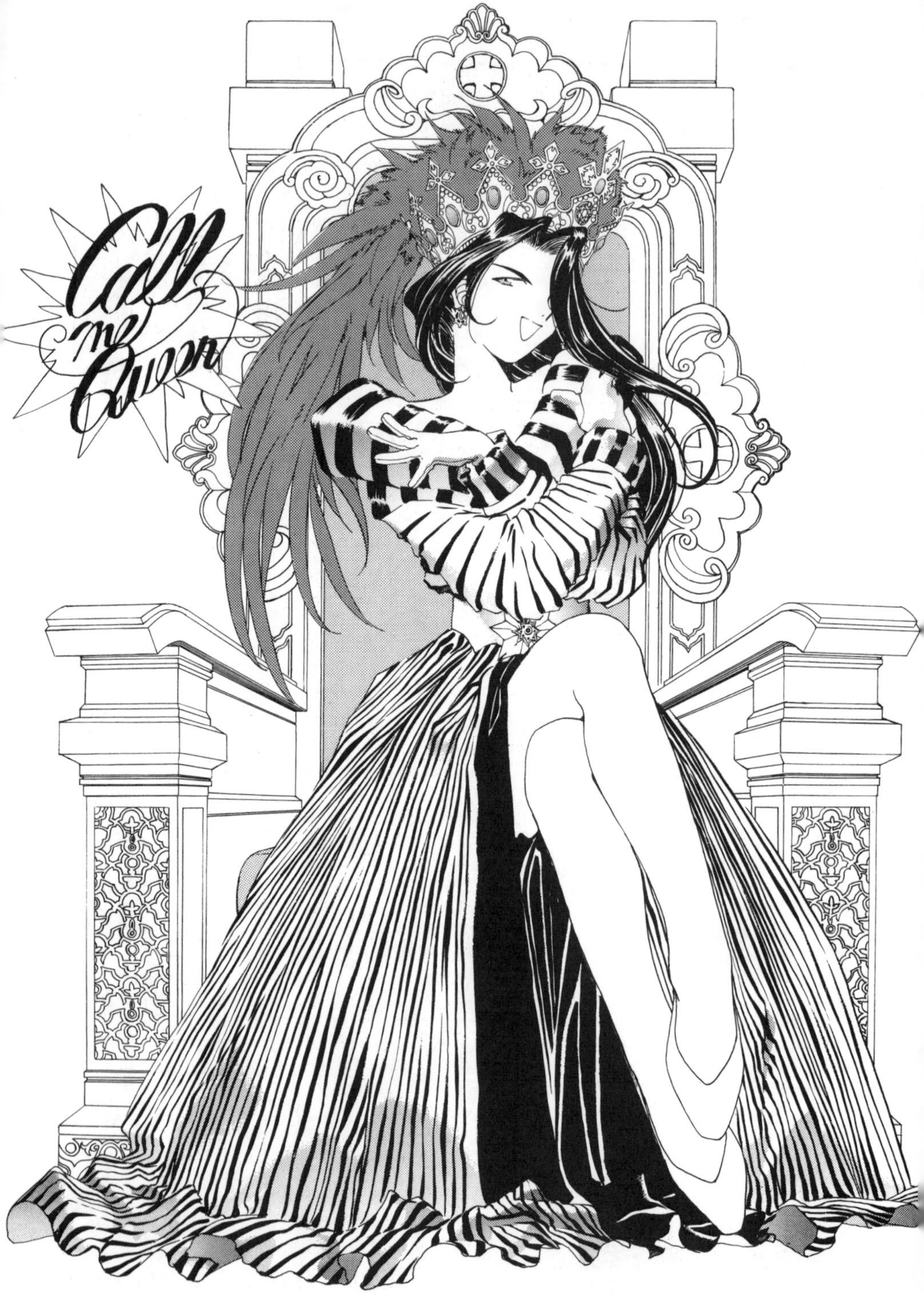
Call me Queen

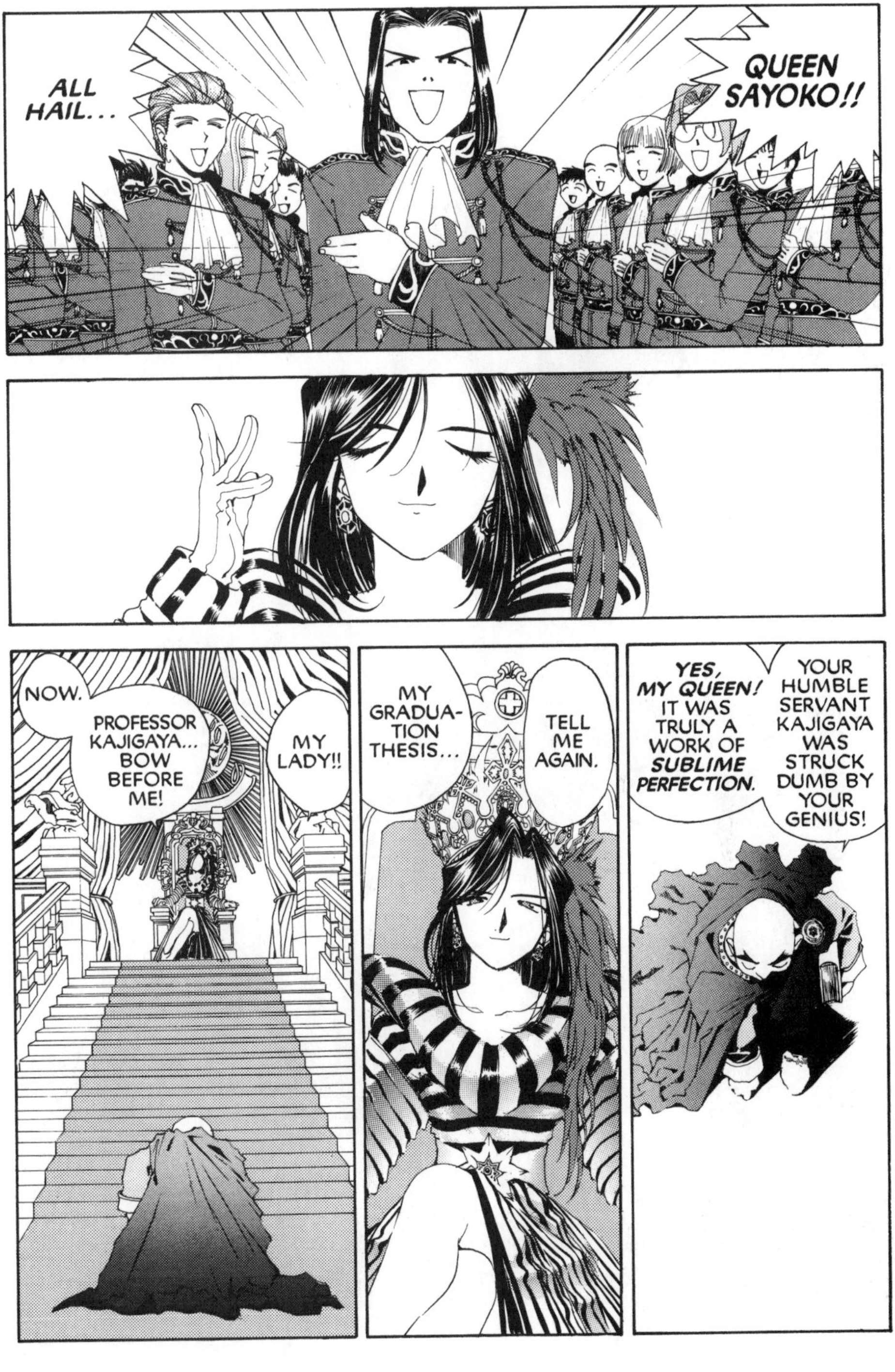
ALL HAIL...
QUEEN SAYOKO!!
NOW.
PROFESSOR KAJIGAYA... BOW BEFORE ME!
MY LADY!!
MY GRADUA-TION THESIS...
TELL ME AGAIN.
YES, MY QUEEN! IT WAS TRULY A WORK OF SUBLIME PERFECTION.
YOUR HUMBLE SERVANT KAJIGAYA WAS STRUCK DUMB BY YOUR GENIUS!

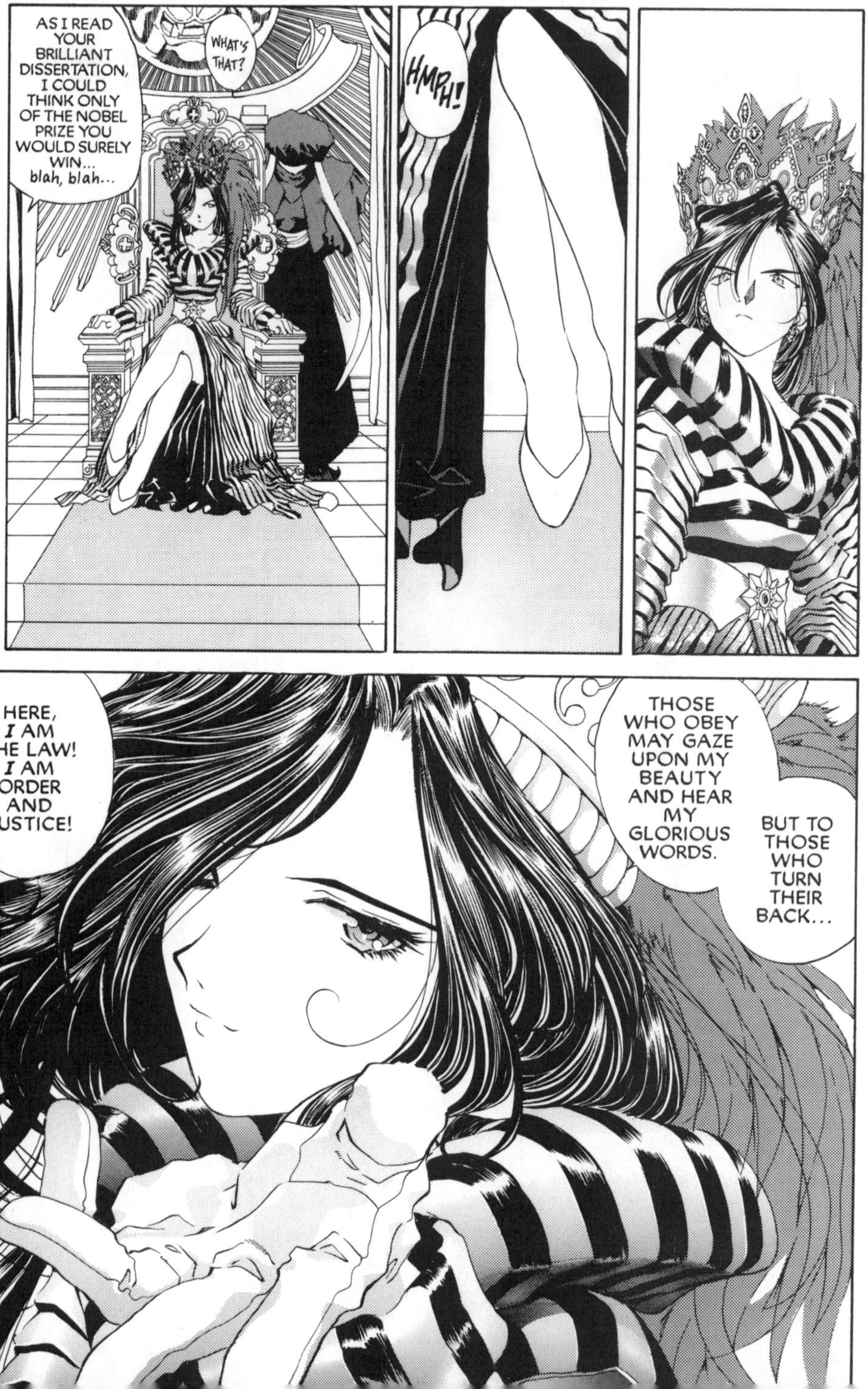
AS I READ YOUR BRILLIANT DISSERTATION, I COULD THINK ONLY OF THE NOBEL PRIZE YOU WOULD SURELY WIN... blah, blah...
WHAT'S THAT?
HMPH!
HERE, *I* AM THE LAW! *I* AM ORDER AND JUSTICE!
THOSE WHO OBEY MAY GAZE UPON MY BEAUTY AND HEAR MY GLORIOUS WORDS.
BUT TO THOSE WHO TURN THEIR BACK...

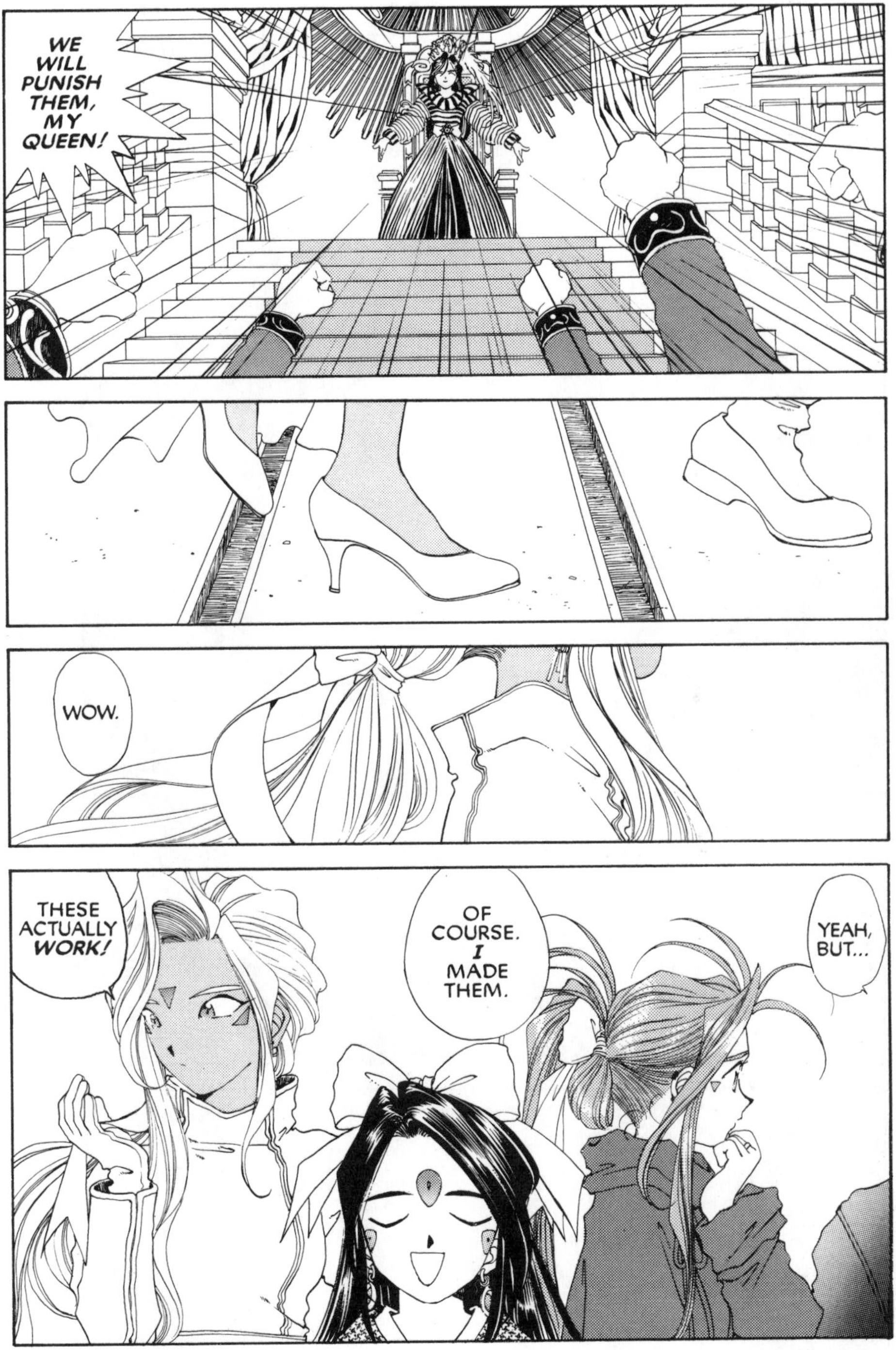
WE WILL PUNISH THEM, MY QUEEN!
WOW.
THESE ACTUALLY *WORK!*
OF COURSE. *I* MADE THEM.
YEAH, BUT...

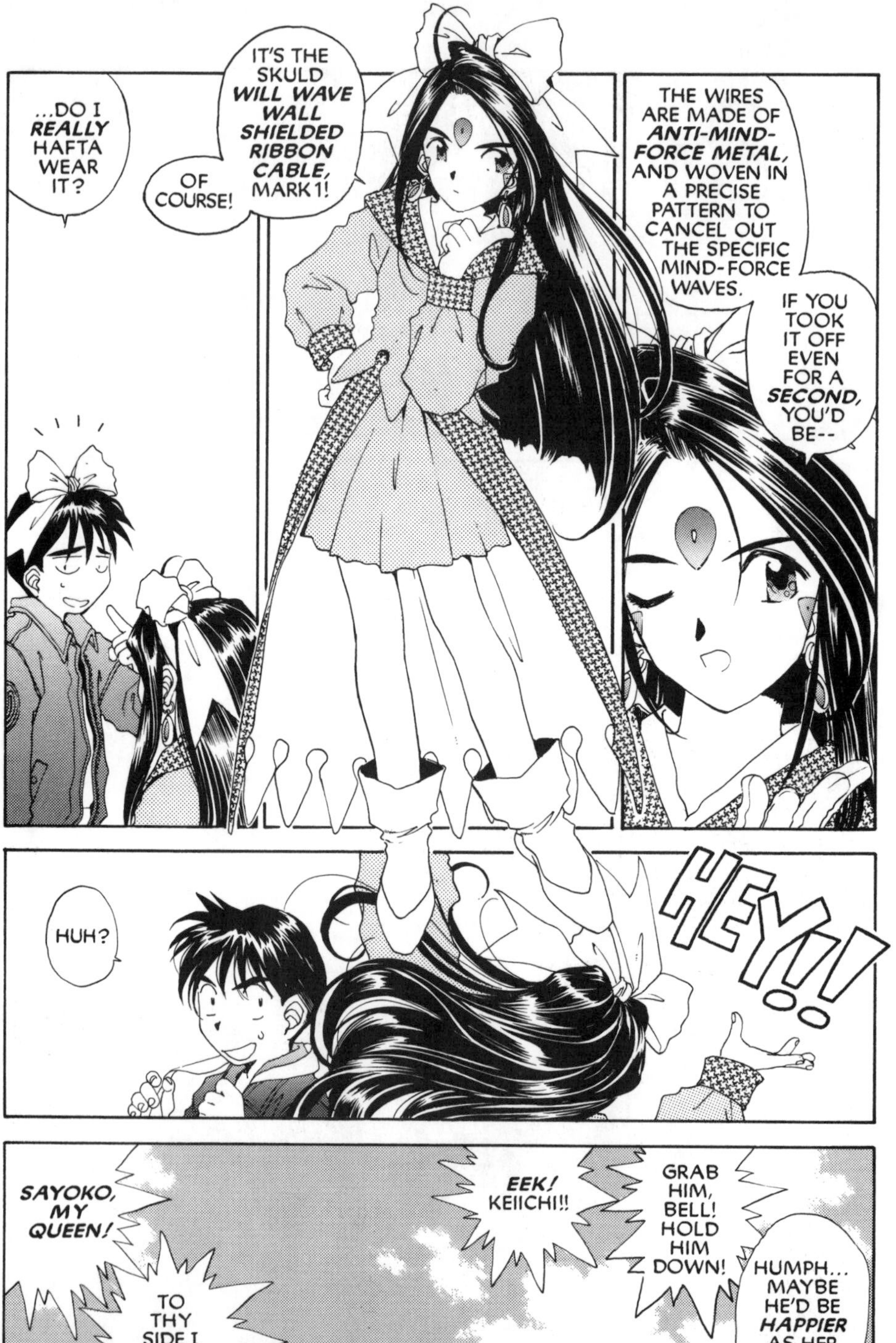
...DO I *REALLY* HAFTA WEAR IT?
OF COURSE!
IT'S THE SKULD ***WILL WAVE WALL SHIELDED RIBBON CABLE,*** MARK 1!
THE WIRES ARE MADE OF ***ANTI-MIND-FORCE METAL,*** AND WOVEN IN A PRECISE PATTERN TO CANCEL OUT THE SPECIFIC MIND-FORCE WAVES.
IF YOU TOOK IT OFF EVEN FOR A ***SECOND,*** YOU'D BE--
HUH?
HEY!!
SAYOKO, MY QUEEN!
TO THY SIDE I COME!
EEK! KEIICHI!!
GRAB HIM, BELL! HOLD HIM DOWN!
HUMPH... MAYBE HE'D BE ***HAPPIER*** AS HER SLAVE...

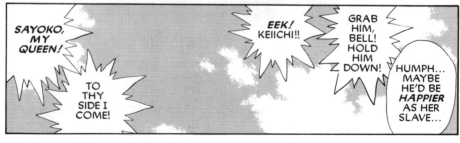

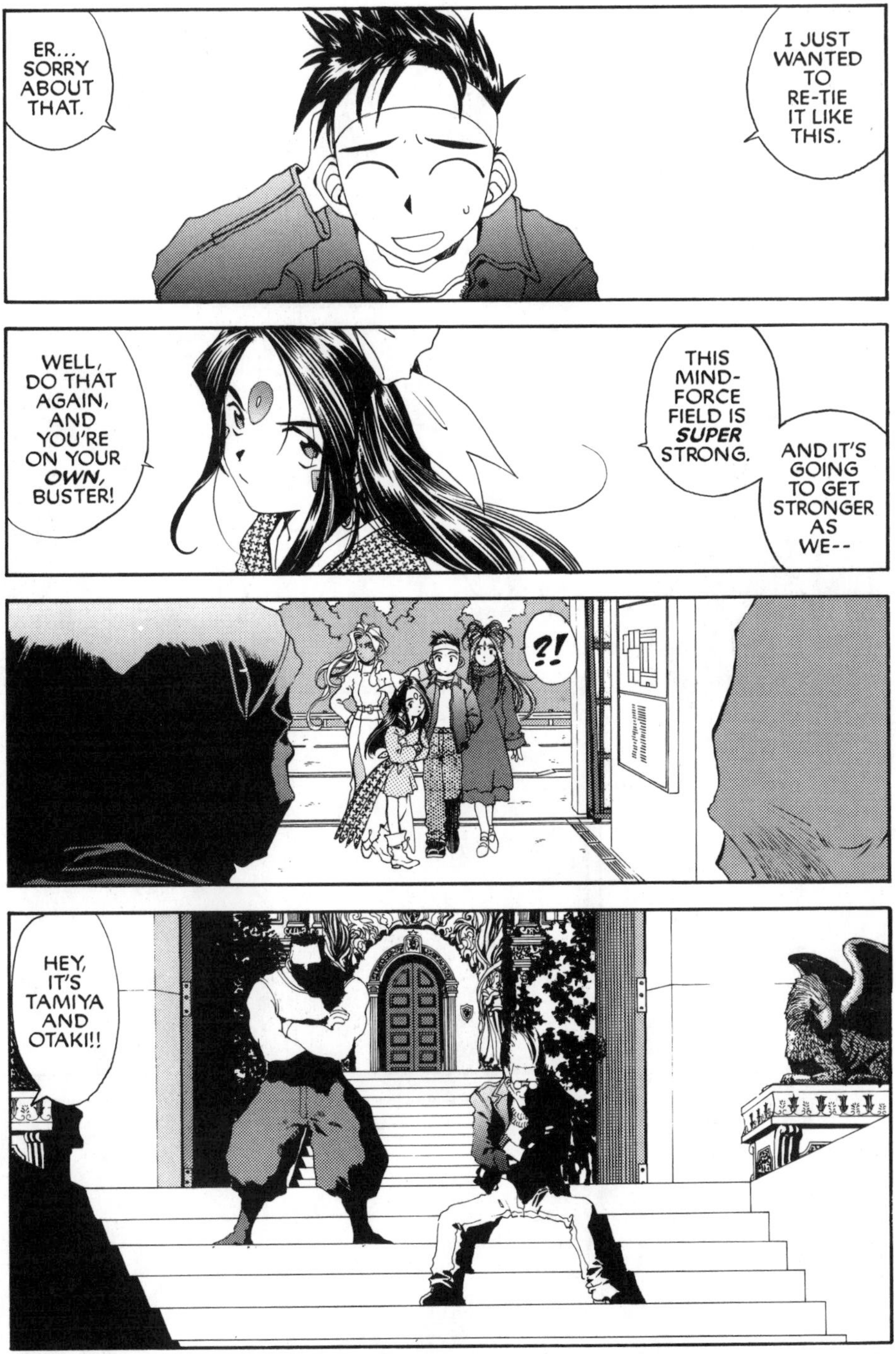
ER... SORRY ABOUT THAT.
I JUST WANTED TO RE-TIE IT LIKE THIS.
WELL, DO THAT AGAIN, AND YOU'RE ON YOUR *OWN,* BUSTER!
THIS MIND-FORCE FIELD IS *SUPER* STRONG.
AND IT'S GOING TO GET STRONGER AS WE--
?!
HEY, IT'S TAMIYA AND OTAKI!!

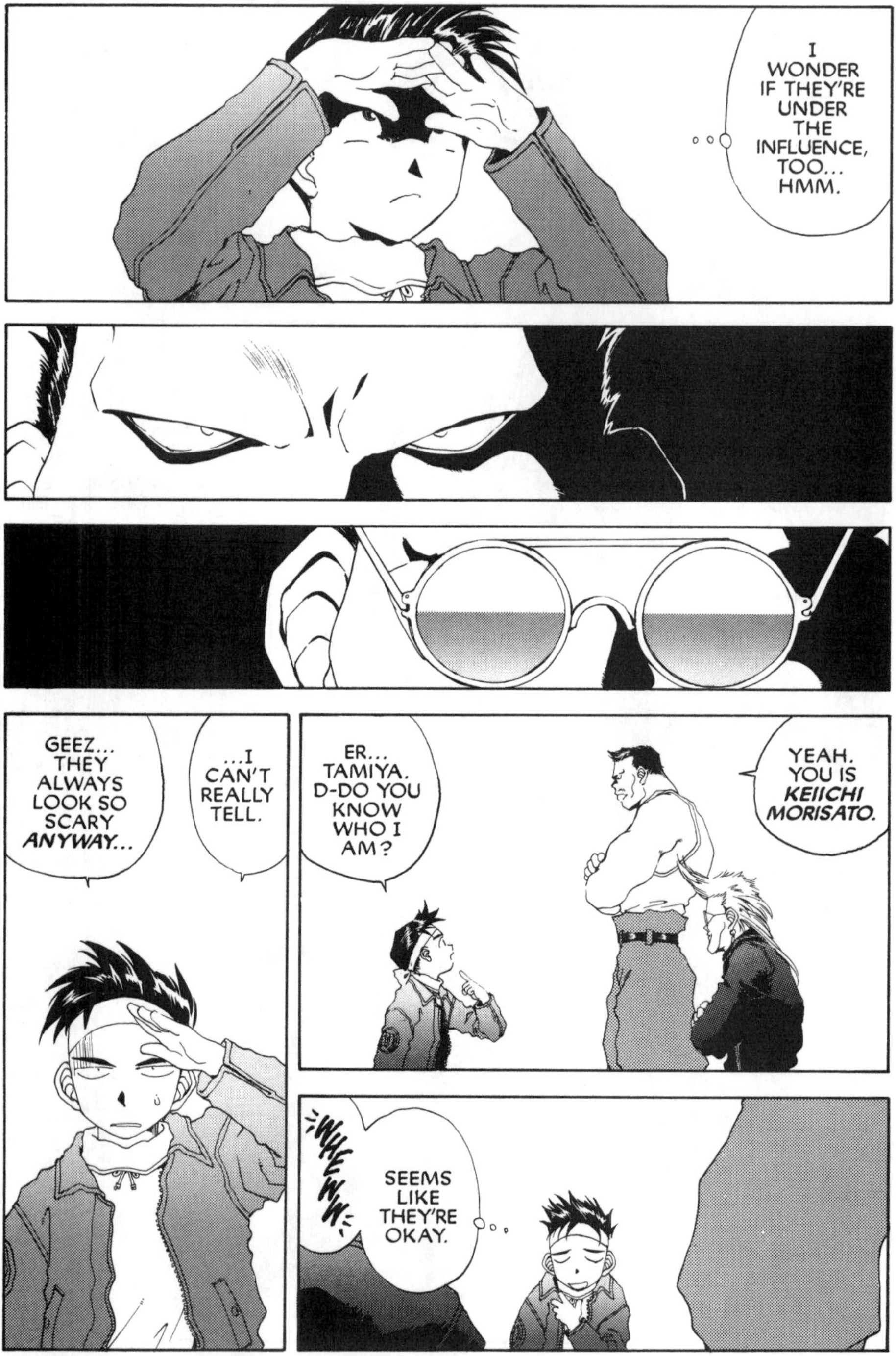
I WONDER IF THEY'RE UNDER THE INFLUENCE, TOO... HMM.
GEEZ... THEY ALWAYS LOOK SO SCARY *ANYWAY...*
...I CAN'T REALLY TELL.
ER... TAMIYA, D-DO YOU KNOW WHO I AM?
YEAH. YOU IS *KEIICHI MORISATO.*
SEEMS LIKE THEY'RE OKAY.

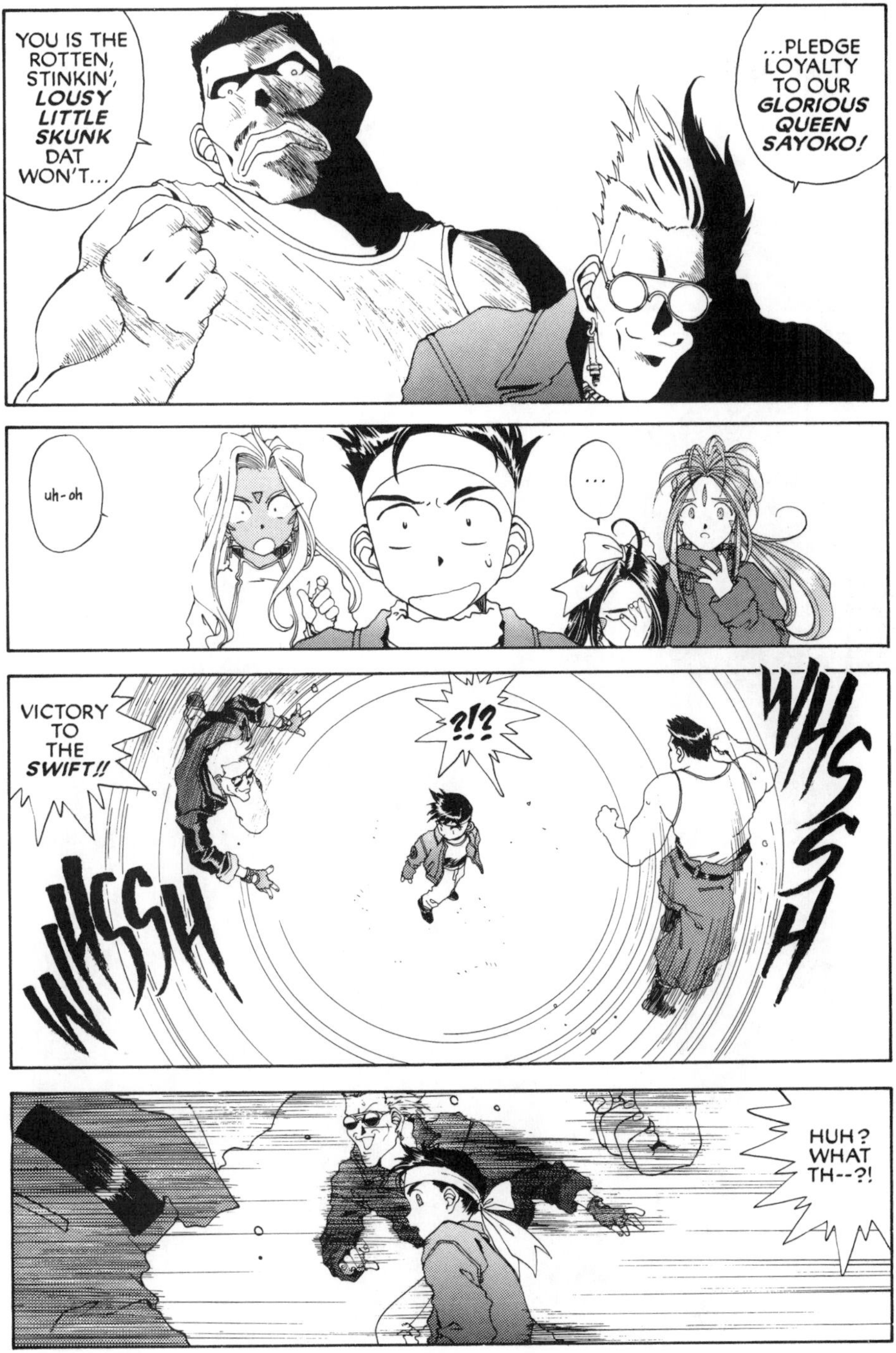
YOU IS THE ROTTEN, STINKIN', LOUSY LITTLE SKUNK DAT WON'T...
...PLEDGE LOYALTY TO OUR GLORIOUS QUEEN SAYOKO!
uh-oh
...
VICTORY TO THE SWIFT!!
?!?
WHSSH
WHSSH
HUH? WHAT TH--?!

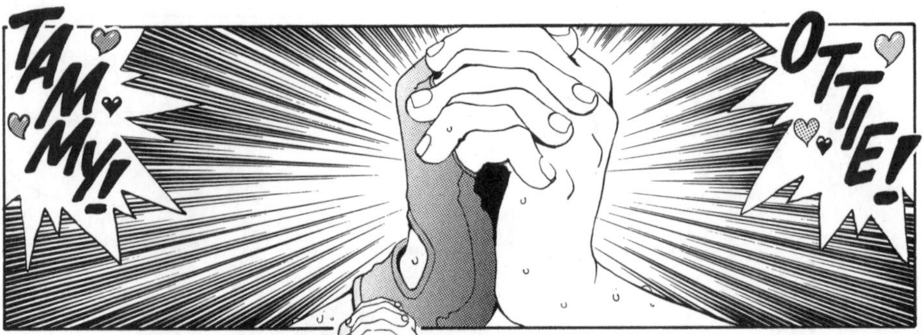
TAMMY!
OTTIE!
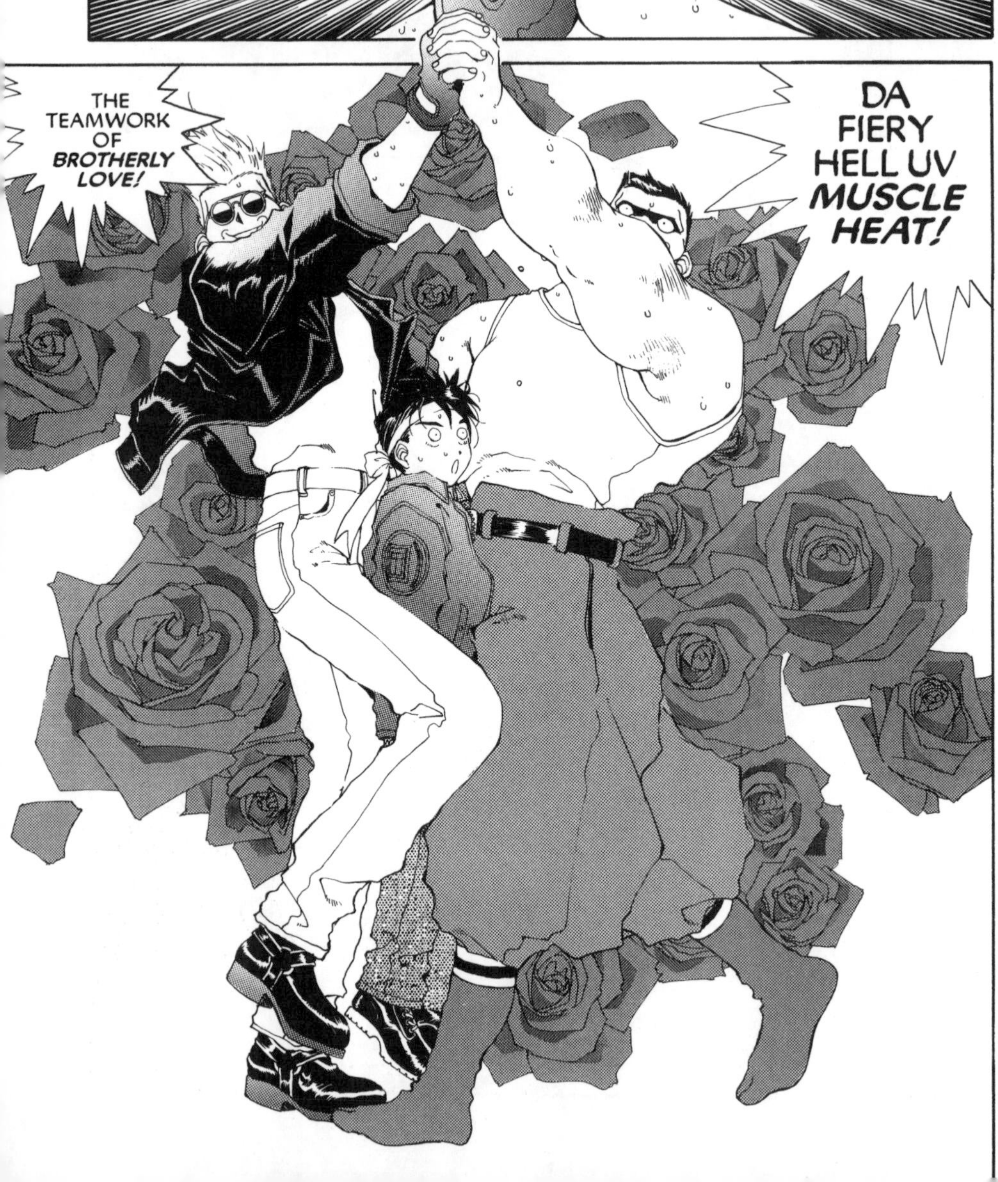
THE TEAMWORK OF BROTHERLY LOVE!
DA FIERY HELL UV MUSCLE HEAT!

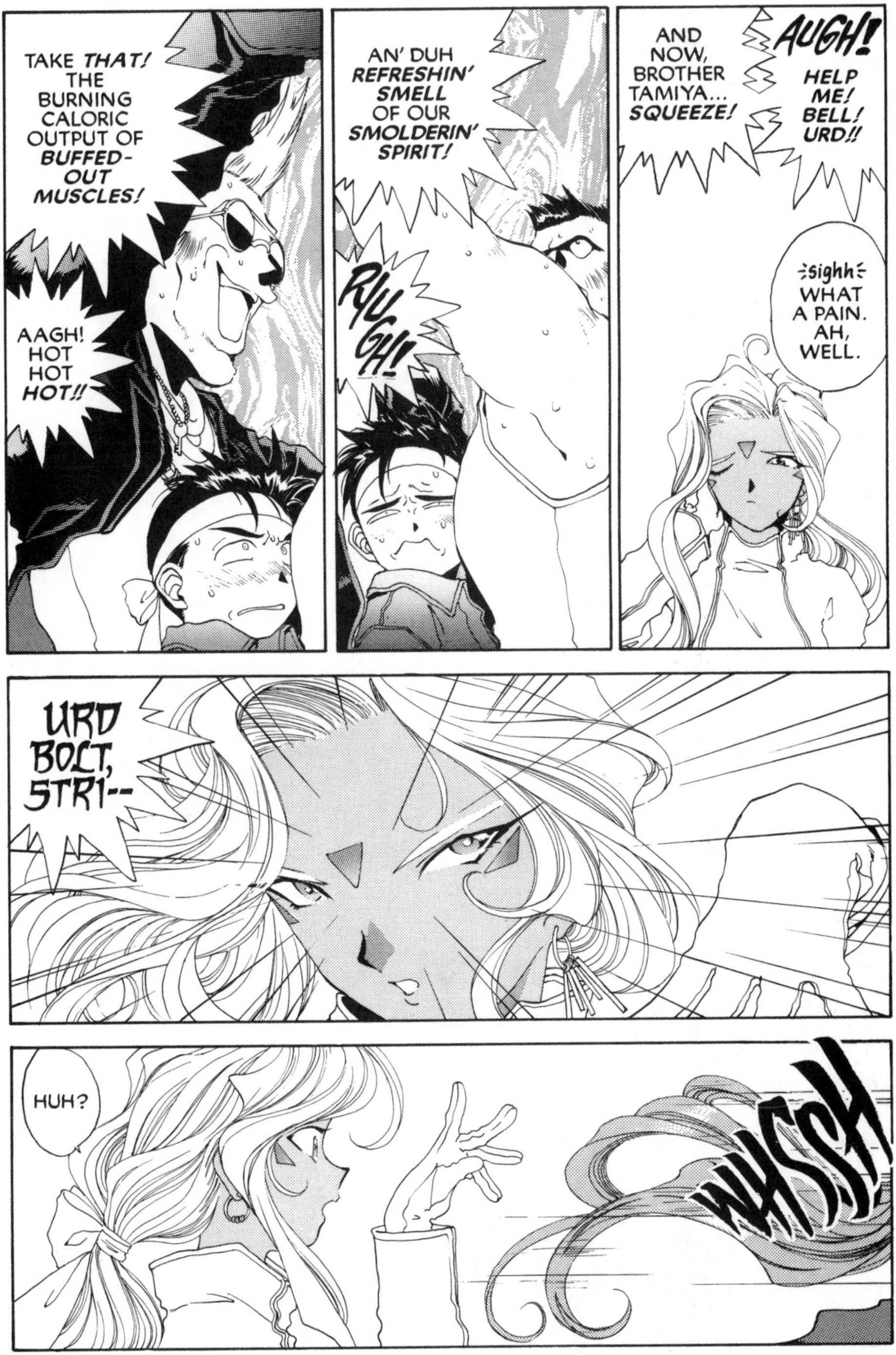
TAKE THAT! THE BURNING CALORIC OUTPUT OF BUFFED-OUT MUSCLES!
AAGH! HOT HOT HOT!!
AN' DUH REFRESHIN' SMELL OF OUR SMOLDERIN' SPIRIT!
RYUGH!
AND NOW, BROTHER TAMIYA... SQUEEZE!
AUGH!
HELP ME! BELL! URD!!
sighh WHAT A PAIN. AH, WELL.
URD BOLT, STRI--
HUH?
WHSSH!

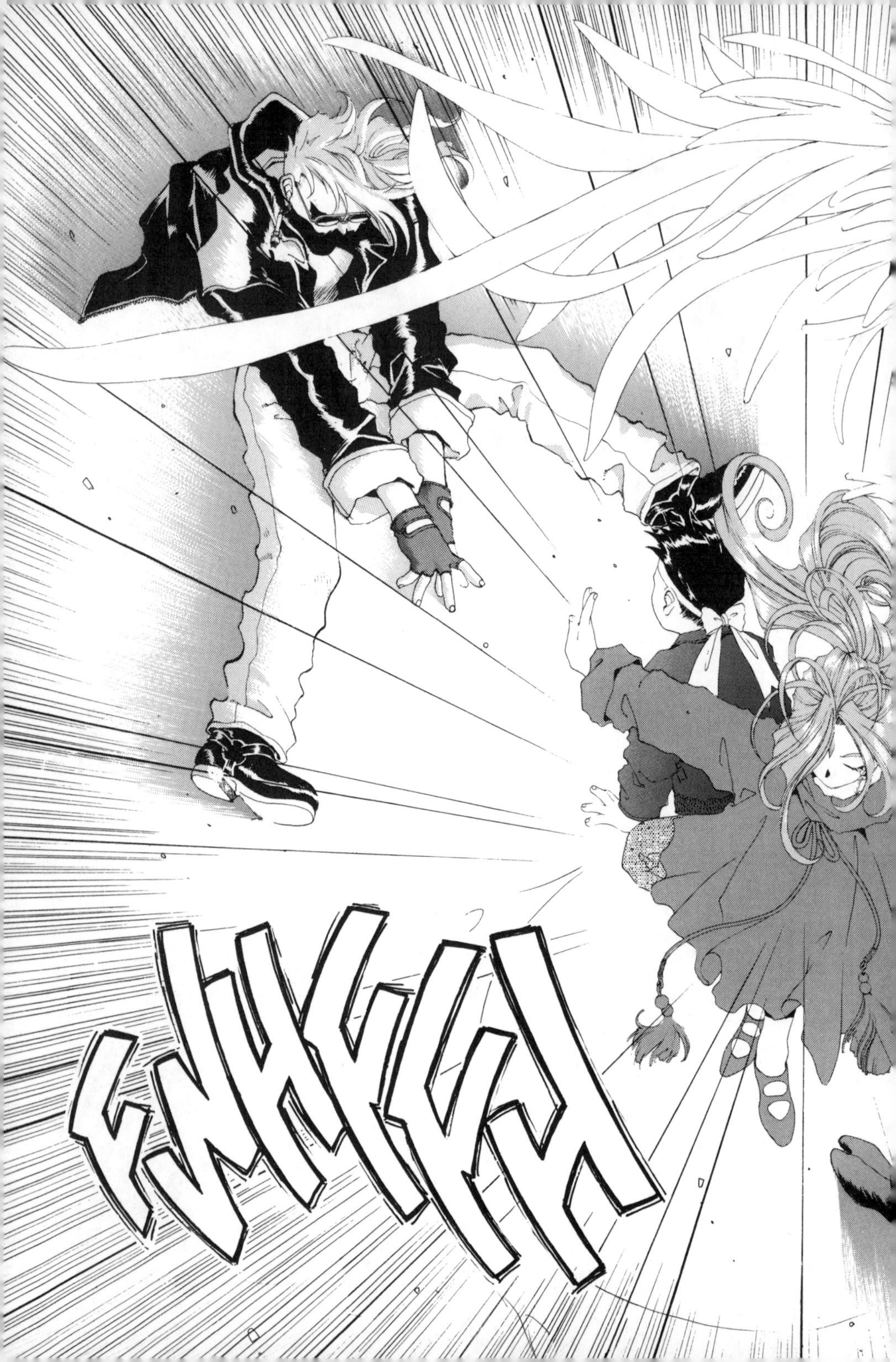

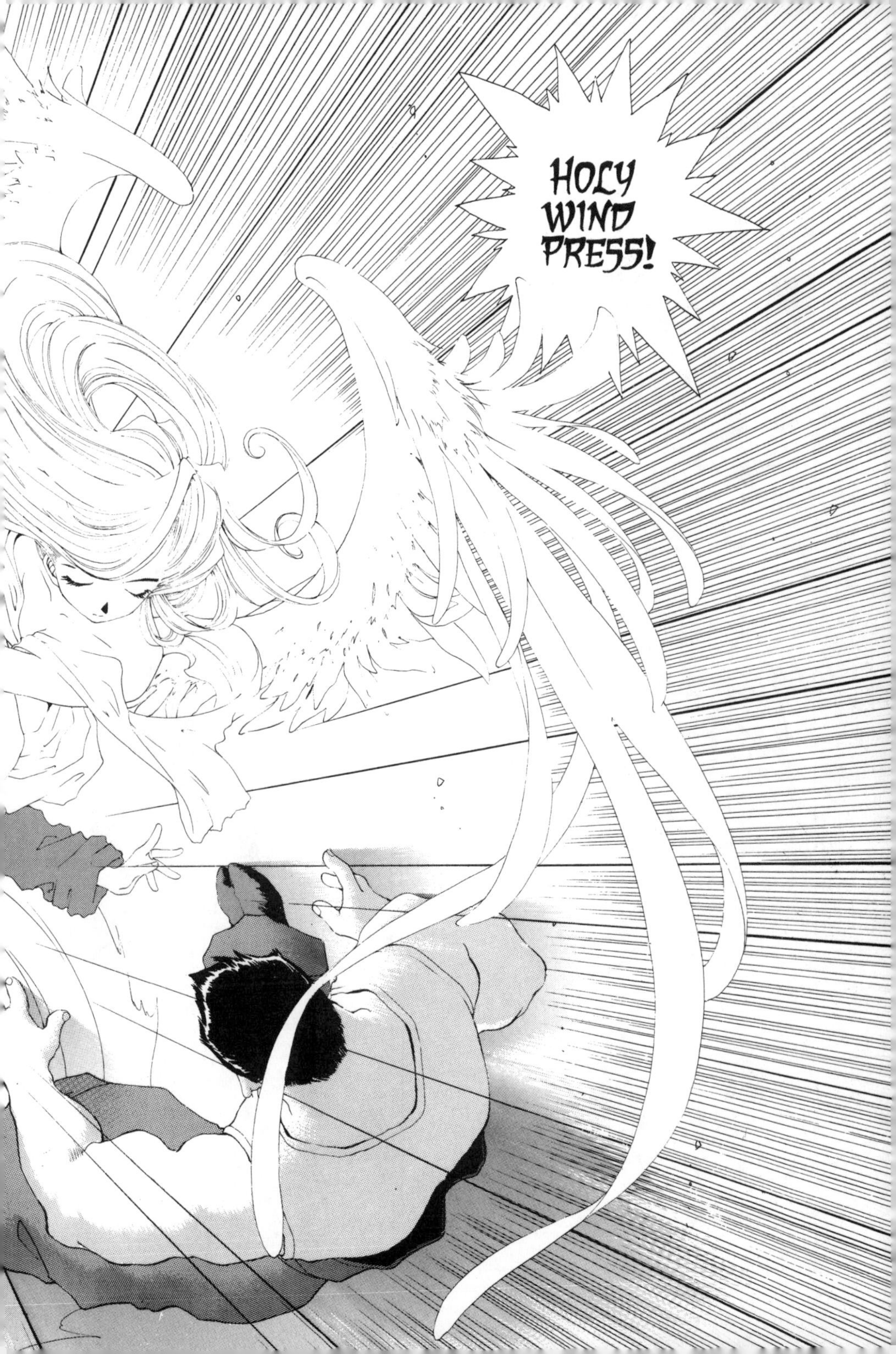
HOLY WIND PRESS!

W-WOW! AN *ATTACK* SPELL?! SIS *NEVER* USES THOSE!

SHE'S ACTUALLY... *ANGRY?*

BELL-DANDY... MY SWEET, SWEET SISTER.

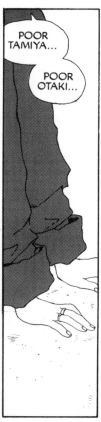

POOR TAMIYA...

POOR OTAKI...

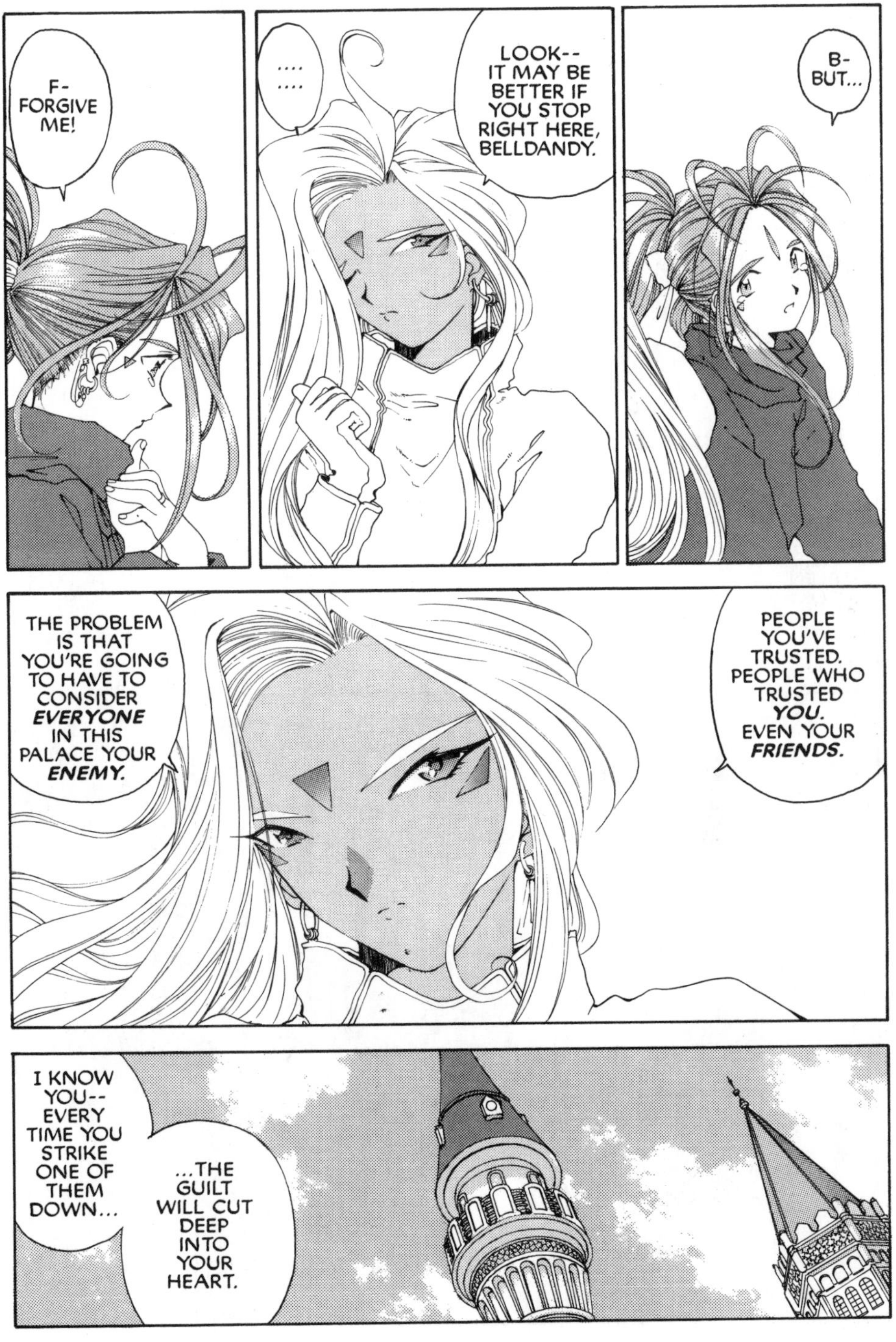
F-FORGIVE ME!
....
....
LOOK-- IT MAY BE BETTER IF YOU STOP RIGHT HERE, BELLDANDY.
B-BUT...
THE PROBLEM IS THAT YOU'RE GOING TO HAVE TO CONSIDER ***EVERYONE*** IN THIS PALACE YOUR ***ENEMY.***
PEOPLE YOU'VE TRUSTED. PEOPLE WHO TRUSTED ***YOU.*** EVEN YOUR ***FRIENDS.***
I KNOW YOU-- EVERY TIME YOU STRIKE ONE OF THEM DOWN...
...THE GUILT WILL CUT DEEP INTO YOUR HEART.

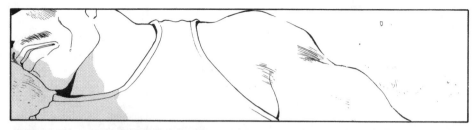

YES,
PERHAPS.
YET,
EVEN
SO...

...I
KNOW
IT MUST
BE
DONE
TO SAVE
THEM.

NO.
INSTEAD
OF
FEARING
IT...

...I
WILL
EMBRACE
THIS
PATH.

I
CANNOT
PERMIT
THIS
DEMONIC
WORK
HERE ON
EARTH.

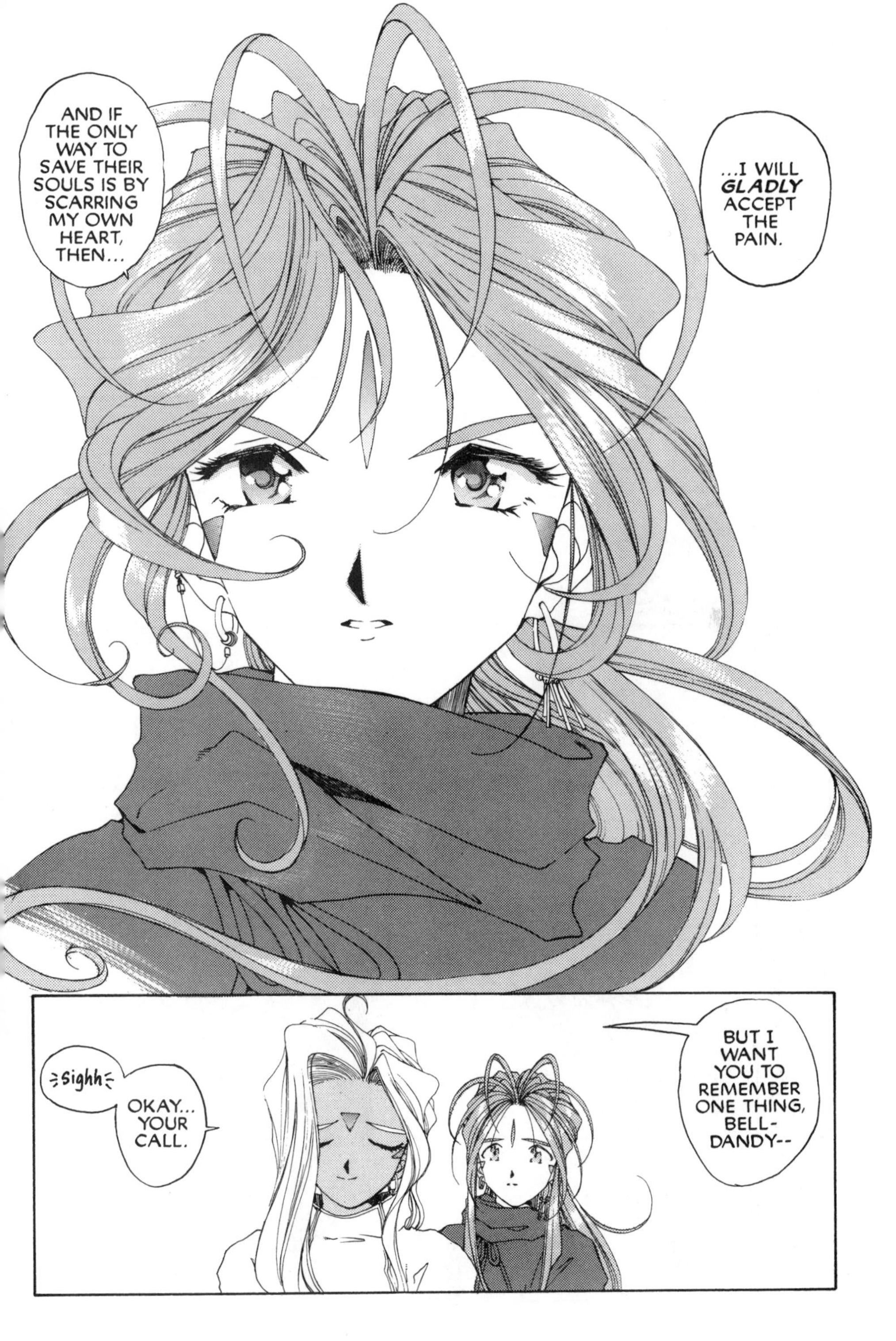
AND IF THE ONLY WAY TO SAVE THEIR SOULS IS BY SCARRING MY OWN HEART, THEN...
...I WILL GLADLY ACCEPT THE PAIN.
sighh
OKAY... YOUR CALL.
BUT I WANT YOU TO REMEMBER ONE THING, BELL-DANDY--

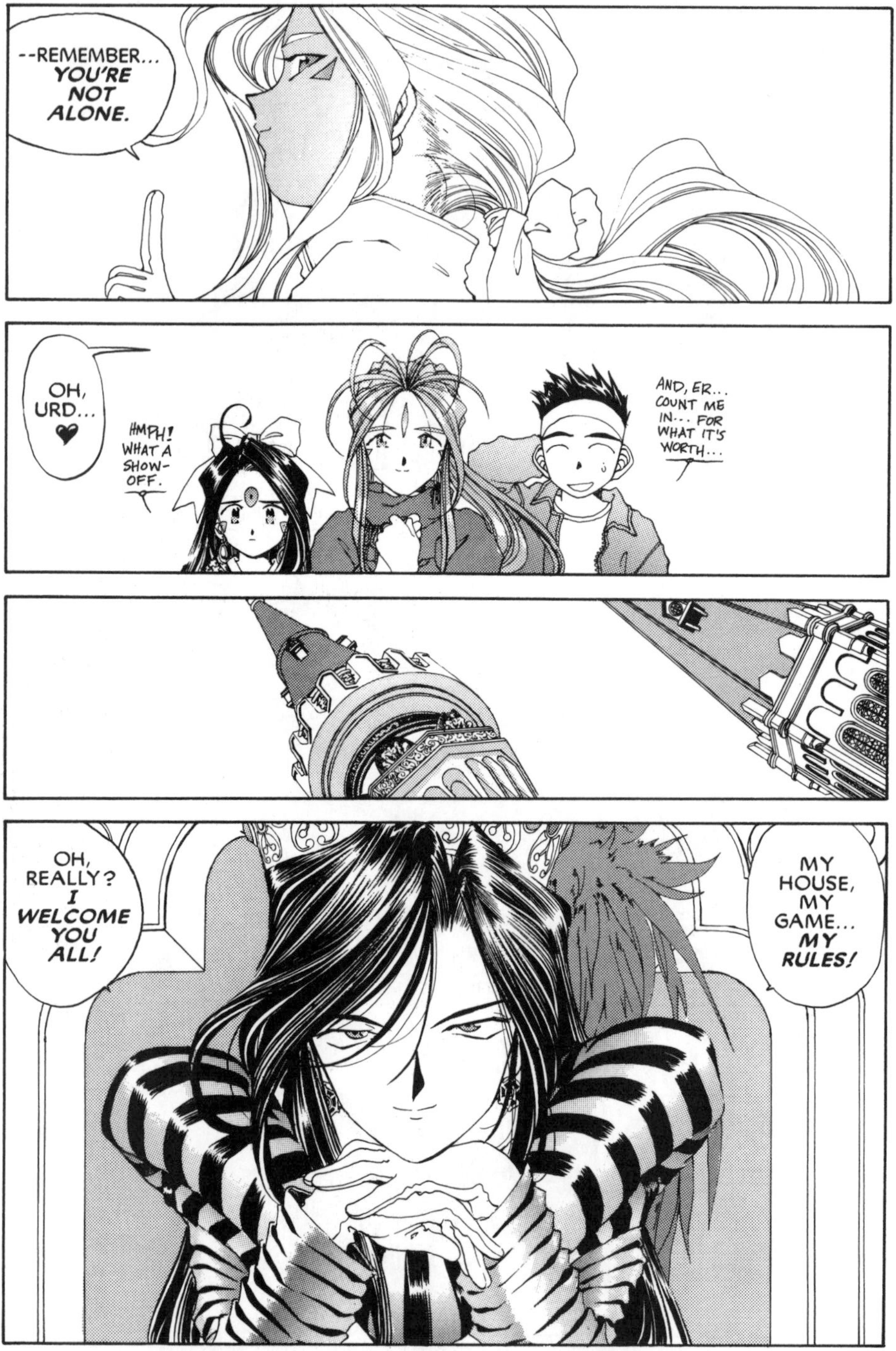
--REMEMBER... YOU'RE NOT ALONE.
OH, URD... ❤
HMPH! WHAT A SHOW-OFF.
AND, ER... COUNT ME IN... FOR WHAT IT'S WORTH...
OH, REALLY? I WELCOME YOU ALL!
MY HOUSE, MY GAME... MY RULES!

And Then There Was One

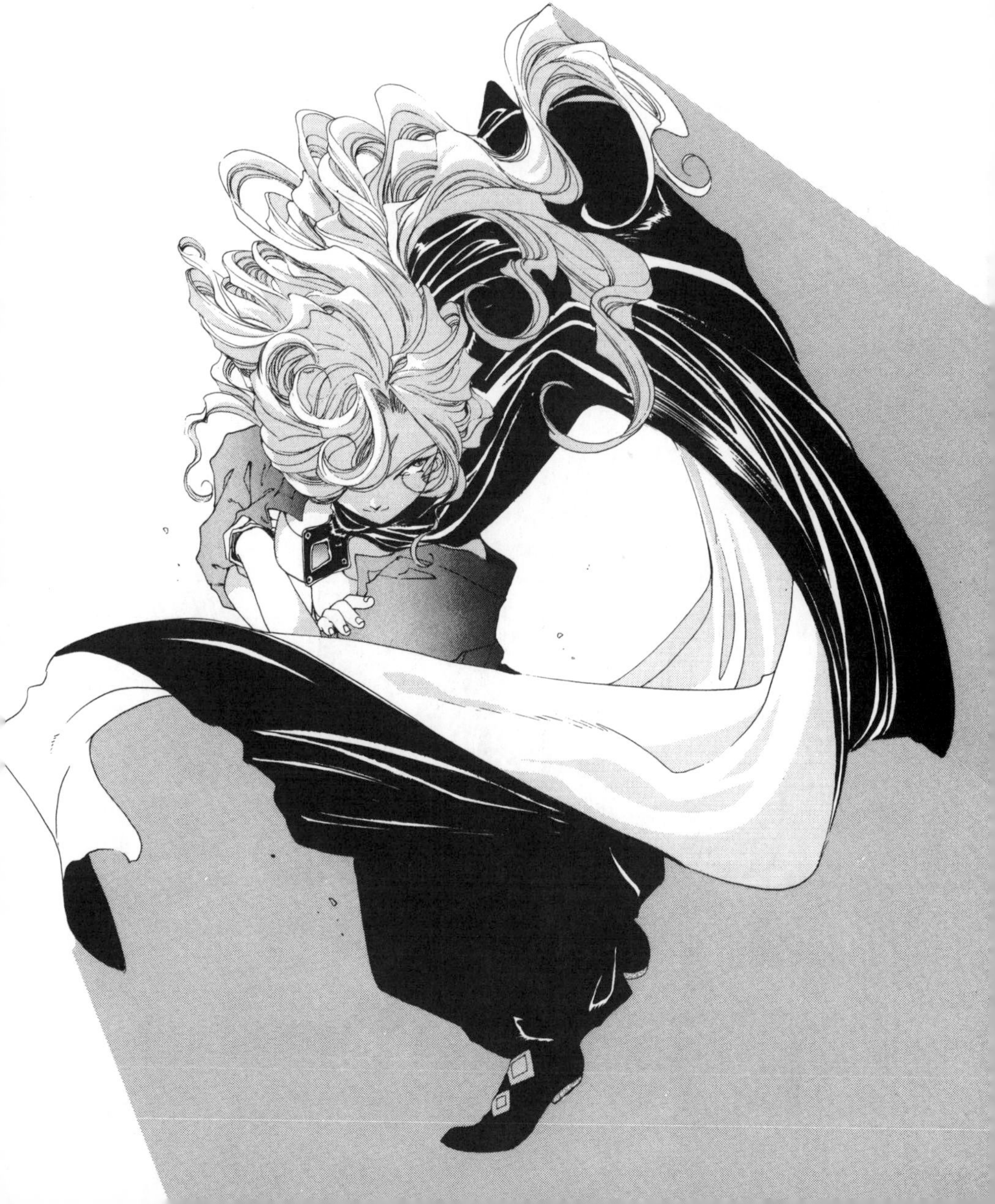

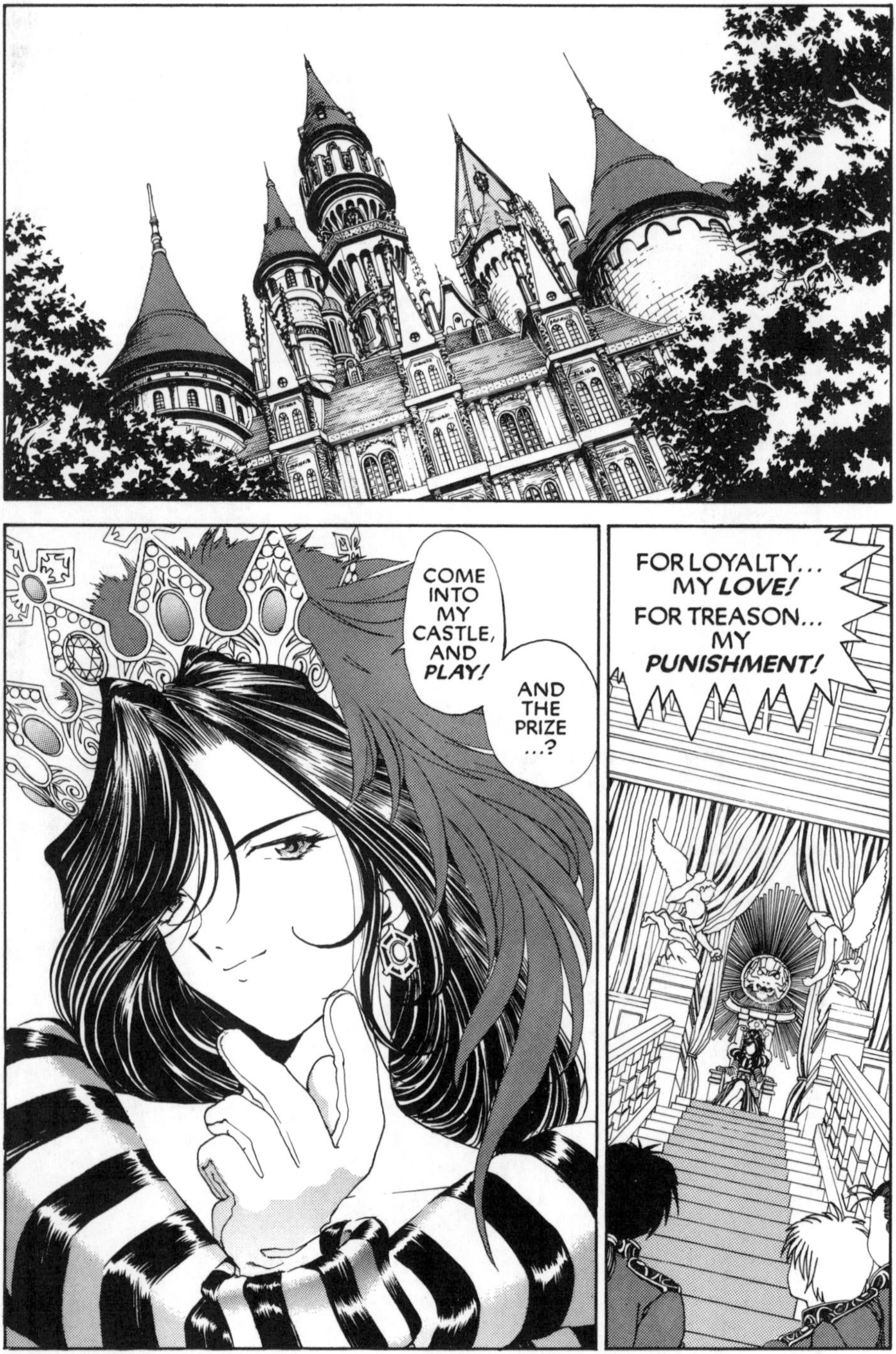
COME INTO MY CASTLE, AND *PLAY!*
AND THE PRIZE ...?
FOR LOYALTY... MY *LOVE!* FOR TREASON... MY *PUNISHMENT!*

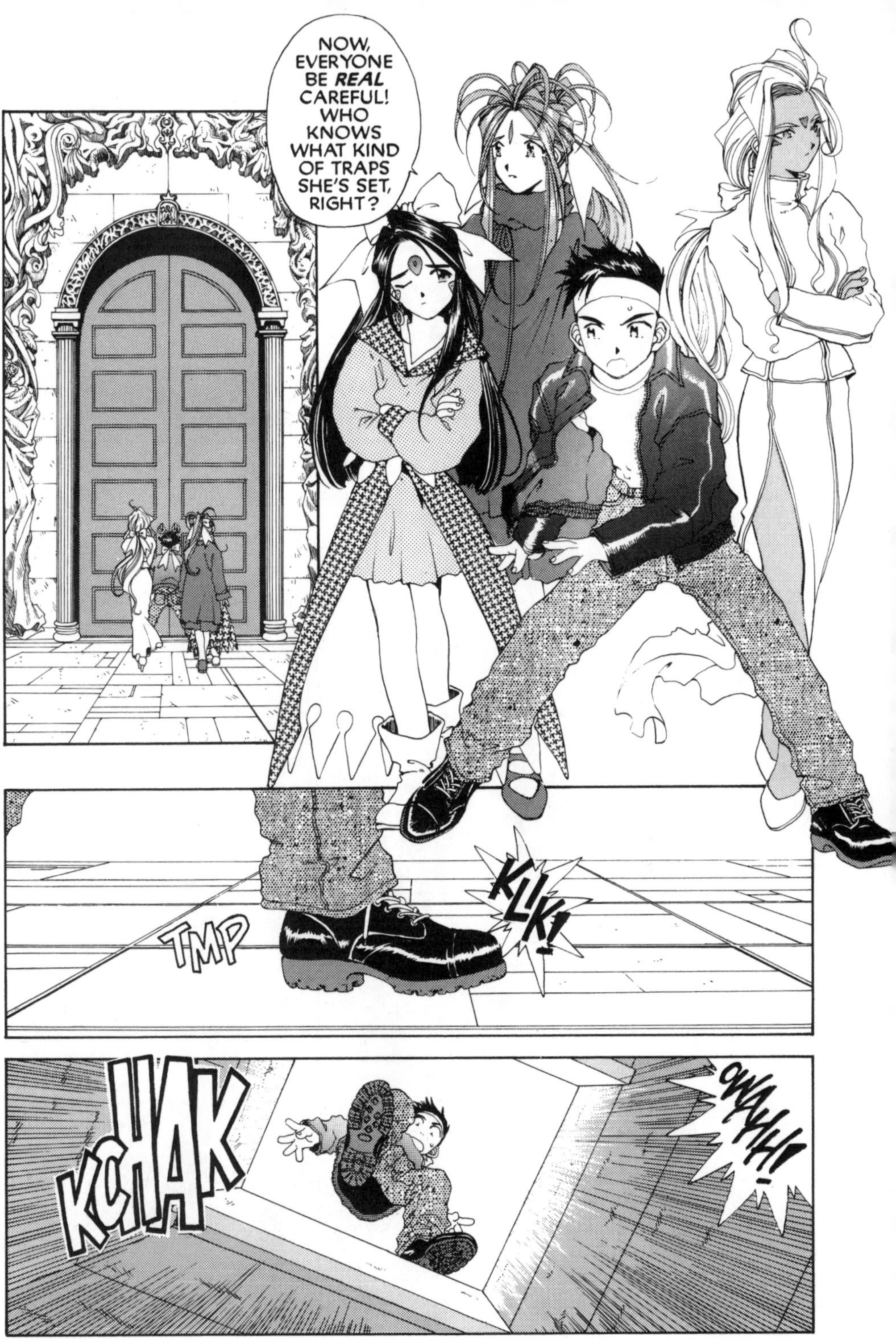
NOW, EVERYONE BE *REAL* CAREFUL! WHO KNOWS WHAT KIND OF TRAPS SHE'S SET, RIGHT?
TMP
KLIK!
KCHAK
OWAHH!

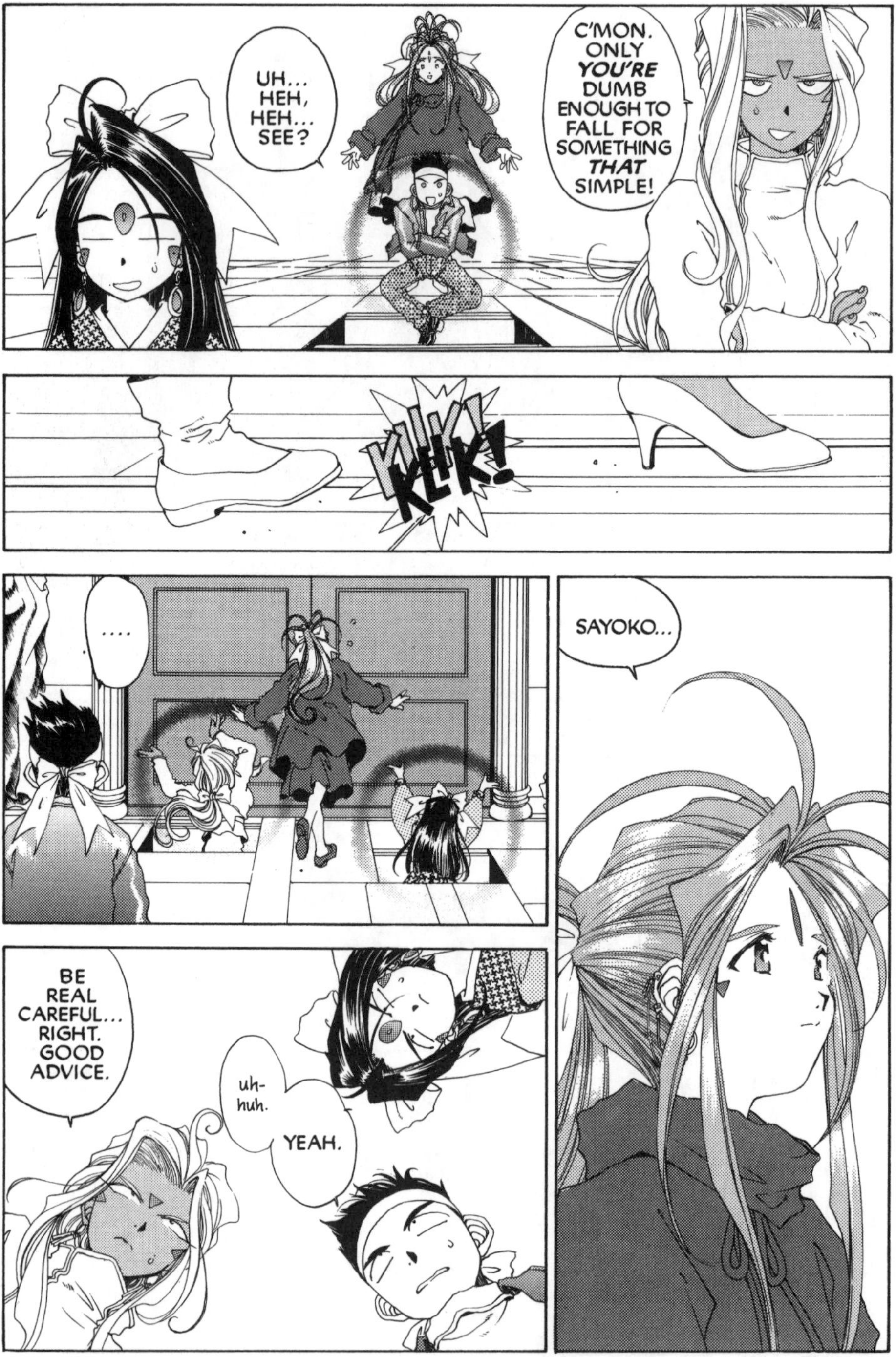
UH... HEH, HEH... SEE?
C'MON. ONLY ***YOU'RE*** DUMB ENOUGH TO FALL FOR SOMETHING ***THAT*** SIMPLE!
KLIK! KLIK!
....
BE REAL CAREFUL... RIGHT. GOOD ADVICE.
uh-huh.
YEAH.
SAYOKO...

DID YOU SO WANT TO BE THE CAMPUS QUEEN...

...YOU'D EVEN JOIN HANDS WITH A *DEMON?*

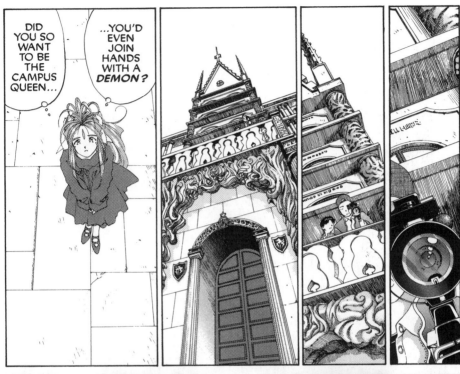

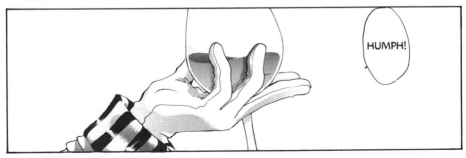

HUMPH!

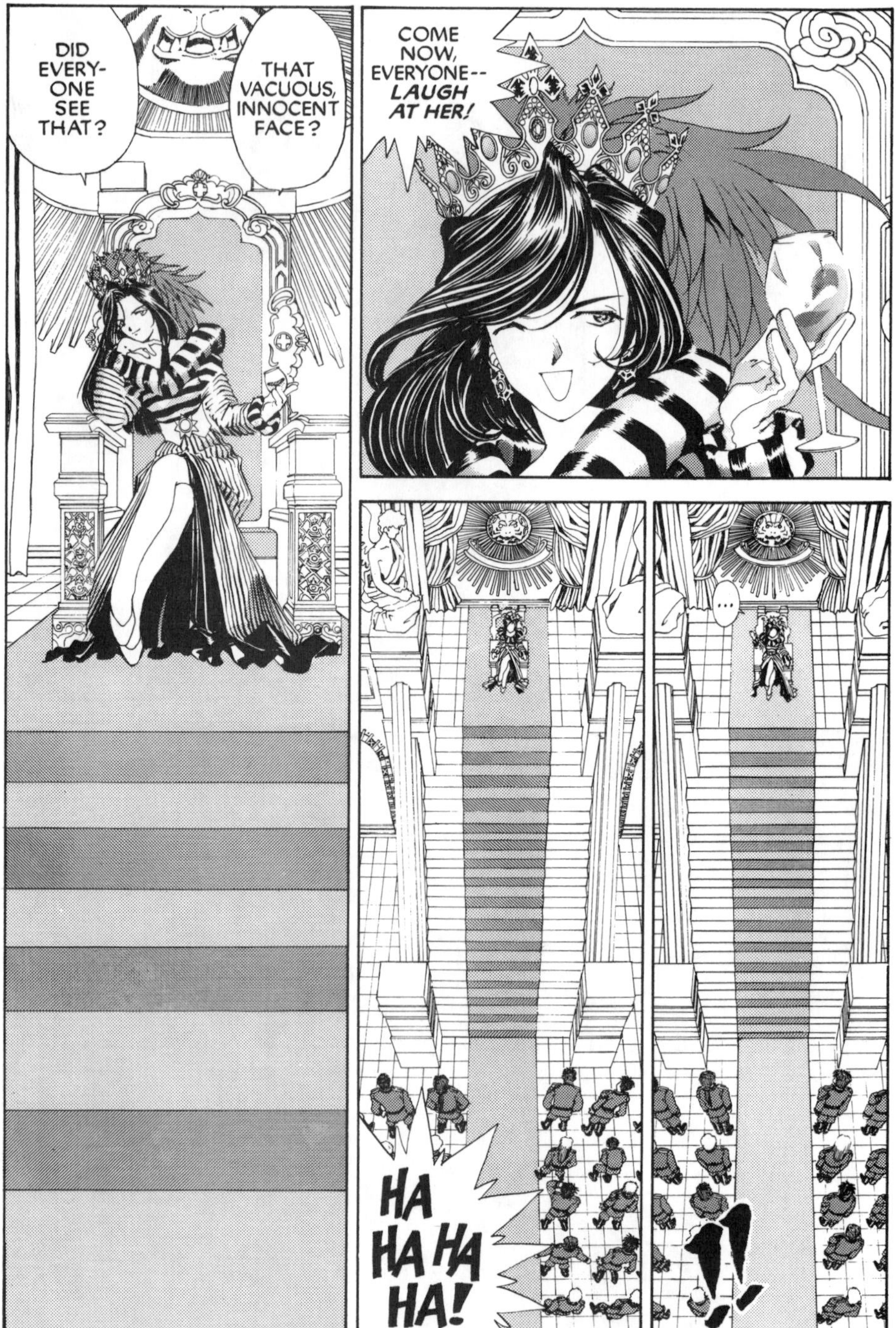
DID EVERY-ONE SEE THAT?
THAT VACUOUS, INNOCENT FACE?
COME NOW, EVERYONE-- *LAUGH AT HER!*
HA HA HA HA HA!
...

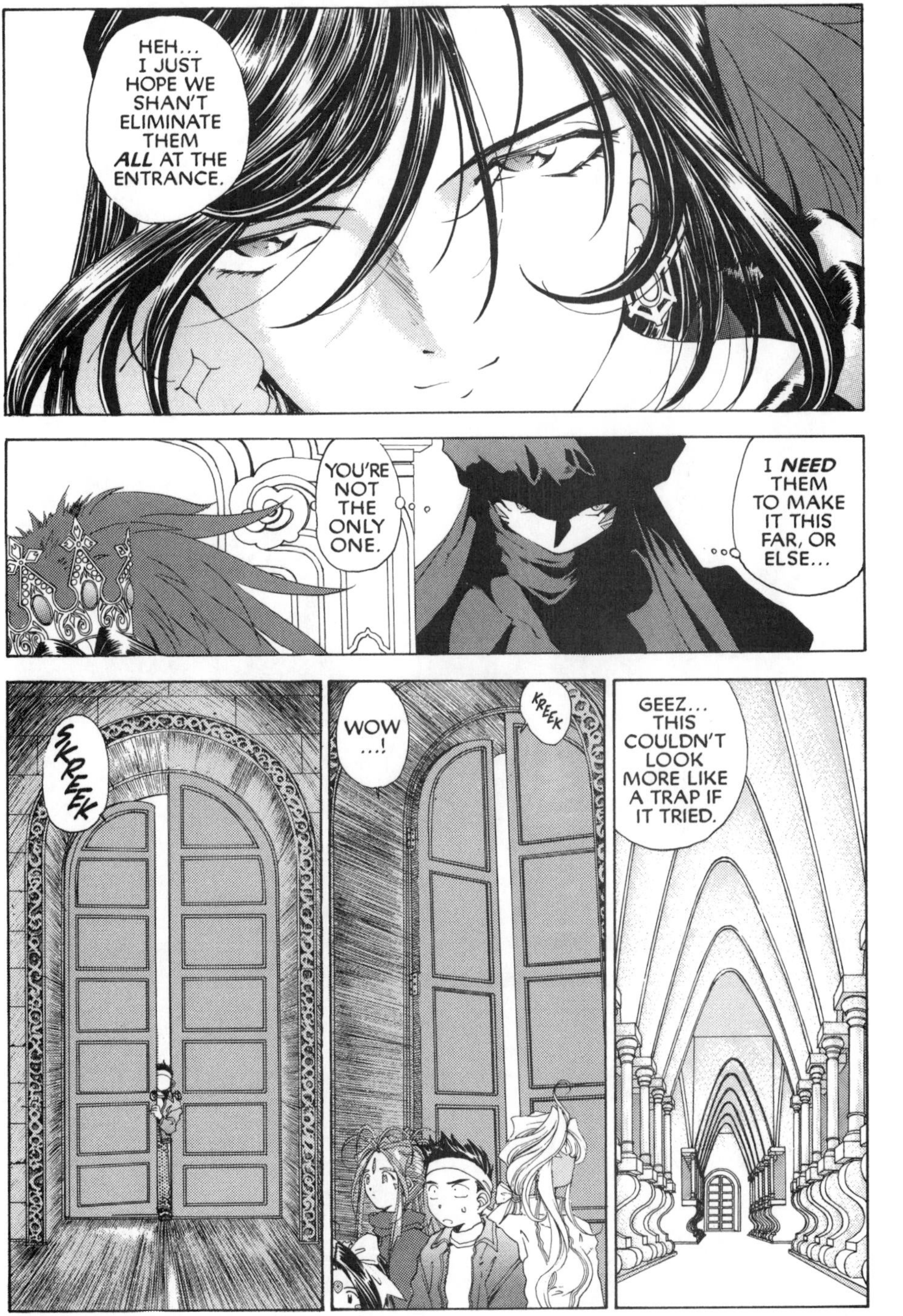
HEH... I JUST HOPE WE SHAN'T ELIMINATE THEM ALL AT THE ENTRANCE.
YOU'RE NOT THE ONLY ONE.
I NEED THEM TO MAKE IT THIS FAR, OR ELSE...
SKREEK
WOW ...!
KREEK
GEEZ... THIS COULDN'T LOOK MORE LIKE A TRAP IF IT TRIED.

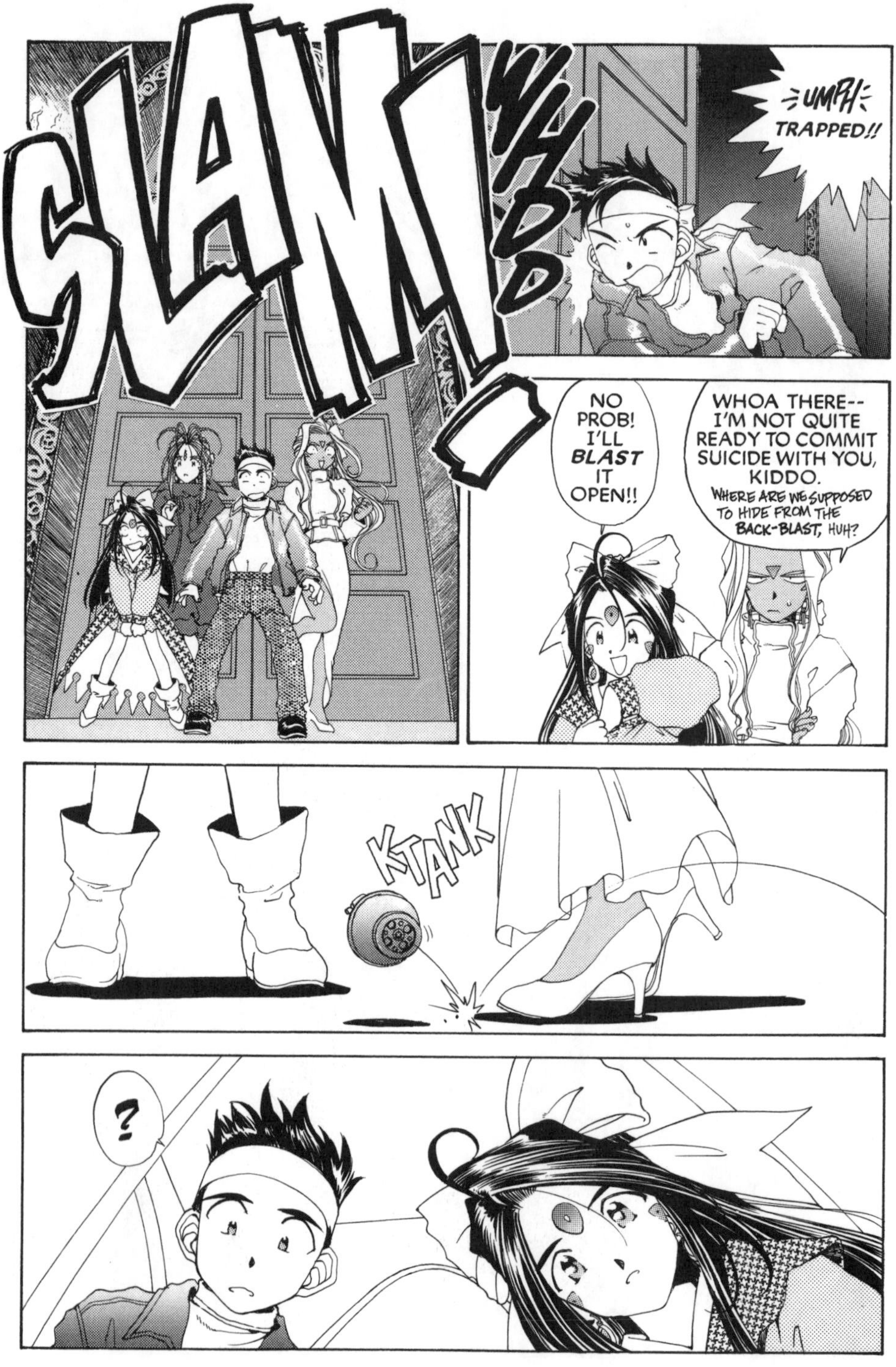
SLAM!
UMPH
TRAPPED!!
NO PROB! I'LL BLAST IT OPEN!!
WHOA THERE-- I'M NOT QUITE READY TO COMMIT SUICIDE WITH YOU, KIDDO.
WHERE ARE WE SUPPOSED TO HIDE FROM THE BACK-BLAST, HUH?
KTANK
?

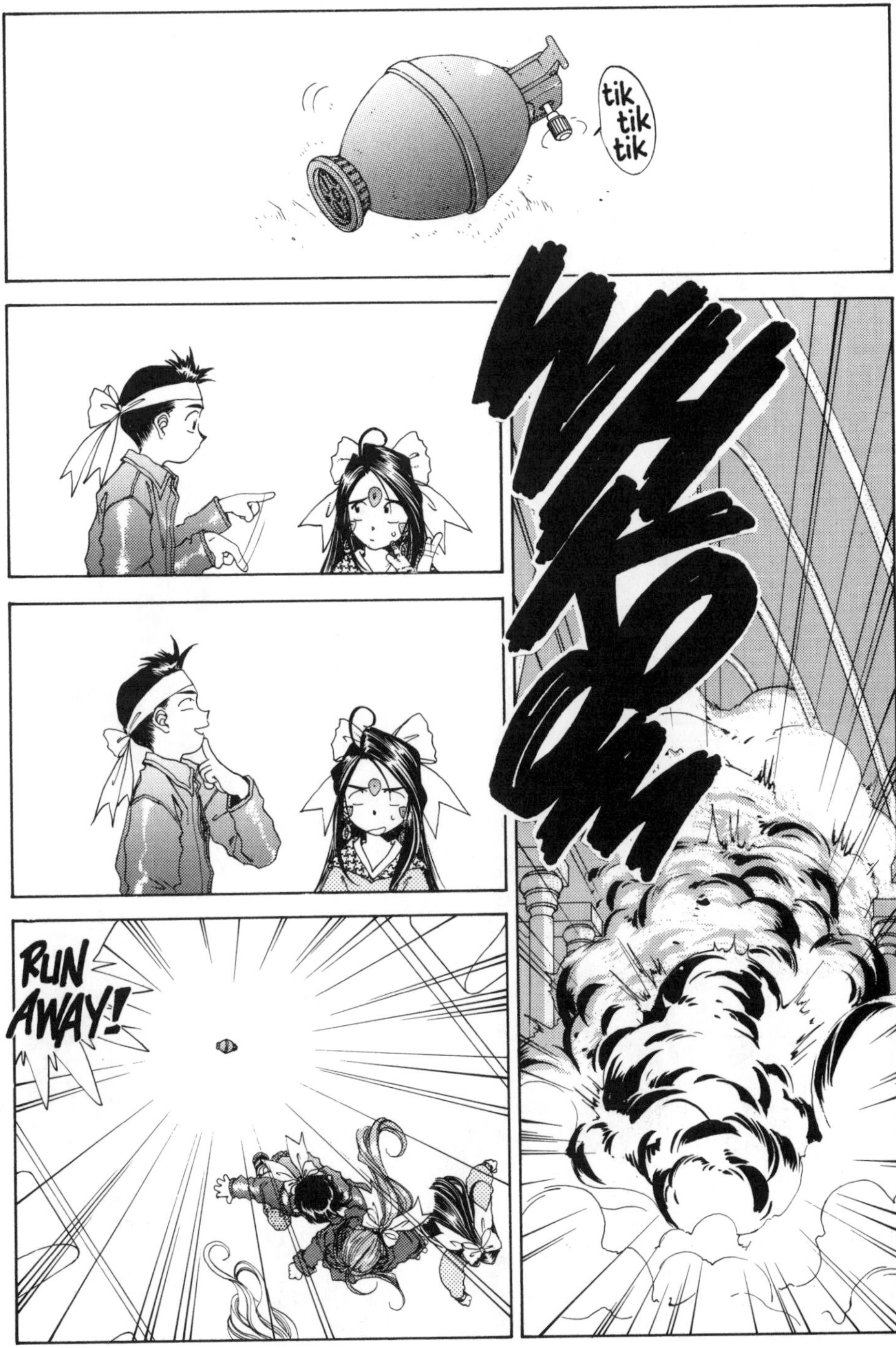
tik tik tik
RUN AWAY!
WHOOOM

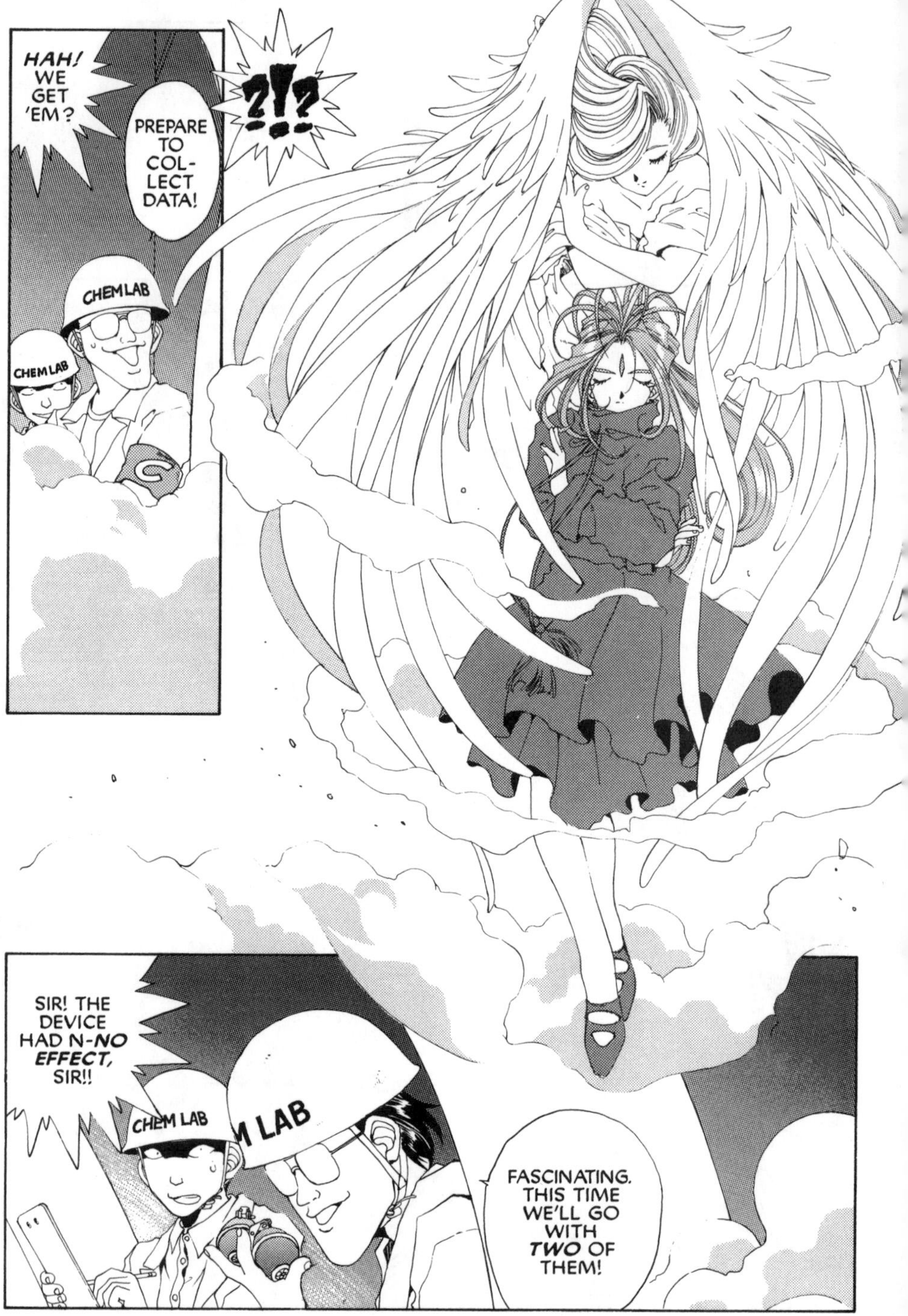

HAH! WE GET 'EM?
PREPARE TO COL-LECT DATA!
?!?
CHEM LAB
CHEM LAB
SIR! THE DEVICE HAD N-NO EFFECT, SIR!!
CHEM LAB
M LAB
FASCINATING. THIS TIME WE'LL GO WITH TWO OF THEM!

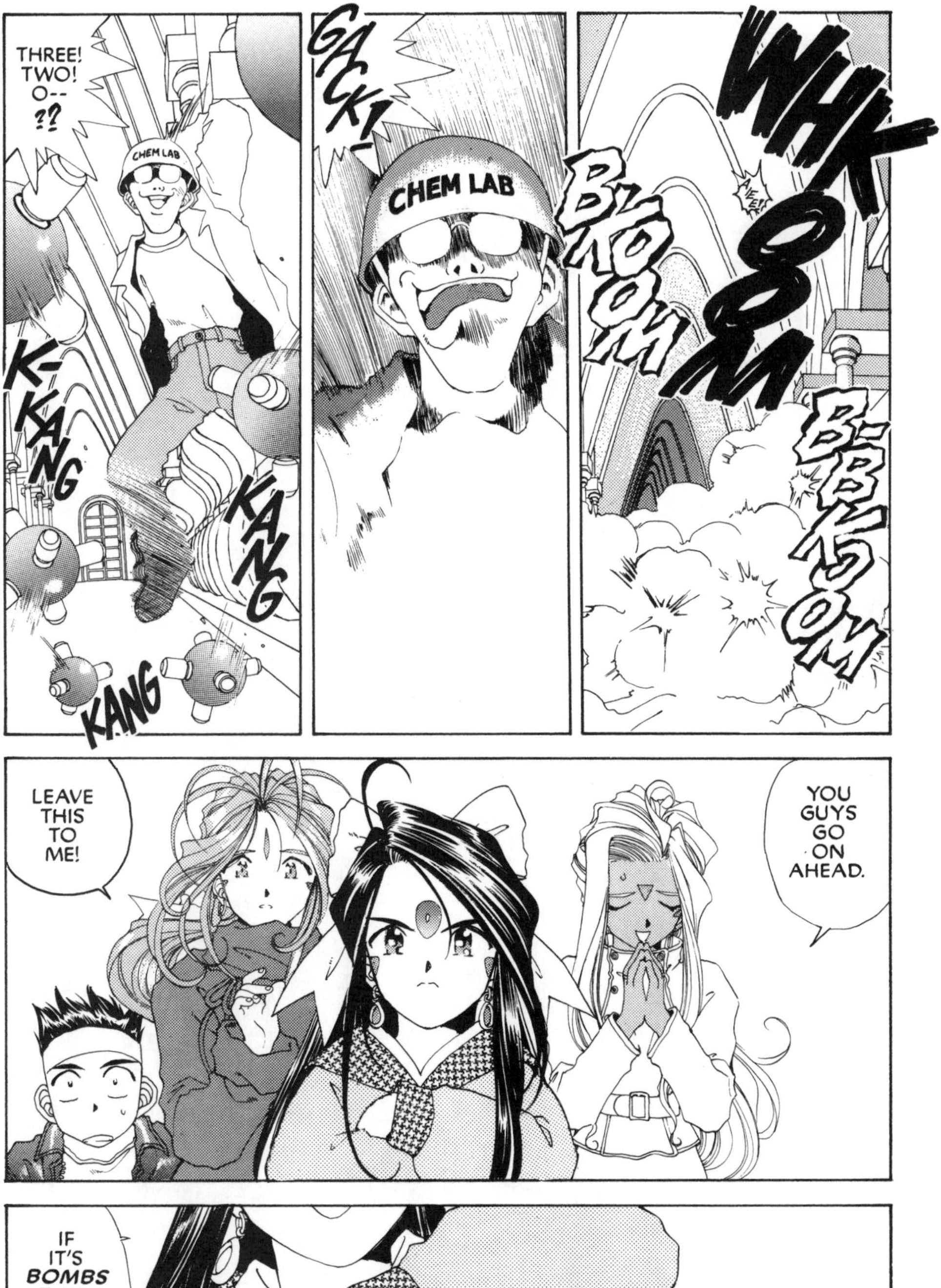
THREE! TWO! O-- ??
CHEM LAB
K-KANG
KANG
KANG
GACK!
CHEM LAB
WHKOOM
BKOOM
AIEE!!
B-BKOOM
LEAVE THIS TO ME!
YOU GUYS GO ON AHEAD.
IF IT'S ***BOMBS*** THEY WANT...

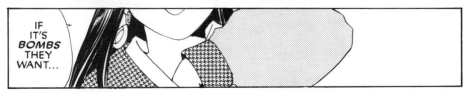

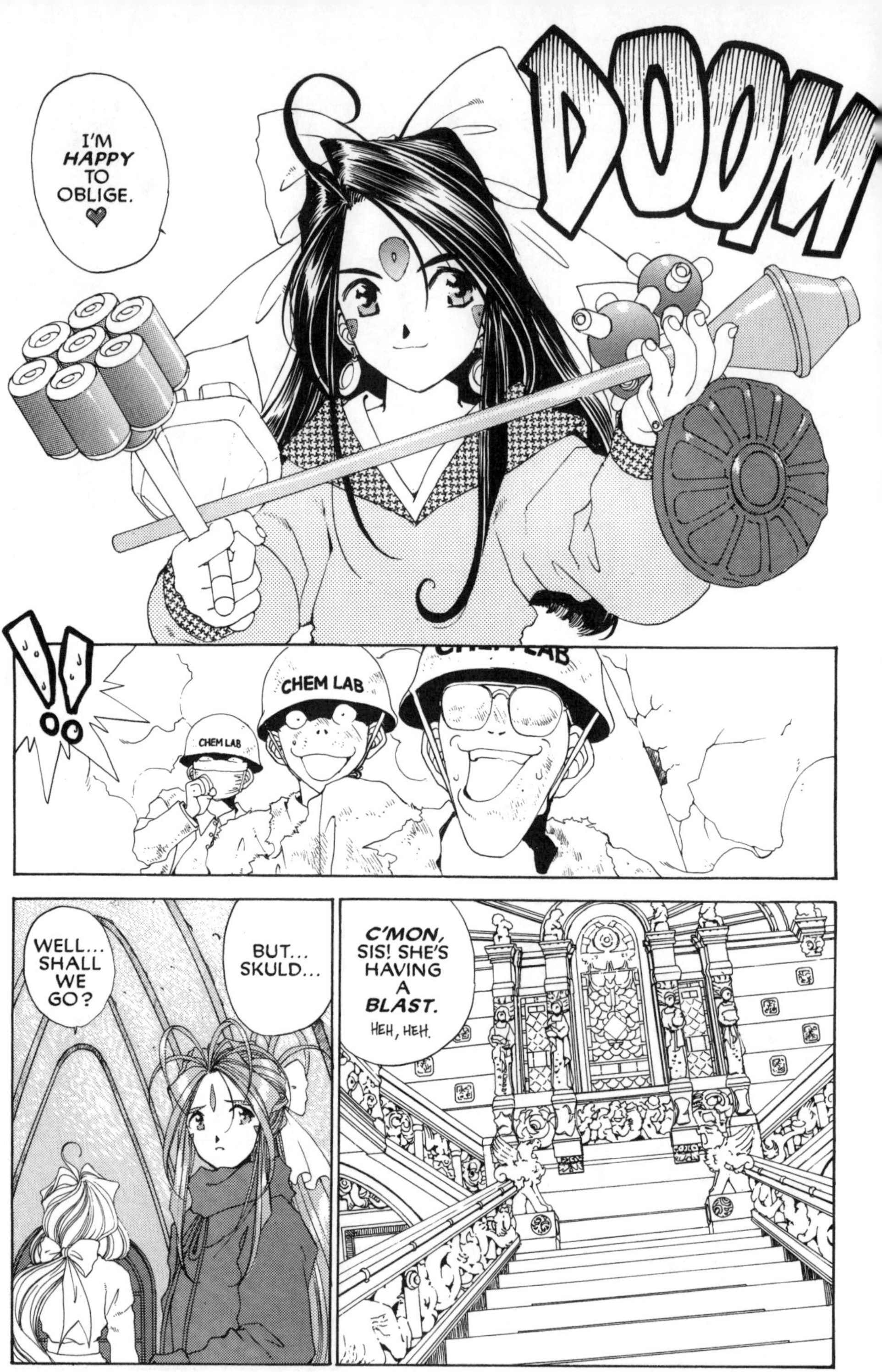
I'M *HAPPY* TO OBLIGE. ♥
DOOM
!!
CHEM LAB
CHEM LAB
WELL... SHALL WE GO?
BUT... SKULD...
C'MON, SIS! SHE'S HAVING A *BLAST.*
HEH, HEH.

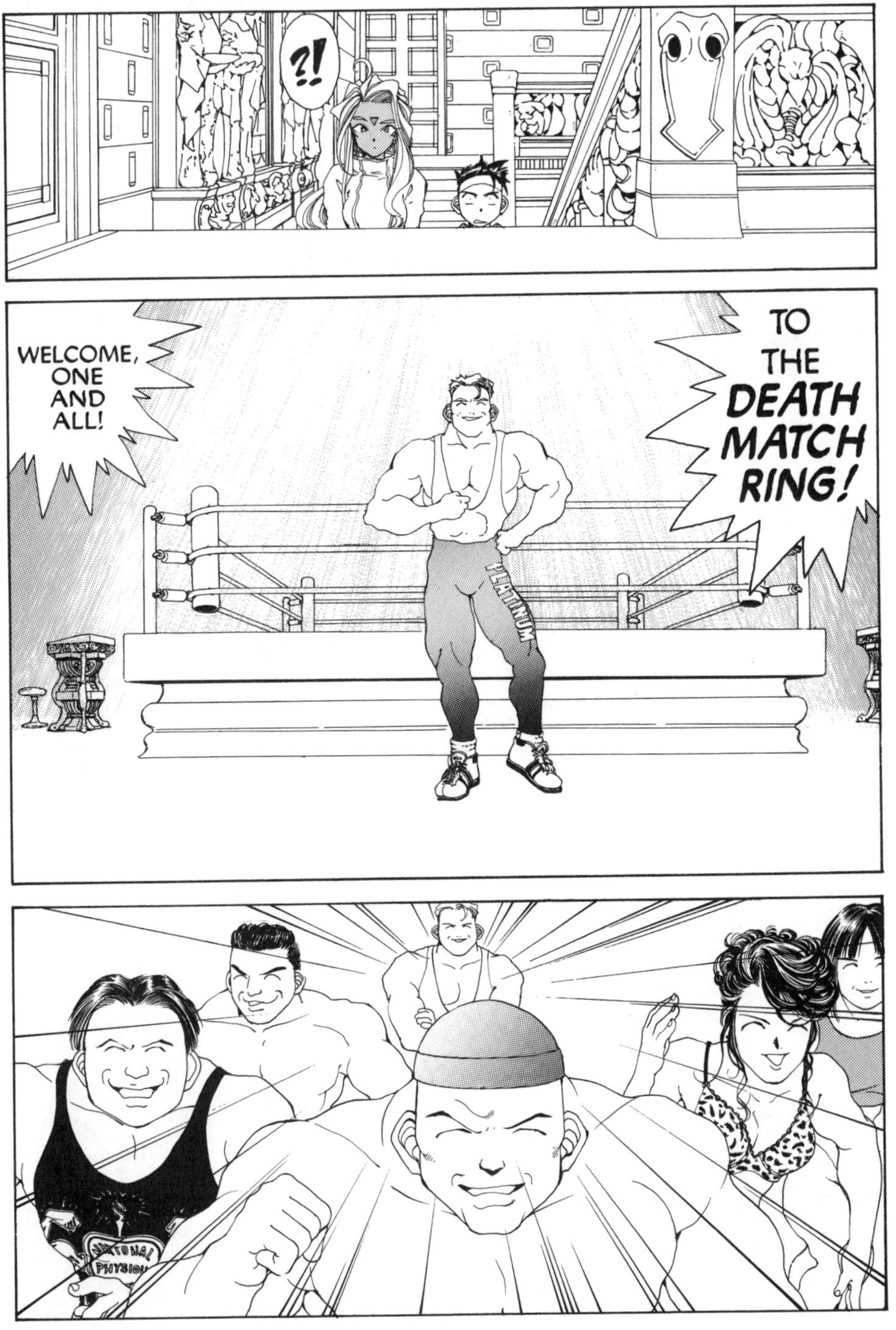
?!
WELCOME, ONE AND ALL!
TO THE DEATH MATCH RING!
PLATINUM

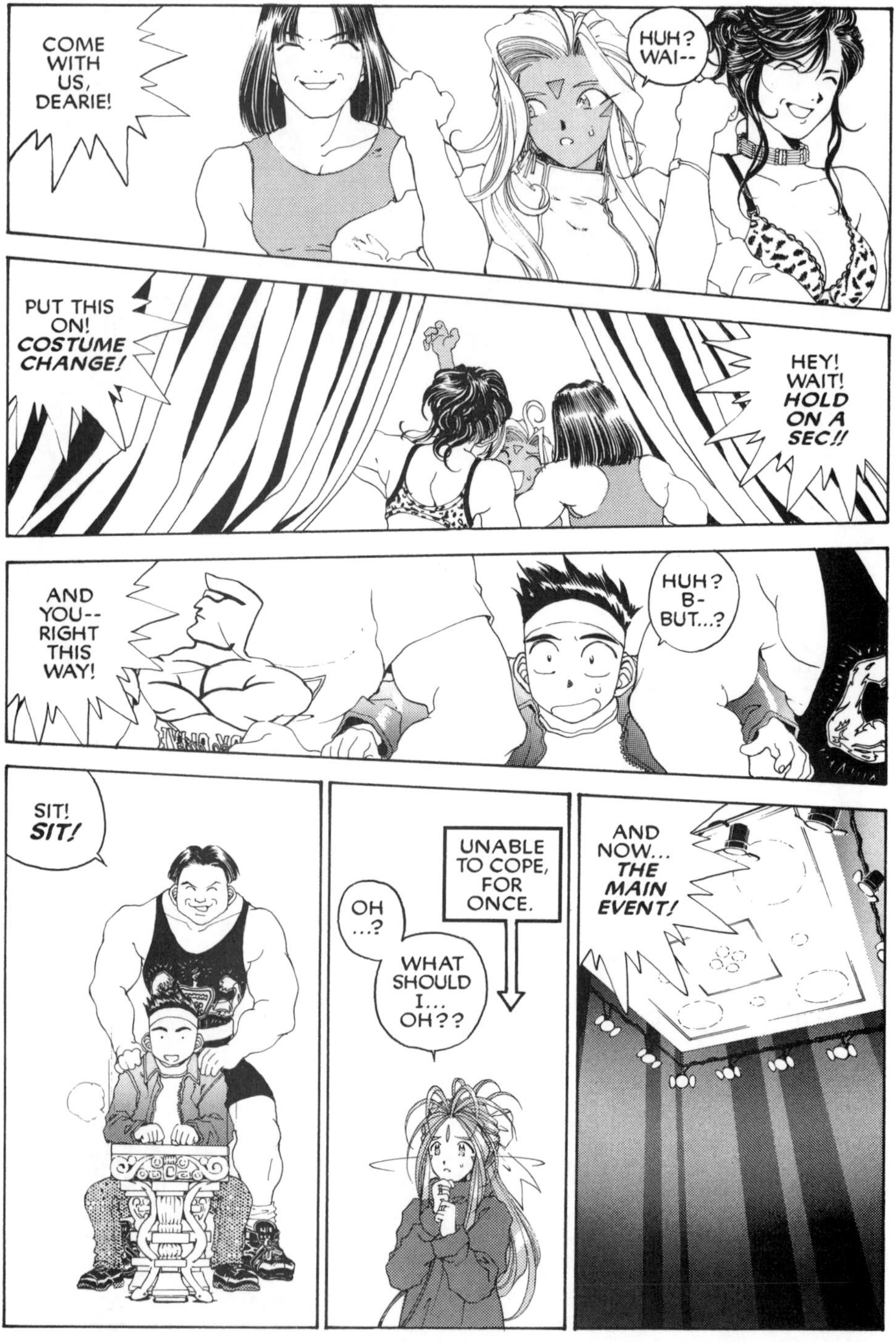
COME WITH US, DEARIE!
HUH? WAI--
PUT THIS ON! *COSTUME CHANGE!*
HEY! WAIT! *HOLD ON A SEC!!*
AND YOU-- RIGHT THIS WAY!
HUH? B- BUT...?
SIT! *SIT!*
UNABLE TO COPE, FOR ONCE.
OH ...?
WHAT SHOULD I... OH??
AND NOW... *THE MAIN EVENT!*

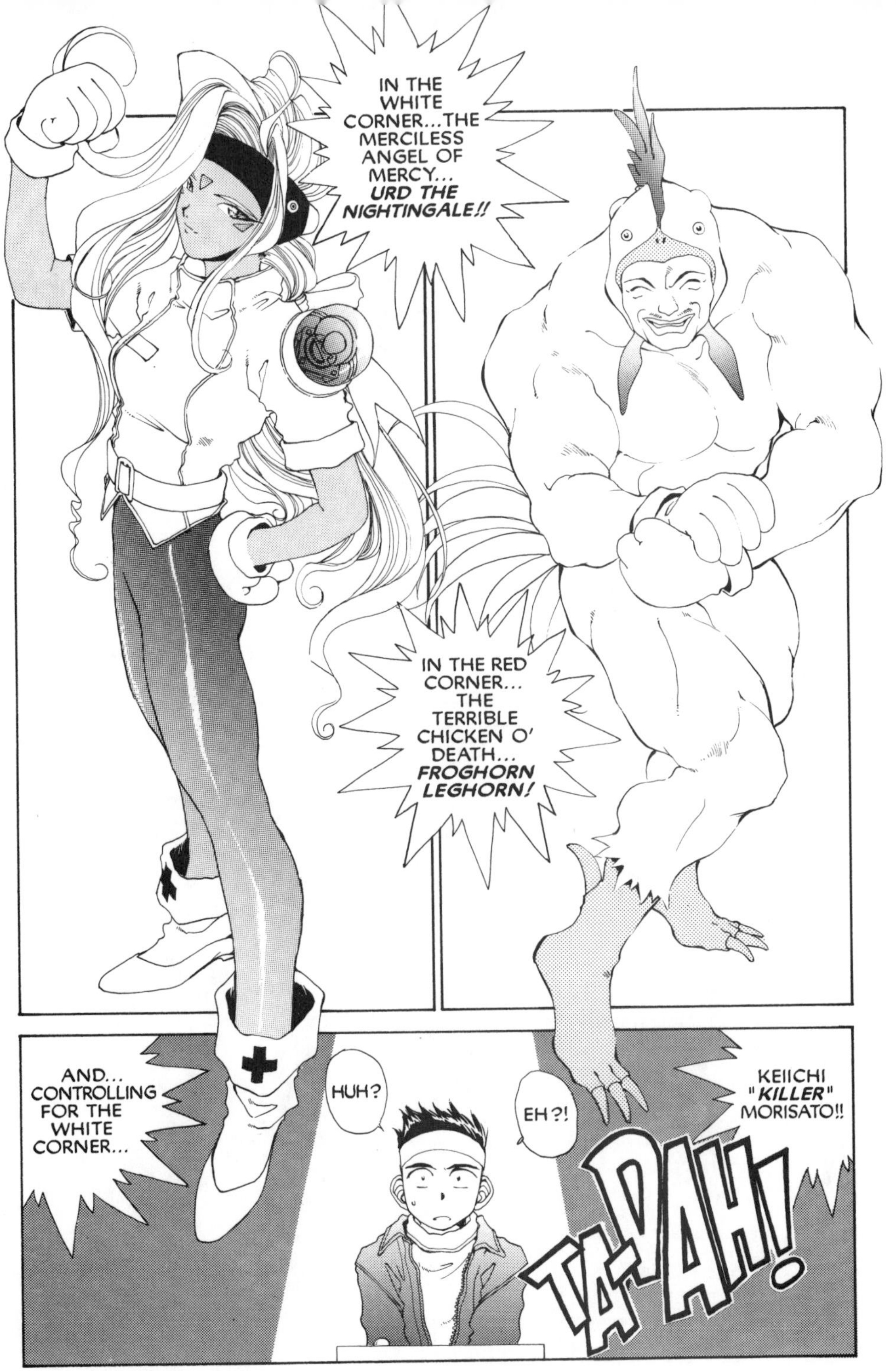
IN THE WHITE CORNER...THE MERCILESS ANGEL OF MERCY... URD THE NIGHTINGALE!!
IN THE RED CORNER... THE TERRIBLE CHICKEN O' DEATH... FROGHORN LEGHORN!
AND... CONTROLLING FOR THE WHITE CORNER...
HUH?
EH?!
KEIICHI "KILLER" MORISATO!!
TA-DAH!

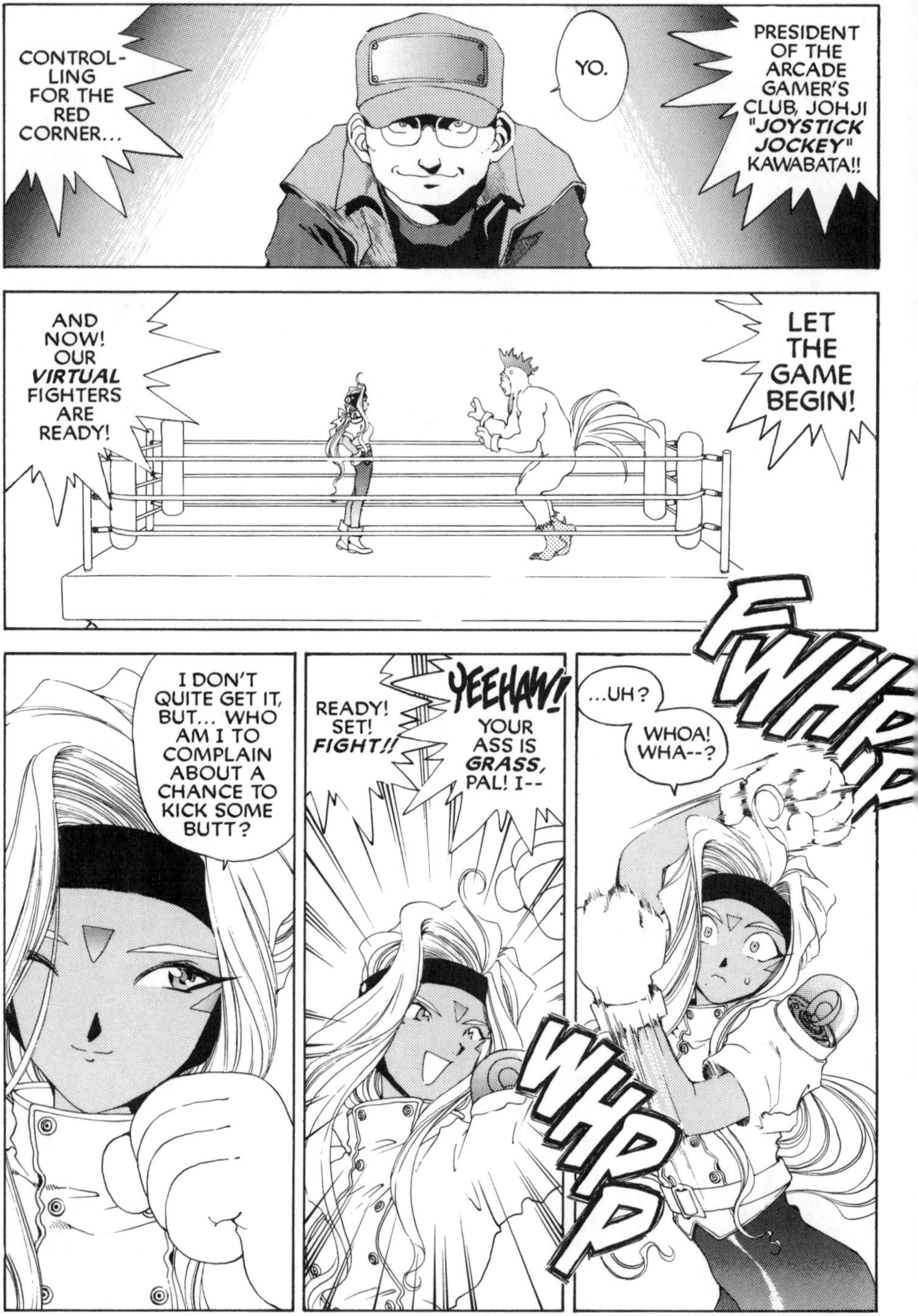
CONTROL-LING FOR THE RED CORNER...
YO.
PRESIDENT OF THE ARCADE GAMER'S CLUB, JOHJI "JOYSTICK JOCKEY" KAWABATA!!
AND NOW! OUR VIRTUAL FIGHTERS ARE READY!
LET THE GAME BEGIN!
I DON'T QUITE GET IT, BUT... WHO AM I TO COMPLAIN ABOUT A CHANCE TO KICK SOME BUTT?
READY! SET! FIGHT!!
YEEHAW!
YOUR ASS IS GRASS, PAL! I--
...UH?
WHOA! WHA--?
WHPP

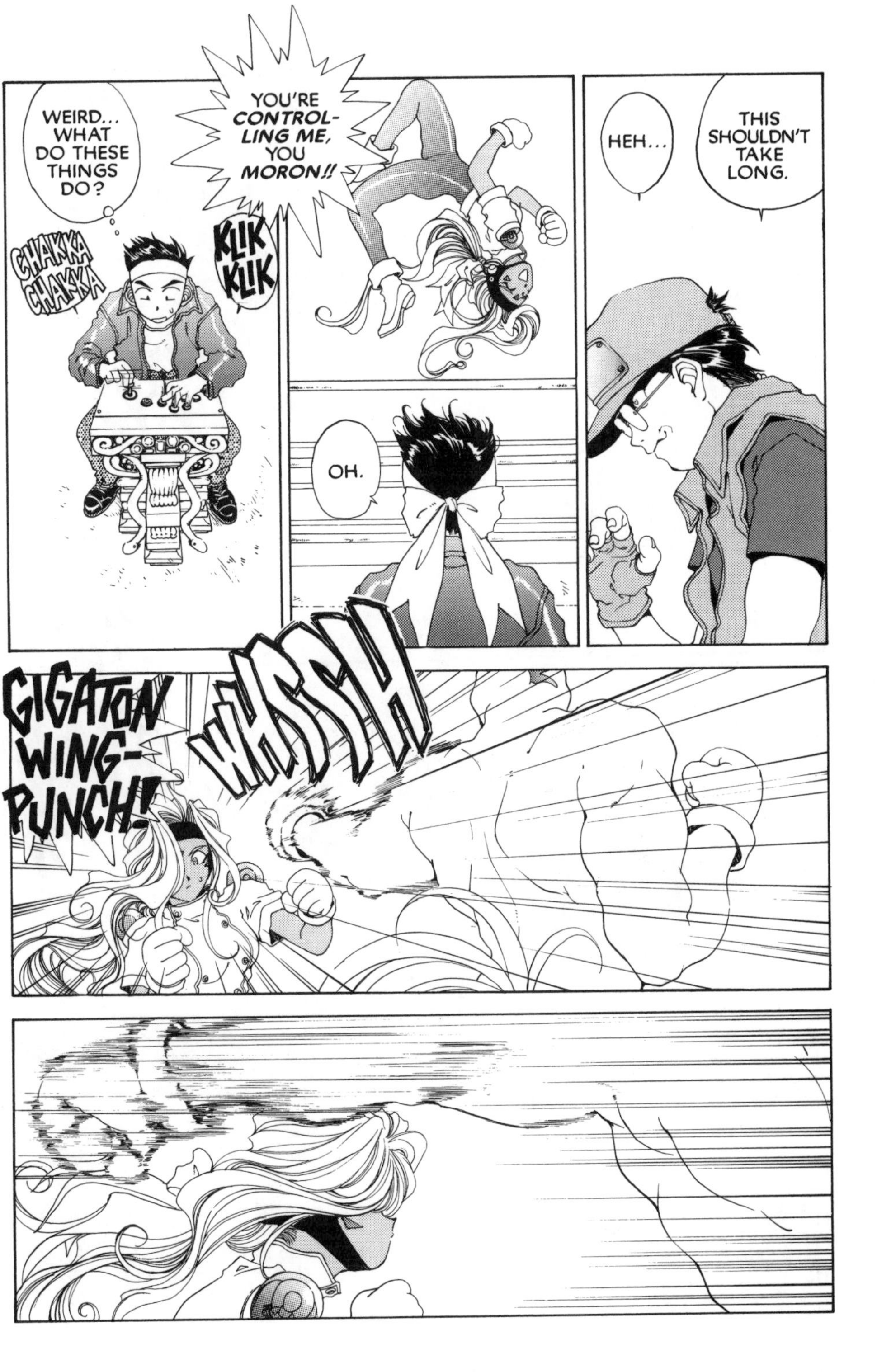
WEIRD... WHAT DO THESE THINGS DO?
CHAKKA CHAKKA
KLIK KLIK
YOU'RE *CONTROL-LING ME,* YOU *MORON!!*
OH.
HEH...
THIS SHOULDN'T TAKE LONG.
GIGATON WING-PUNCH!
WHSSH

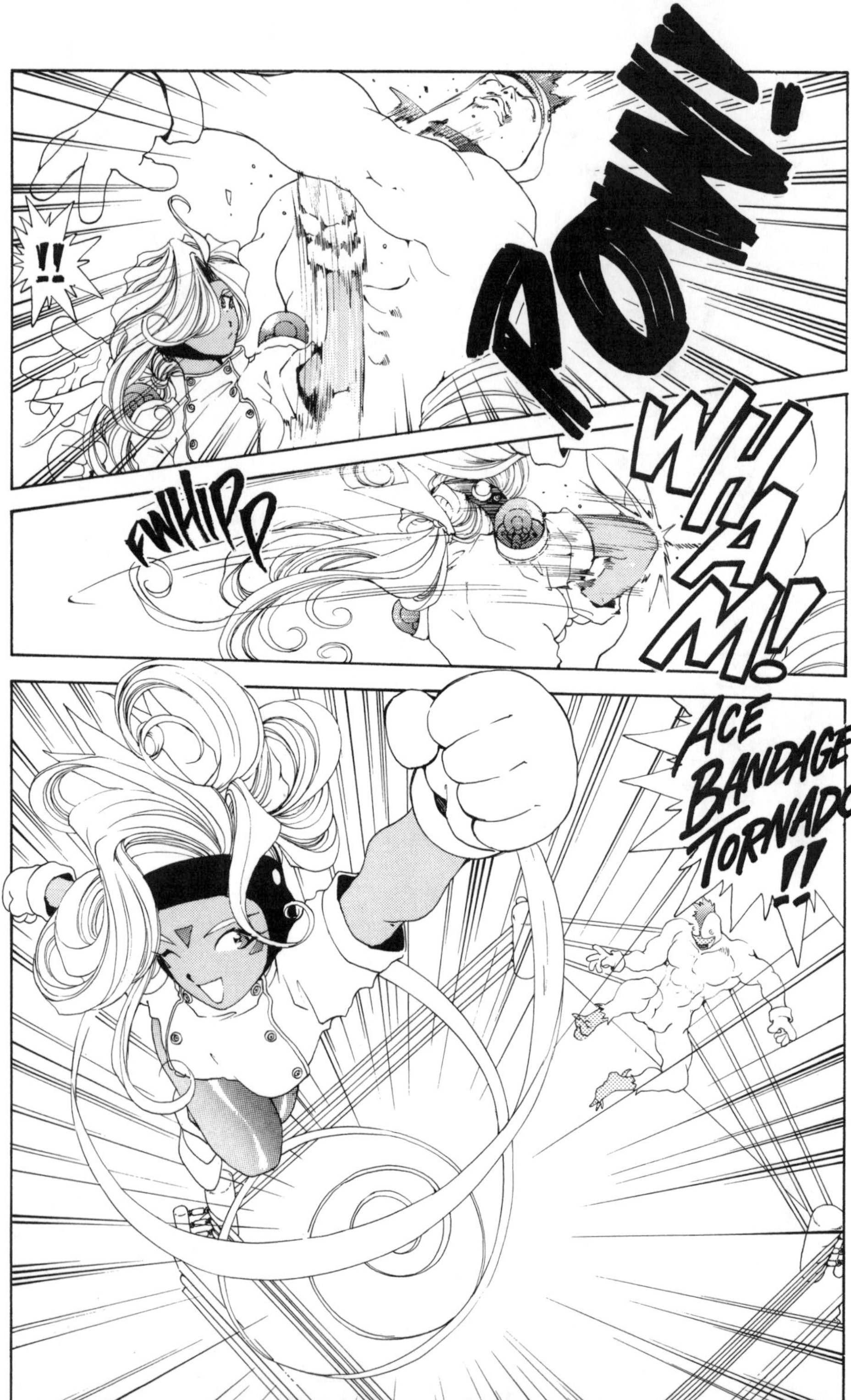
POW!
!!
WHAM!
FWHIPP
ACE BANDAGE TORNADO!!

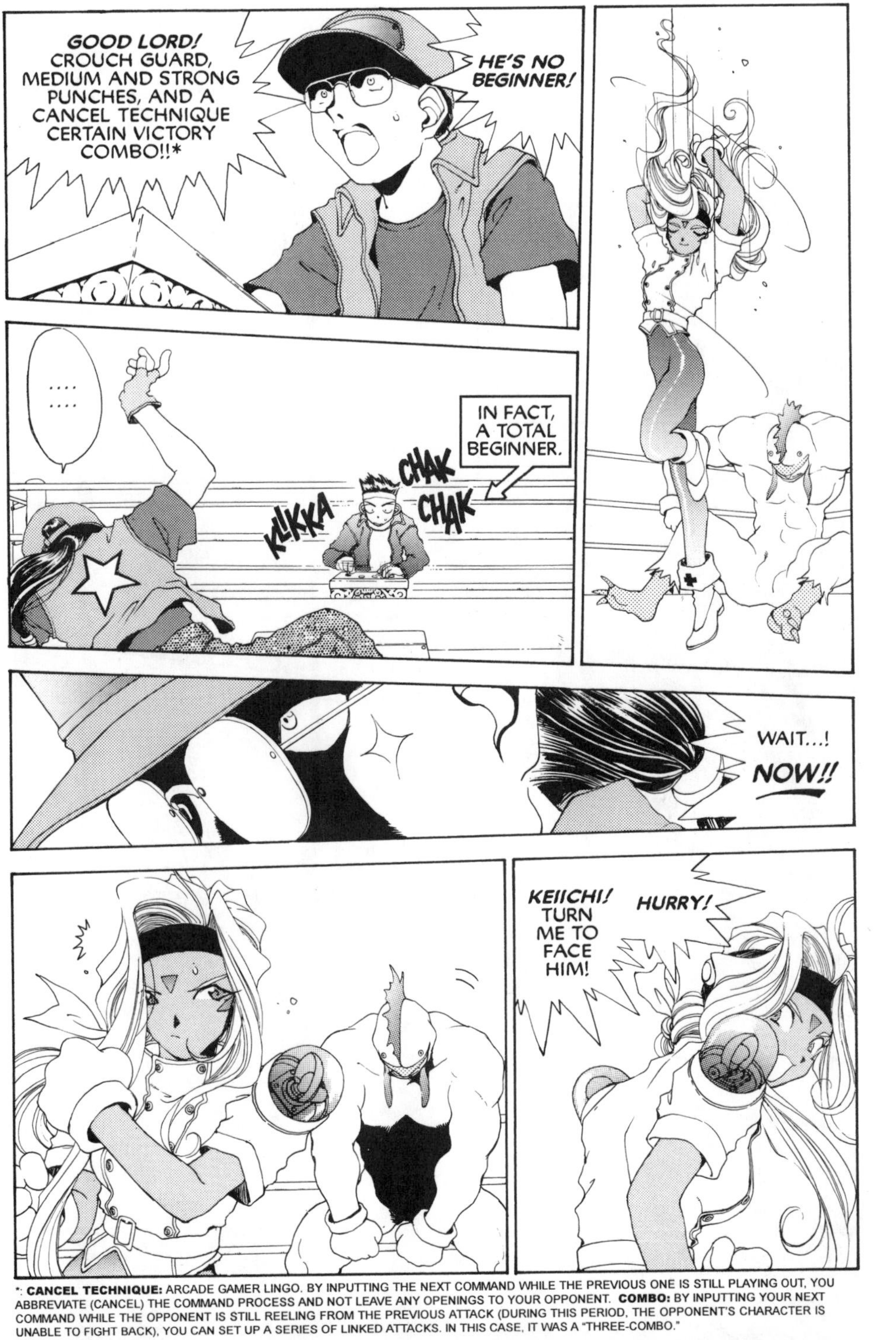
GOOD LORD! CROUCH GUARD, MEDIUM AND STRONG PUNCHES, AND A CANCEL TECHNIQUE CERTAIN VICTORY COMBO!!*
HE'S NO BEGINNER!
....
....
IN FACT, A TOTAL BEGINNER.
KLIKKA
CHAK
CHAK
WAIT...!
NOW!!
KEIICHI! TURN ME TO FACE HIM!
HURRY!

*: **CANCEL TECHNIQUE:** ARCADE GAMER LINGO. BY INPUTTING THE NEXT COMMAND WHILE THE PREVIOUS ONE IS STILL PLAYING OUT, YOU ABBREVIATE (CANCEL) THE COMMAND PROCESS AND NOT LEAVE ANY OPENINGS TO YOUR OPPONENT. **COMBO:** BY INPUTTING YOUR NEXT COMMAND WHILE THE OPPONENT IS STILL REELING FROM THE PREVIOUS ATTACK (DURING THIS PERIOD, THE OPPONENT'S CHARACTER IS UNABLE TO FIGHT BACK), YOU CAN SET UP A SERIES OF LINKED ATTACKS. IN THIS CASE, IT WAS A "THREE-COMBO."

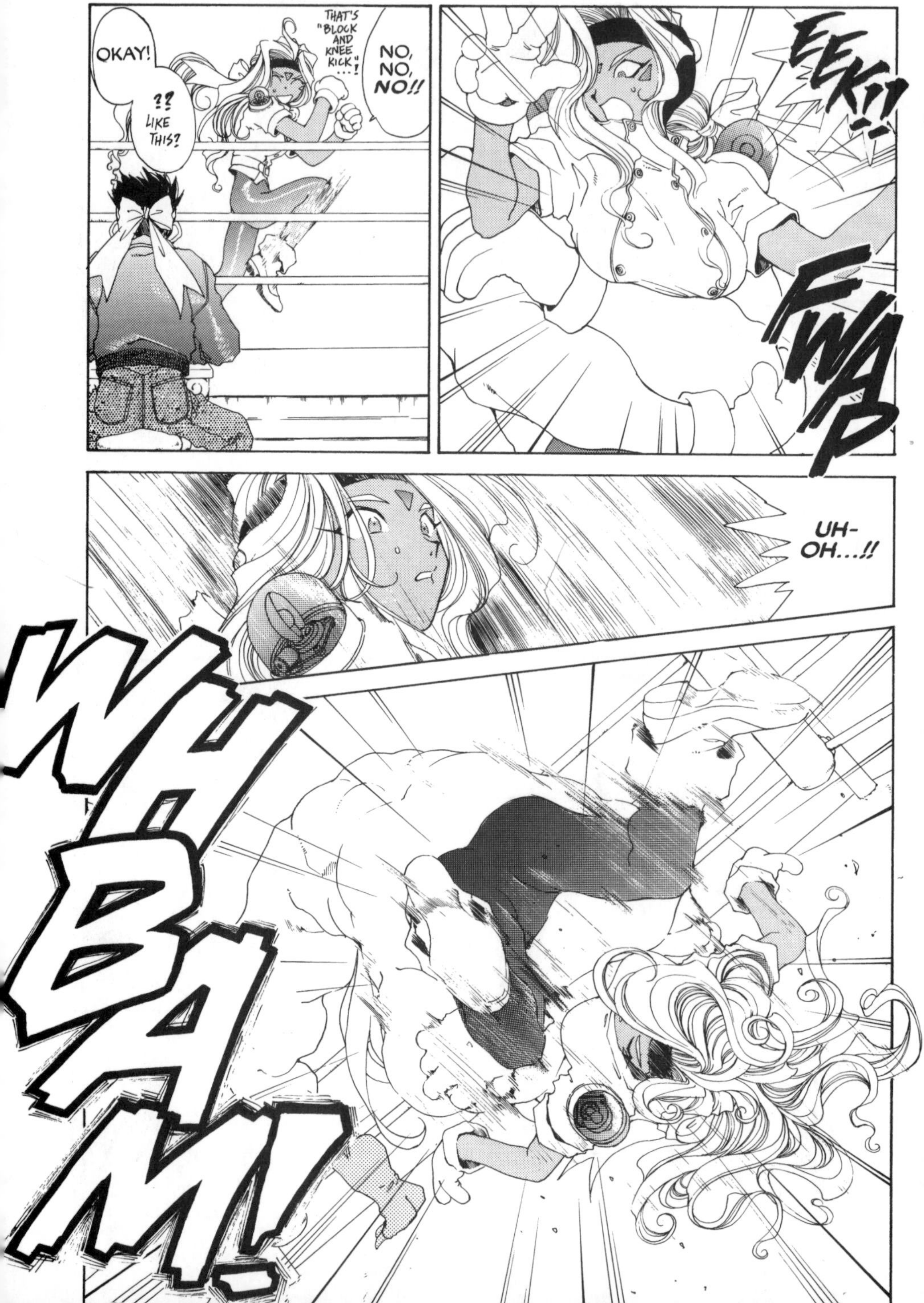

OKAY!
?? LIKE THIS?
THAT'S "BLOCK AND KNEE KICK"....!
NO, NO, NO!!
EEK!!
FWAP
UH-OH...!!
WHBAM!

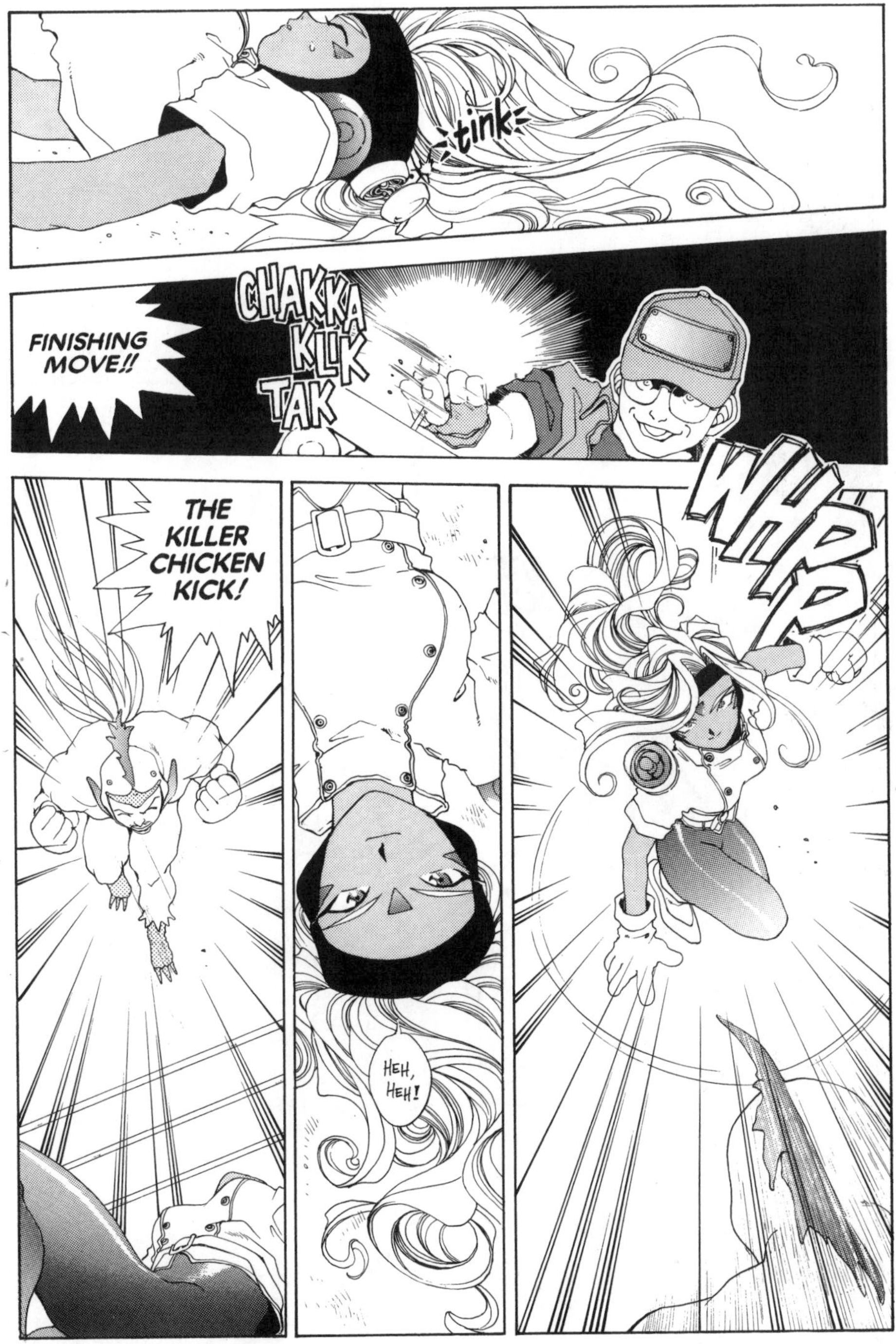
tink
FINISHING MOVE!!
CHAKKA KLIK TAK
WHPP
THE KILLER CHICKEN KICK!
HEH, HEH!

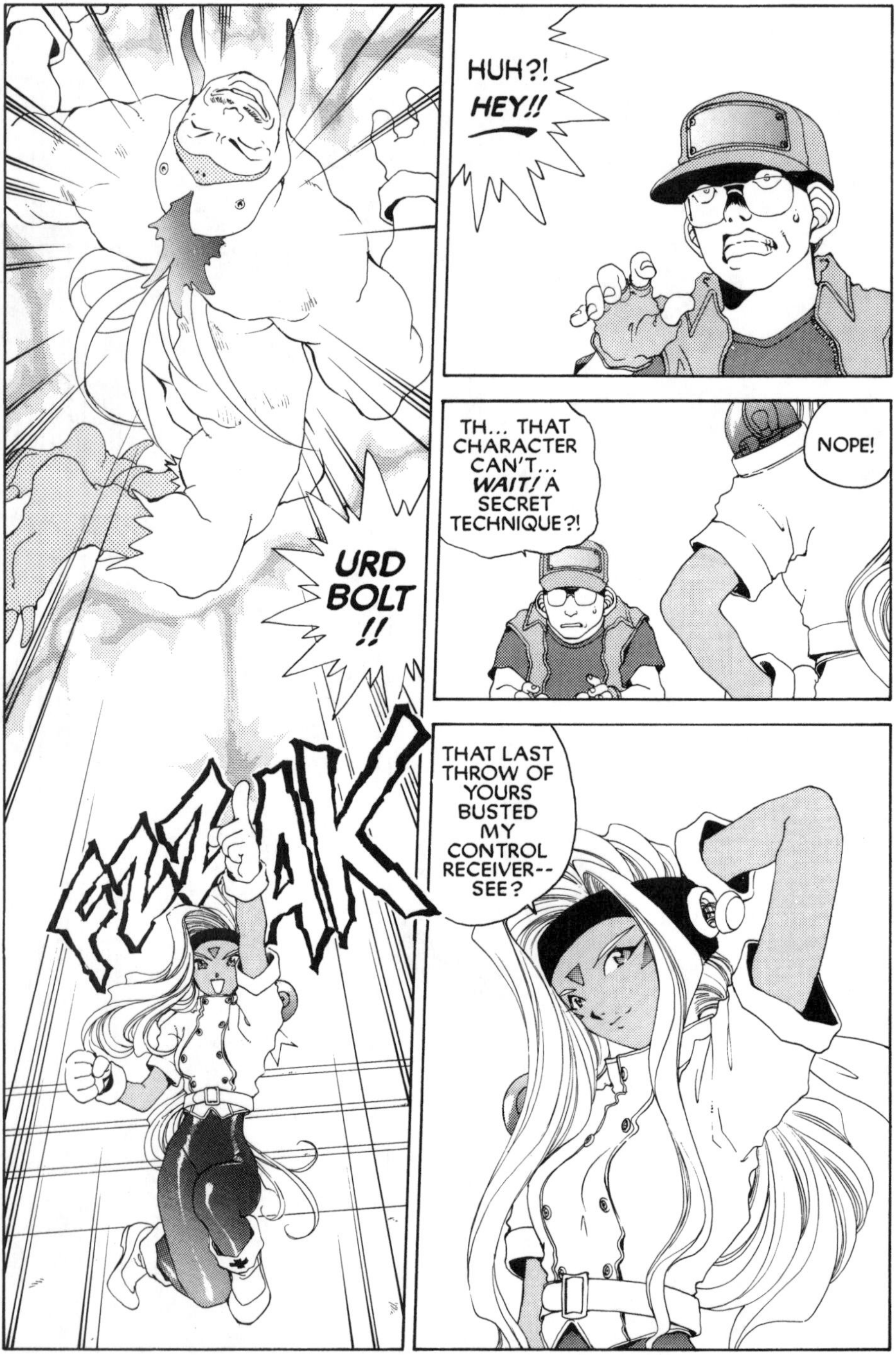
URD BOLT !!
FZZZAK
HUH?! HEY!!
TH... THAT CHARACTER CAN'T... WAIT! A SECRET TECHNIQUE?!
NOPE!
THAT LAST THROW OF YOURS BUSTED MY CONTROL RECEIVER-- SEE?

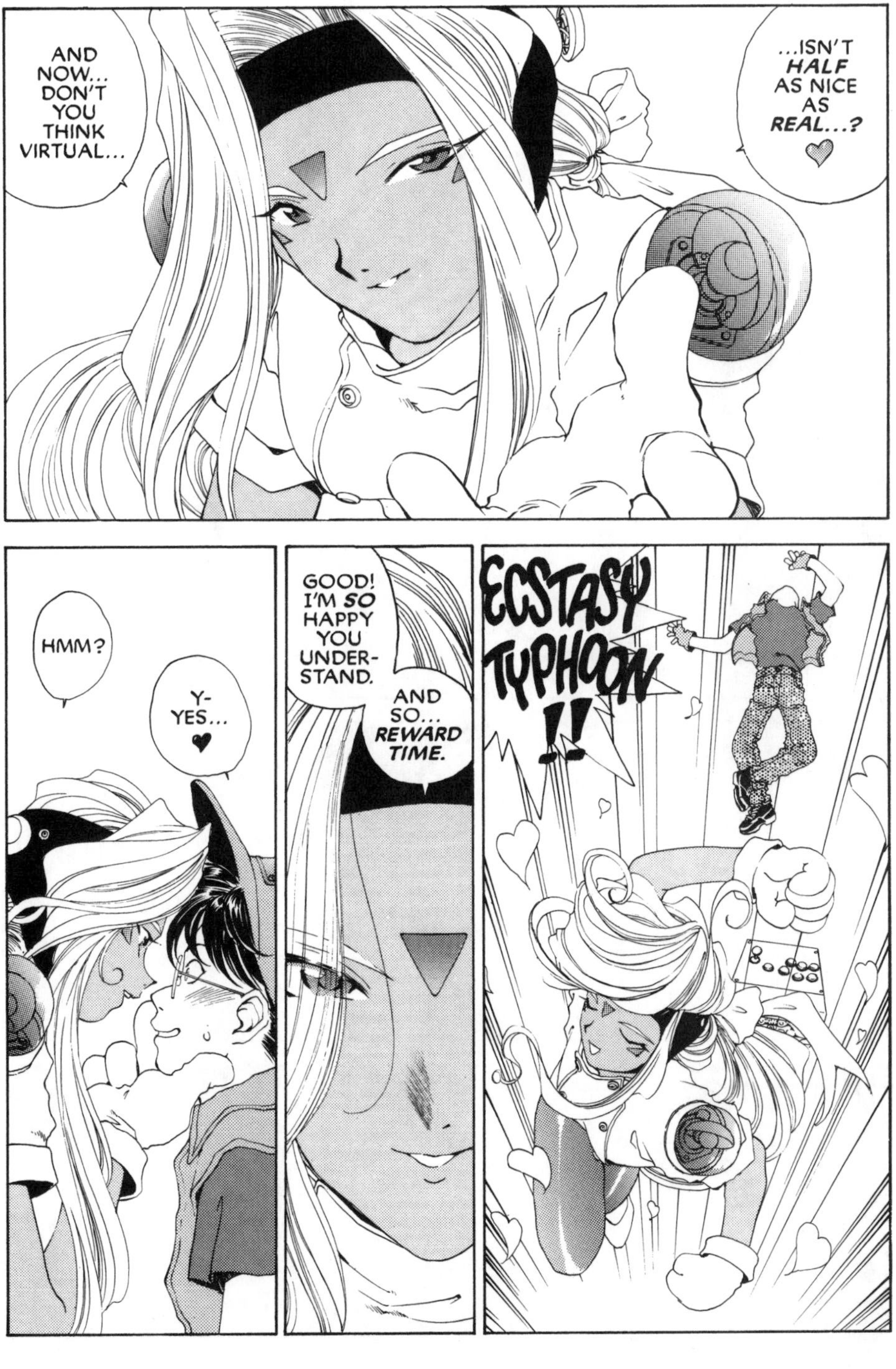
AND NOW... DON'T YOU THINK VIRTUAL...
...ISN'T *HALF* AS NICE AS *REAL...?* ♥
HMM?
Y-YES... ♥
GOOD! I'M *SO* HAPPY YOU UNDER-STAND.
AND SO... *REWARD TIME.*
ECSTASY TYPHOON!!

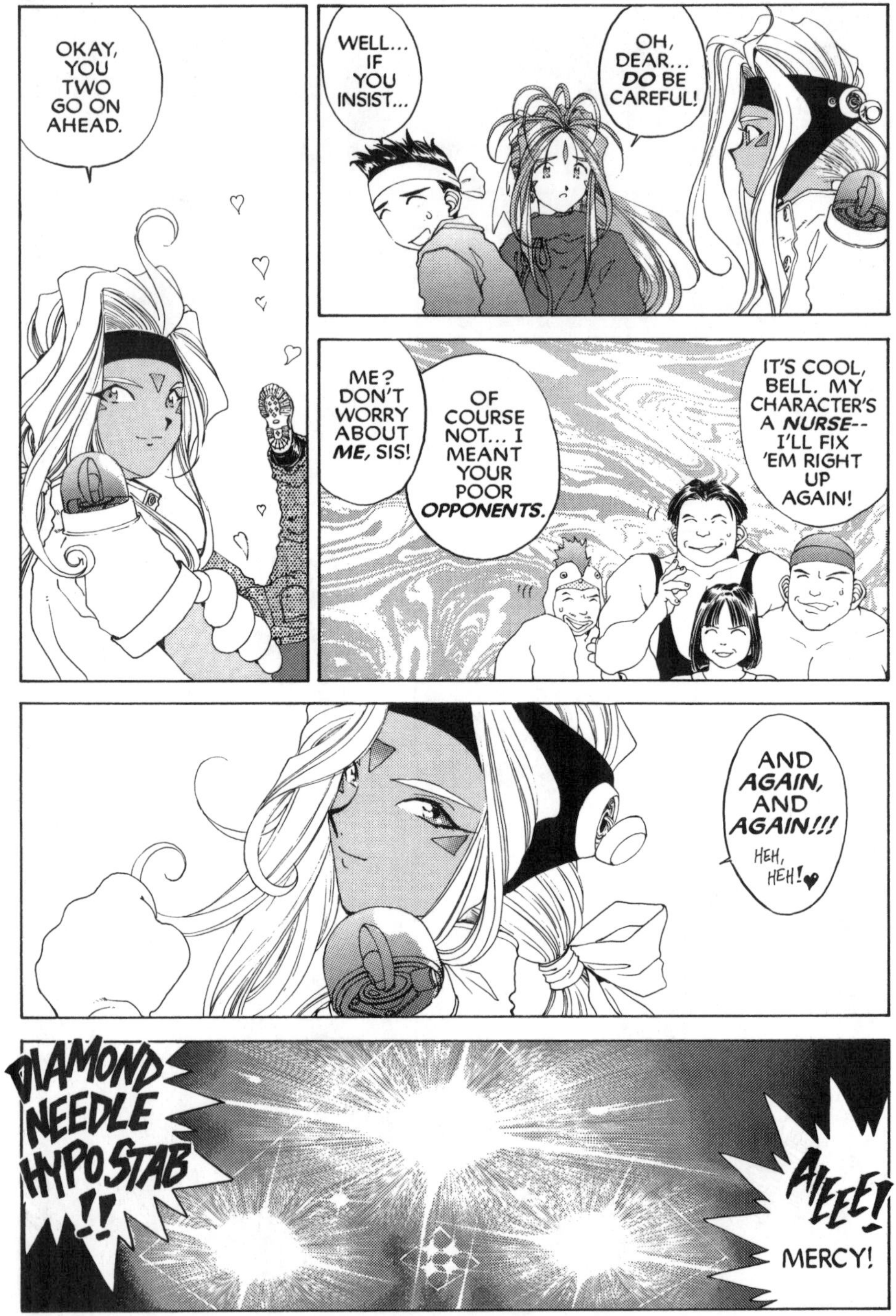

OKAY, YOU TWO GO ON AHEAD.
WELL... IF YOU INSIST...
OH, DEAR... DO BE CAREFUL!
ME? DON'T WORRY ABOUT ME, SIS!
OF COURSE NOT... I MEANT YOUR POOR OPPONENTS.
IT'S COOL, BELL. MY CHARACTER'S A NURSE-- I'LL FIX 'EM RIGHT UP AGAIN!
AND AGAIN, AND AGAIN!!!
HEH, HEH!
DIAMOND NEEDLE HYPO STAB!!
AIEEE!
MERCY!

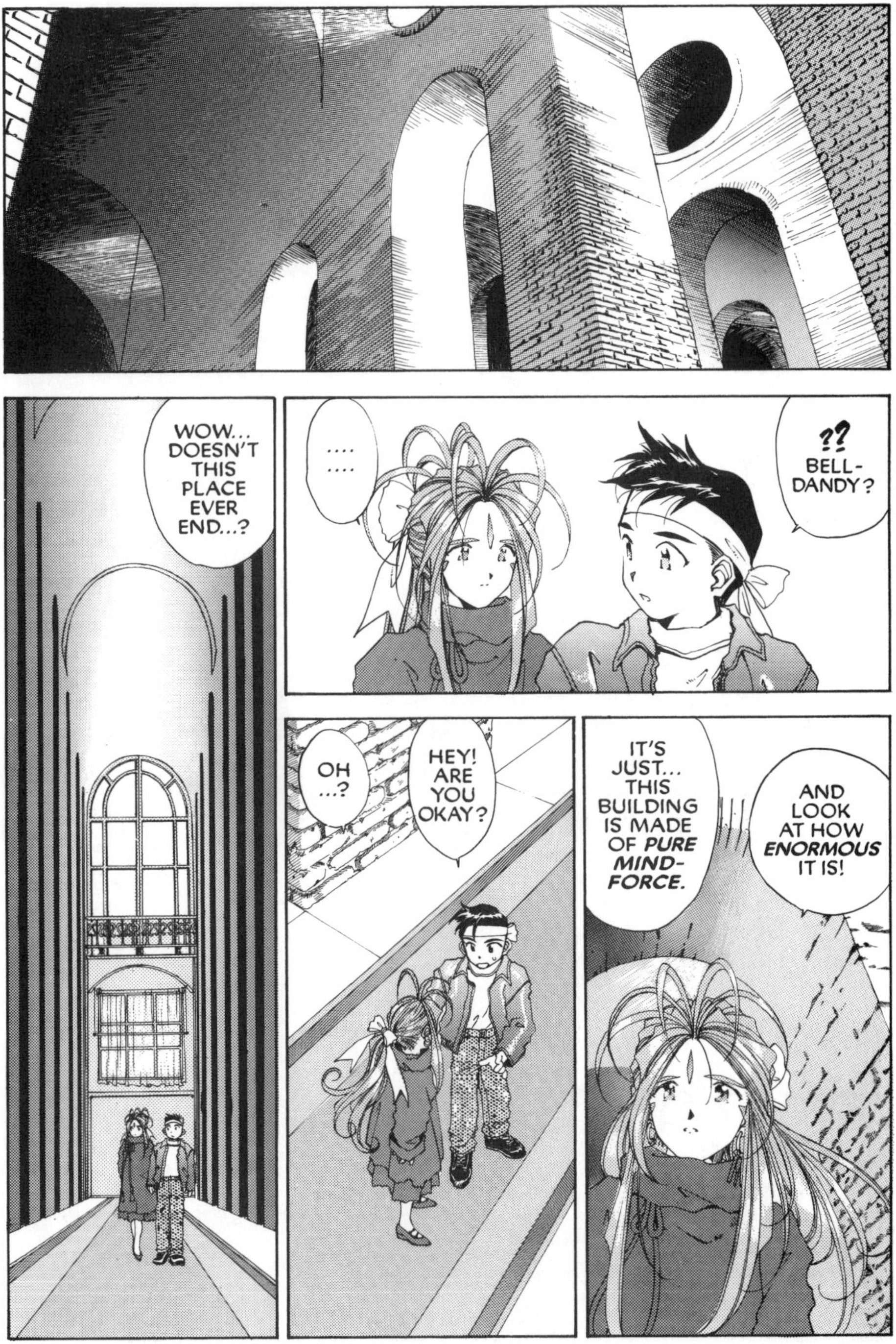
WOW... DOESN'T THIS PLACE EVER END...?
....
....
??
BELL-DANDY?
OH ...?
HEY! ARE YOU OKAY?
IT'S JUST... THIS BUILDING IS MADE OF *PURE MIND-FORCE.*
AND LOOK AT HOW *ENORMOUS* IT IS!

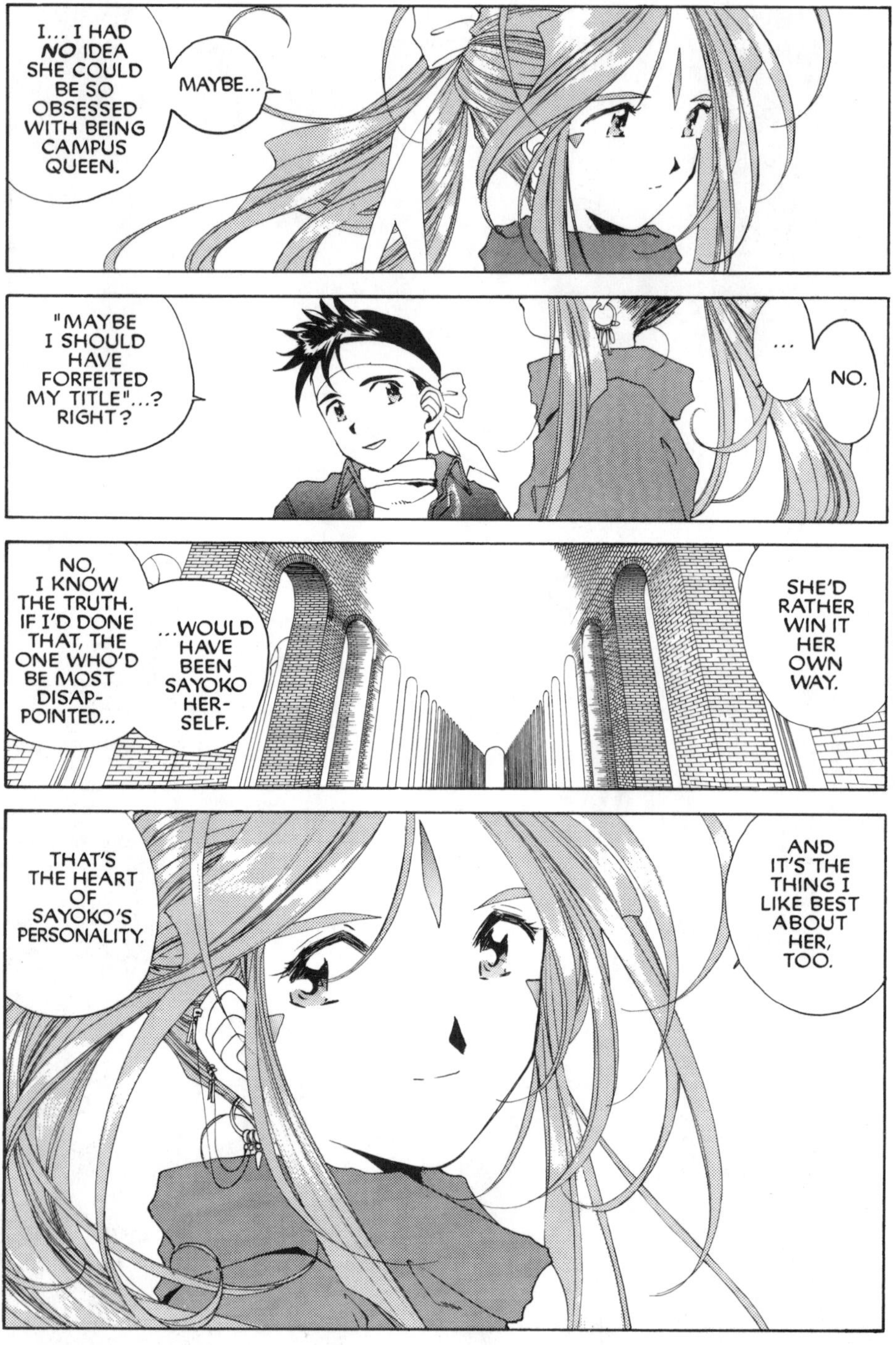
I... I HAD NO IDEA SHE COULD BE SO OBSESSED WITH BEING CAMPUS QUEEN.
MAYBE...
"MAYBE I SHOULD HAVE FORFEITED MY TITLE"...? RIGHT?
... NO.
NO, I KNOW THE TRUTH. IF I'D DONE THAT, THE ONE WHO'D BE MOST DISAP-POINTED...
...WOULD HAVE BEEN SAYOKO HER-SELF.
SHE'D RATHER WIN IT HER OWN WAY.
THAT'S THE HEART OF SAYOKO'S PERSONALITY.
AND IT'S THE THING I LIKE BEST ABOUT HER, TOO.

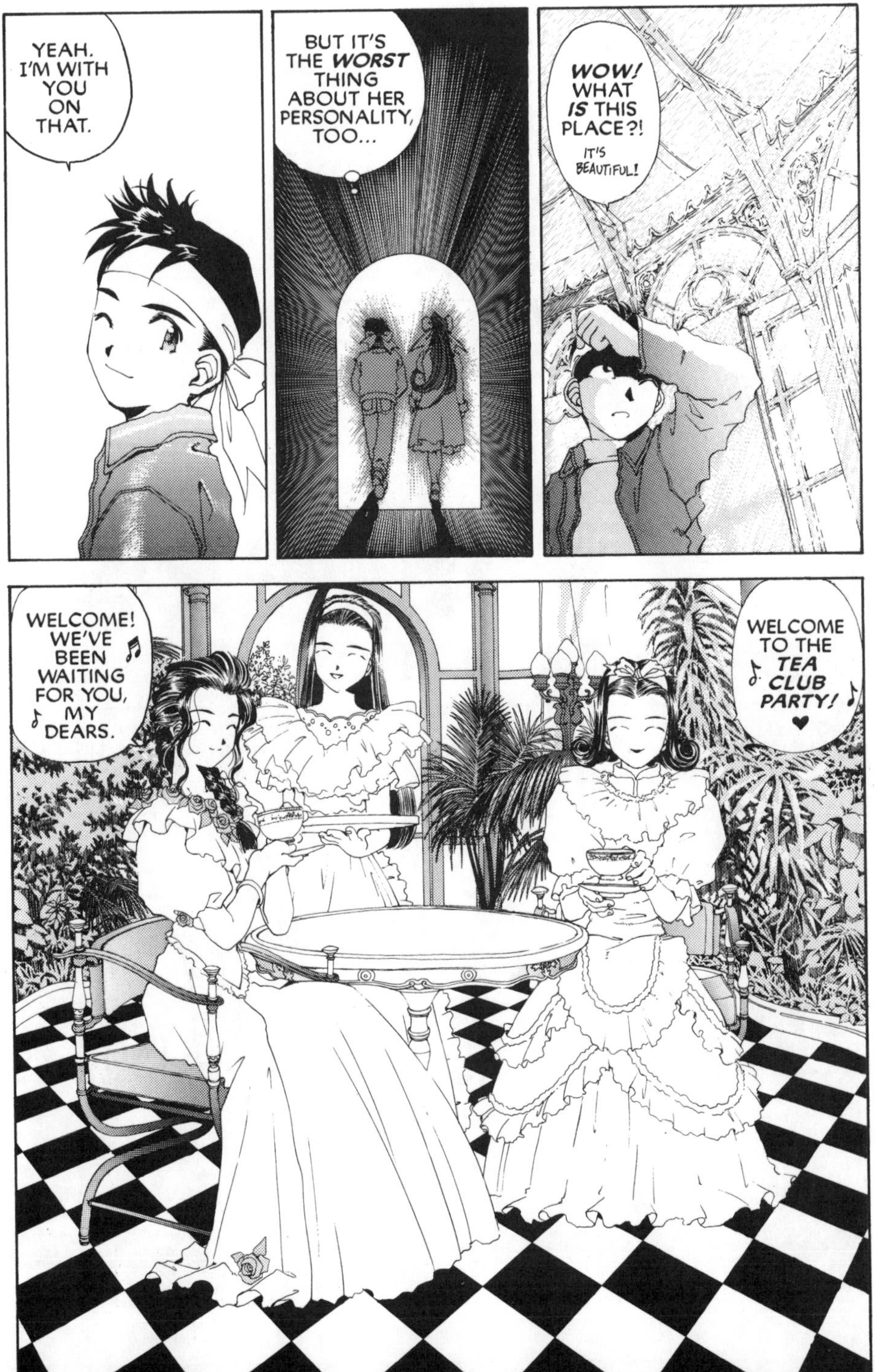
YEAH. I'M WITH YOU ON THAT.
BUT IT'S THE ***WORST*** THING ABOUT HER PERSONALITY, TOO...
WOW! WHAT ***IS*** THIS PLACE?!
IT'S BEAUTIFUL!
WELCOME! WE'VE BEEN WAITING FOR YOU, MY DEARS. ♪
WELCOME TO THE ***TEA CLUB PARTY!*** ♪ ♥

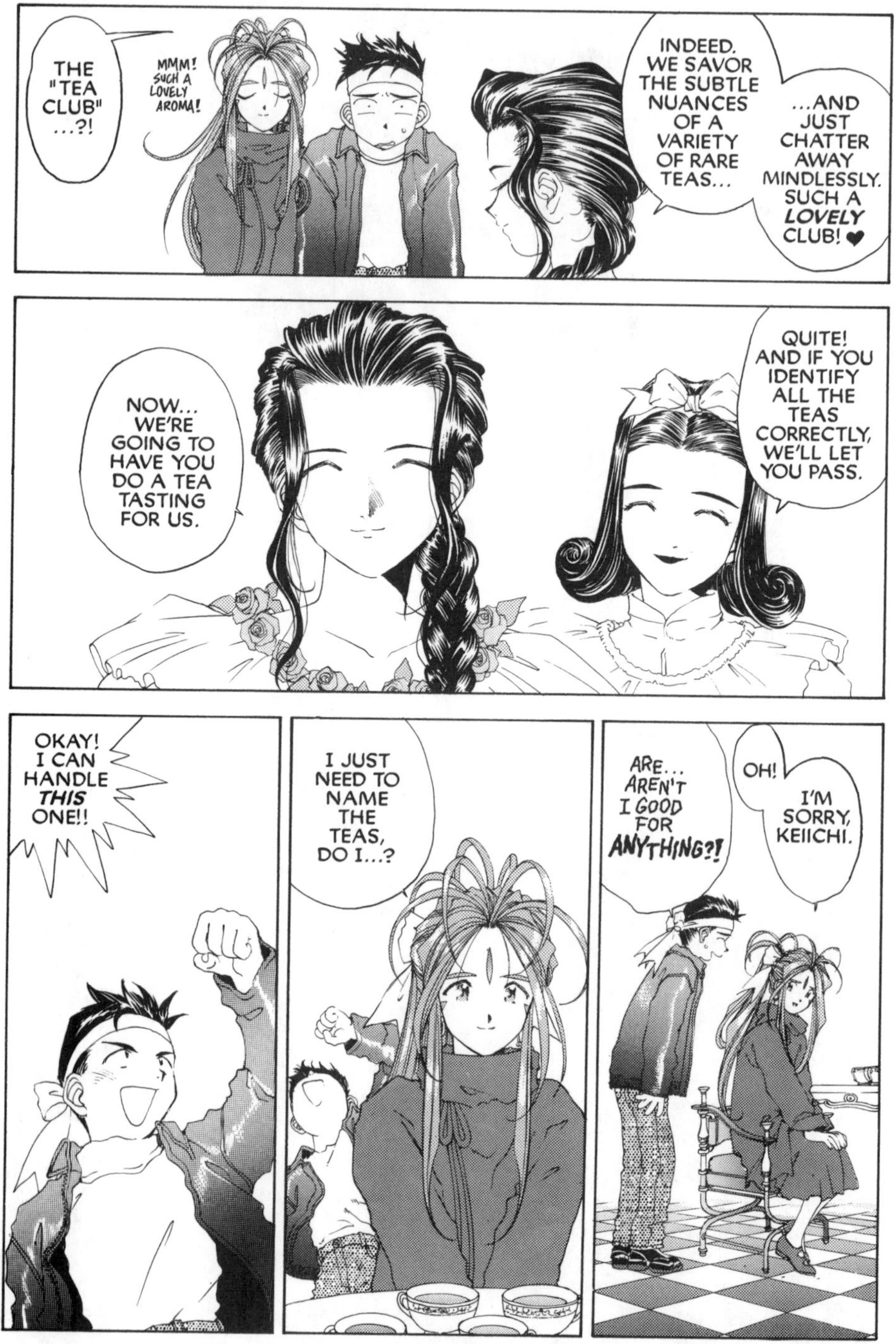
THE "TEA CLUB" ...?!
MMM! SUCH A LOVELY AROMA!
INDEED. WE SAVOR THE SUBTLE NUANCES OF A VARIETY OF RARE TEAS...
...AND JUST CHATTER AWAY MINDLESSLY. SUCH A *LOVELY* CLUB! ❤
NOW... WE'RE GOING TO HAVE YOU DO A TEA TASTING FOR US.
QUITE! AND IF YOU IDENTIFY ALL THE TEAS CORRECTLY, WE'LL LET YOU PASS.
OKAY! I CAN HANDLE *THIS* ONE!!
I JUST NEED TO NAME THE TEAS, DO I...?
ARE... AREN'T I GOOD FOR **ANYTHING?!**
OH!
I'M SORRY, KEIICHI.

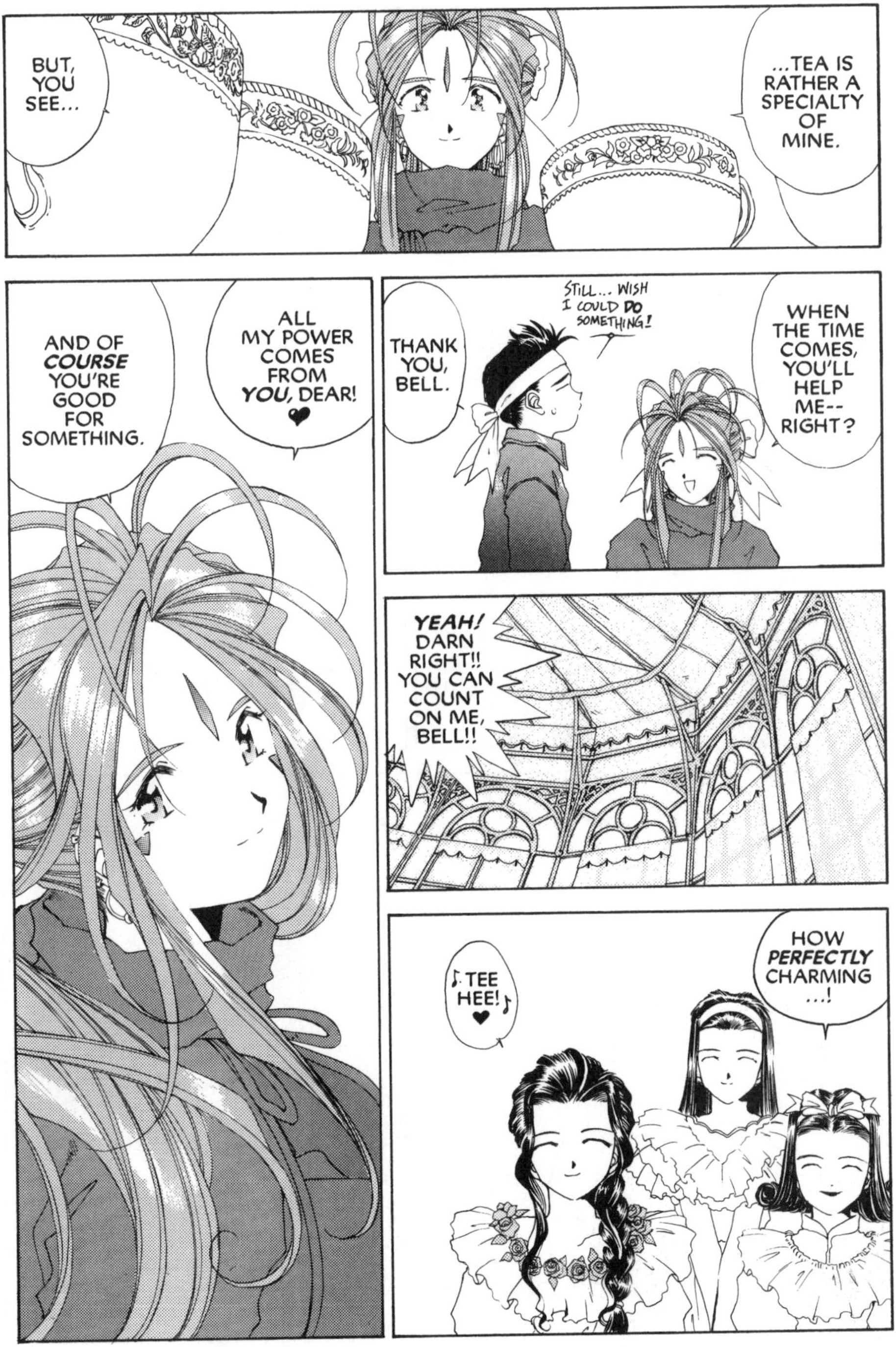
BUT, YOU SEE...
...TEA IS RATHER A SPECIALTY OF MINE.
AND OF COURSE YOU'RE GOOD FOR SOMETHING.
ALL MY POWER COMES FROM YOU, DEAR!
THANK YOU, BELL.
STILL... WISH I COULD DO SOMETHING!
WHEN THE TIME COMES, YOU'LL HELP ME--RIGHT?
YEAH! DARN RIGHT!! YOU CAN COUNT ON ME, BELL!!
TEE HEE!
HOW PERFECTLY CHARMING ...!

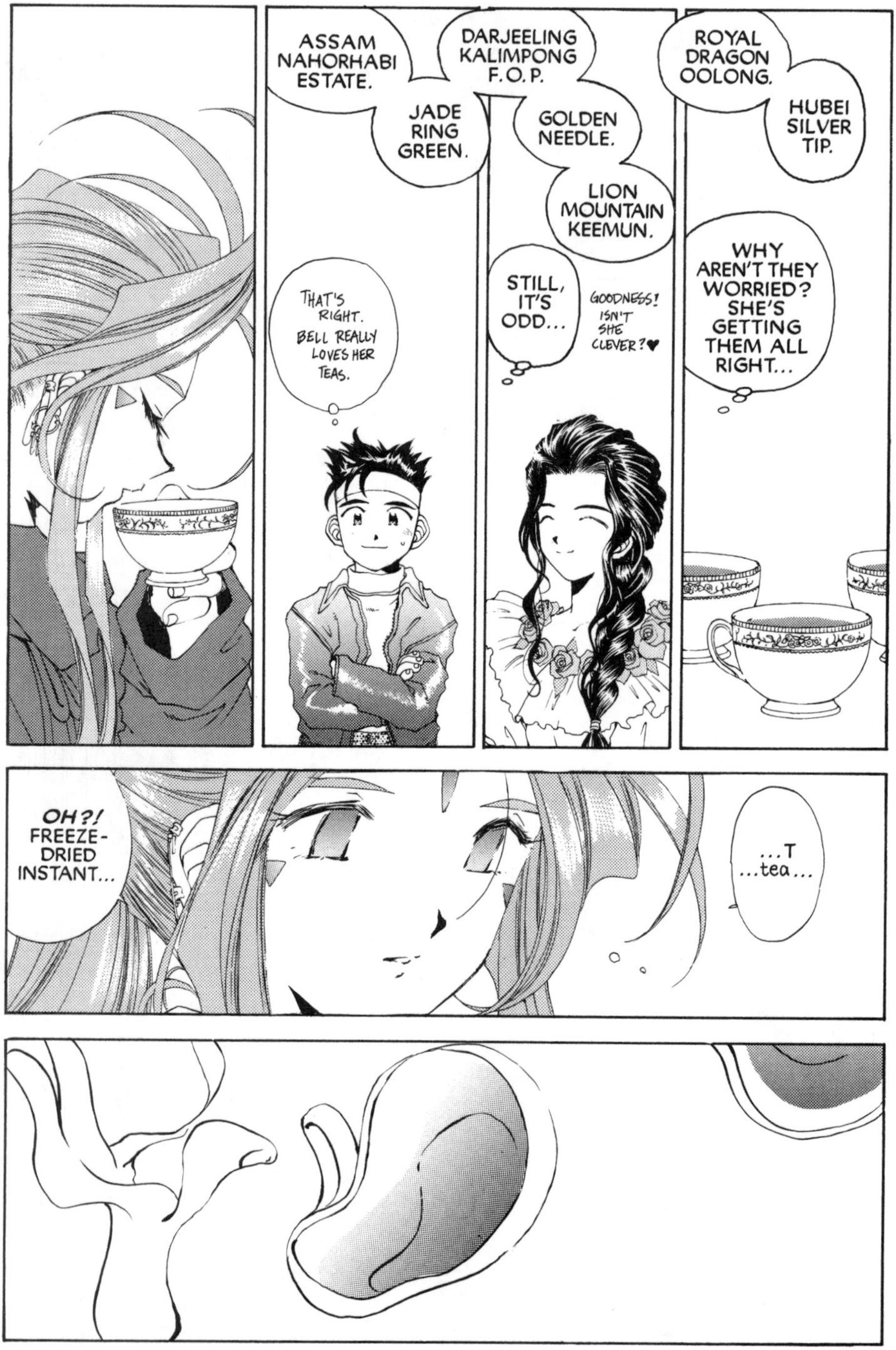
ASSAM NAHORHABI ESTATE.
JADE RING GREEN.
DARJEELING KALIMPONG F.O.P.
THAT'S RIGHT. BELL REALLY LOVES HER TEAS.
GOLDEN NEEDLE.
LION MOUNTAIN KEEMUN.
STILL, IT'S ODD...
GOODNESS! ISN'T SHE CLEVER?♥
ROYAL DRAGON OOLONG.
HUBEI SILVER TIP.
WHY AREN'T THEY WORRIED? SHE'S GETTING THEM ALL RIGHT...
OH?! FREEZE-DRIED INSTANT...
...T ...tea...

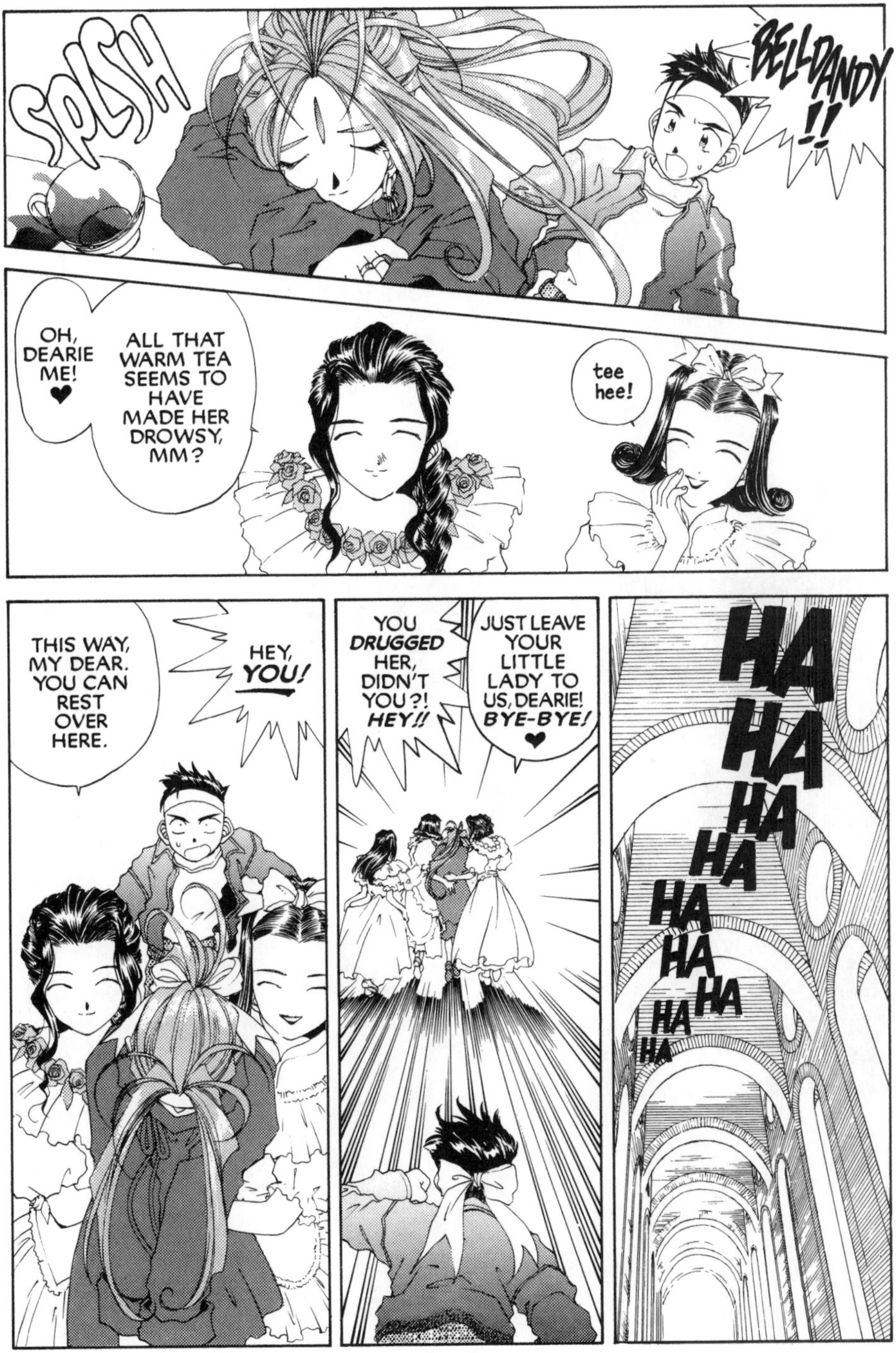
SPLSH
BELLDANDY!!
OH, DEARIE ME! ❤
ALL THAT WARM TEA SEEMS TO HAVE MADE HER DROWSY, MM?
tee hee!
THIS WAY, MY DEAR. YOU CAN REST OVER HERE.
HEY, YOU!
YOU DRUGGED HER, DIDN'T YOU?! HEY!!
JUST LEAVE YOUR LITTLE LADY TO US, DEARIE! BYE-BYE! ❤
HA HA HA HA HA HA HA HA HA HA HA

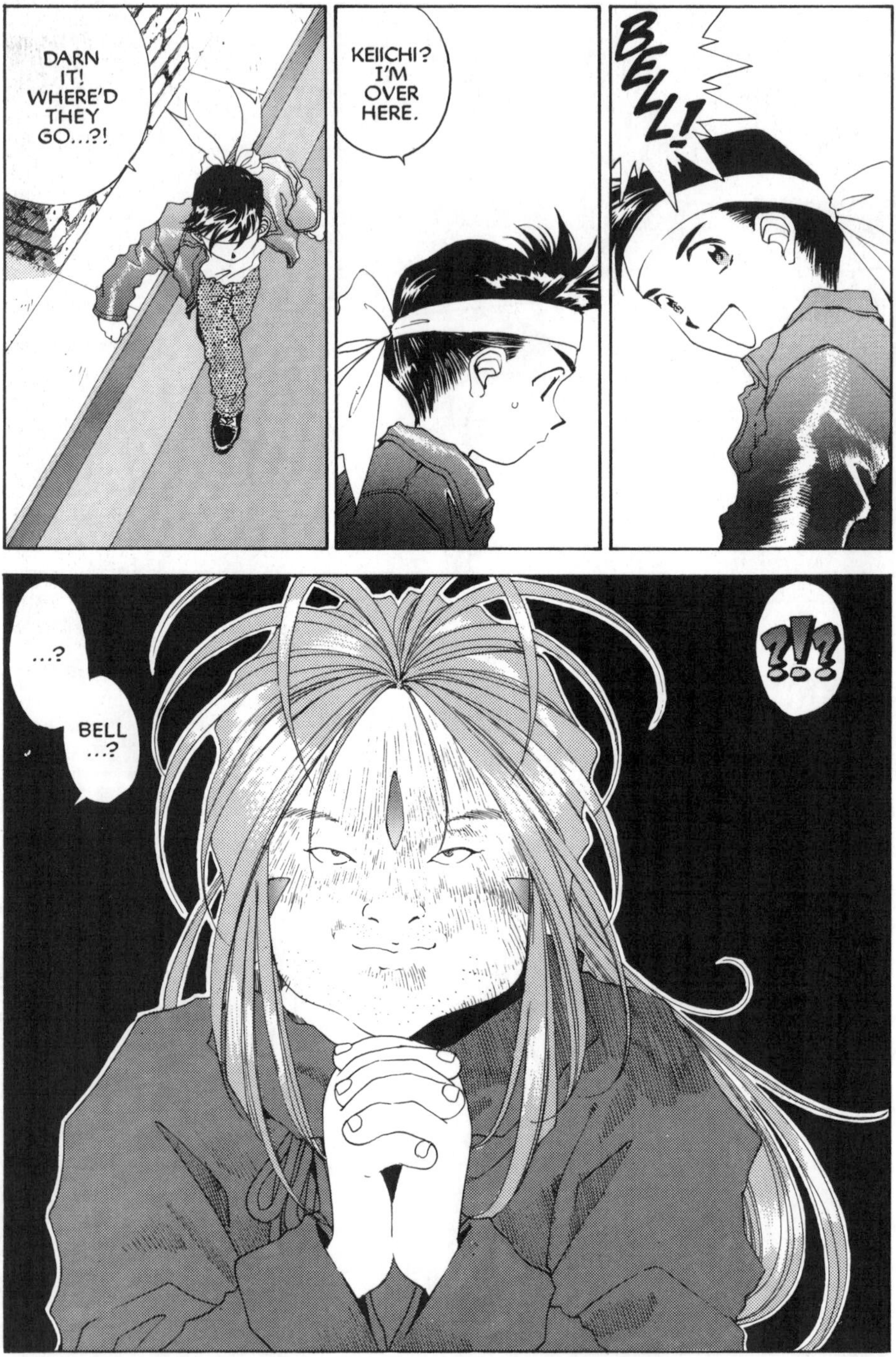
DARN IT! WHERE'D THEY GO...?!
KEIICHI? I'M OVER HERE.
BELL!
...?
BELL ...?
?!!?

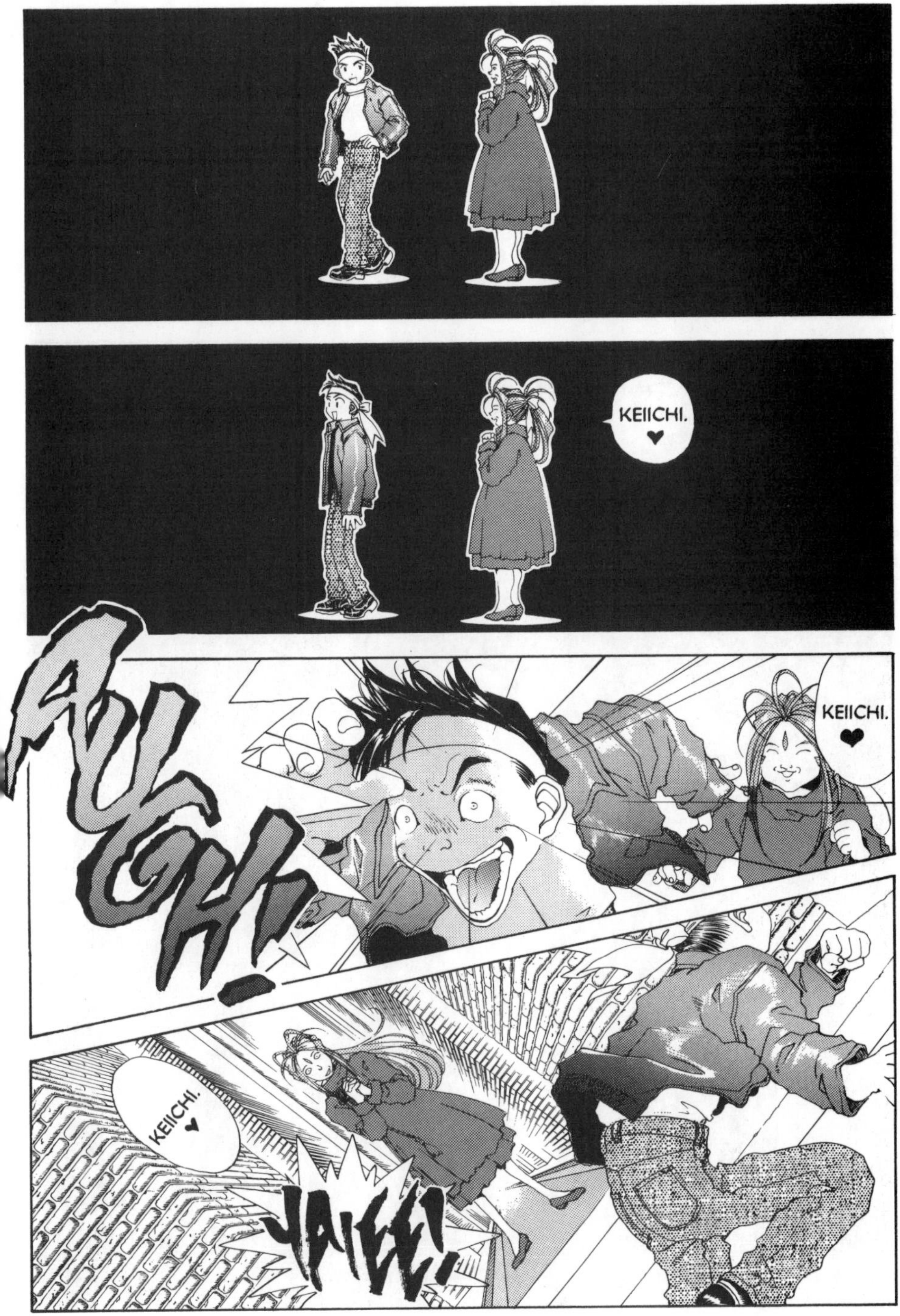
KEIICHI. ♥
AU... GH!
KEIICHI. ♥
KEIICHI. ♥
YAIEEE!

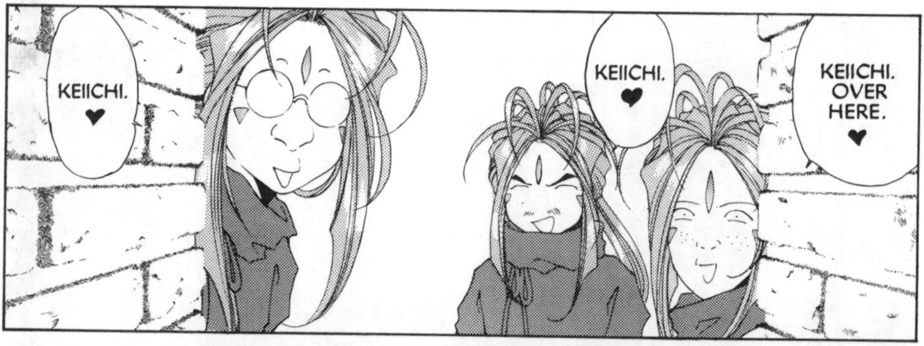
KEIICHI. ♥
KEIICHI. ♥
KEIICHI. OVER HERE. ♥

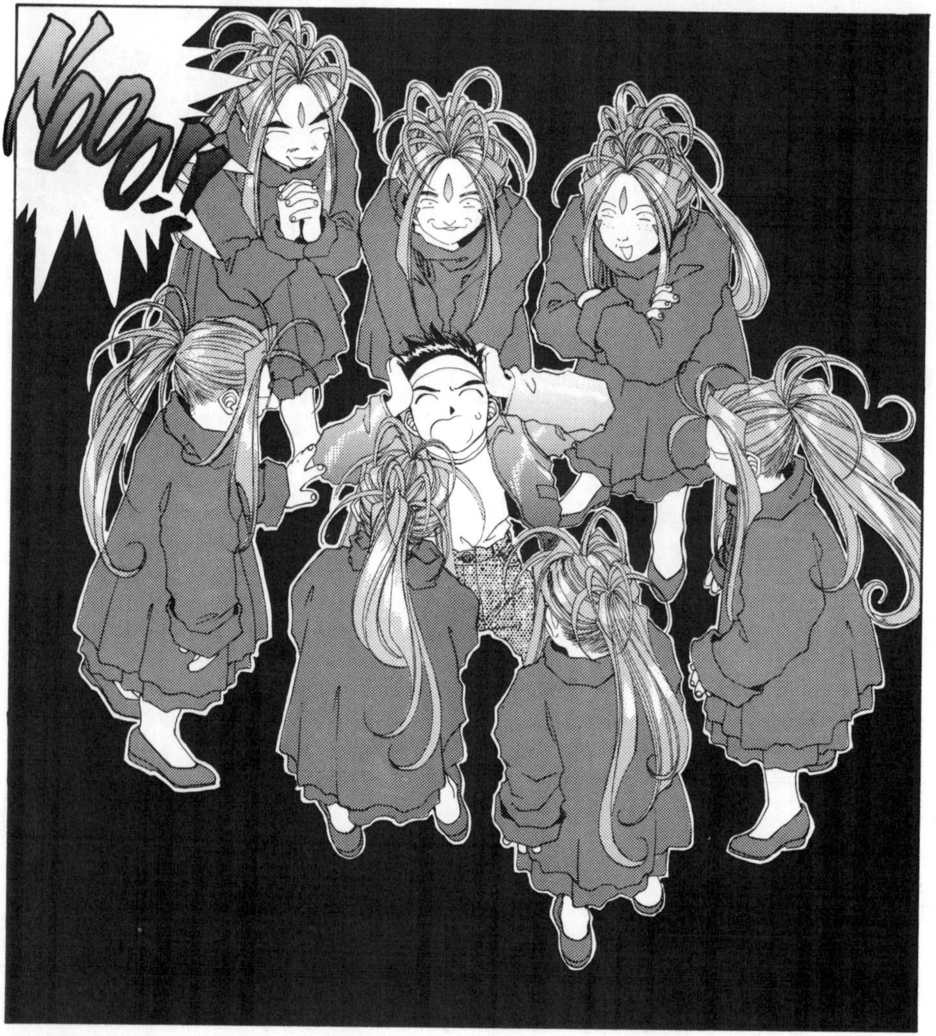
NOOO!!

Sayoko or Bust

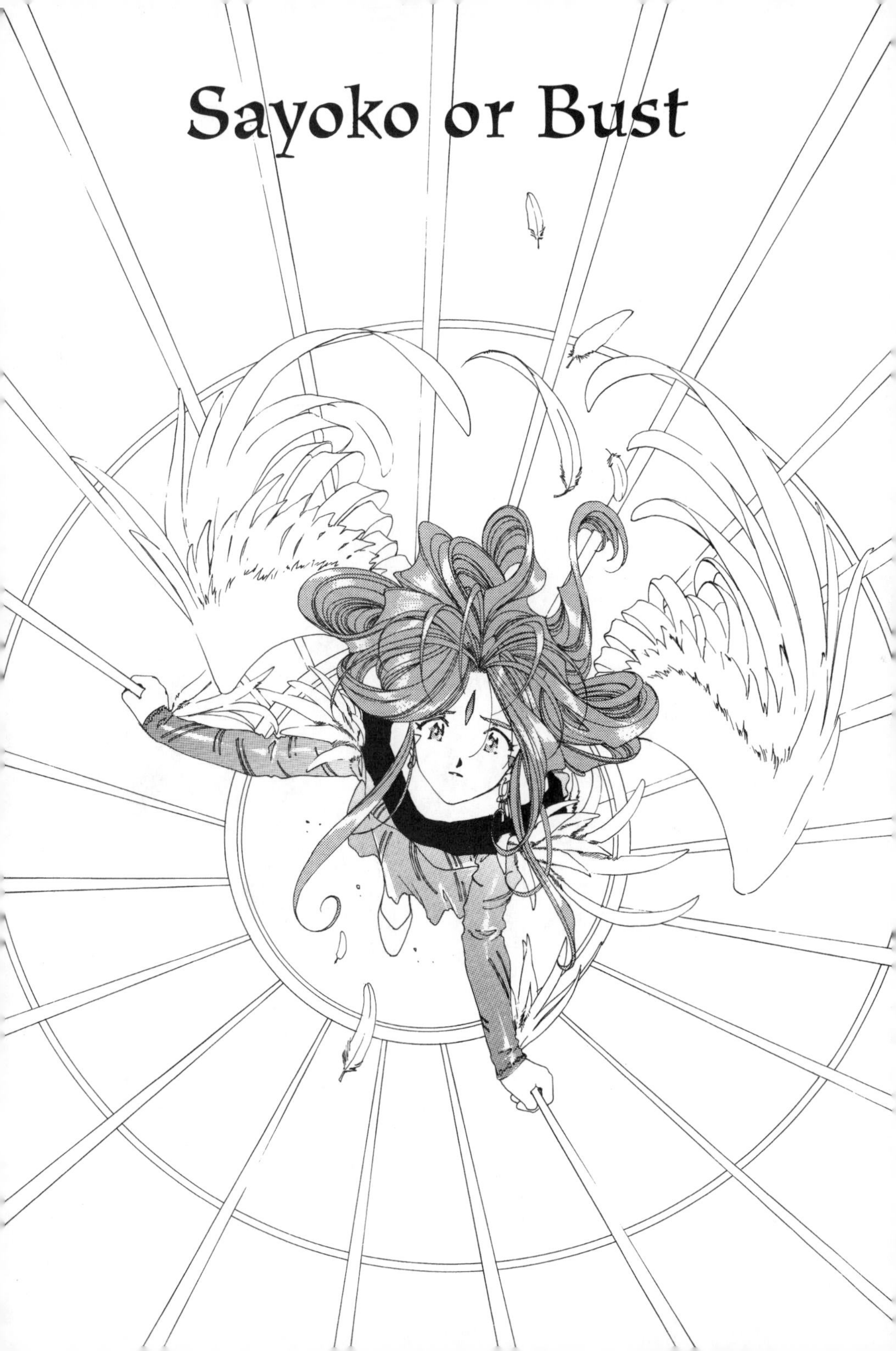

OH, KEIICHI, MY DEAREST!
KEIICHI ...!
KEIICHI, IT'S ME!
HUNNY-BUNNY!
YAIEE!!
YOU HAVEN'T FORGOTTEN ME, HAVE YOU, KEIICHI?
GET OFF!!

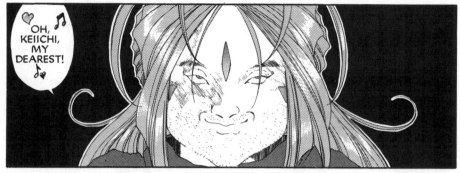

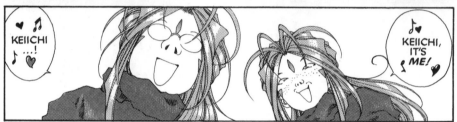

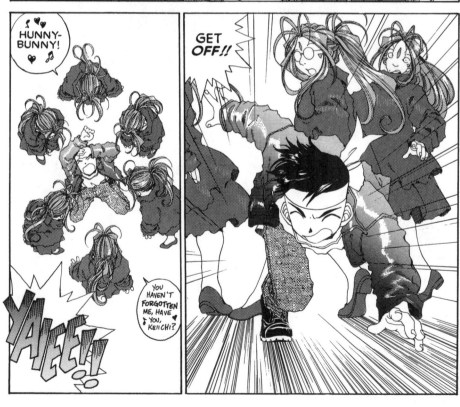

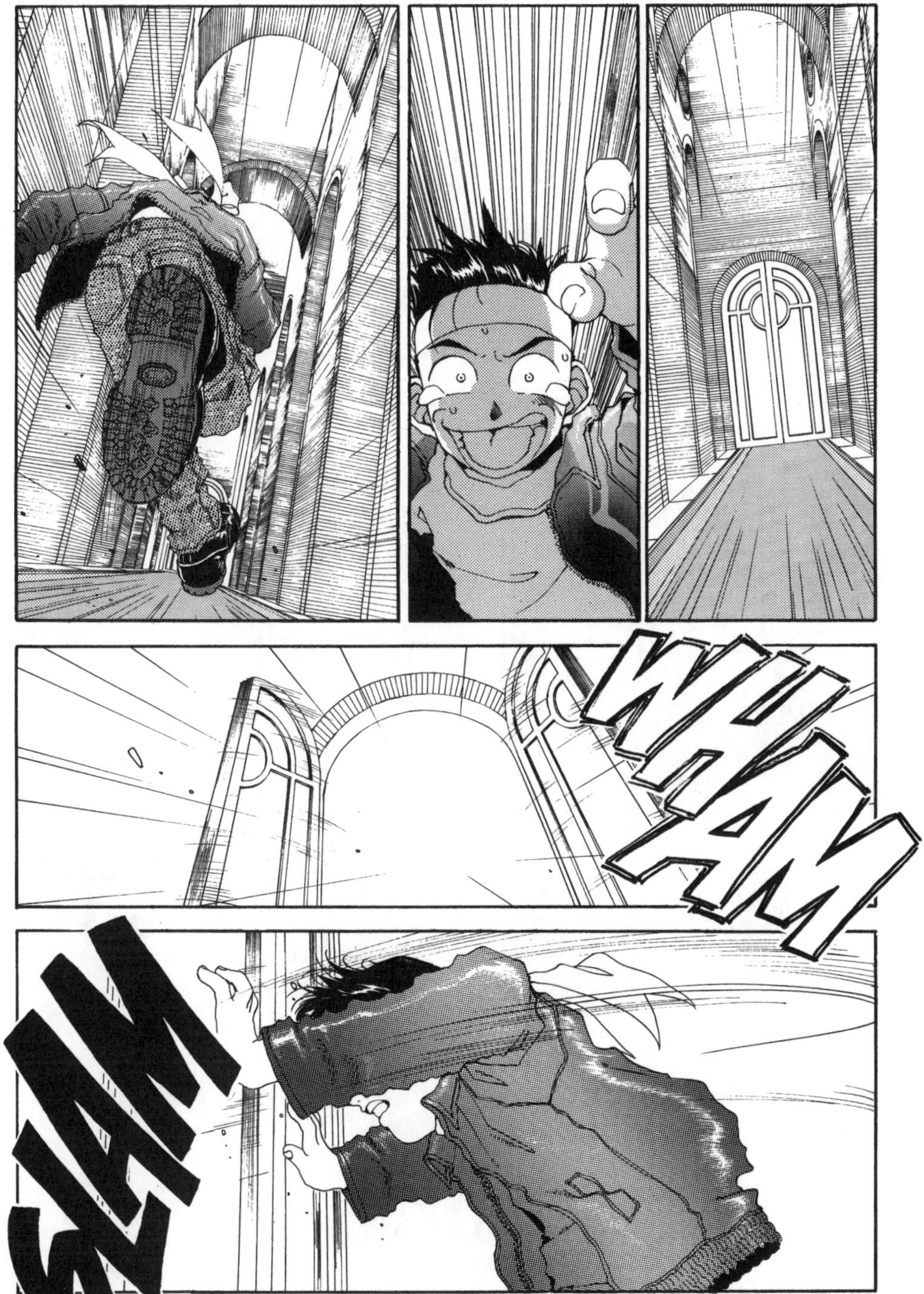
WHAM
SLAM

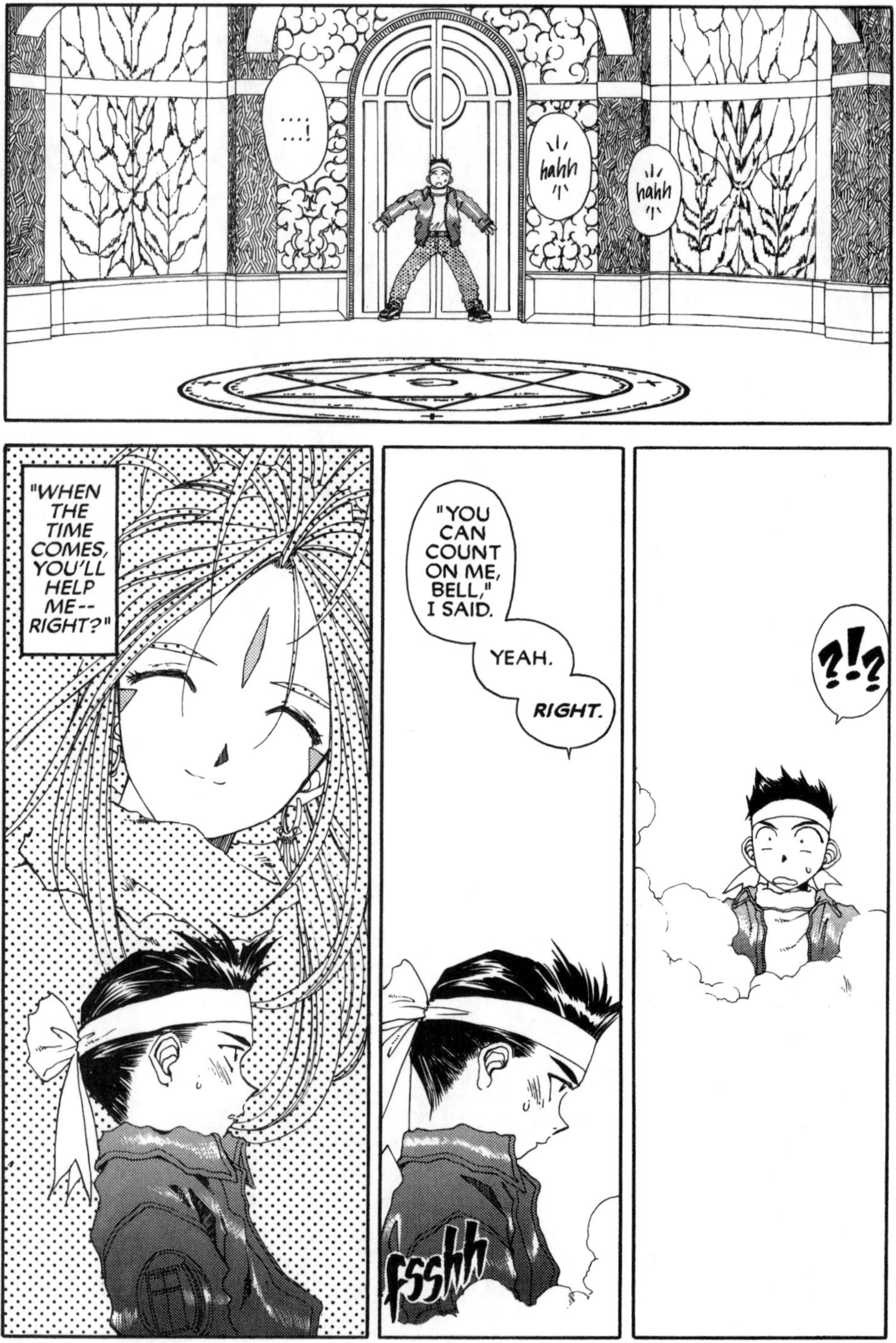
....!
hahh
hahh
"WHEN THE TIME COMES, YOU'LL HELP ME--RIGHT?"
"YOU CAN COUNT ON ME, BELL," I SAID.
YEAH.
RIGHT.
fsshh
?!?

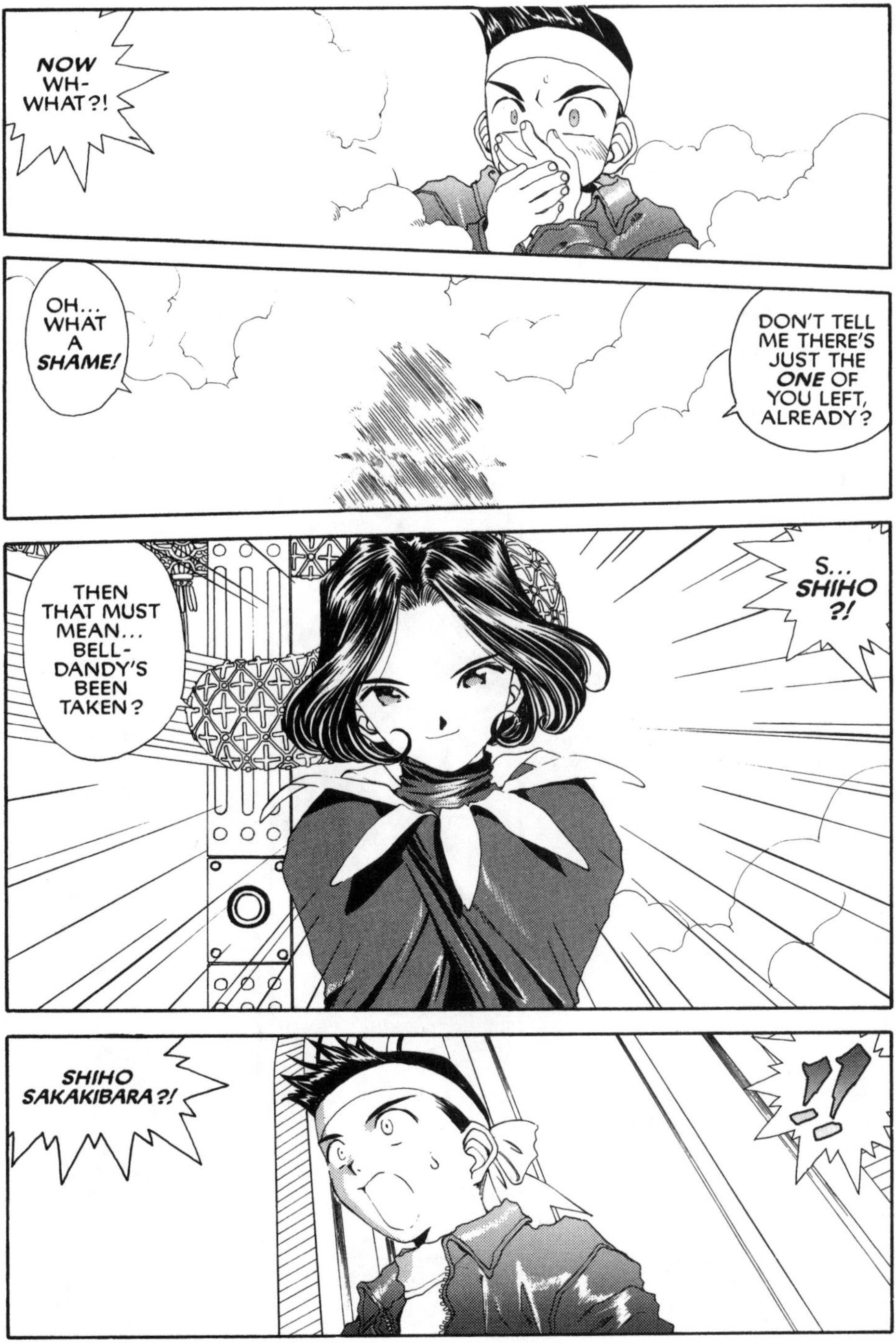
NOW WH- WHAT?!
OH... WHAT A SHAME!
DON'T TELL ME THERE'S JUST THE ONE OF YOU LEFT, ALREADY?
THEN THAT MUST MEAN... BELL-DANDY'S BEEN TAKEN?
S... SHIHO ?!
SHIHO SAKAKIBARA?!
!!

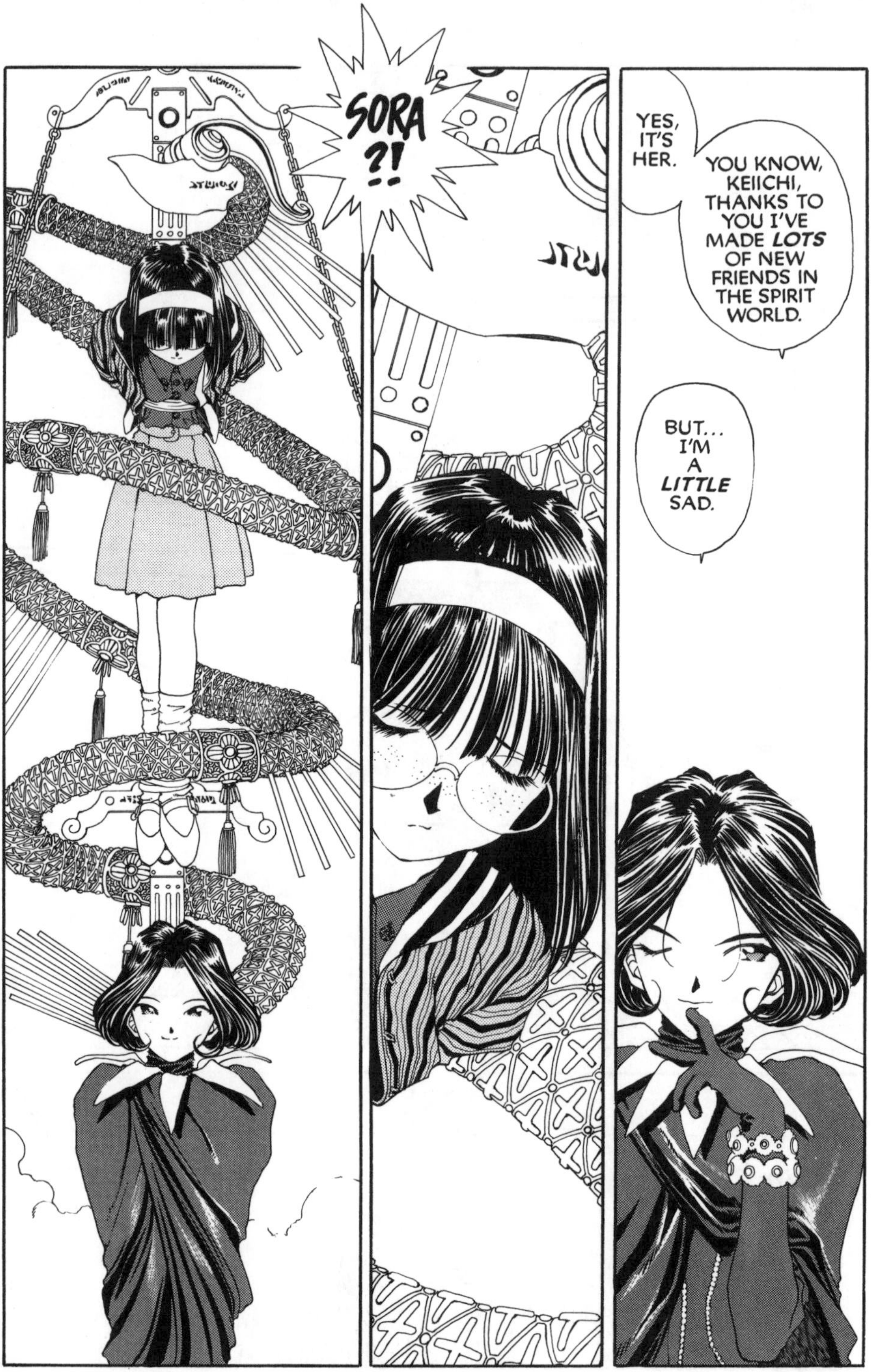
SORA ?!
YES, IT'S HER.
YOU KNOW, KEIICHI, THANKS TO YOU I'VE MADE *LOTS* OF NEW FRIENDS IN THE SPIRIT WORLD.
BUT... I'M A *LITTLE* SAD.

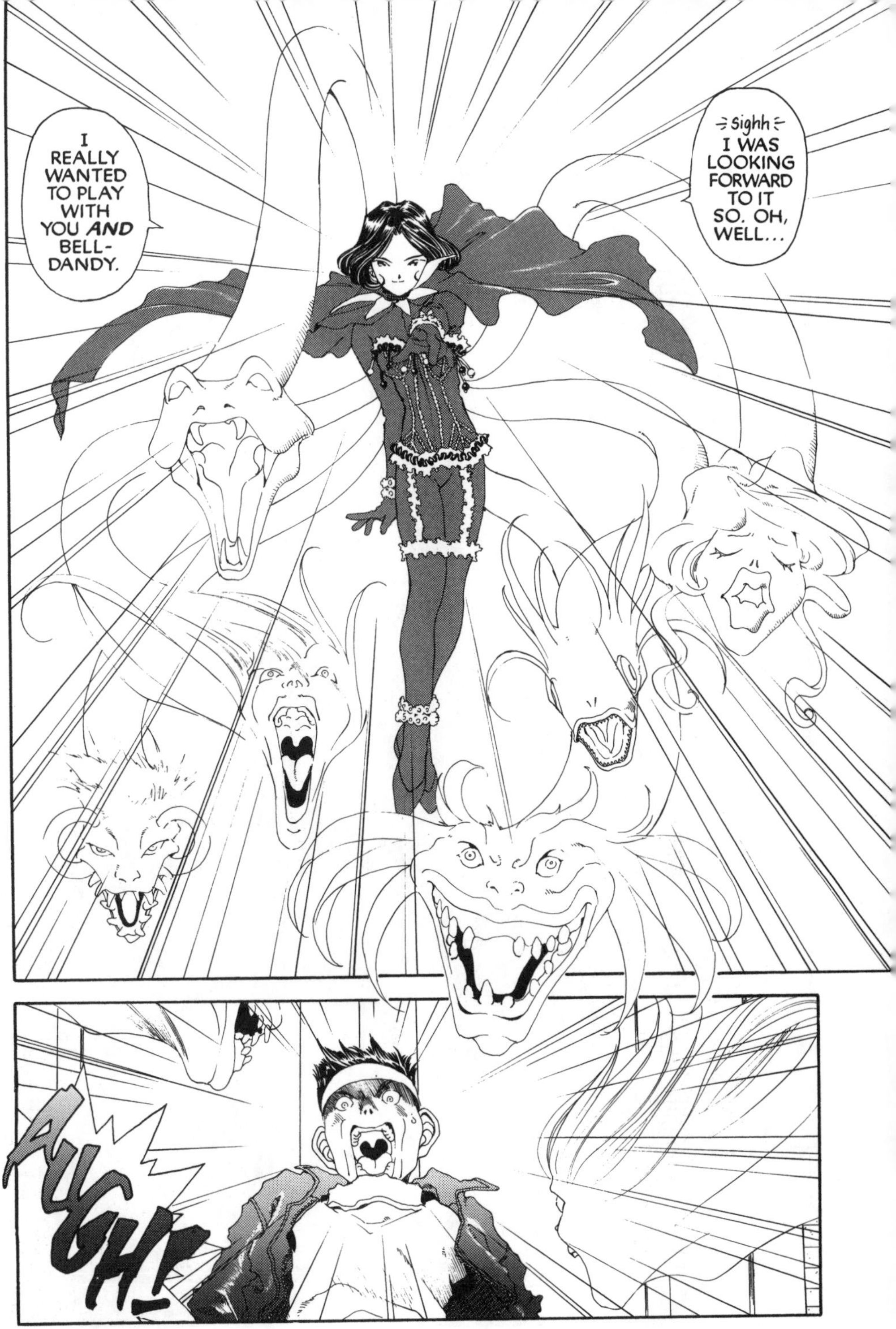
I REALLY WANTED TO PLAY WITH YOU *AND* BELL-DANDY.
≡ Sighh ≡ I WAS LOOKING FORWARD TO IT SO. OH, WELL...
AUGH!

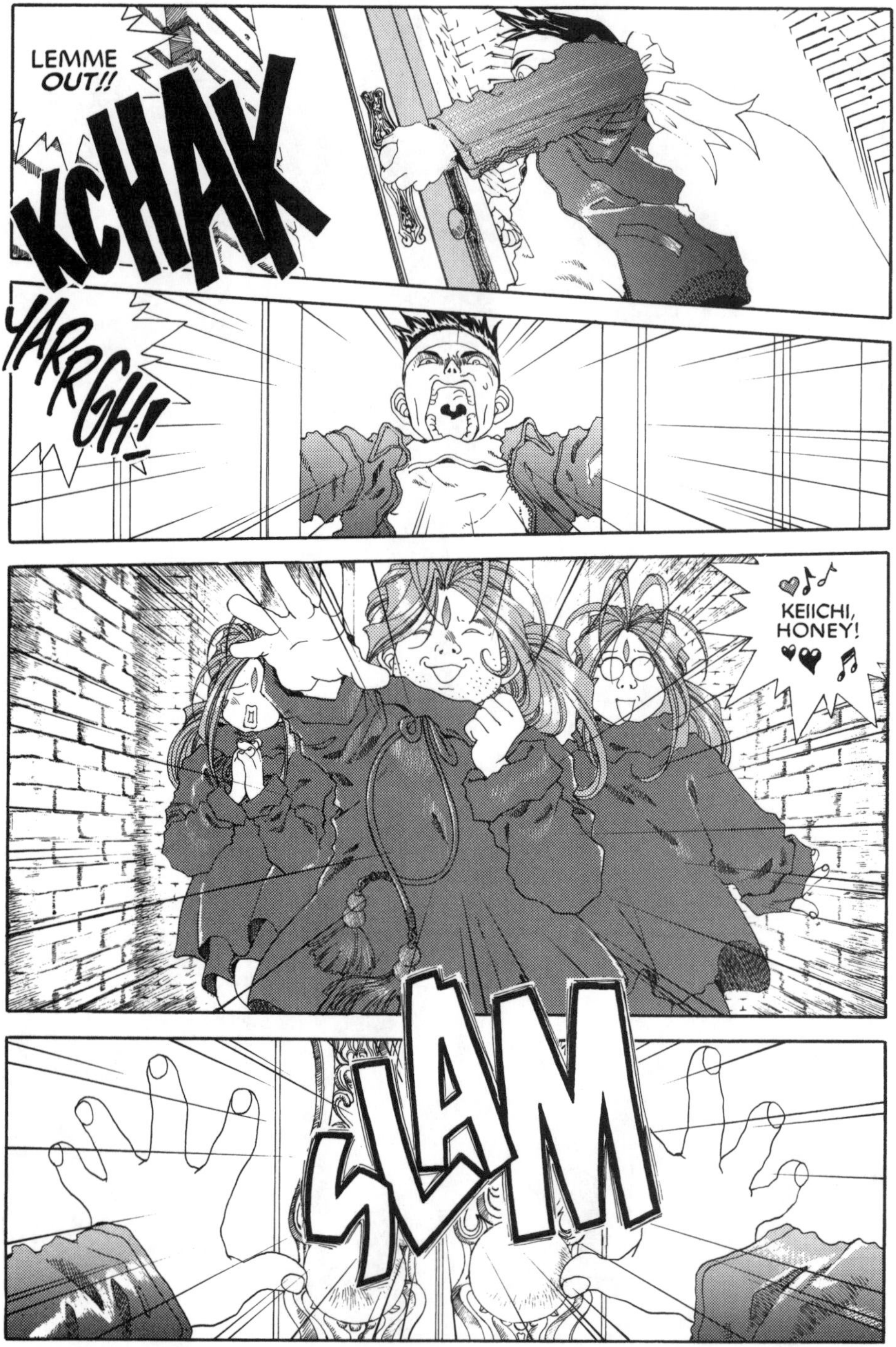
LEMME OUT!!
KCHAK
YARRGH!
KEIICHI, HONEY!
SLAM

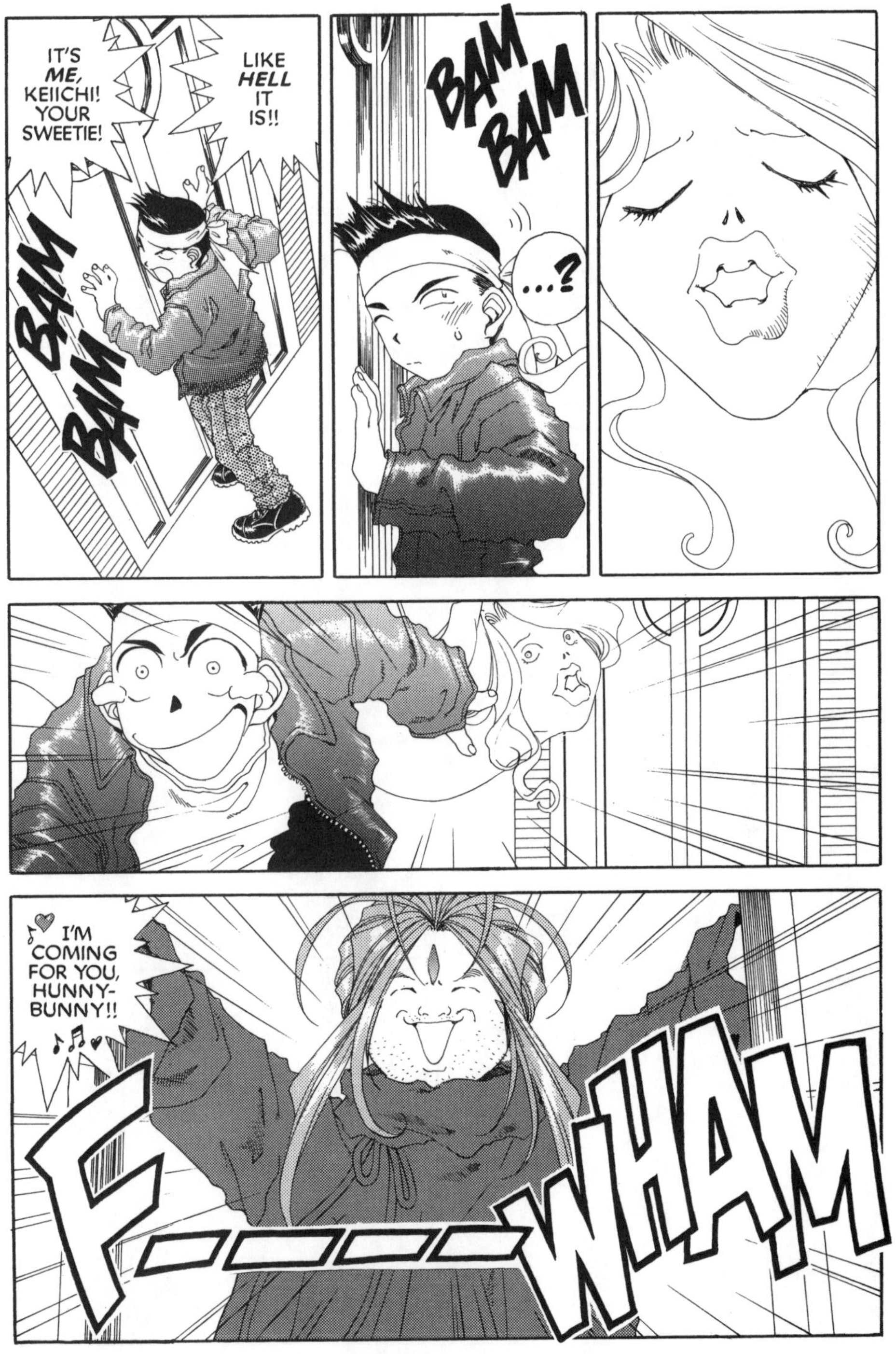

IT'S ME, KEIICHI! YOUR SWEETIE!
LIKE HELL IT IS!!
BAM BAM
BAM BAM
...?
I'M COMING FOR YOU, HUNNY-BUNNY!!
F-----WHAM

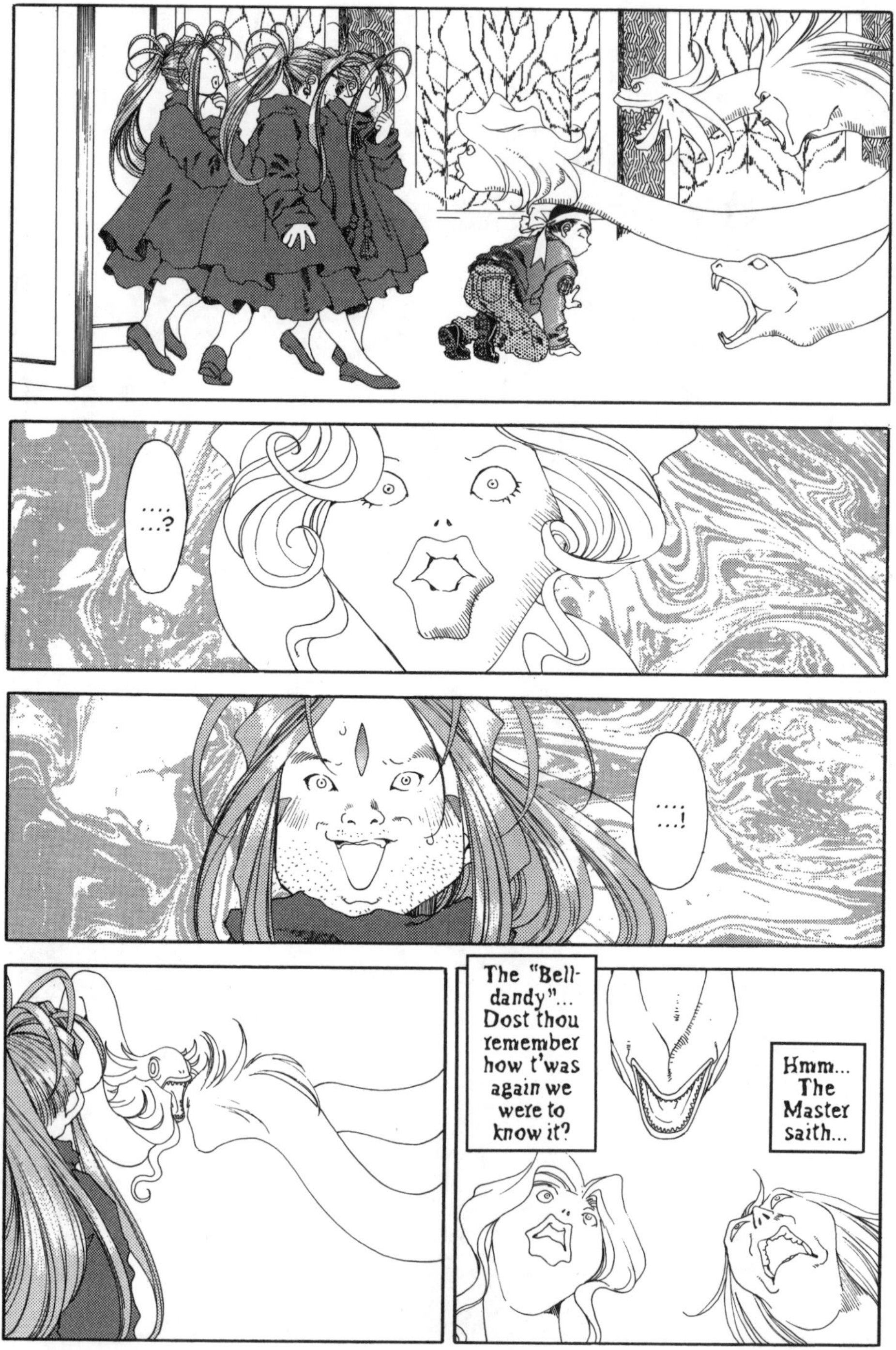
......?
......!
The "Bell-dandy"... Dost thou remember how t'was again we were to know it?
Hmm... The Master saith...

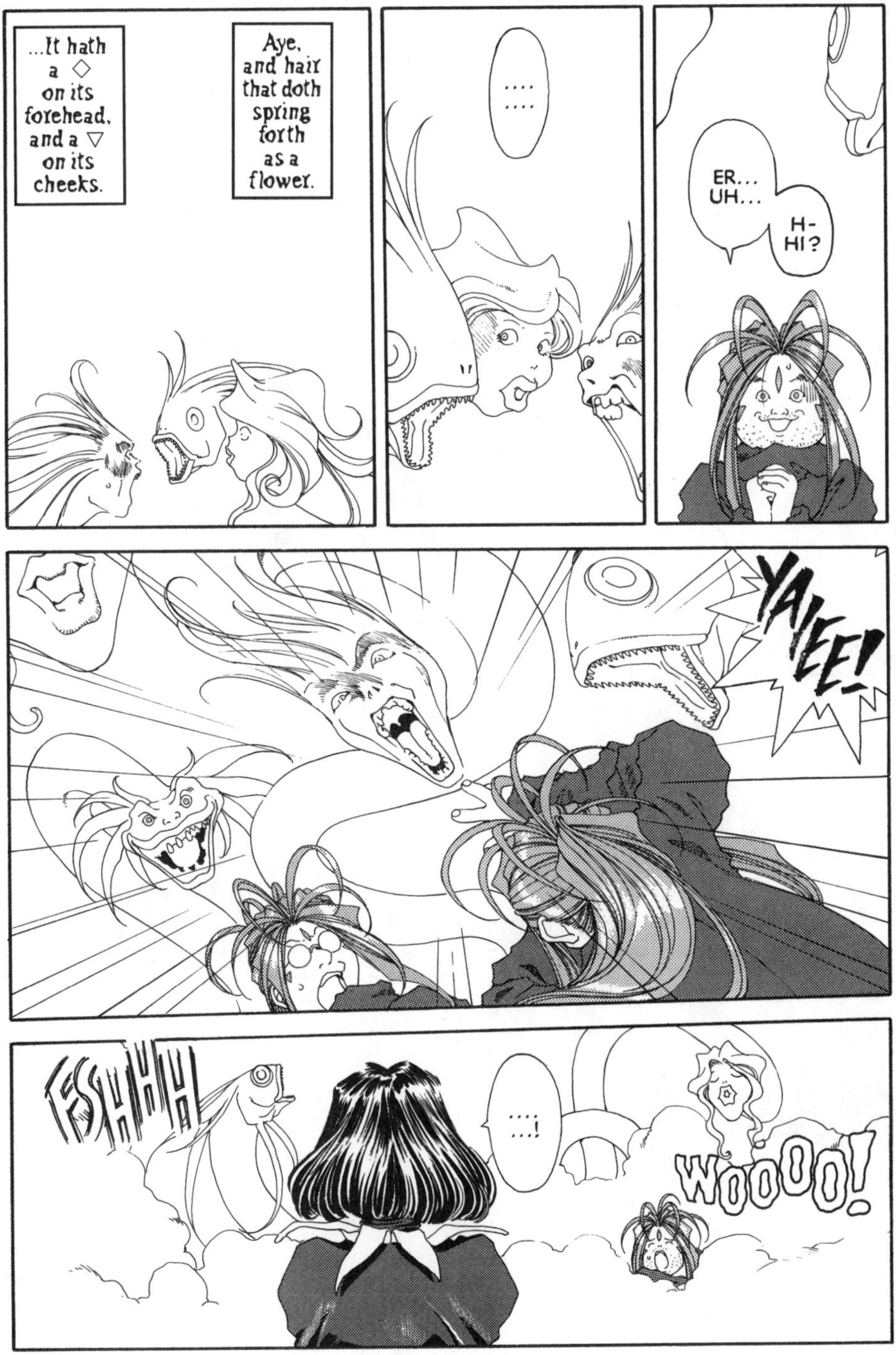
...It hath a ◇ on its forehead, and a ▽ on its cheeks.
Aye, and hair that doth spring forth as a flower.
....
ER... UH...
H-HI?
YAIEE!
FSHHHA
....; ...!
WOOOO!

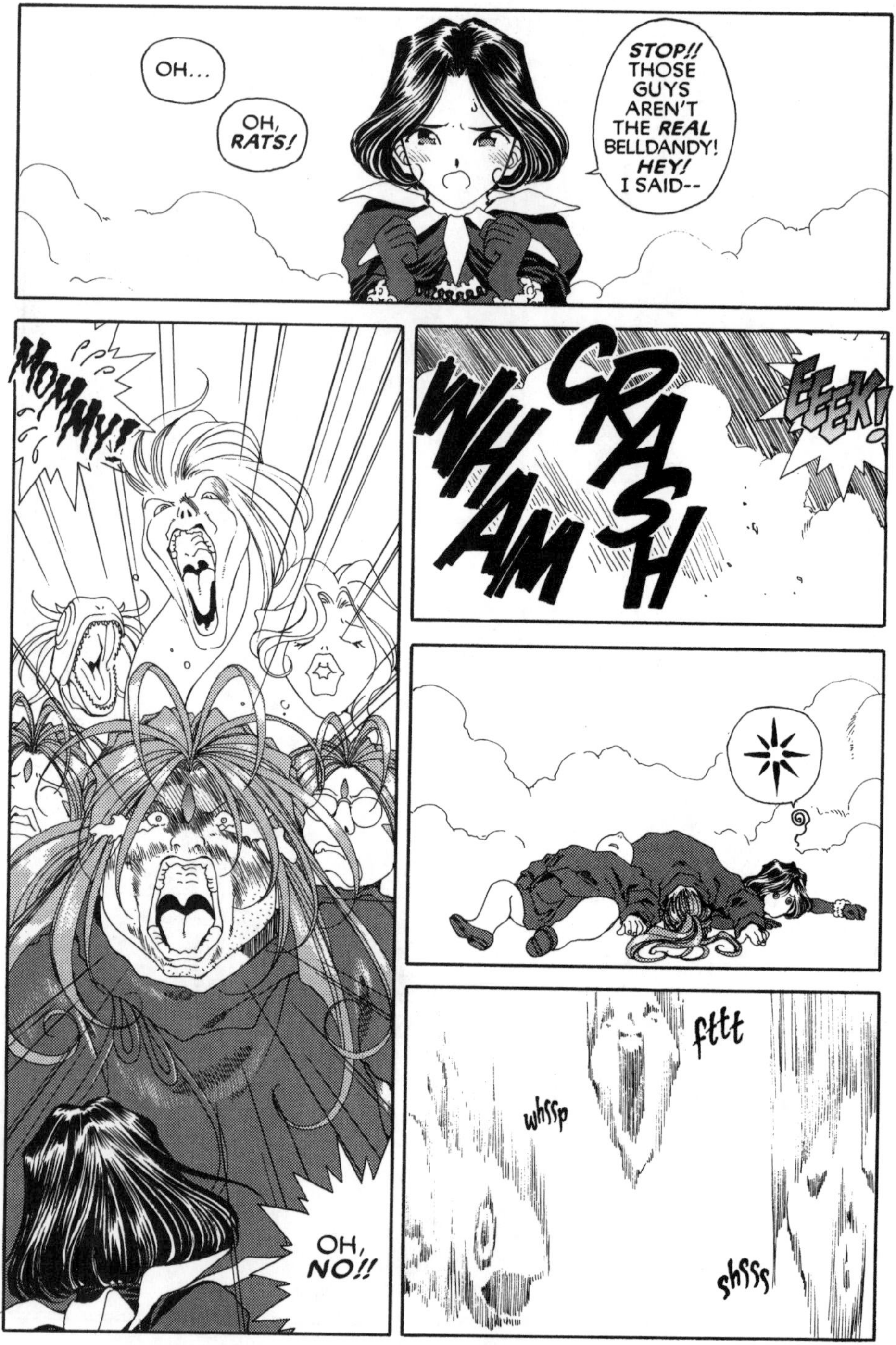
OH...
OH, *RATS!*
STOP!! THOSE GUYS AREN'T THE *REAL* BELLDANDY! *HEY!* I SAID--
MOMMY!
OH, *NO!!*
WHAM
CRASH
EEEK!
fttt
whssp
shsss

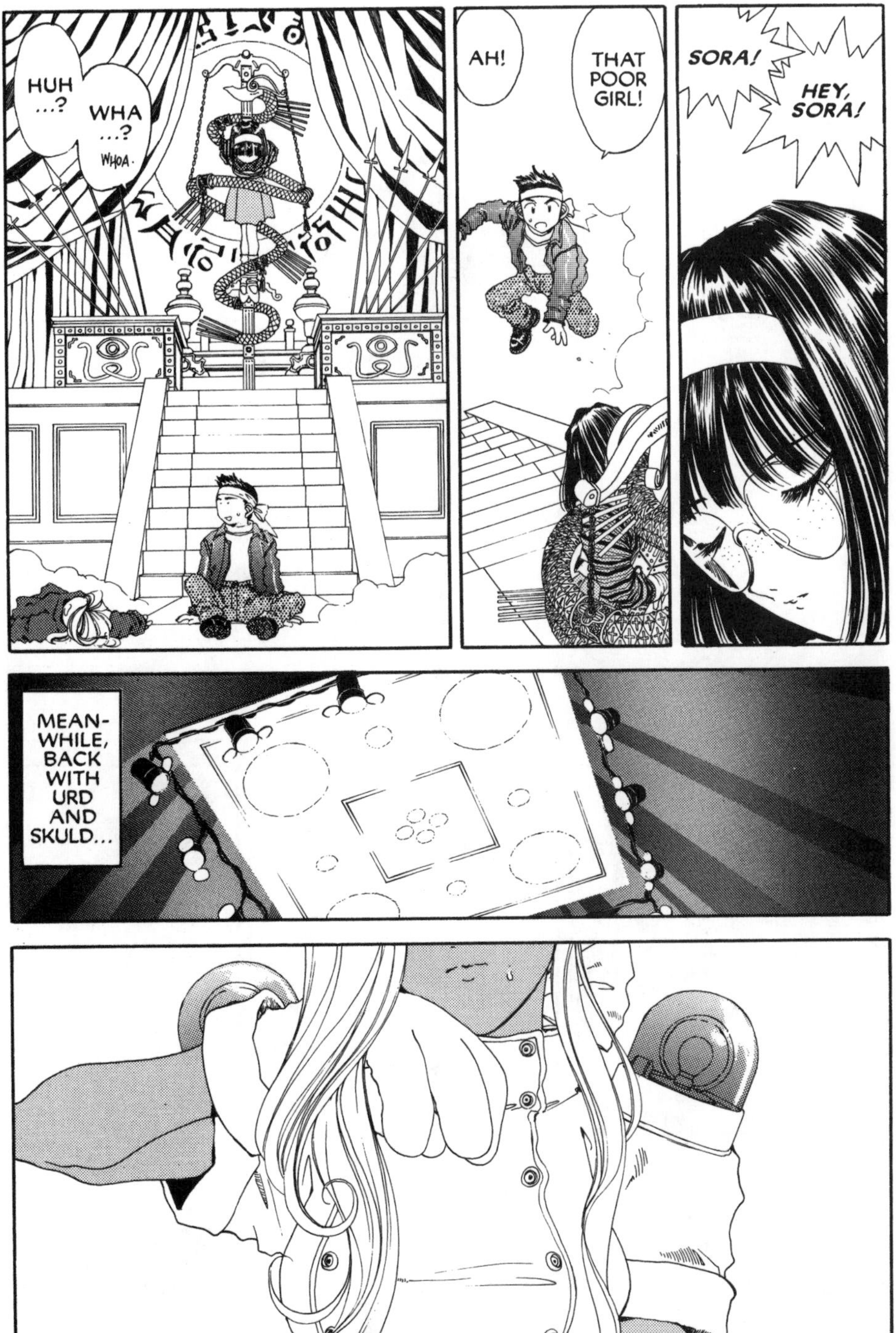
HUH ...?
WHA ...?
WHOA.
AH!
THAT POOR GIRL!
SORA!
HEY, SORA!
MEAN-WHILE, BACK WITH URD AND SKULD...

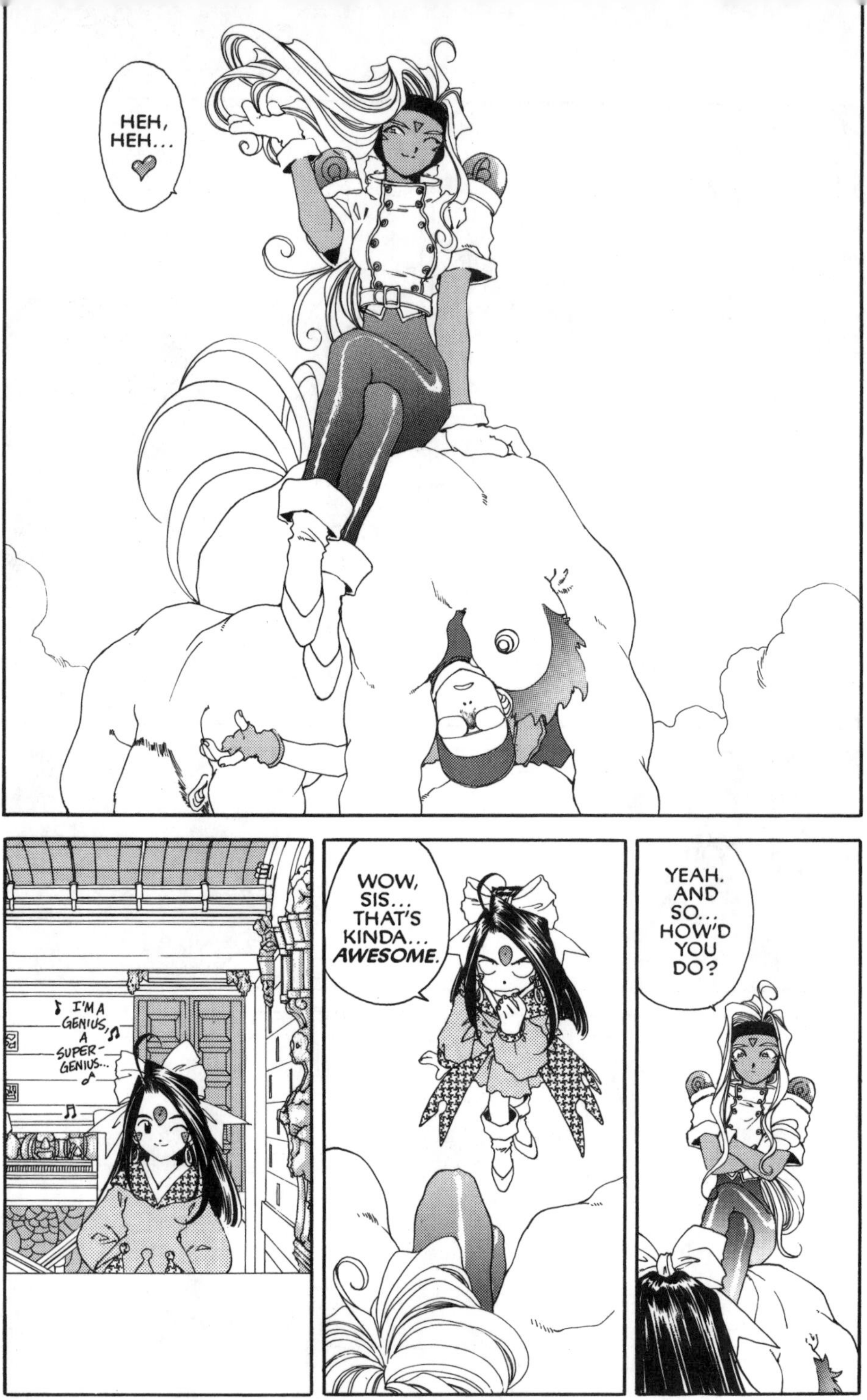
HEH, HEH... ♥
♪ I'M A GENIUS, ♫ A SUPER-GENIUS... ♪
WOW, SIS... THAT'S KINDA... ***AWESOME.***
YEAH. AND SO... HOW'D YOU DO?

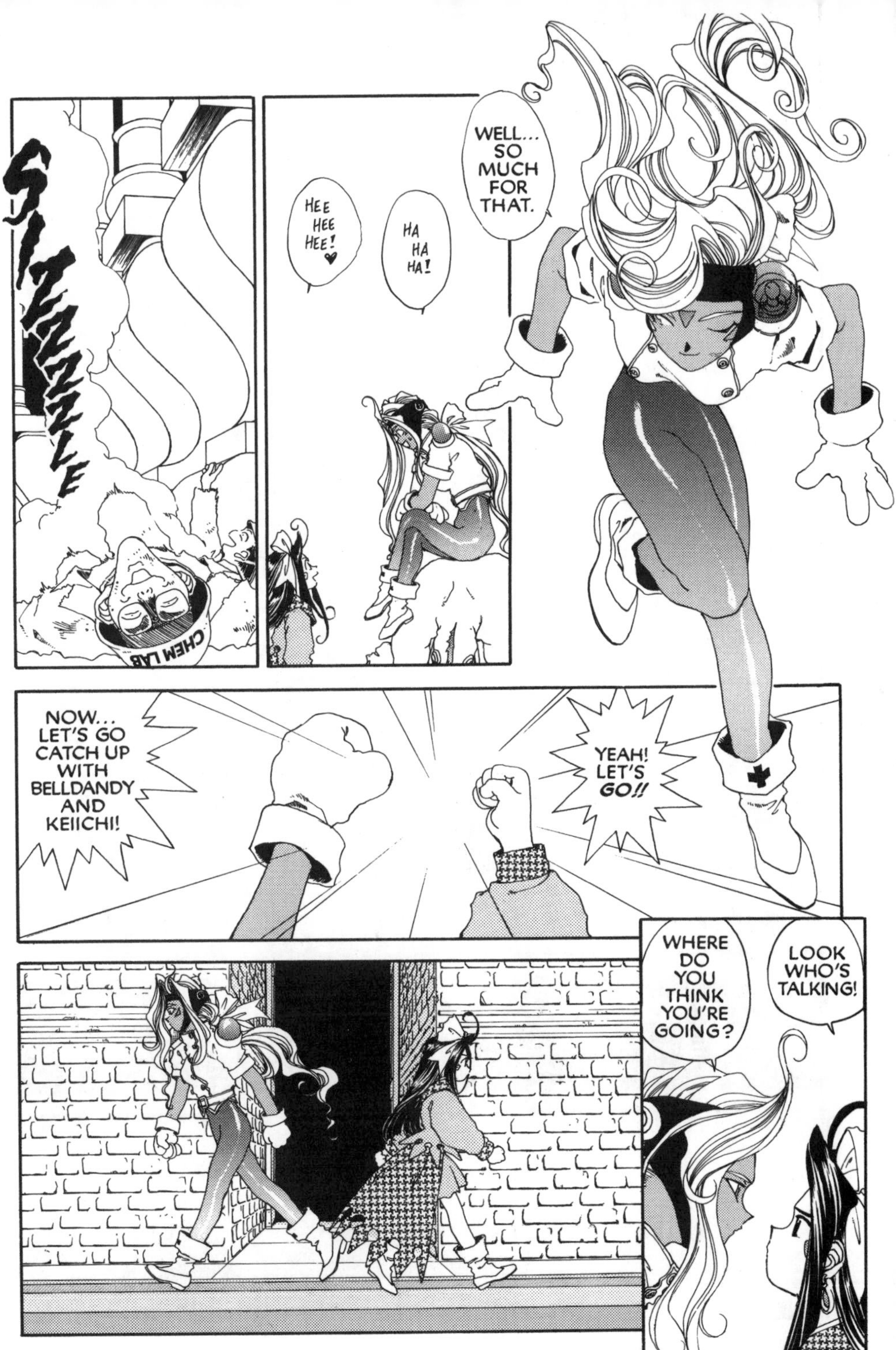
SIZZZZZLE
CHEM LAB
HEE HEE HEE! ♥
HA HA HA!
WELL... SO MUCH FOR THAT.
NOW... LET'S GO CATCH UP WITH BELLDANDY AND KEIICHI!
YEAH! LET'S GO!!
WHERE DO YOU THINK YOU'RE GOING?
LOOK WHO'S TALKING!

THERE'S **DANGER** THAT WAY-- ACCORDING TO MY **URD SENSE!**

HAH! IN THAT CASE, IT'S PROBABLY **MORE** DANGEROUS OVER THERE!

OH, **YEAH?!** AND WHO FELL INTO THAT ENTRANCE-HALL TRAP?!

WE BOTH DID, REMEMBER?!

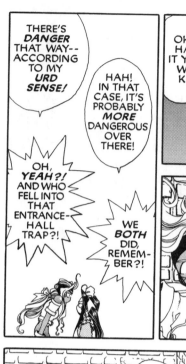

OKAY, HAVE IT YOUR WAY, KID!

MAYBE I **WILL!**

WHADDA YA THINK? STICK TOGETHER?

YEAH, MAYBE. SURE.

....-RA ....?

SORA ...?!

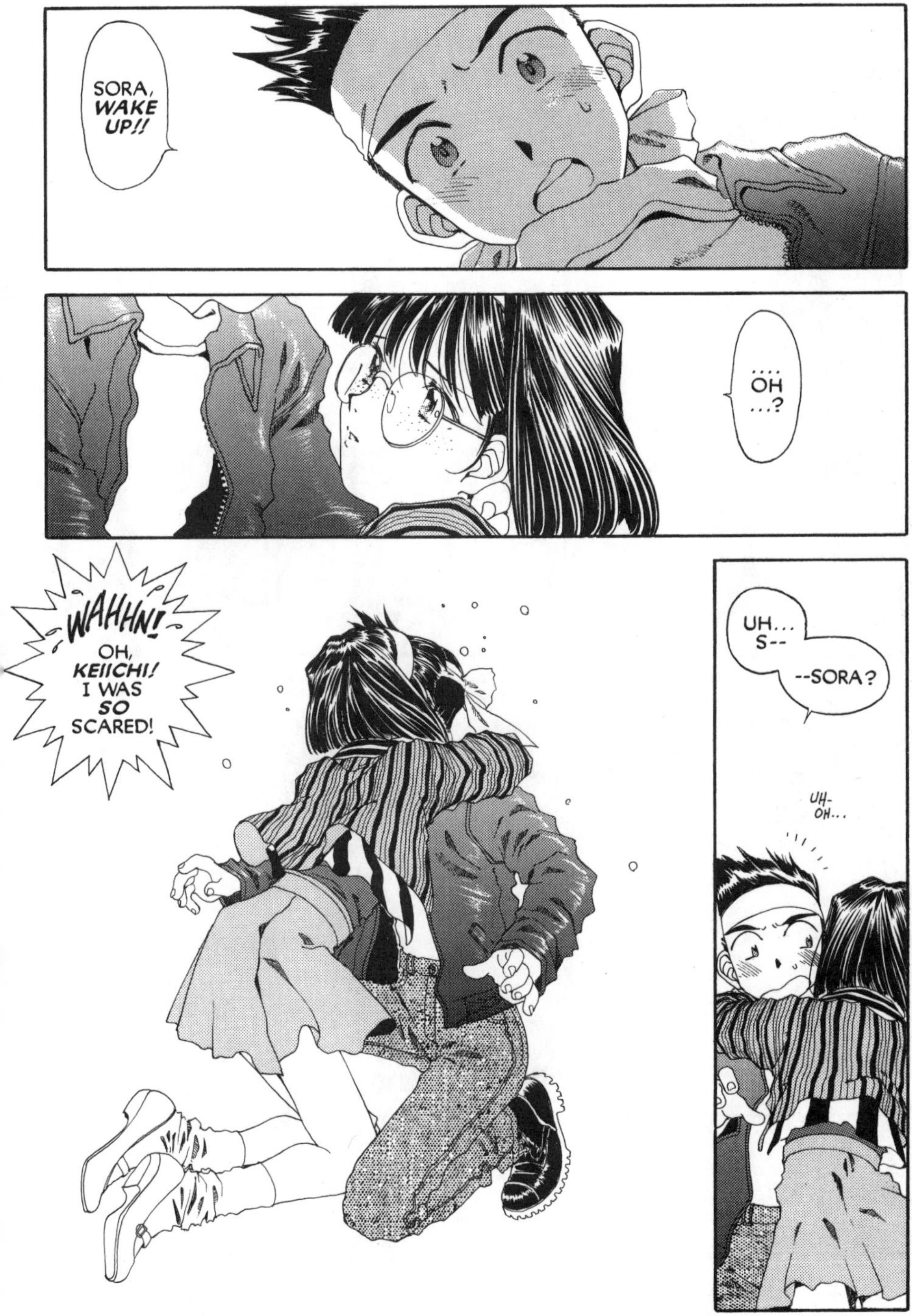
SORA, WAKE UP!!
....OH ...?
WAHHN! OH, KEIICHI! I WAS SO SCARED!
UH... S--
--SORA?
UH-OH...

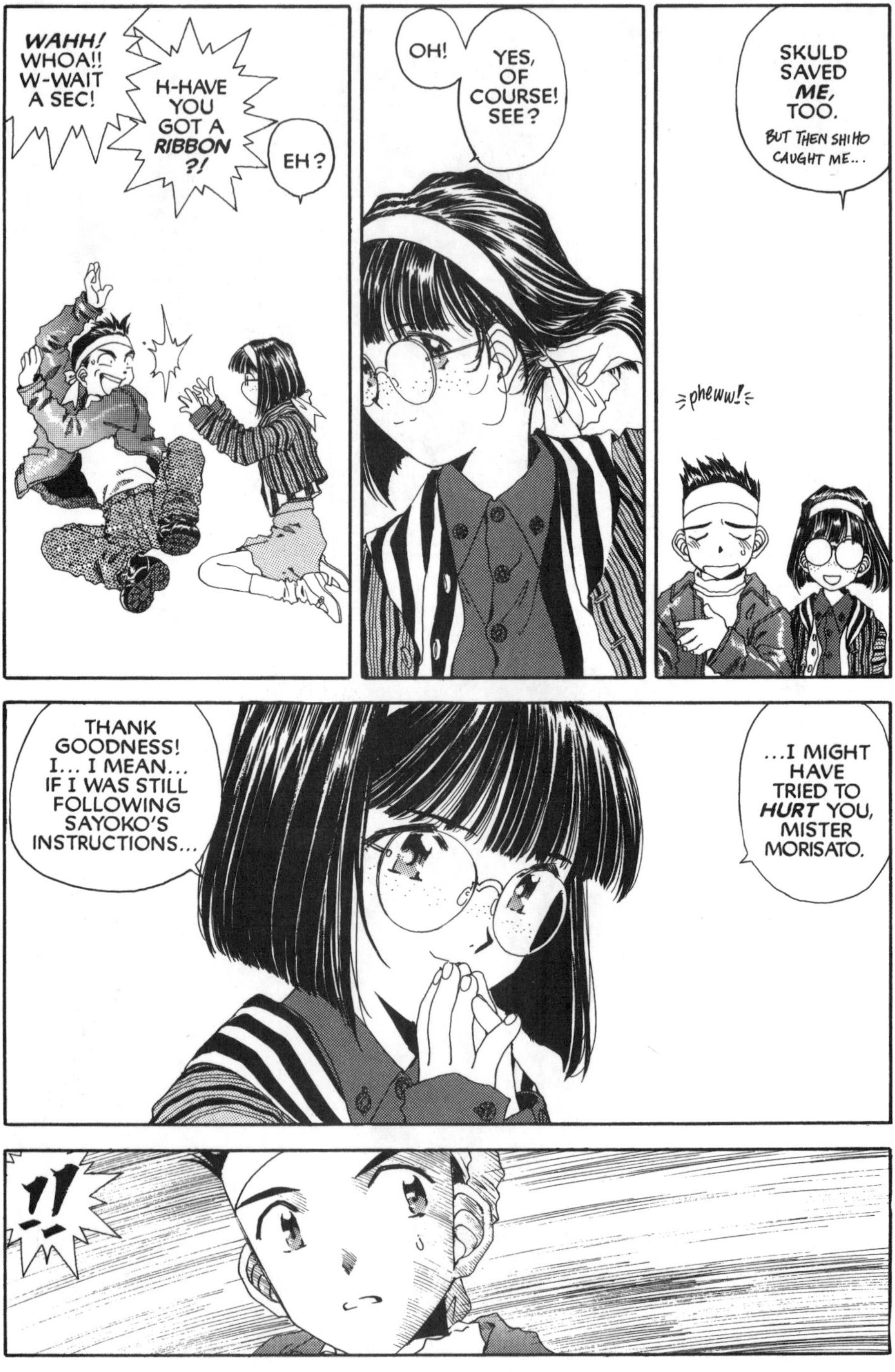
WAHH! WHOA!! W-WAIT A SEC!
H-HAVE YOU GOT A RIBBON ?!
EH?
OH!
YES, OF COURSE! SEE?
SKULD SAVED ME, TOO.
BUT THEN SHIHO CAUGHT ME...
phewww!
THANK GOODNESS! I... I MEAN... IF I WAS STILL FOLLOWING SAYOKO'S INSTRUCTIONS...
...I MIGHT HAVE TRIED TO HURT YOU, MISTER MORISATO.
!!

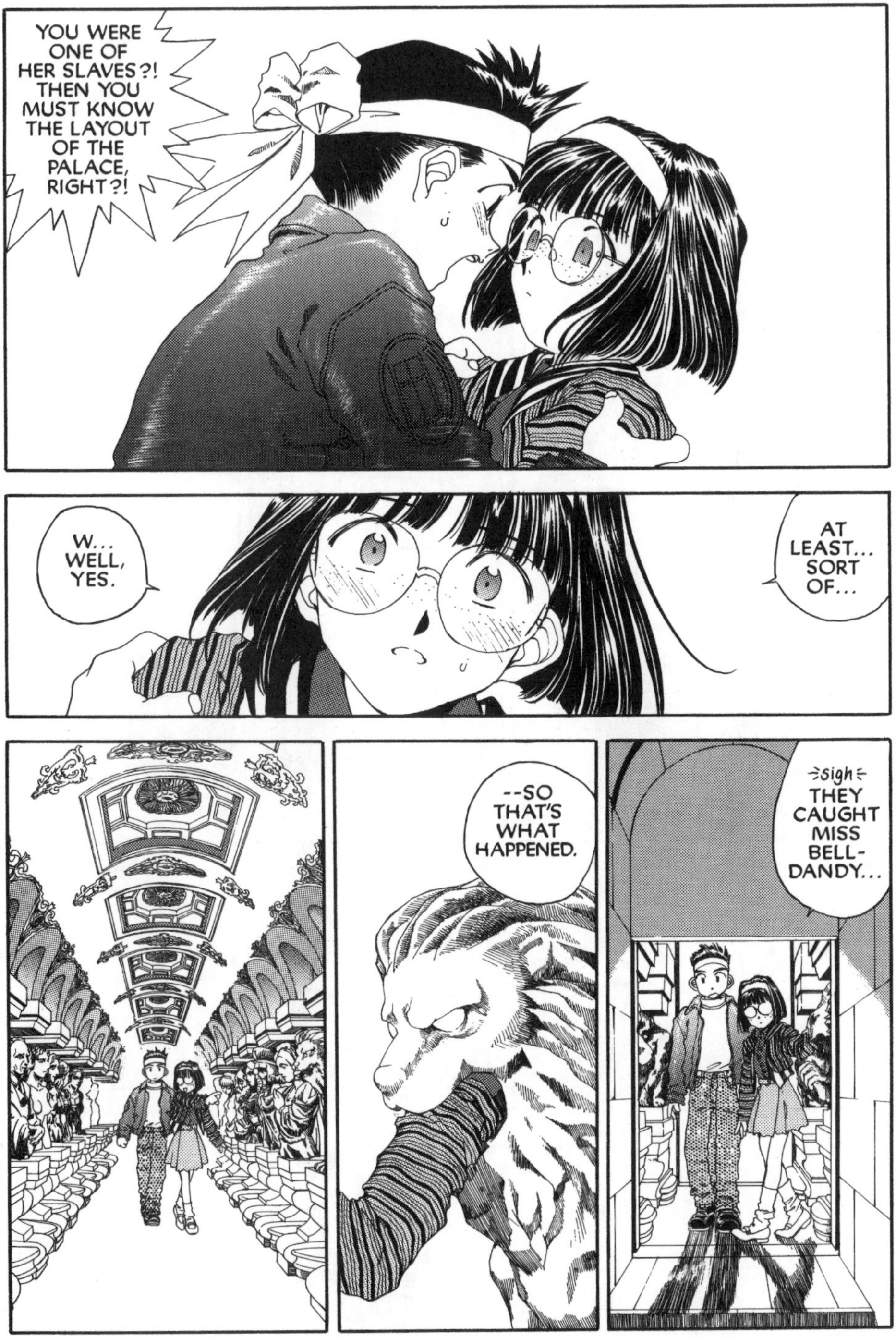
YOU WERE ONE OF HER SLAVES?! THEN YOU MUST KNOW THE LAYOUT OF THE PALACE, RIGHT?!
W... WELL, YES.
AT LEAST... SORT OF...
--SO THAT'S WHAT HAPPENED.
sigh
THEY CAUGHT MISS BELL-DANDY...

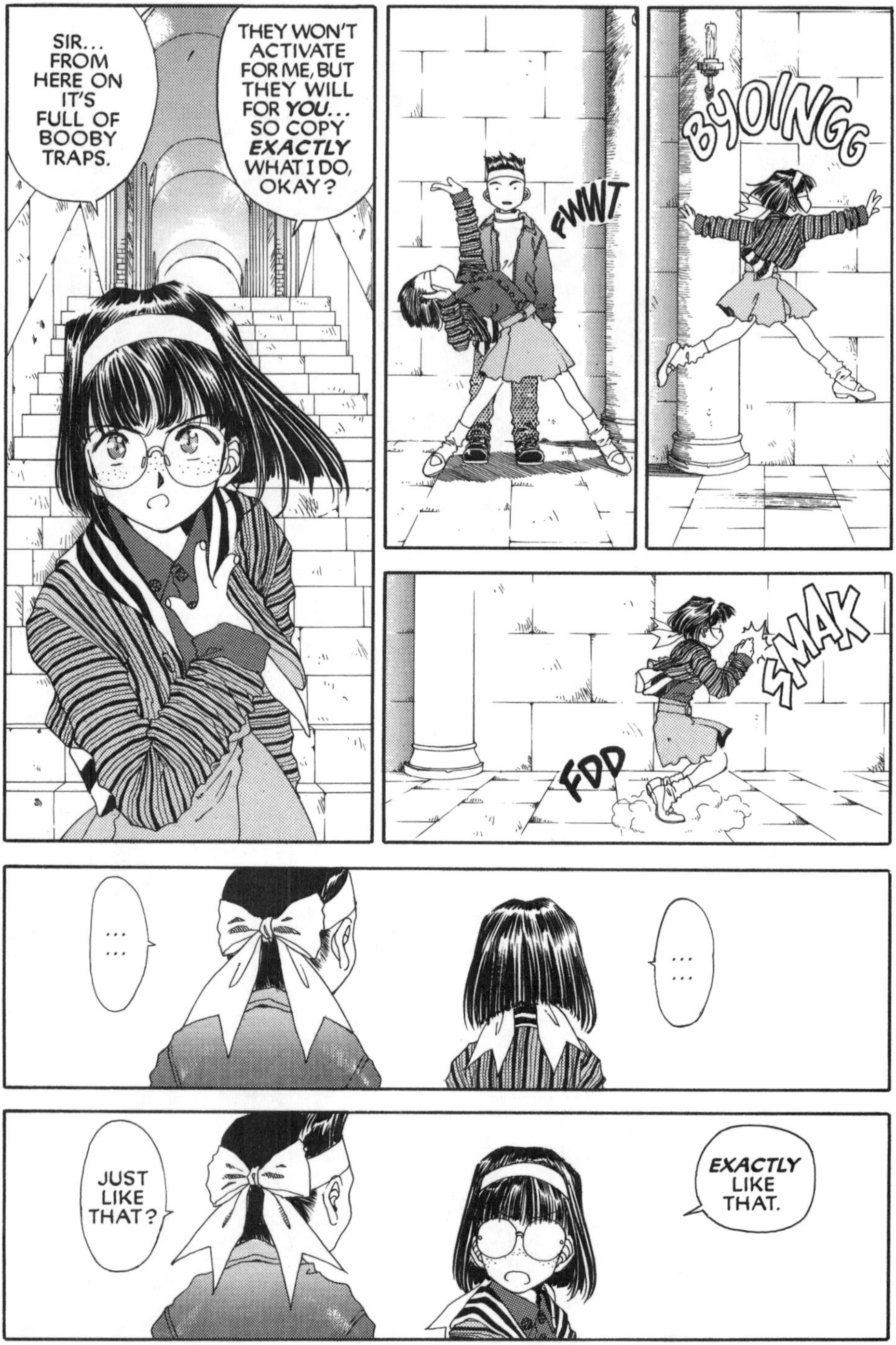
SIR... FROM HERE ON IT'S FULL OF BOOBY TRAPS.
THEY WON'T ACTIVATE FOR ME, BUT THEY WILL FOR *YOU*... SO COPY ***EXACTLY*** WHAT I DO, OKAY?
FWWT
BYOINGG
SMAK
FDD
......
......
JUST LIKE THAT?
EXACTLY LIKE THAT.

OKAYYY...

ARM UP KINDA LIKE SO... UH...

SIR, I REALLY MUST INSIST YOU TAKE THIS *QUITE SERIOUSLY.*

OKAY, OKAY.

SHEESH.

THEN... HERE WE GO!

WHOA ...?

WHSSH

FWTT
FWTT
FWTT
FWTT

YEEOW!

BYOINGG

KSHAK

FOO

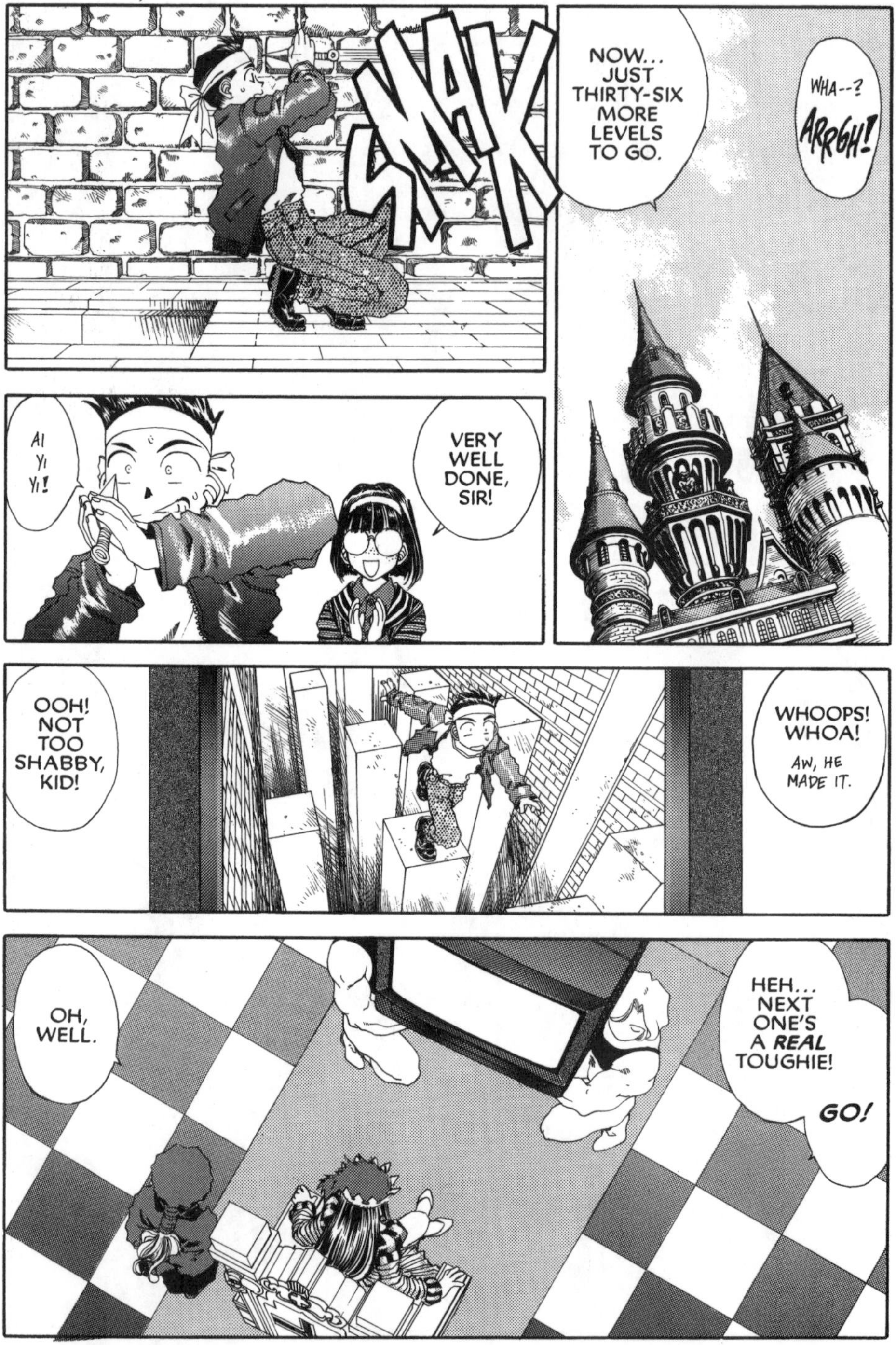
SMAK
AI YI YI!
VERY WELL DONE, SIR!
NOW... JUST THIRTY-SIX MORE LEVELS TO GO.
WHA--? ARRGH!
OOH! NOT TOO SHABBY, KID!
WHOOPS! WHOA!
AW, HE MADE IT.
OH, WELL.
HEH... NEXT ONE'S A *REAL* TOUGHIE!
GO!

AAH?! LUCK! PURE LUCK!

OH, PHOOEY!

MY LADY SAYOKO...

...WHAT DO YOU PLAN TO DO WITH THE PRISONER BELL-DANDY?

I GAVE HER TO SOME OF MY BOYS TO PLAY WITH.

BUT IF YOU WANT HER, GO AHEAD. I'M BUSY RIGHT NOW.

OOH! GOOD ONE!

THANK YOU, YOUR MAJESTY!

EEEK! NOT THAT ONE!

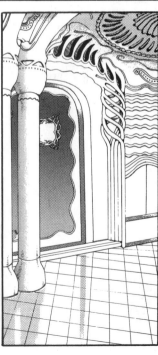

Imperial Model
Club Research
Center

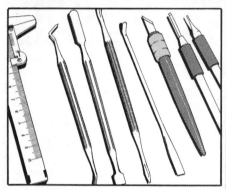

DIRECTOR, SIR! SILICONE MOLDING COMPOUND PREPARATION IS COMPLETE!

EXCELLENT!

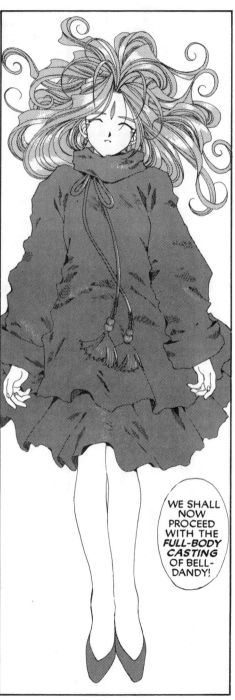

WE SHALL NOW PROCEED WITH THE *FULL-BODY CASTING* OF BELL-DANDY!

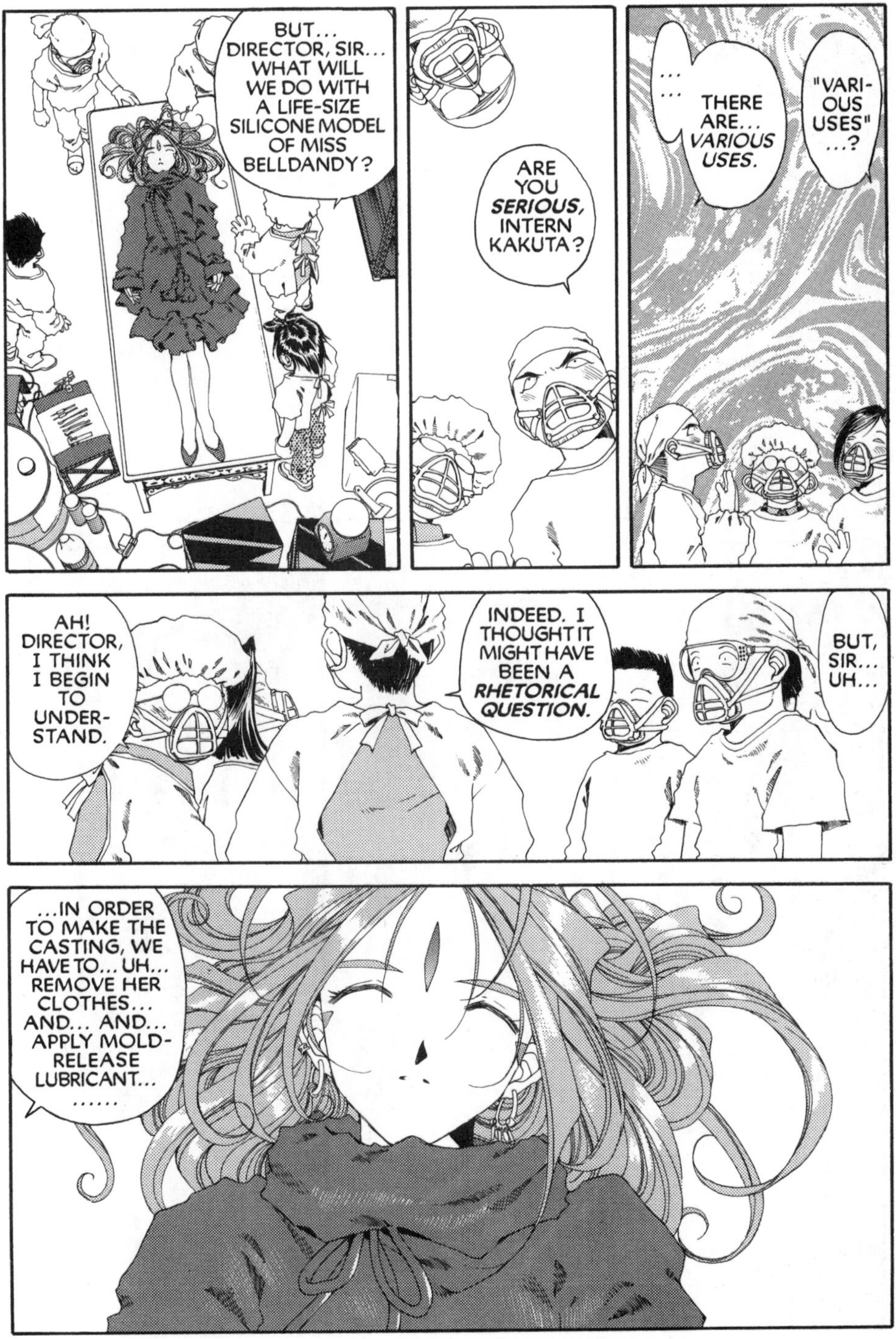
BUT... DIRECTOR, SIR... WHAT WILL WE DO WITH A LIFE-SIZE SILICONE MODEL OF MISS BELLDANDY?
ARE YOU *SERIOUS,* INTERN KAKUTA?
...
...
THERE ARE... *VARIOUS USES.*
"VARIOUS USES" ...?
AH! DIRECTOR, I THINK I BEGIN TO UNDERSTAND.
INDEED. I THOUGHT IT MIGHT HAVE BEEN A *RHETORICAL QUESTION.*
BUT, SIR... UH...
...IN ORDER TO MAKE THE CASTING, WE HAVE TO... UH... REMOVE HER CLOTHES... AND... AND... APPLY MOLD-RELEASE LUBRICANT... ......

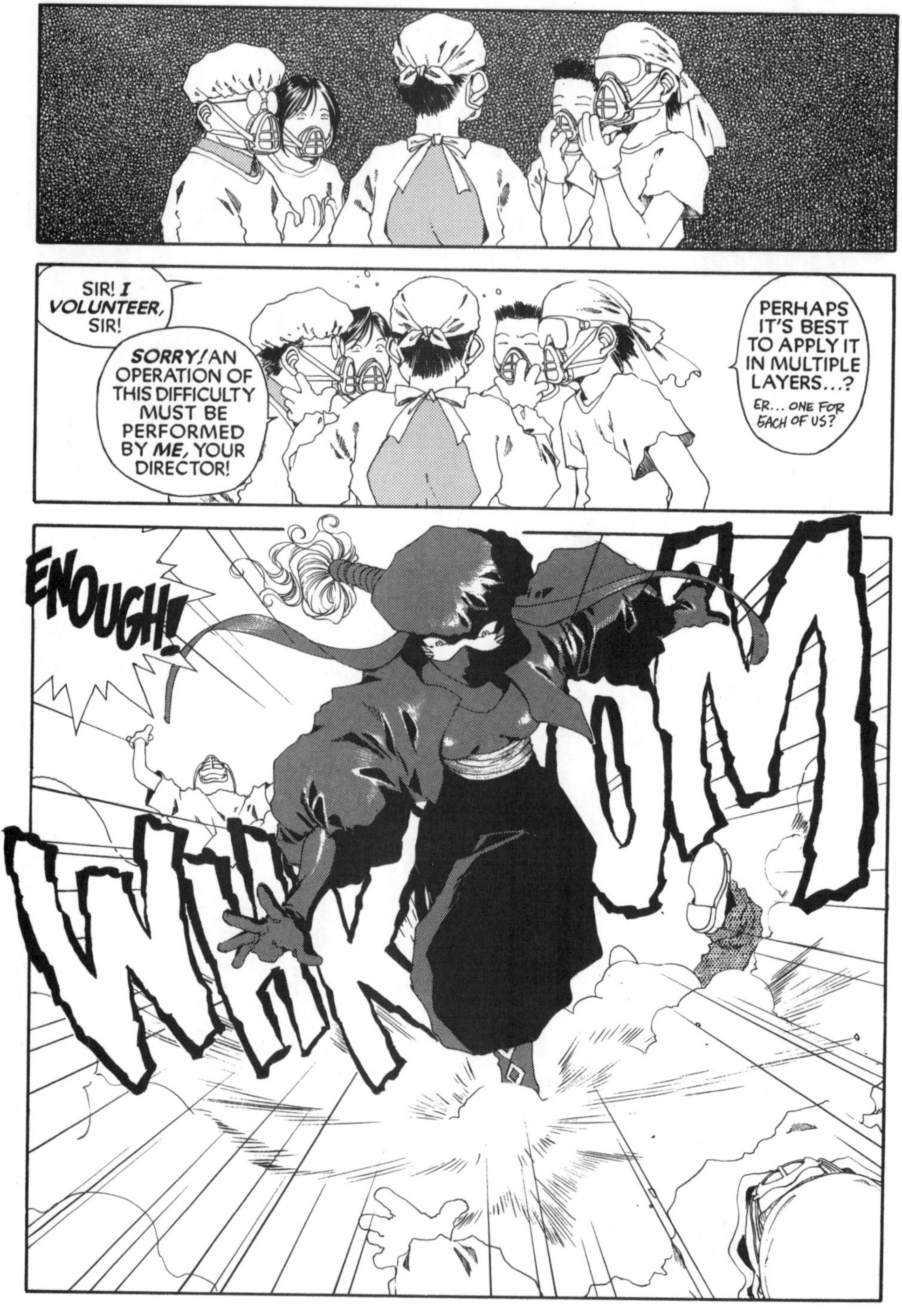
SIR! *I VOLUNTEER,* SIR!
SORRY! AN OPERATION OF THIS DIFFICULTY MUST BE PERFORMED BY *ME,* YOUR DIRECTOR!
PERHAPS IT'S BEST TO APPLY IT IN MULTIPLE LAYERS...?
ER... ONE FOR EACH OF US?
ENOUGH!

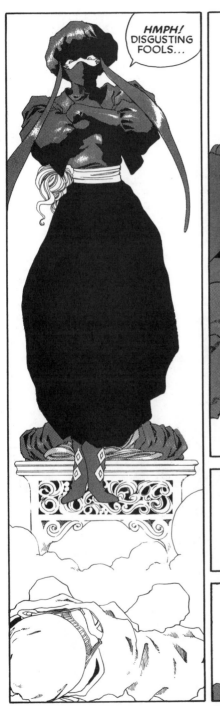

HMPH! DISGUSTING FOOLS...

HEH, HEH... TIME TO *WAKE,* MY SLEEPING BEAUTY!

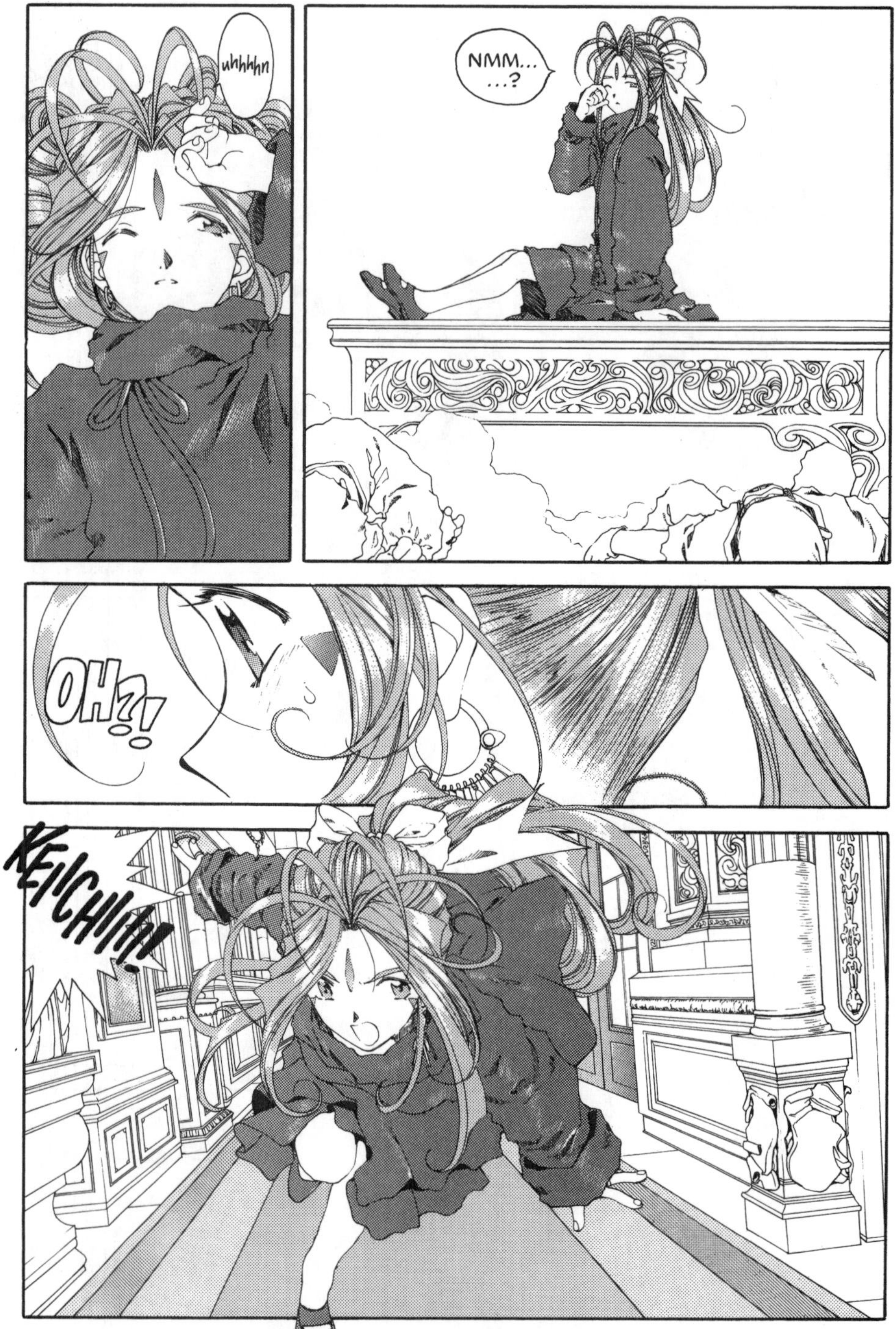
uhhhhn
NMM... ...?
OH?!
KEIICHIII!!

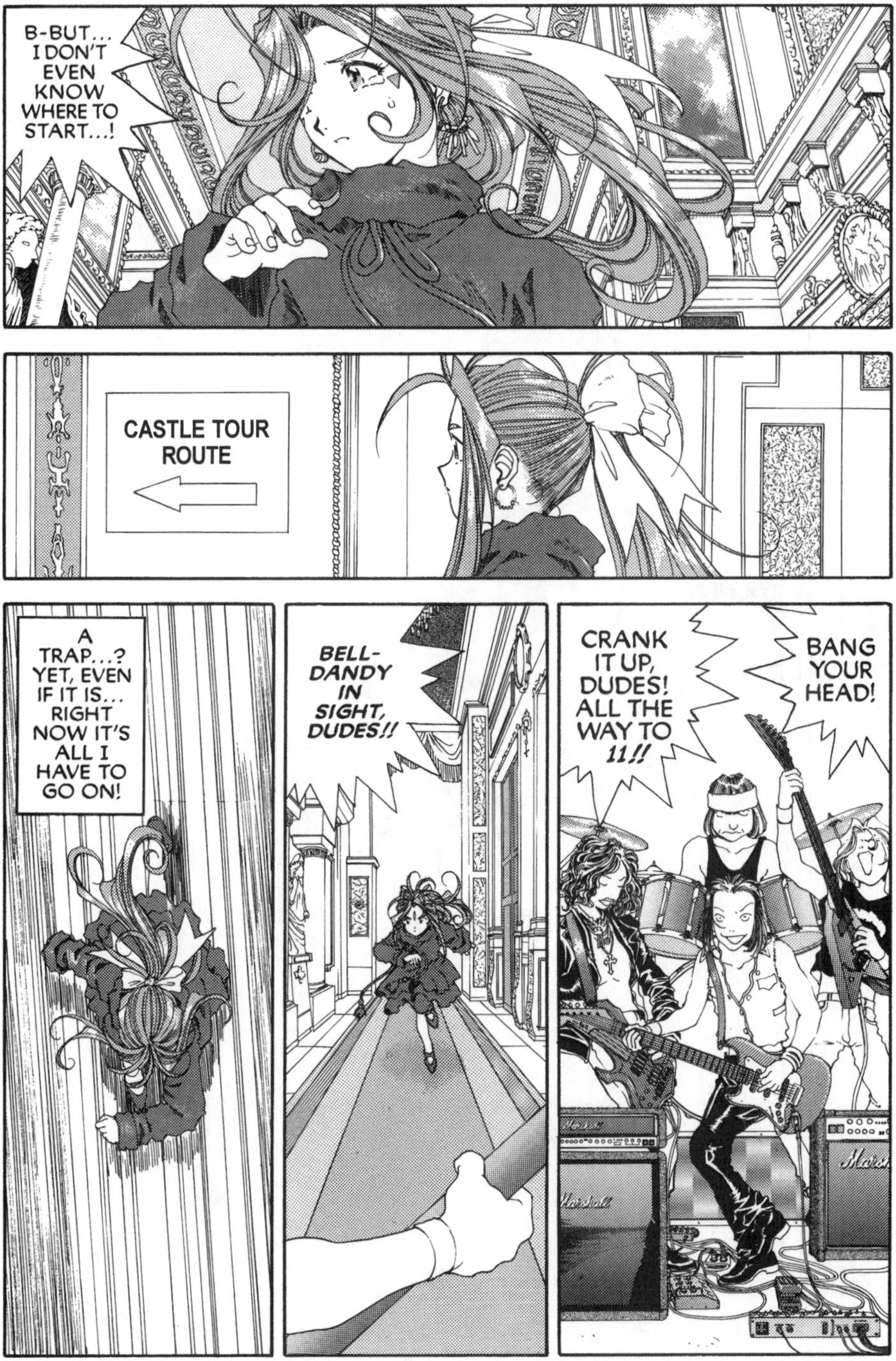
B-BUT... I DON'T EVEN KNOW WHERE TO START...!
CASTLE TOUR ROUTE
A TRAP...? YET, EVEN IF IT IS... RIGHT NOW IT'S ALL I HAVE TO GO ON!
BELL-DANDY IN SIGHT, DUDES!!
CRANK IT UP, DUDES! ALL THE WAY TO *11!!*
BANG YOUR HEAD!

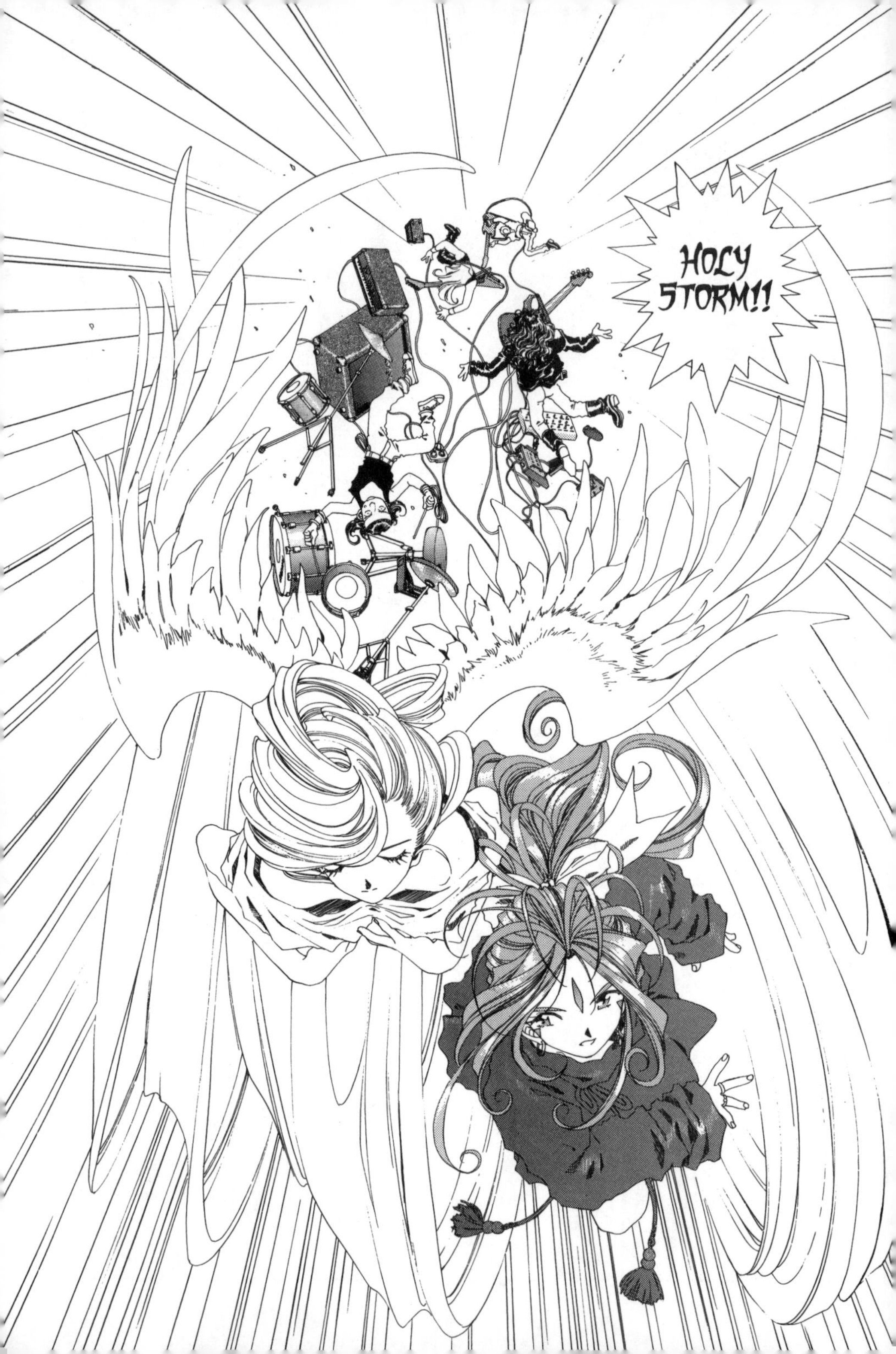
HOLY STORM!!

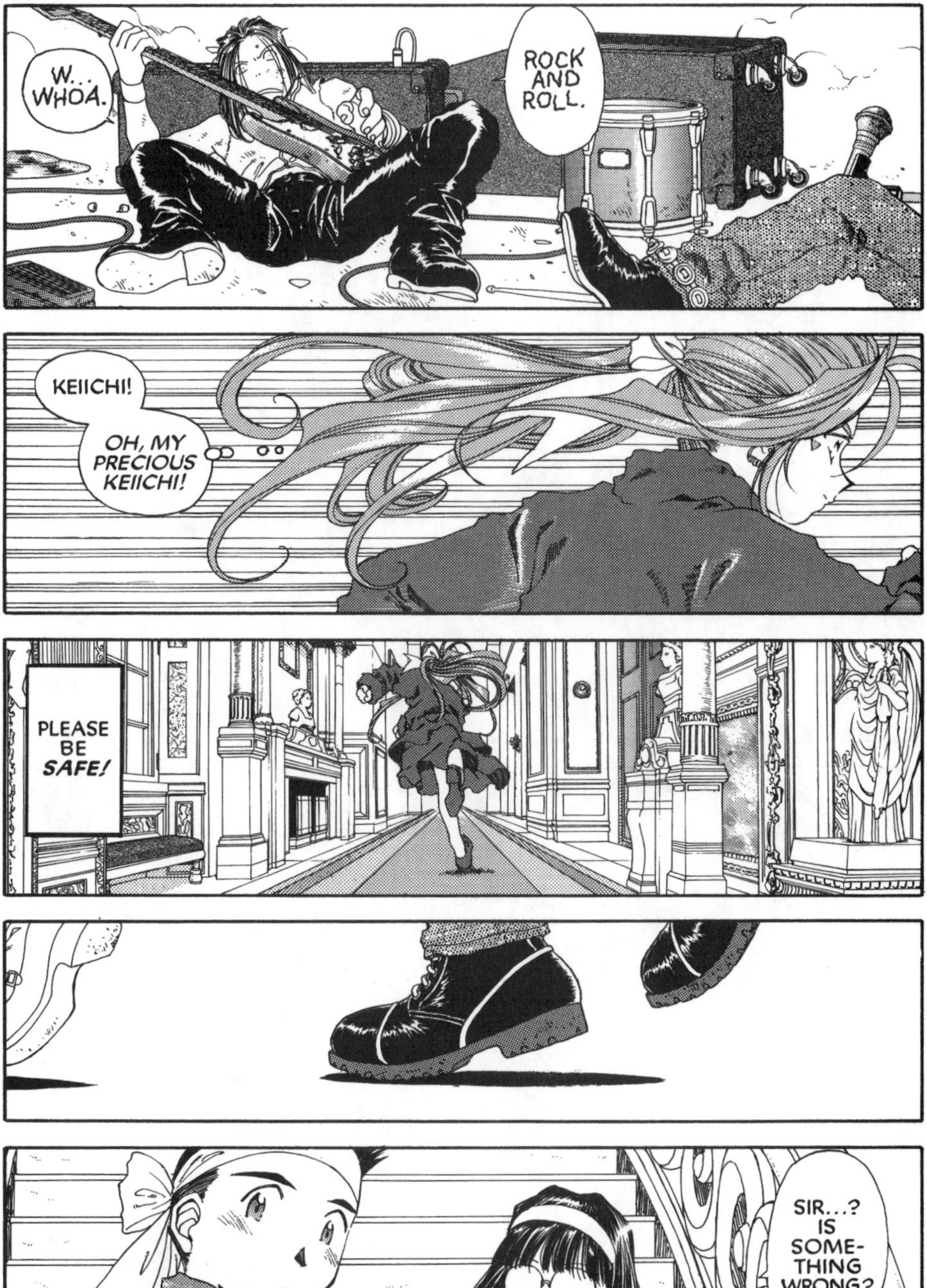
W... WHOA.
ROCK AND ROLL.
KEIICHI!
OH, MY PRECIOUS KEIICHI!
PLEASE BE ***SAFE!***
SIR...? IS SOME-THING WRONG?

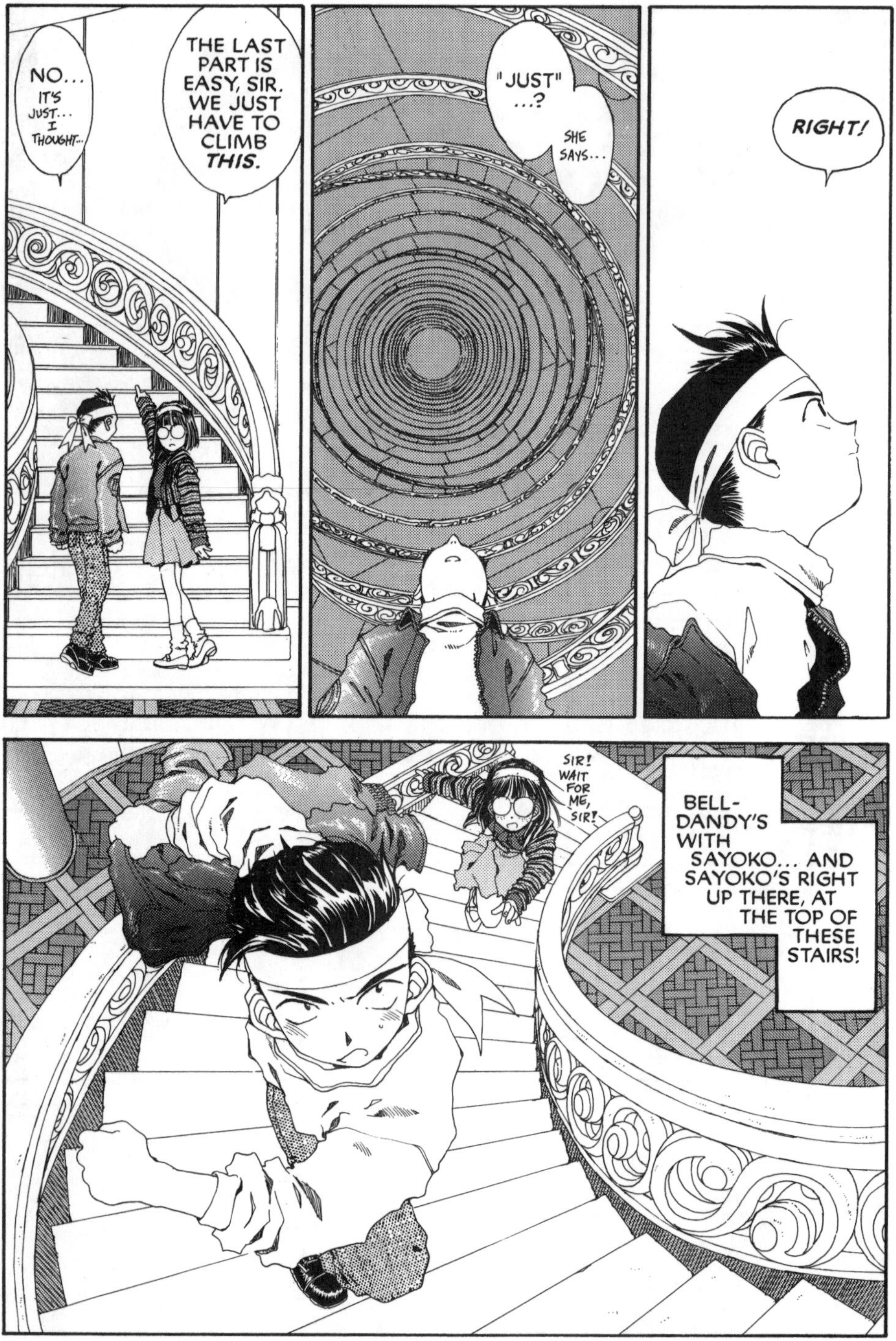
NO... IT'S JUST... I THOUGHT...
THE LAST PART IS EASY, SIR. WE JUST HAVE TO CLIMB *THIS*.
"JUST" ...?
SHE SAYS...
RIGHT!
SIR! WAIT FOR ME, SIR!
BELL-DANDY'S WITH SAYOKO... AND SAYOKO'S RIGHT UP THERE, AT THE TOP OF THESE STAIRS!

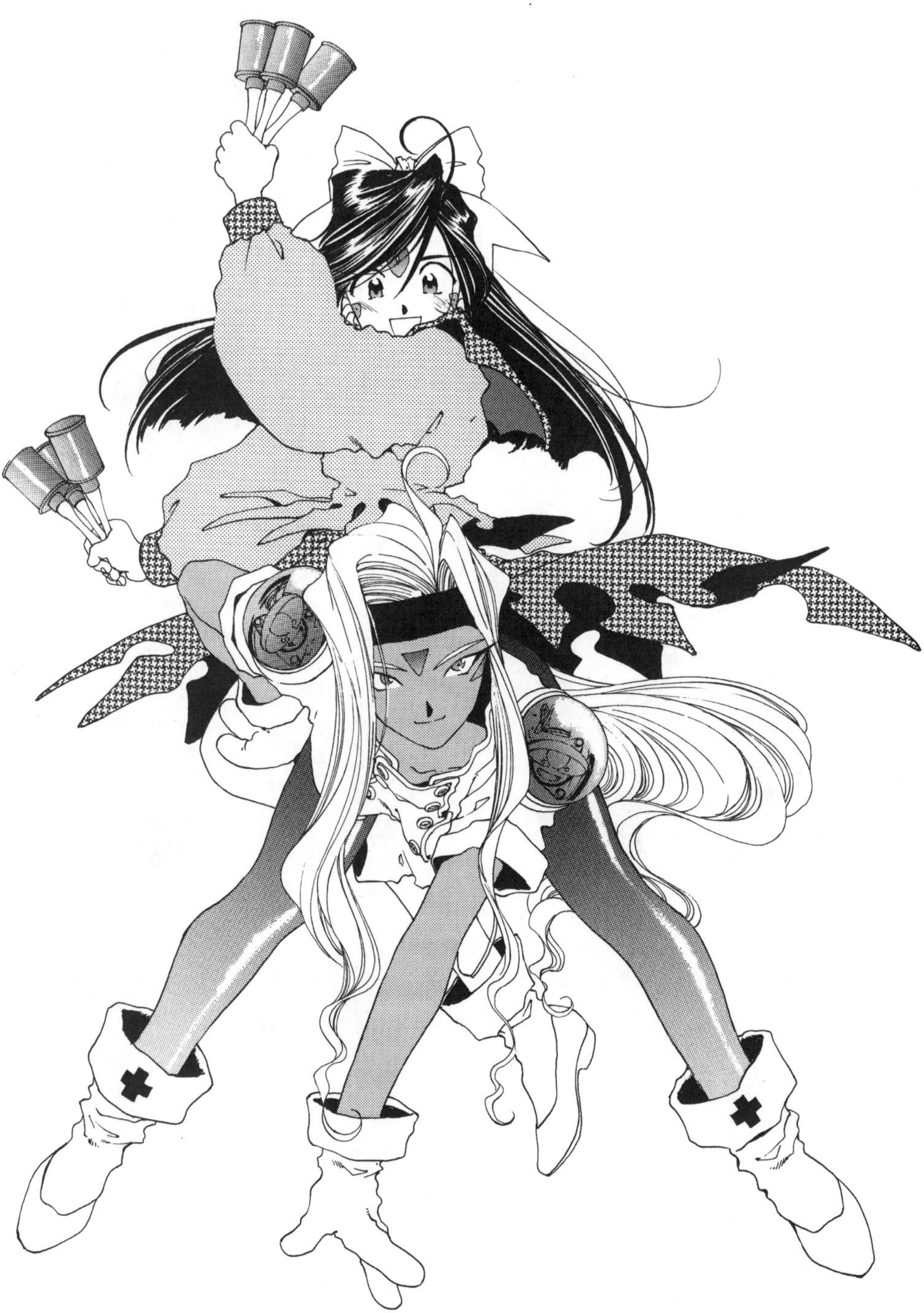

At Sayoko's Side

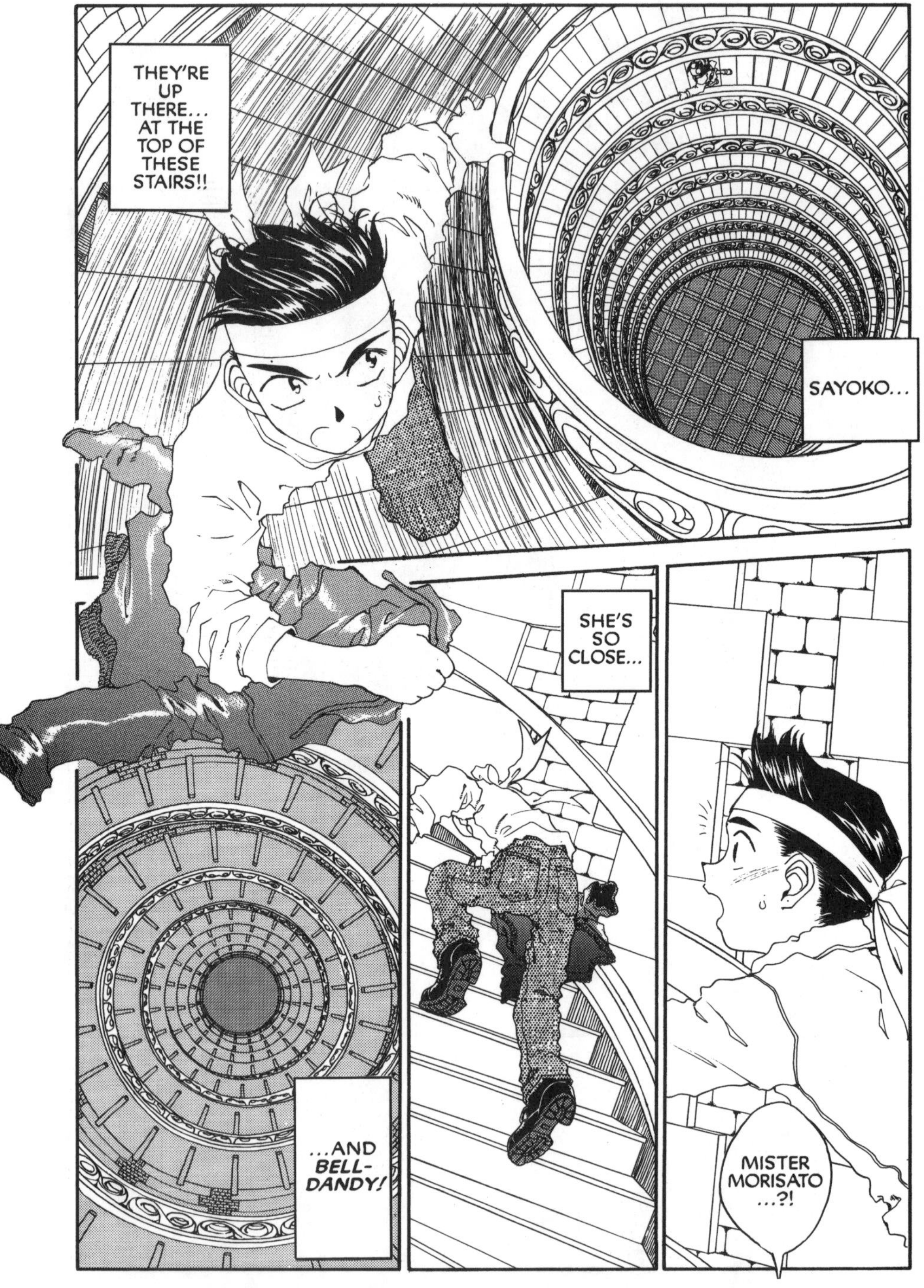
THEY'RE UP THERE... AT THE TOP OF THESE STAIRS!!
SAYOKO...
...AND BELL-DANDY!
SHE'S SO CLOSE...
MISTER MORISATO ...?!

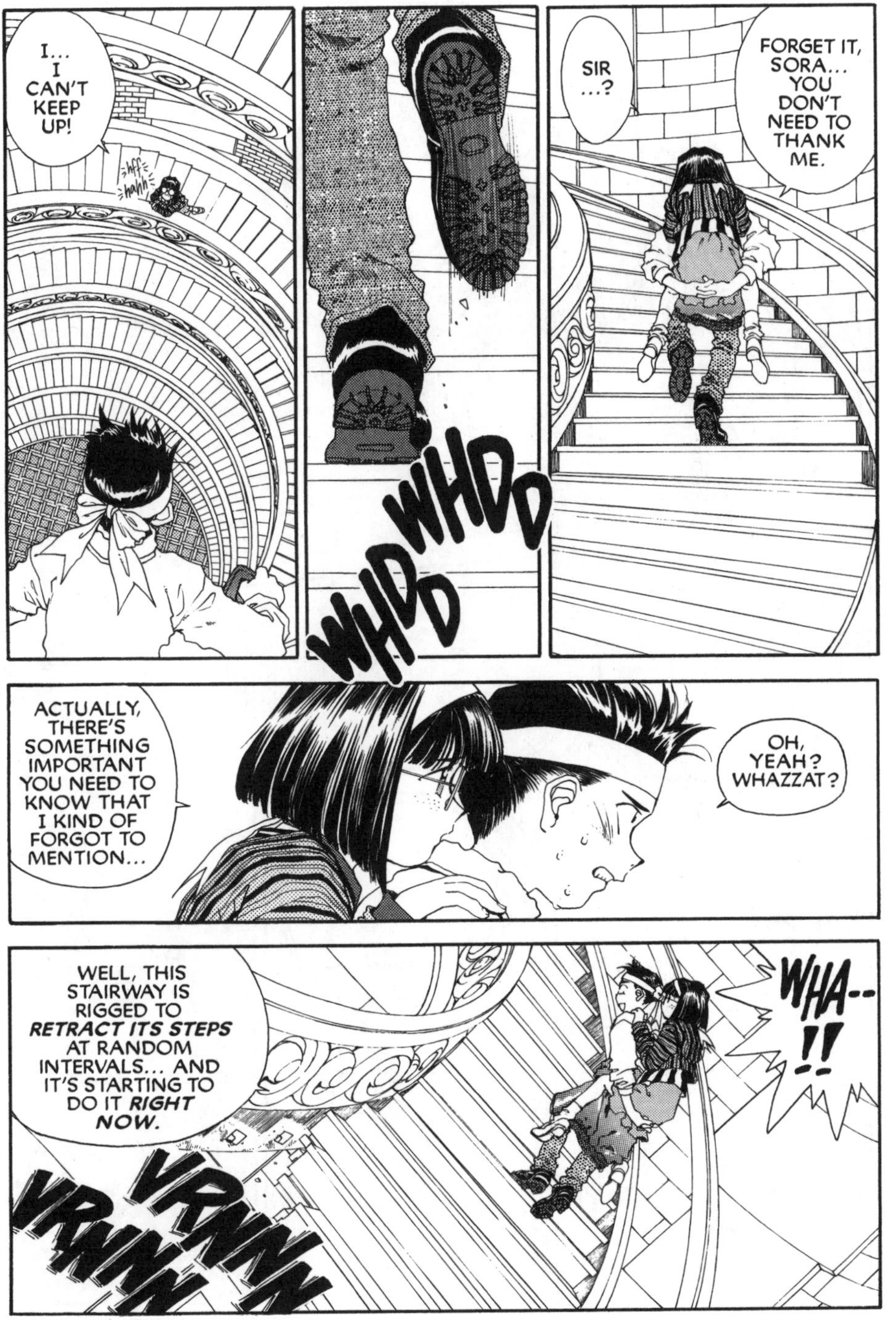
I... I CAN'T KEEP UP!
hff hahh
SIR ...?
FORGET IT, SORA... YOU DON'T NEED TO THANK ME.
WHDD WHDD
ACTUALLY, THERE'S SOMETHING IMPORTANT YOU NEED TO KNOW THAT I KIND OF FORGOT TO MENTION...
OH, YEAH? WHAZZAT?
WELL, THIS STAIRWAY IS RIGGED TO ***RETRACT ITS STEPS*** AT RANDOM INTERVALS... AND IT'S STARTING TO DO IT ***RIGHT NOW.***
WHA--!!
VRNNN VRNNN

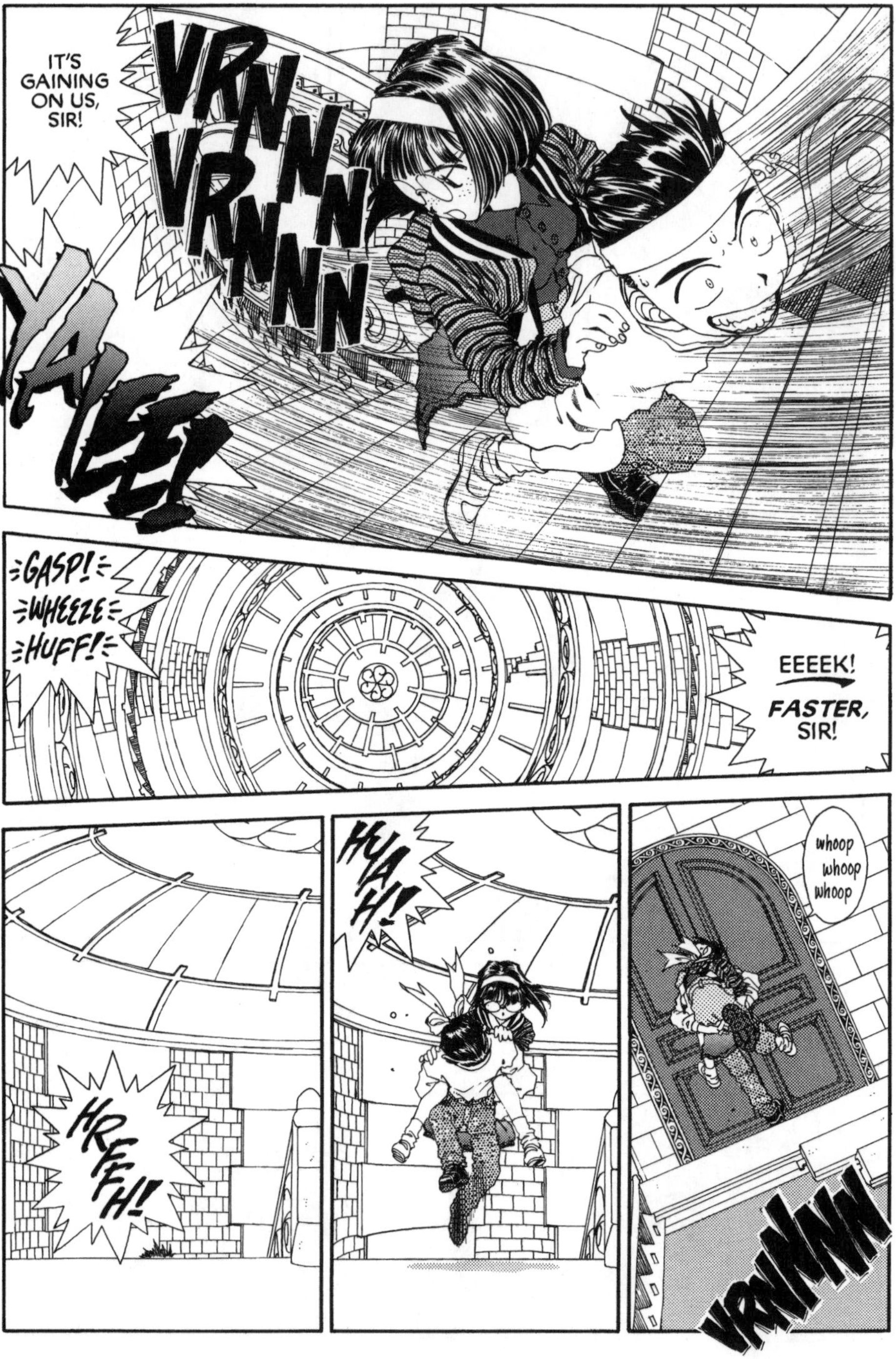
IT'S GAINING ON US, SIR!
VRNNNN
VRNNNN
YAIEE!
GASP!
WHEEZE
HUFF!
EEEEK!
FASTER, SIR!
HRFFH!
HYAH!
whoop whoop whoop
VRNNNN

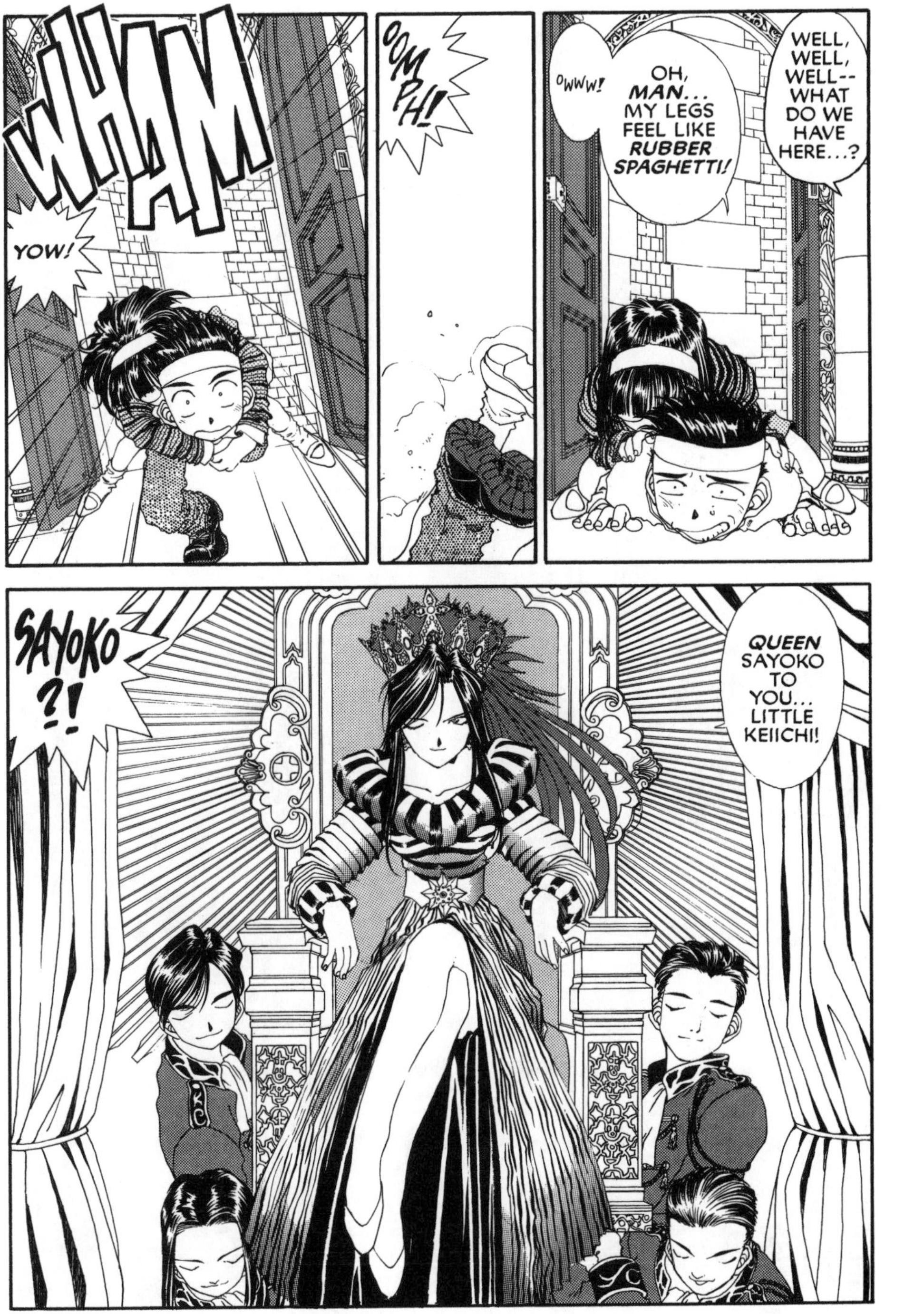
WHAM
YOW!
OOMPH!
OWWW!
OH, MAN... MY LEGS FEEL LIKE RUBBER SPAGHETTI!
WELL, WELL, WELL-- WHAT DO WE HAVE HERE...?
SAYOKO ?!
QUEEN SAYOKO TO YOU... LITTLE KEIICHI!

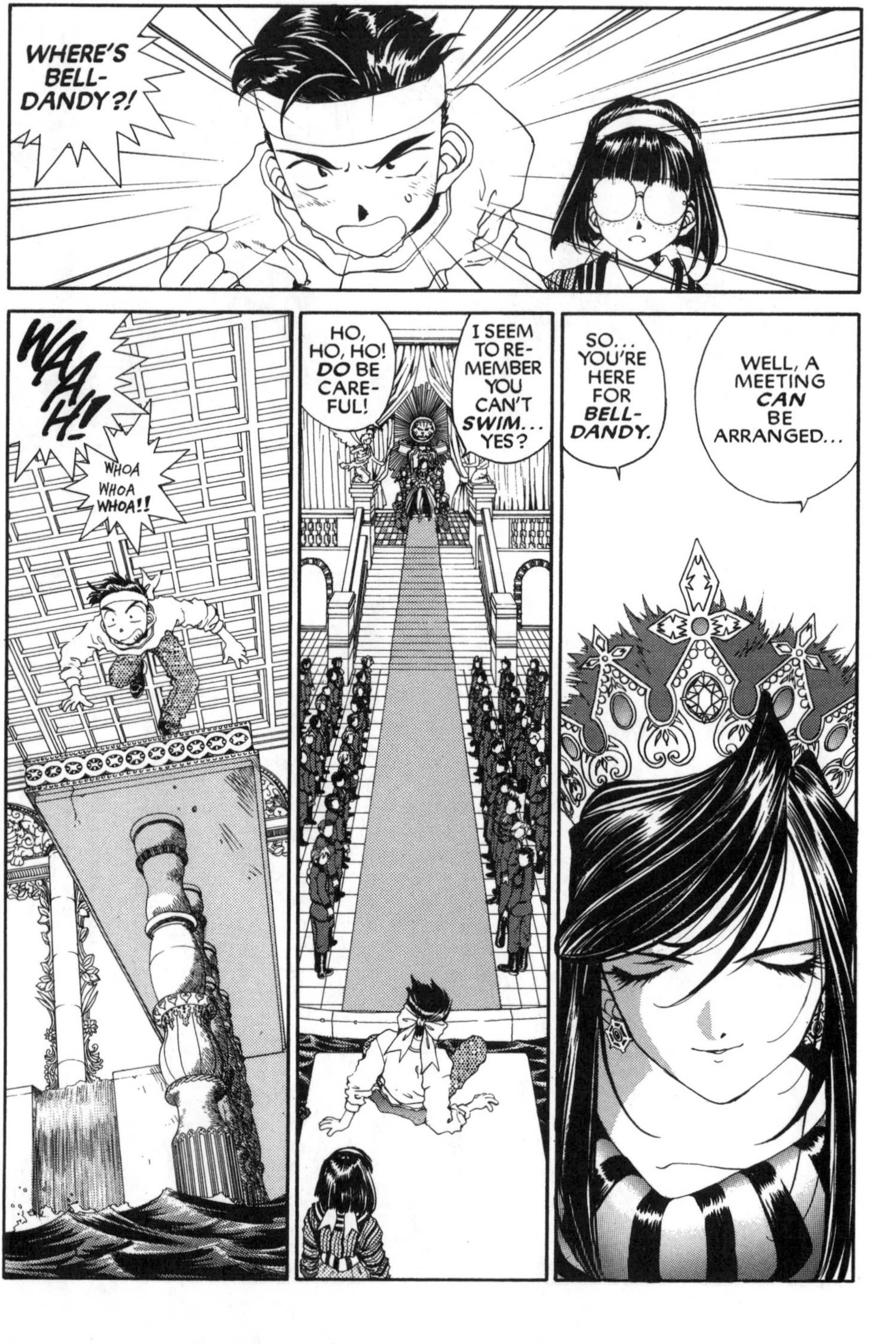
WHERE'S BELL-DANDY?!
WAAAH!!
WHOA WHOA WHOA!!
HO, HO, HO! DO BE CARE-FUL!
I SEEM TO RE-MEMBER YOU CAN'T SWIM... YES?
SO... YOU'RE HERE FOR BELL-DANDY.
WELL, A MEETING CAN BE ARRANGED...

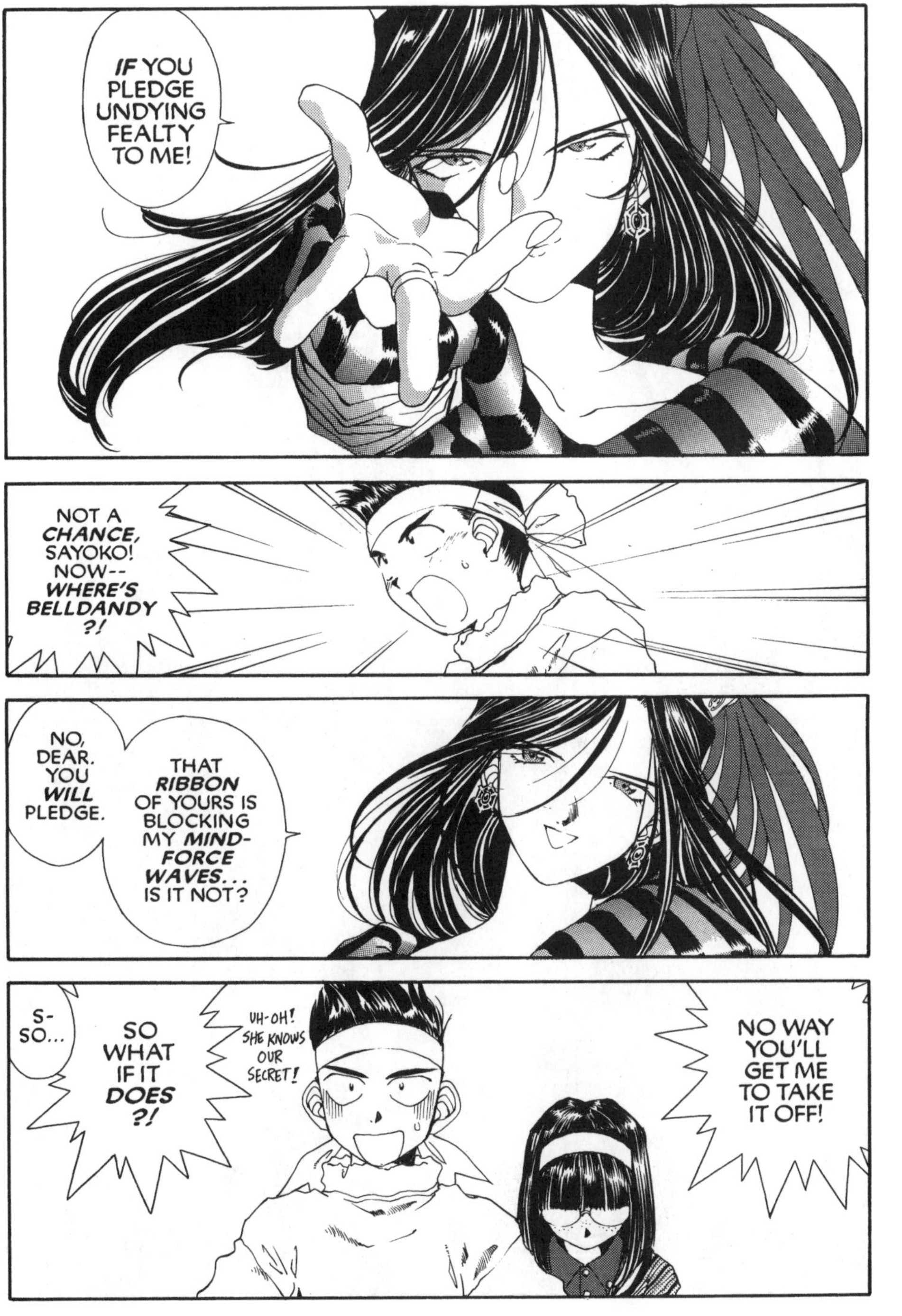
IF YOU PLEDGE UNDYING FEALTY TO ME!
NOT A CHANCE, SAYOKO! NOW-- WHERE'S BELLDANDY ?!
NO, DEAR. YOU WILL PLEDGE.
THAT RIBBON OF YOURS IS BLOCKING MY MIND-FORCE WAVES... IS IT NOT?
S- SO...
SO WHAT IF IT DOES ?!
UH-OH! SHE KNOWS OUR SECRET!
NO WAY YOU'LL GET ME TO TAKE IT OFF!

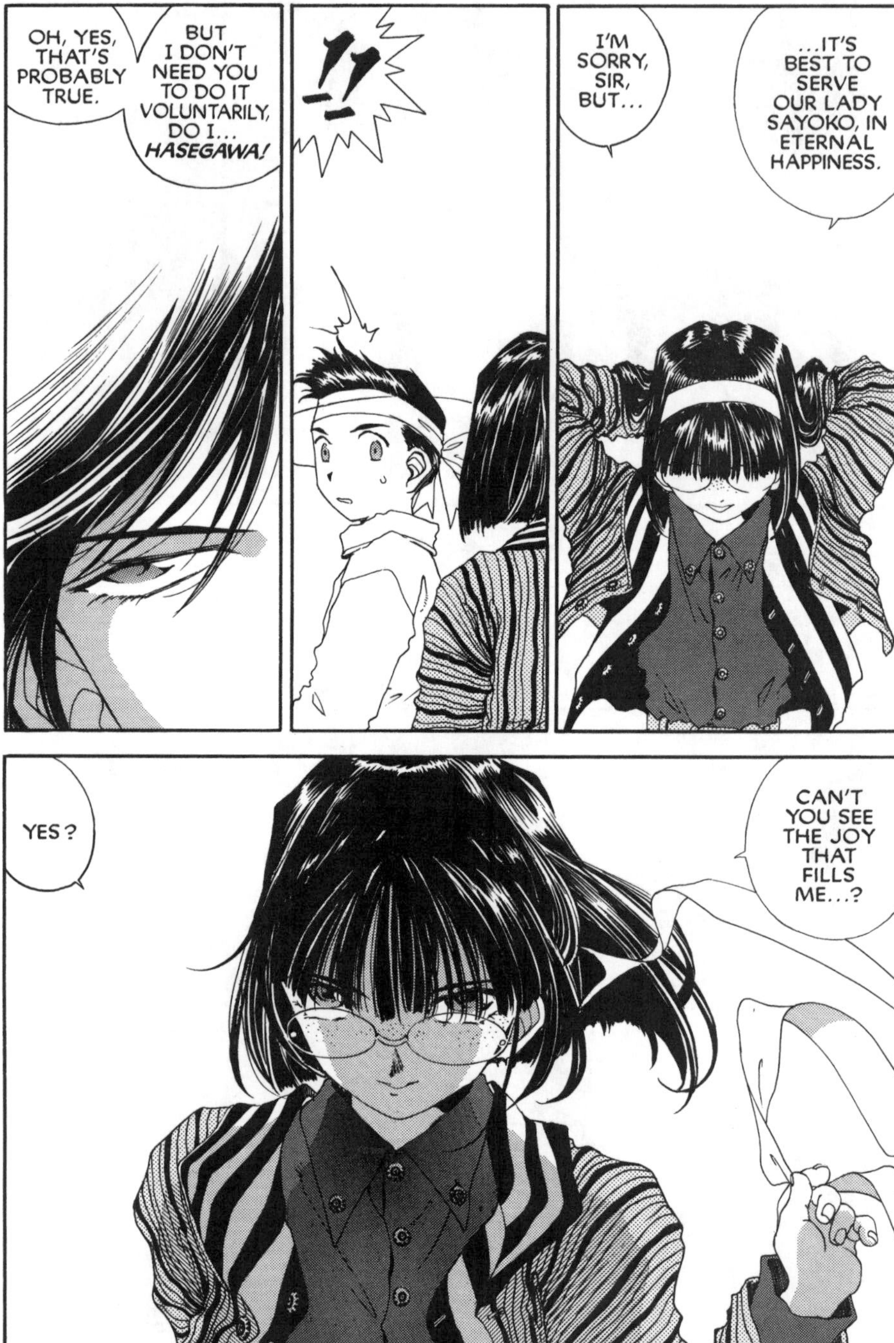
OH, YES, THAT'S PROBABLY TRUE.
BUT I DON'T NEED YOU TO DO IT VOLUNTARILY, DO I... *HASEGAWA!*
!!
I'M SORRY, SIR, BUT...
...IT'S BEST TO SERVE OUR LADY SAYOKO, IN ETERNAL HAPPINESS.
YES?
CAN'T YOU SEE THE JOY THAT FILLS ME...?

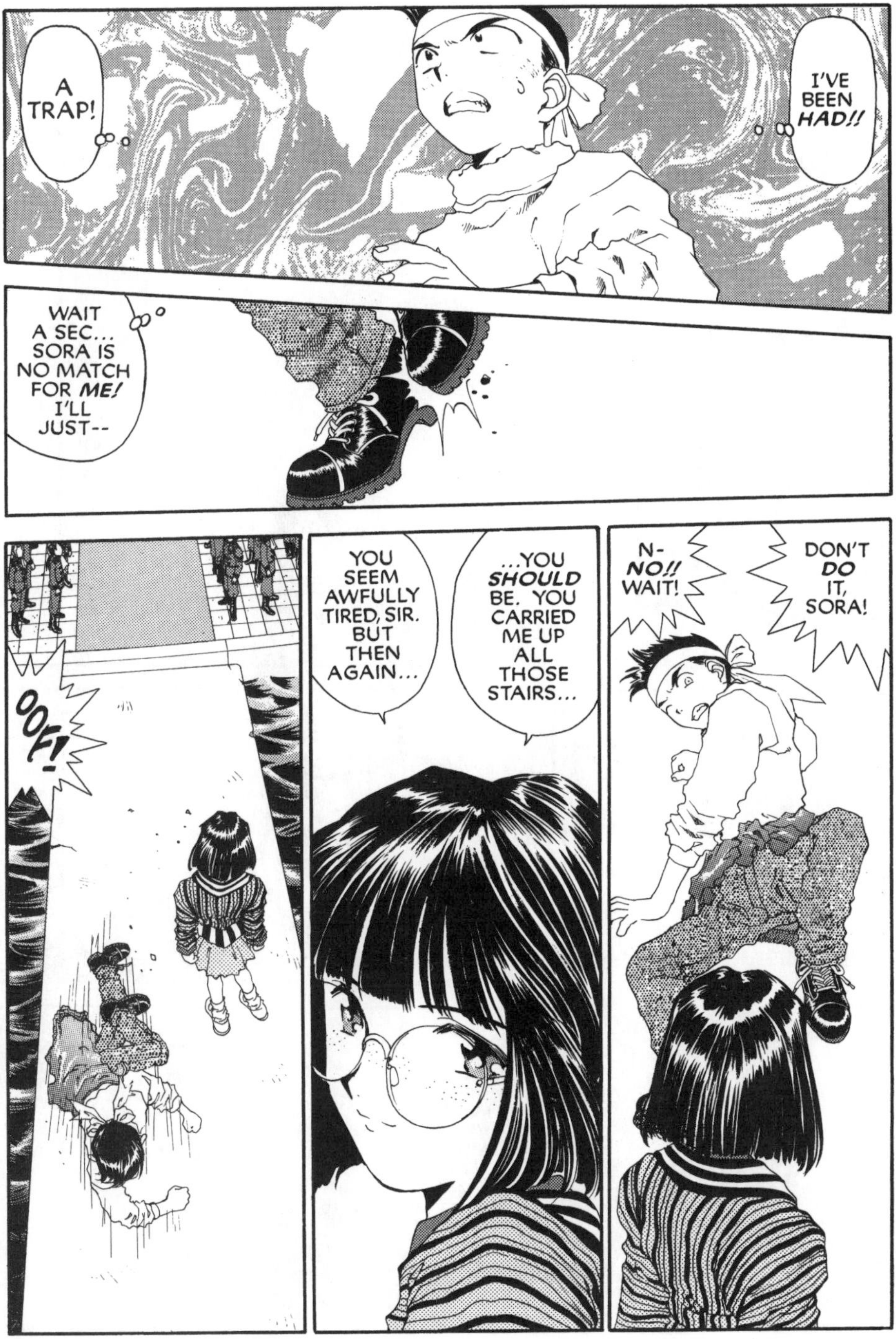
A TRAP!
I'VE BEEN HAD!!
WAIT A SEC... SORA IS NO MATCH FOR ME! I'LL JUST--
OOF!
YOU SEEM AWFULLY TIRED, SIR. BUT THEN AGAIN...
...YOU SHOULD BE. YOU CARRIED ME UP ALL THOSE STAIRS...
N- NO!! WAIT!
DON'T DO IT, SORA!

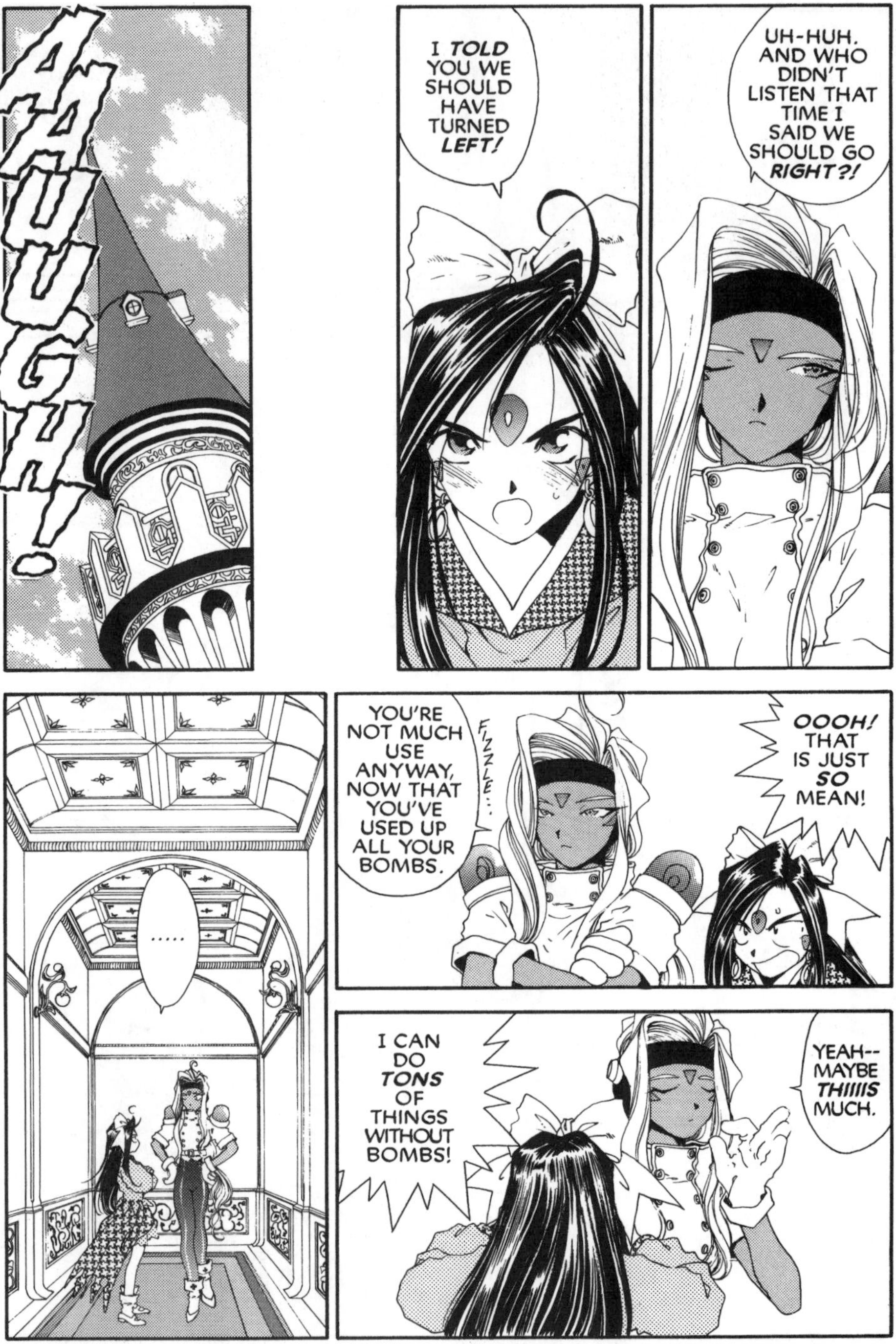
AAUUGH!
I TOLD YOU WE SHOULD HAVE TURNED LEFT!
UH-HUH. AND WHO DIDN'T LISTEN THAT TIME I SAID WE SHOULD GO RIGHT?!
......
YOU'RE NOT MUCH USE ANYWAY, NOW THAT YOU'VE USED UP ALL YOUR BOMBS.
FIZZLE...
OOOH! THAT IS JUST SO MEAN!
I CAN DO TONS OF THINGS WITHOUT BOMBS!
YEAH-- MAYBE THIIIIS MUCH.

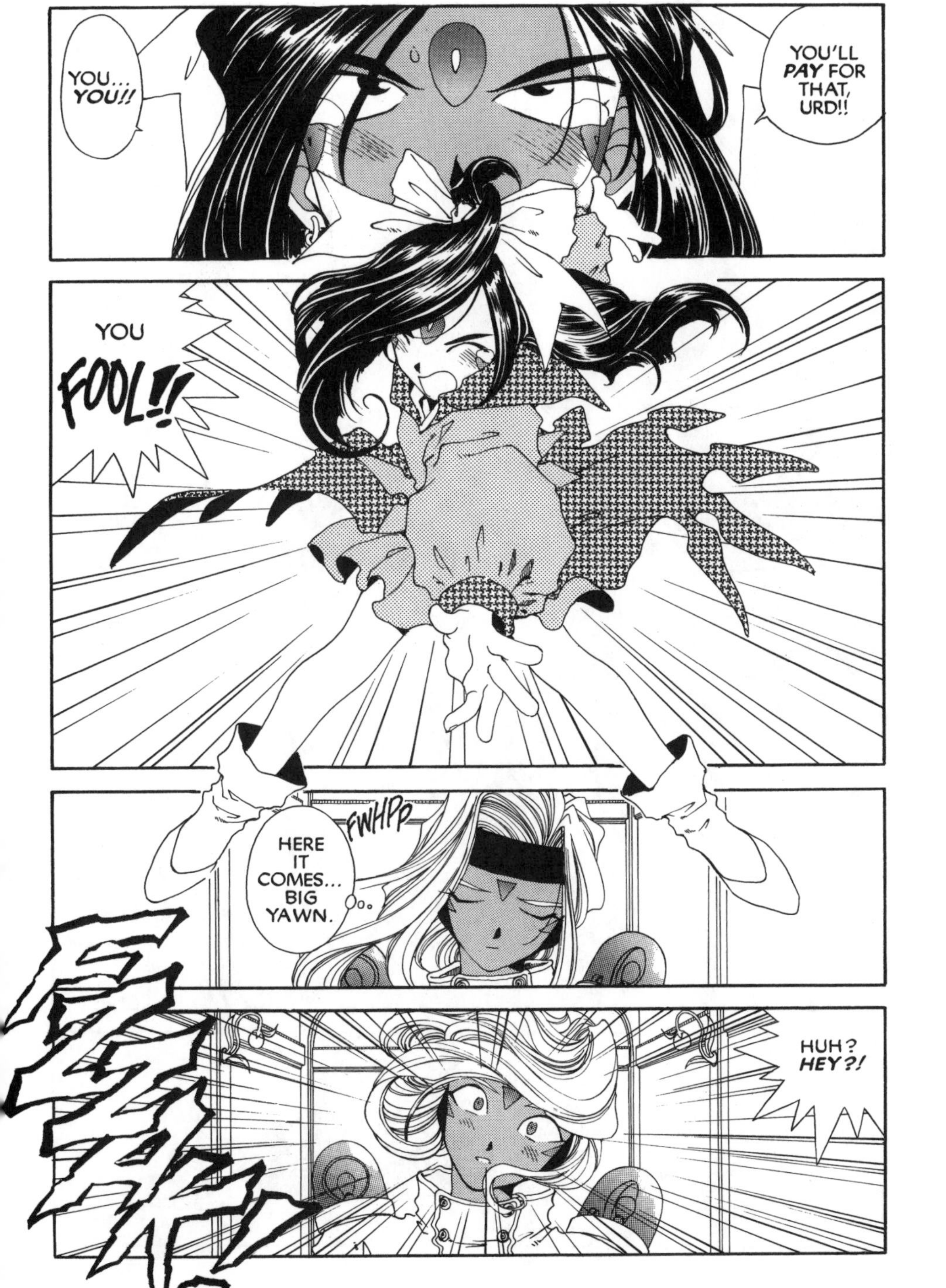
YOU... *YOU!!*
YOU'LL *PAY* FOR THAT, URD!!
YOU FOOL!!
FWHPP
HERE IT COMES... BIG YAWN.
HUH? *HEY?!*

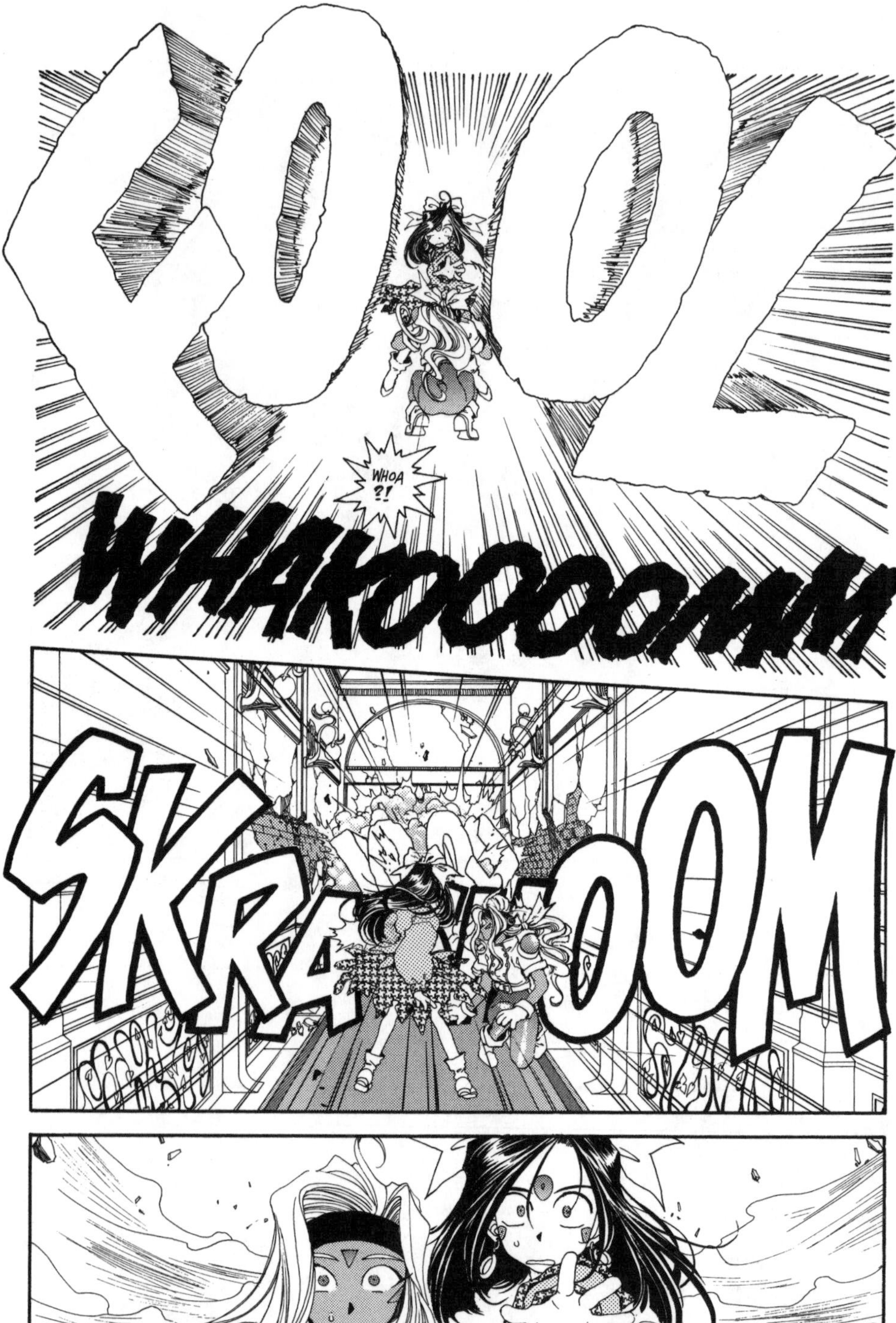
WHOA ?!
WHAKOOOOMM

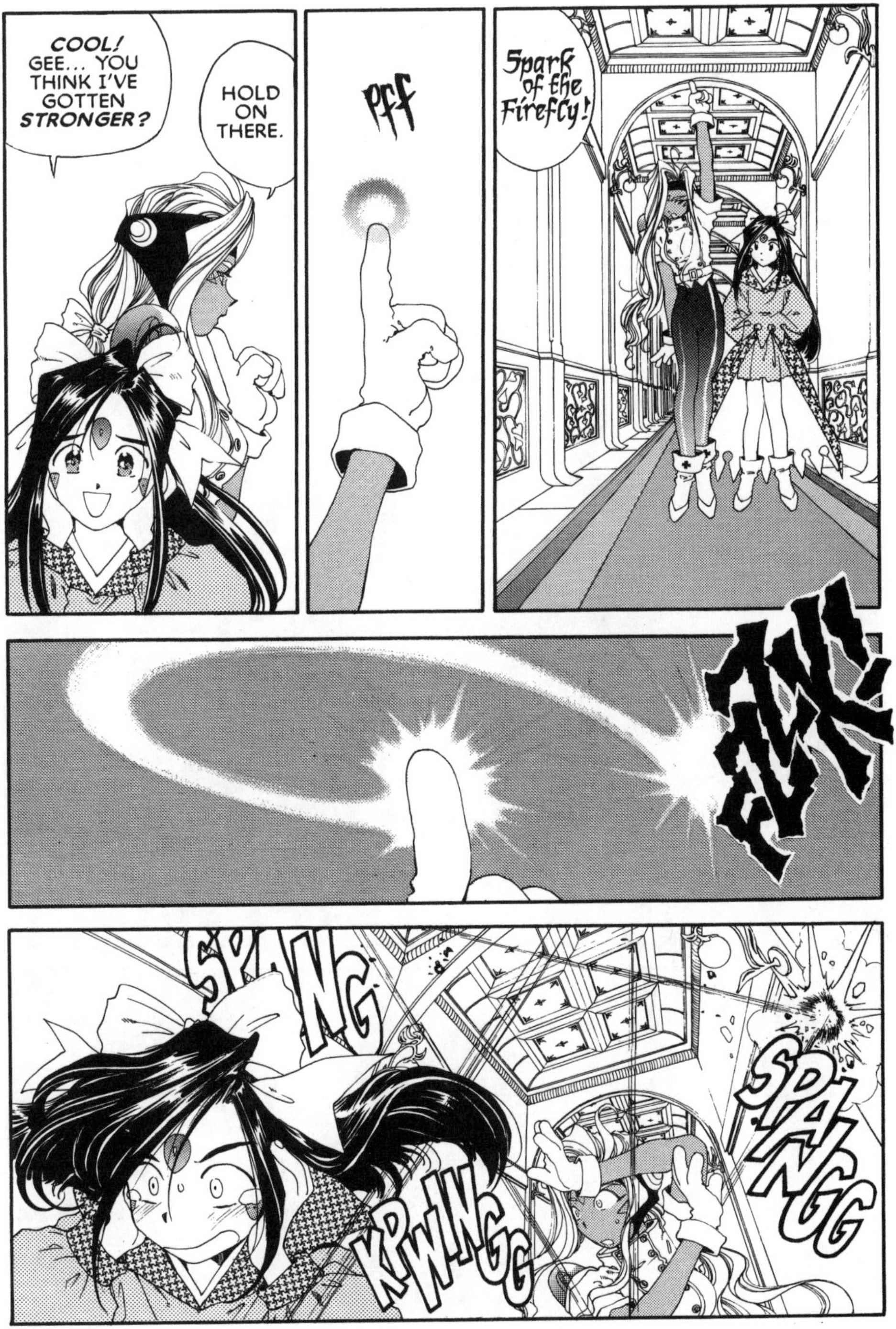
COOL! GEE... YOU THINK I'VE GOTTEN STRONGER?
HOLD ON THERE.
PFF
Spark of the Firefly!
SPANG
SPANGG
KPWINGG

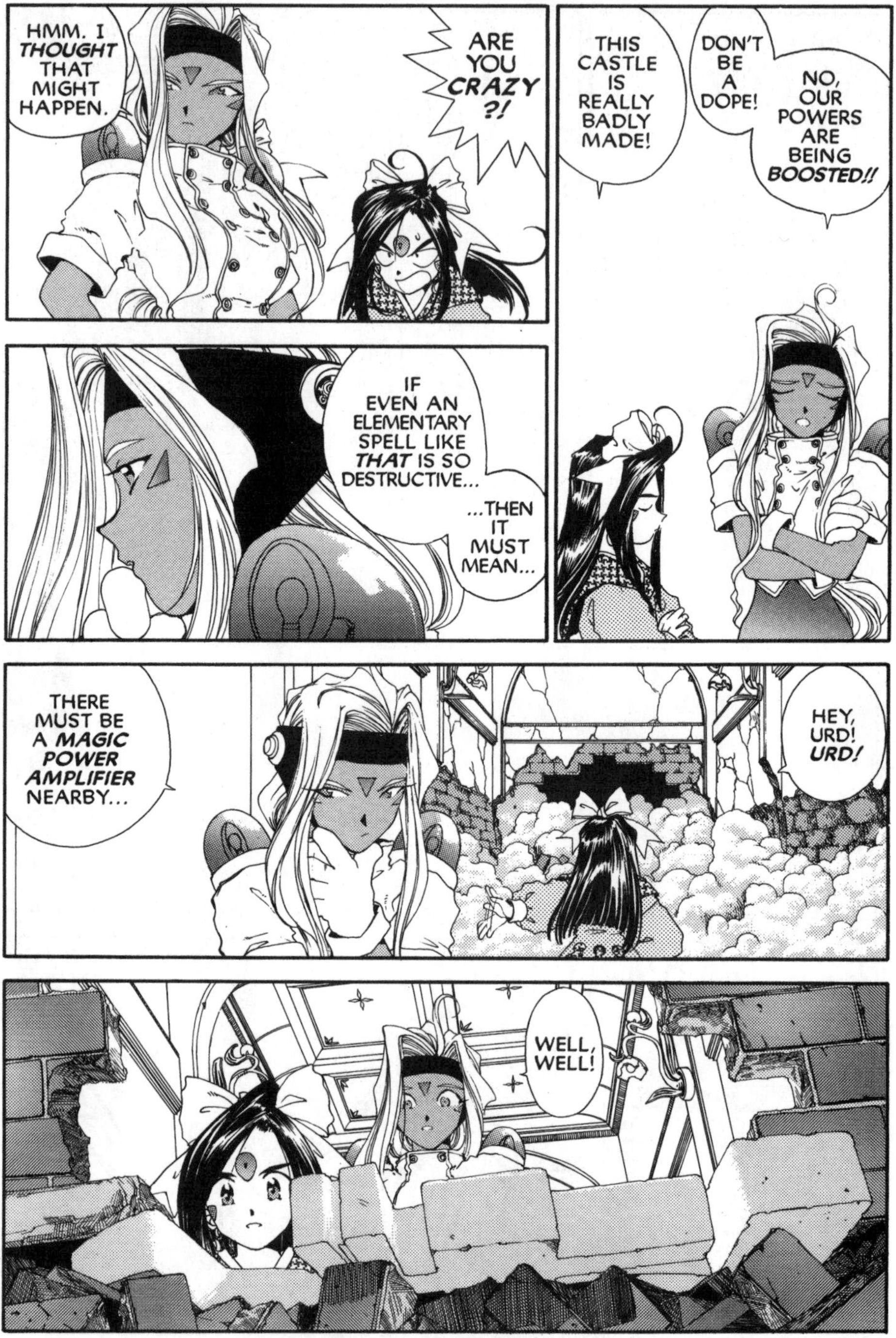
HMM. I *THOUGHT* THAT MIGHT HAPPEN.
ARE YOU *CRAZY* ?!
IF EVEN AN ELEMENTARY SPELL LIKE *THAT* IS SO DESTRUCTIVE...
...THEN IT MUST MEAN...
THIS CASTLE IS REALLY BADLY MADE!
DON'T BE A DOPE!
NO, OUR POWERS ARE BEING *BOOSTED!!*
THERE MUST BE A *MAGIC POWER AMPLIFIER* NEARBY...
HEY, URD! *URD!*
WELL, WELL!

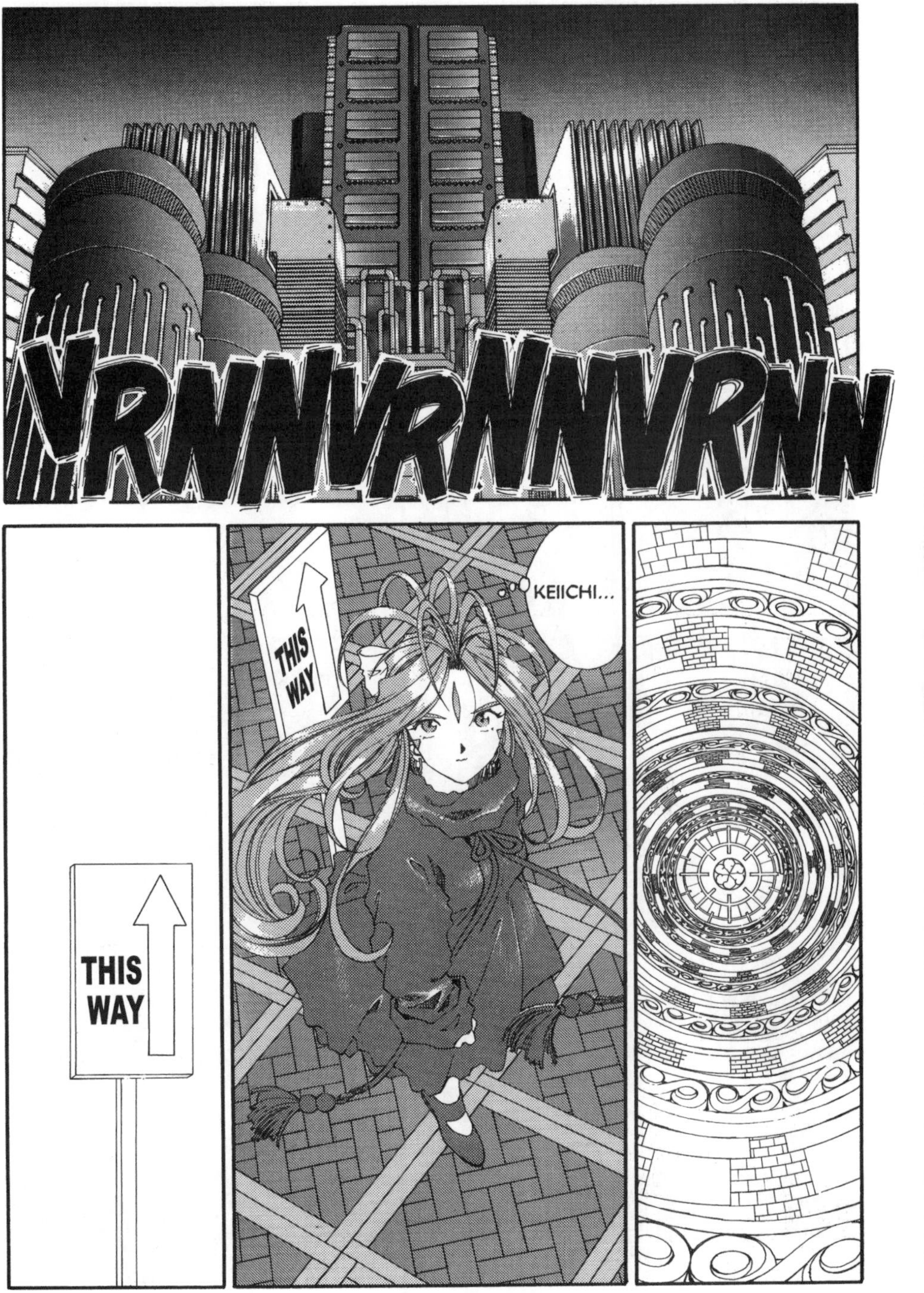
VRNNVRNNVRNN
THIS WAY
THIS WAY
KEIICHI...

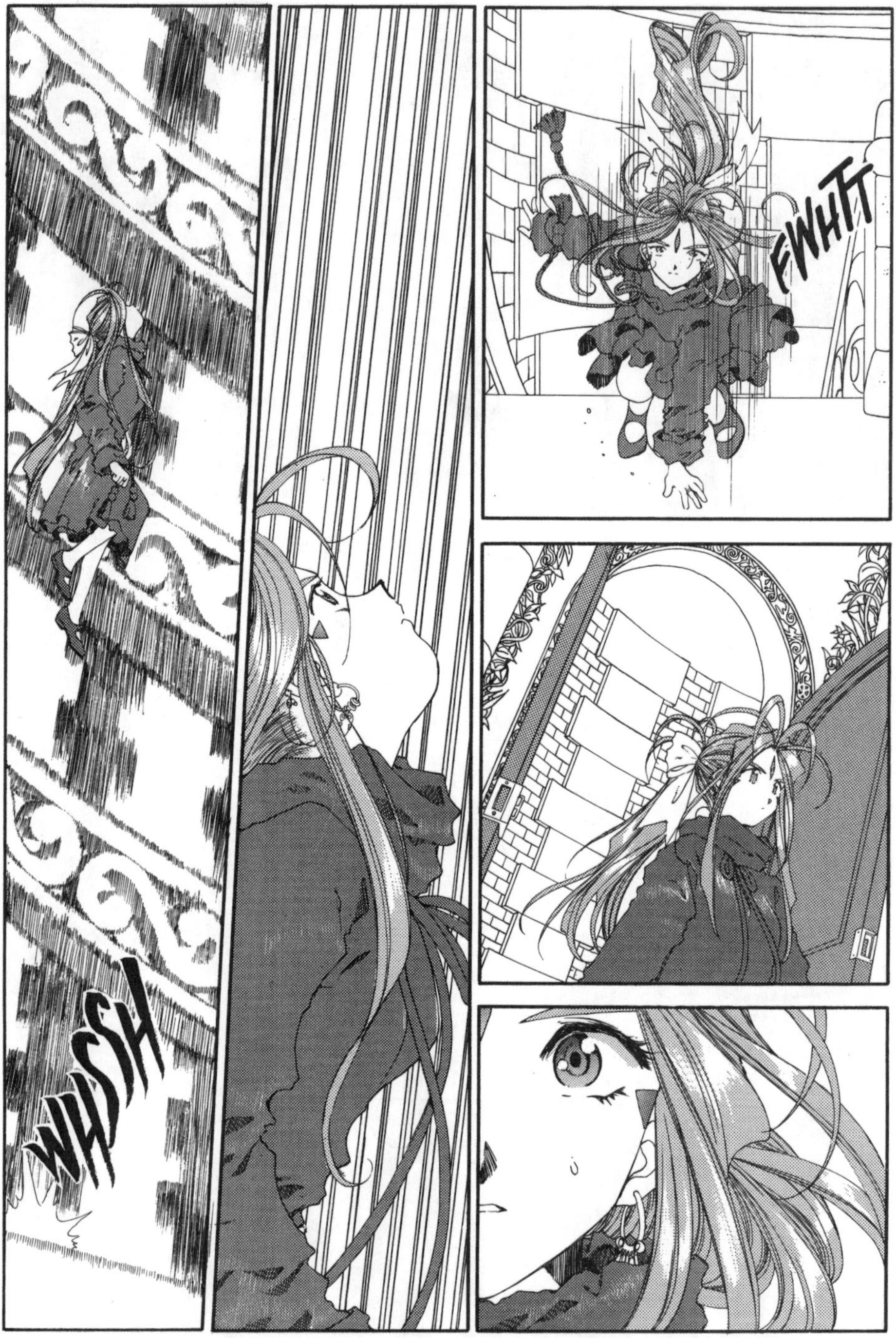
WHSH
FWHTT

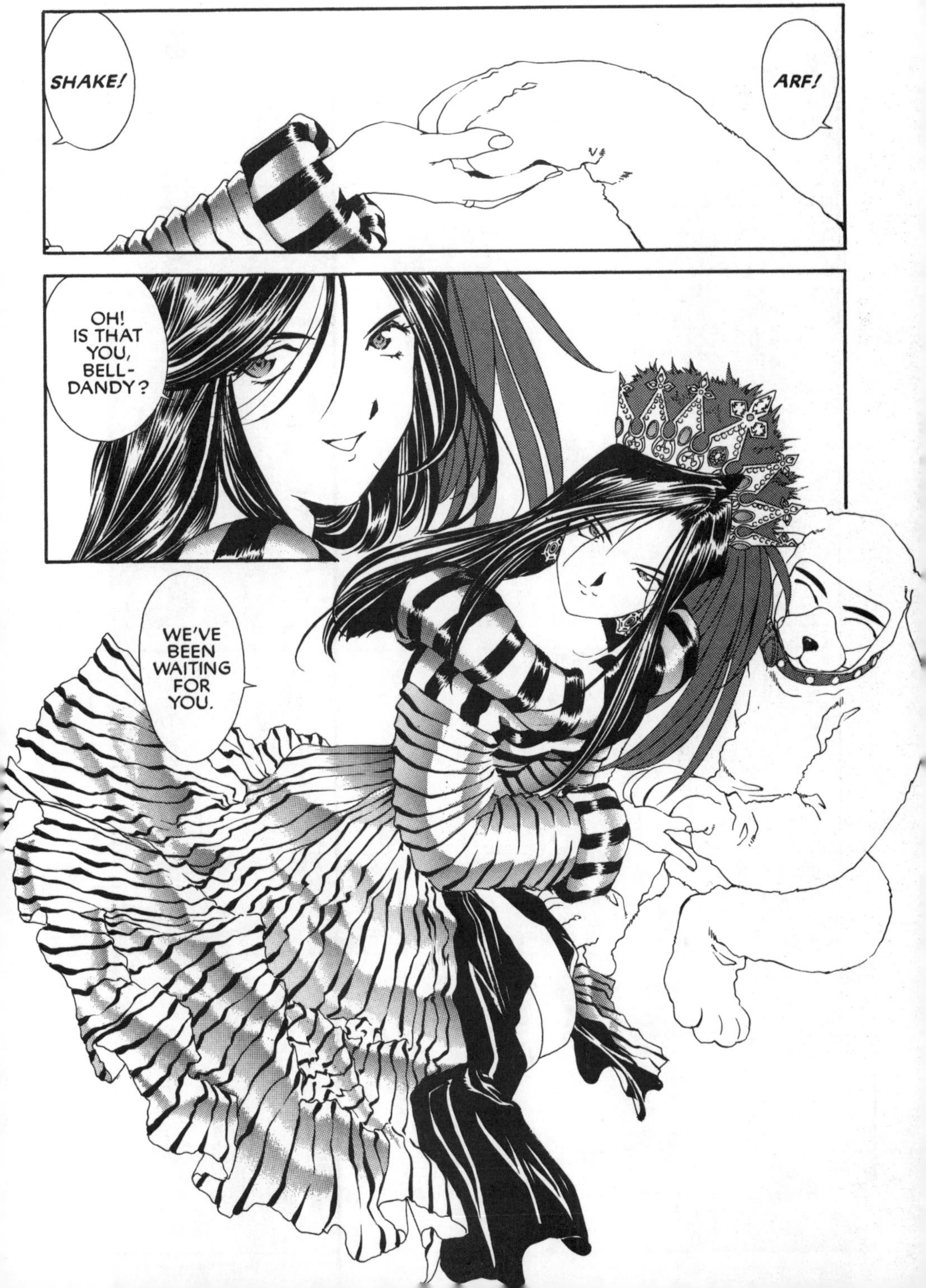
SHAKE!
ARF!
OH! IS THAT YOU, BELL-DANDY?
WE'VE BEEN WAITING FOR YOU.

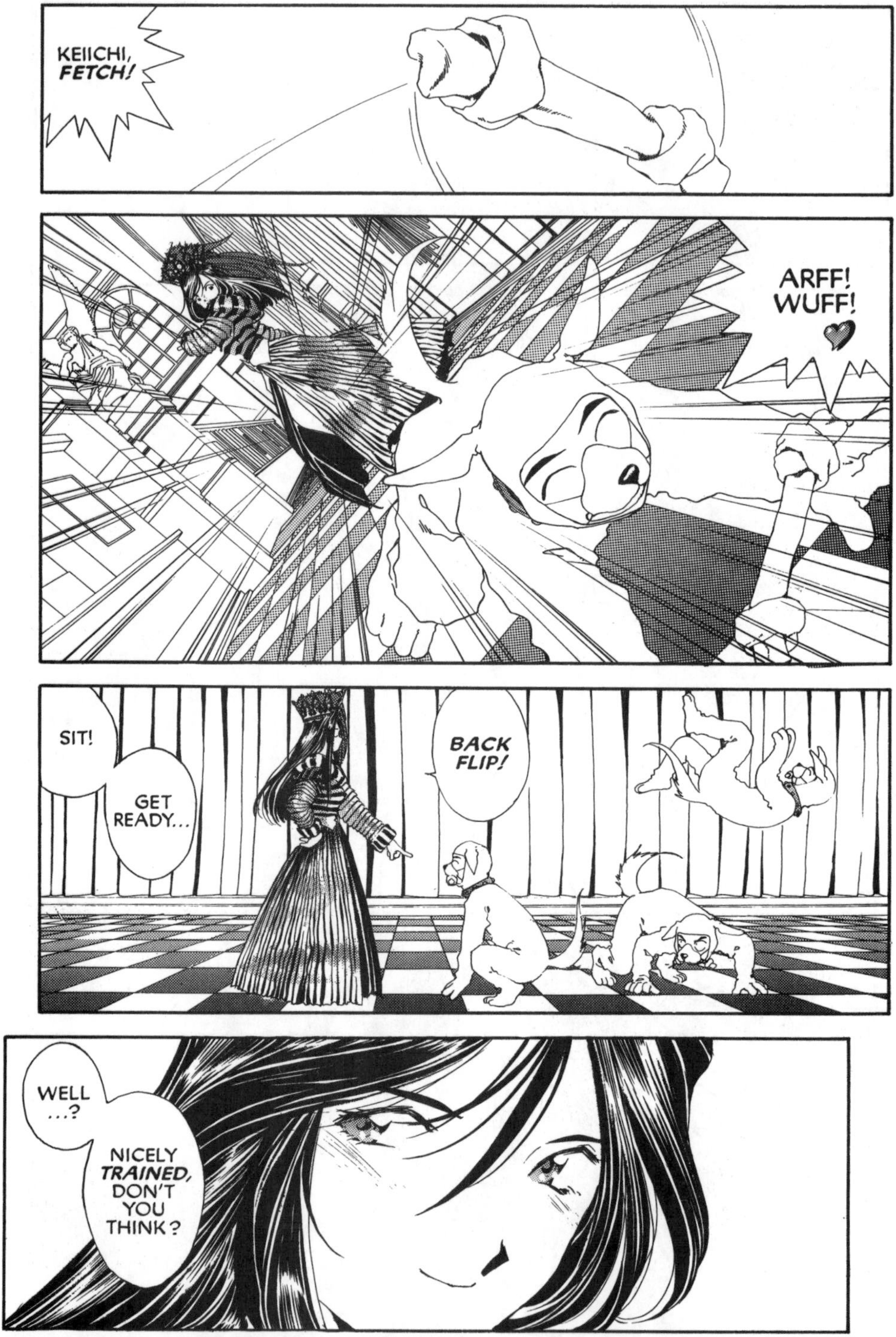
KEIICHI, *FETCH!*
ARFF! WUFF! ♥
SIT!
GET READY...
BACK FLIP!
WELL ...?
NICELY *TRAINED,* DON'T YOU THINK?

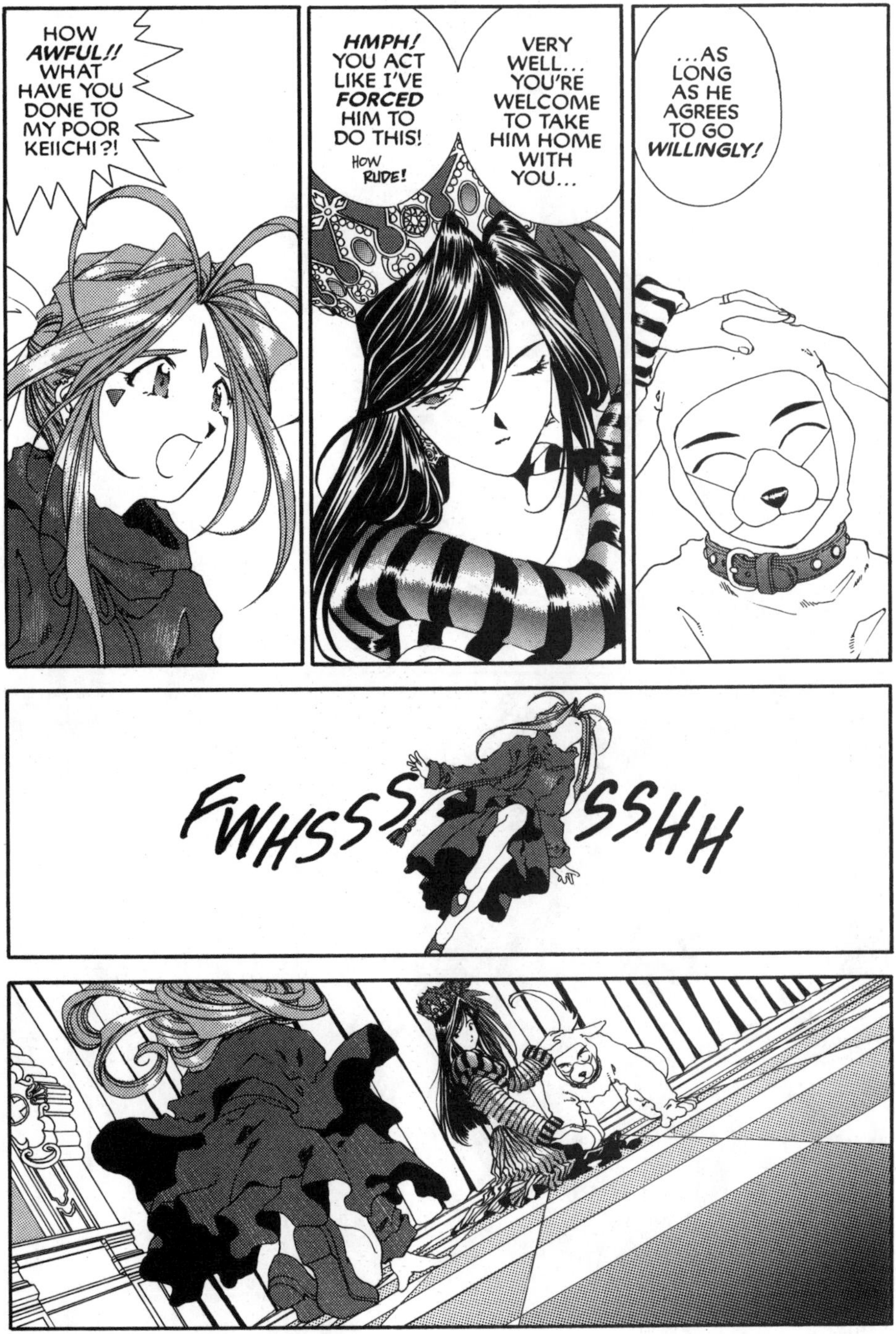
HOW AWFUL!! WHAT HAVE YOU DONE TO MY POOR KEIICHI?!
HMPH! YOU ACT LIKE I'VE FORCED HIM TO DO THIS!
HOW RUDE!
VERY WELL... YOU'RE WELCOME TO TAKE HIM HOME WITH YOU...
...AS LONG AS HE AGREES TO GO WILLINGLY!
FWHSSSSSHH

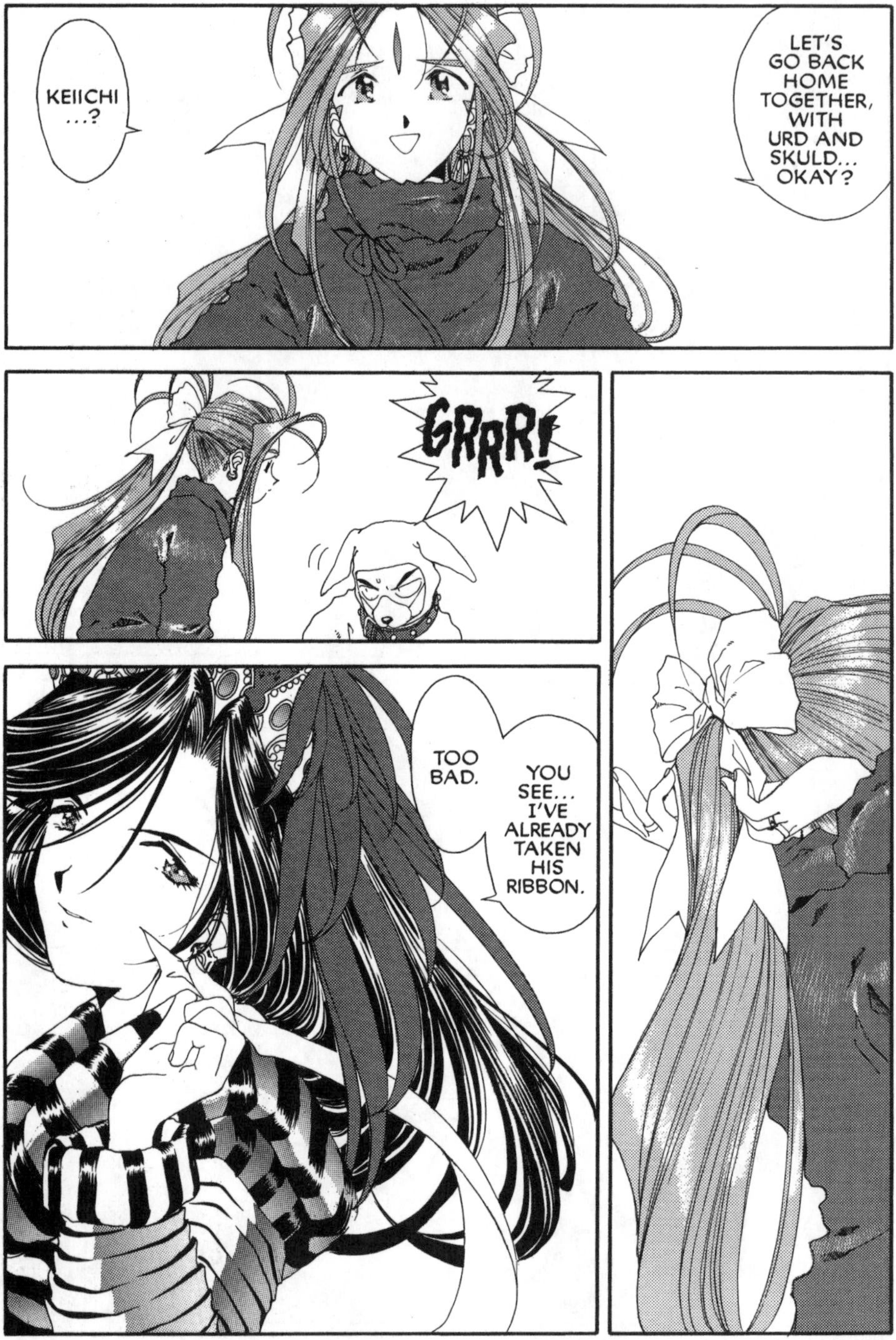
KEIICHI ...?
LET'S GO BACK HOME TOGETHER, WITH URD AND SKULD... OKAY?
GRRR!
TOO BAD.
YOU SEE... I'VE ALREADY TAKEN HIS RIBBON.

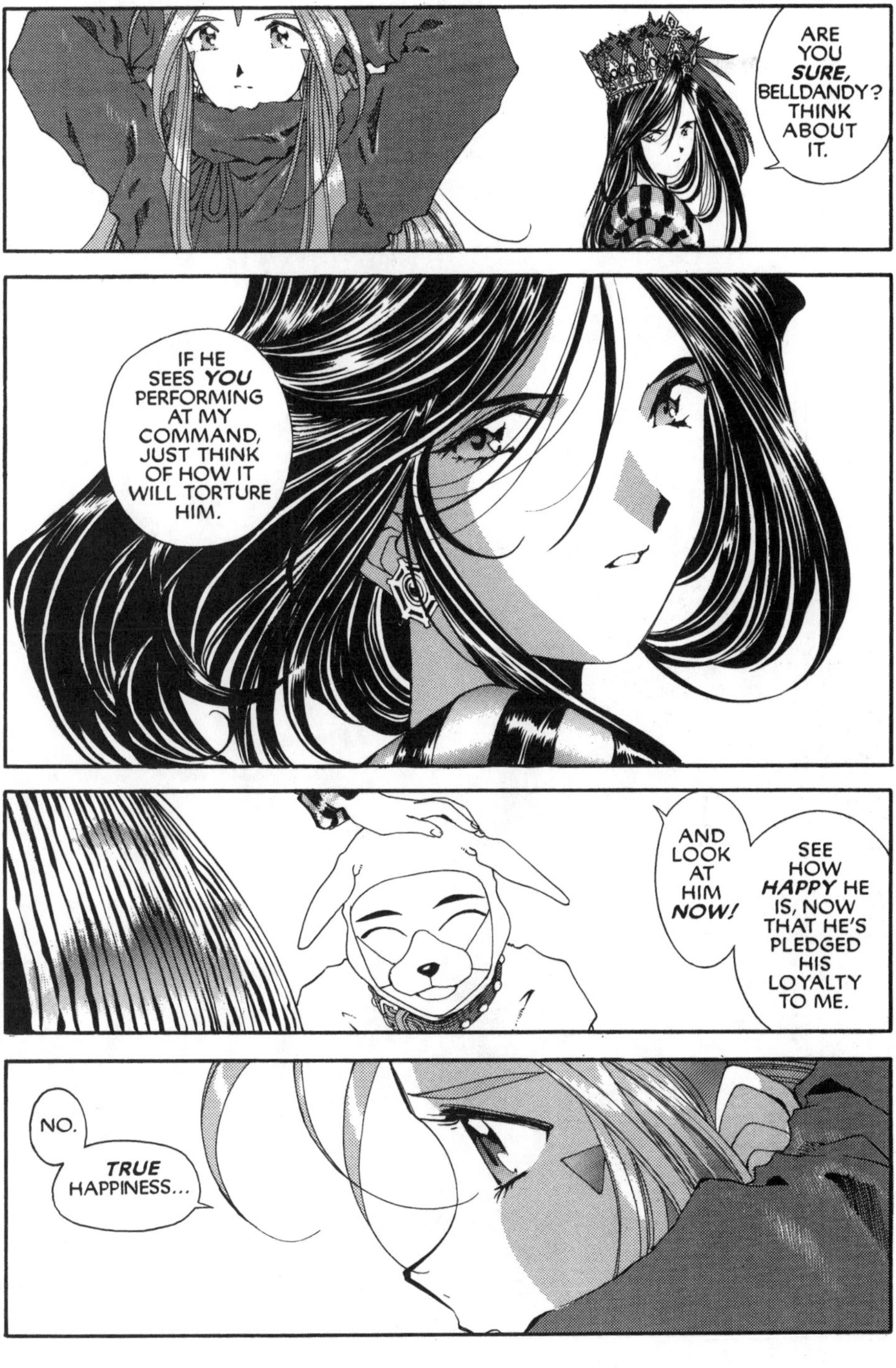
ARE YOU SURE, BELLDANDY? THINK ABOUT IT.
IF HE SEES YOU PERFORMING AT MY COMMAND, JUST THINK OF HOW IT WILL TORTURE HIM.
AND LOOK AT HIM NOW!
SEE HOW HAPPY HE IS, NOW THAT HE'S PLEDGED HIS LOYALTY TO ME.
NO.
TRUE HAPPINESS...

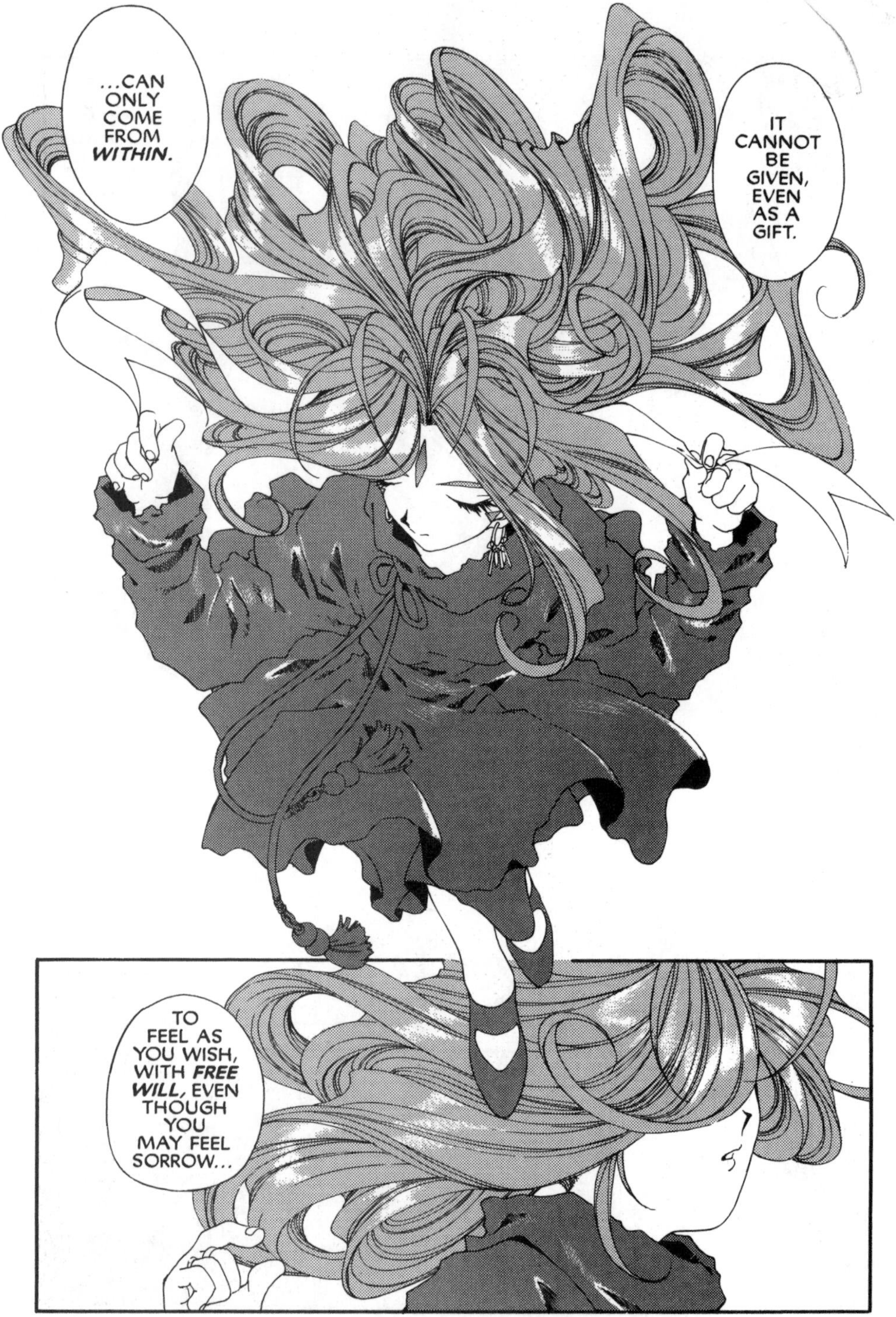
...CAN ONLY COME FROM *WITHIN*.
IT CANNOT BE GIVEN, EVEN AS A GIFT.
TO FEEL AS YOU WISH, WITH *FREE WILL*, EVEN THOUGH YOU MAY FEEL SORROW...

...IS WORTH *INFINITELY* MORE...

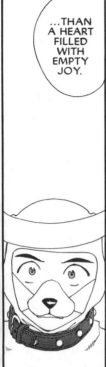

...THAN A HEART FILLED WITH EMPTY JOY.

MY DEAREST KEIICHI...

...YOU'LL UNDER-STAND.

I KNOW YOU WILL...

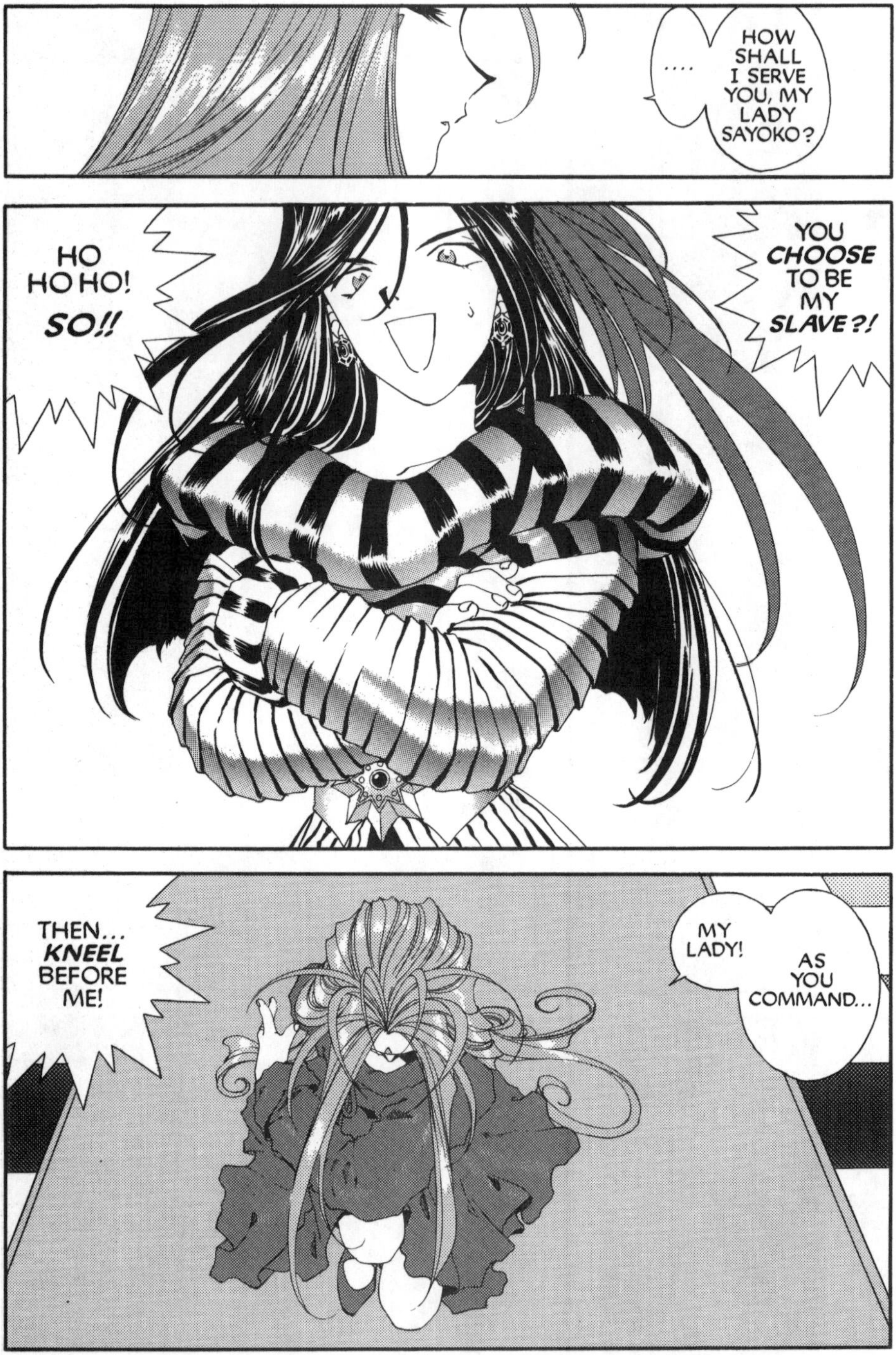
. . . .
HOW SHALL I SERVE YOU, MY LADY SAYOKO?
HO HO HO! ***SO!!***
YOU ***CHOOSE*** TO BE MY ***SLAVE?!***
THEN... ***KNEEL*** BEFORE ME!
MY LADY!
AS YOU COMMAND...

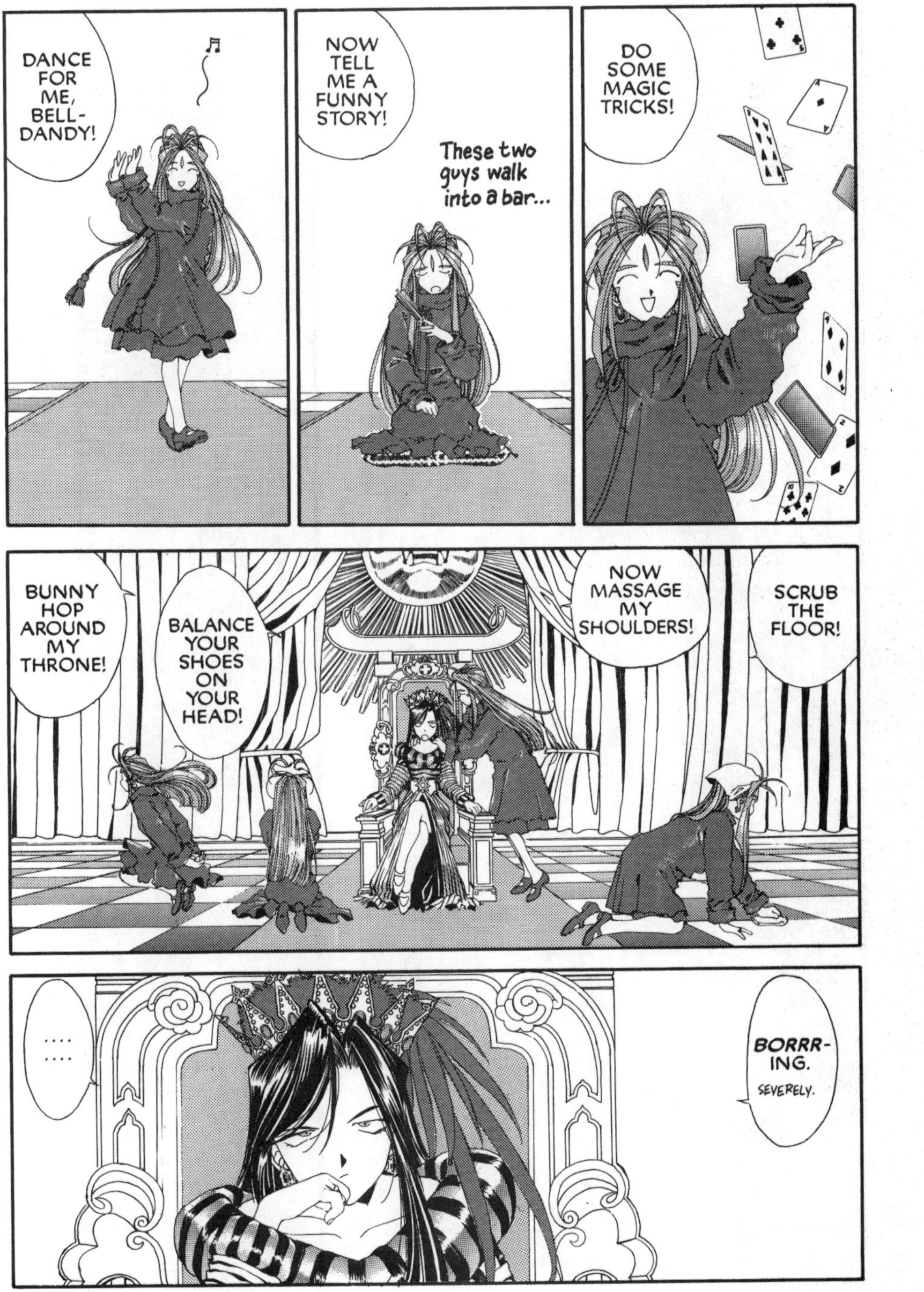
DANCE FOR ME, BELL-DANDY!
♫
NOW TELL ME A FUNNY STORY!
These two guys walk into a bar...
DO SOME MAGIC TRICKS!
BUNNY HOP AROUND MY THRONE!
BALANCE YOUR SHOES ON YOUR HEAD!
NOW MASSAGE MY SHOULDERS!
SCRUB THE FLOOR!
....
BORRR-ING.
SEVERELY.

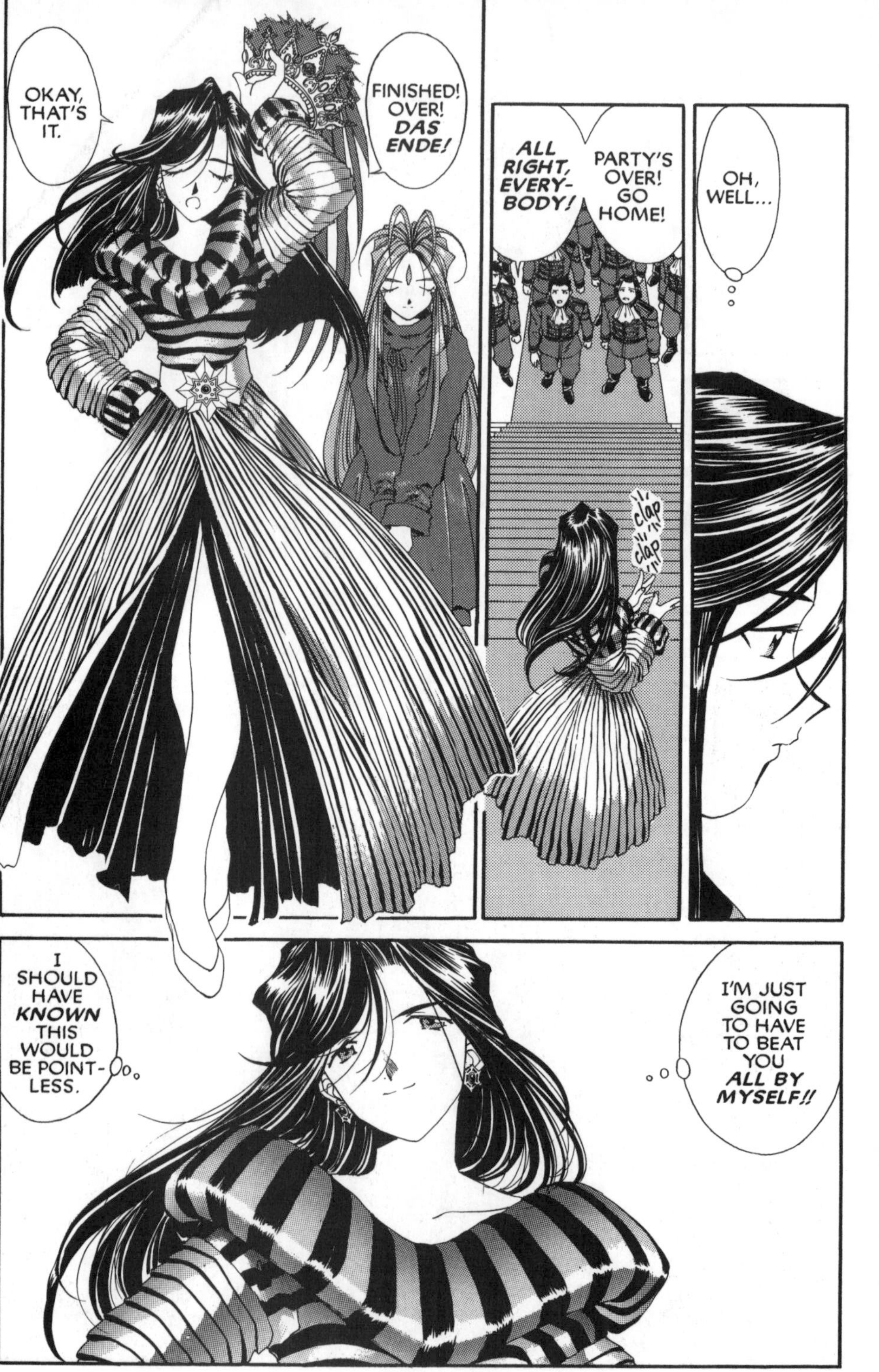

OKAY, THAT'S IT.
FINISHED! OVER! *DAS ENDE!*
ALL RIGHT, EVERY-BODY!
PARTY'S OVER! GO HOME!
clap clap
OH, WELL...
I SHOULD HAVE *KNOWN* THIS WOULD BE POINT-LESS.
I'M JUST GOING TO HAVE TO BEAT YOU *ALL BY MYSELF!!*

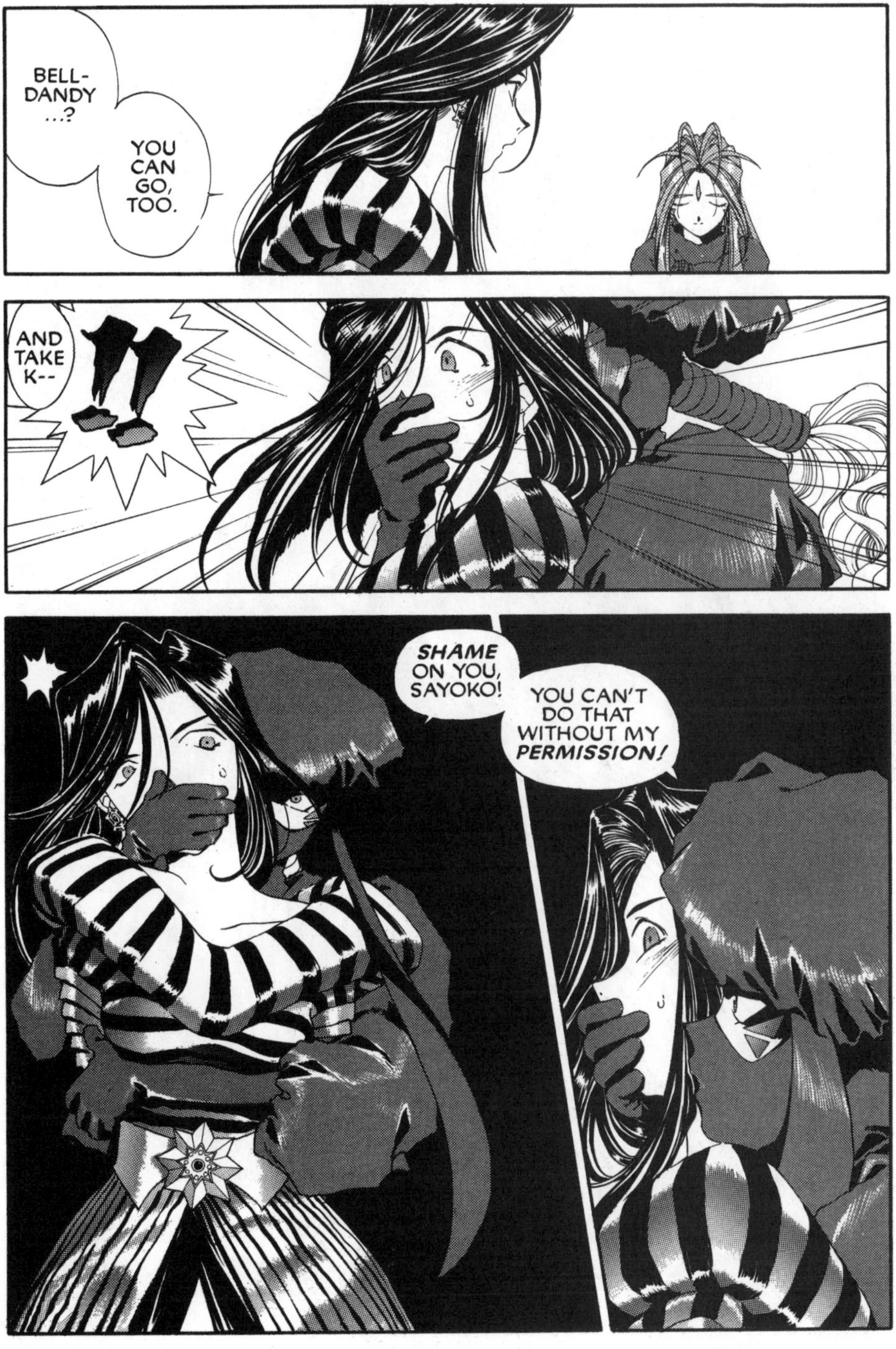
BELL-DANDY ...?
YOU CAN GO, TOO.
AND TAKE K--
SHAME ON YOU, SAYOKO!
YOU CAN'T DO THAT WITHOUT MY PERMISSION!

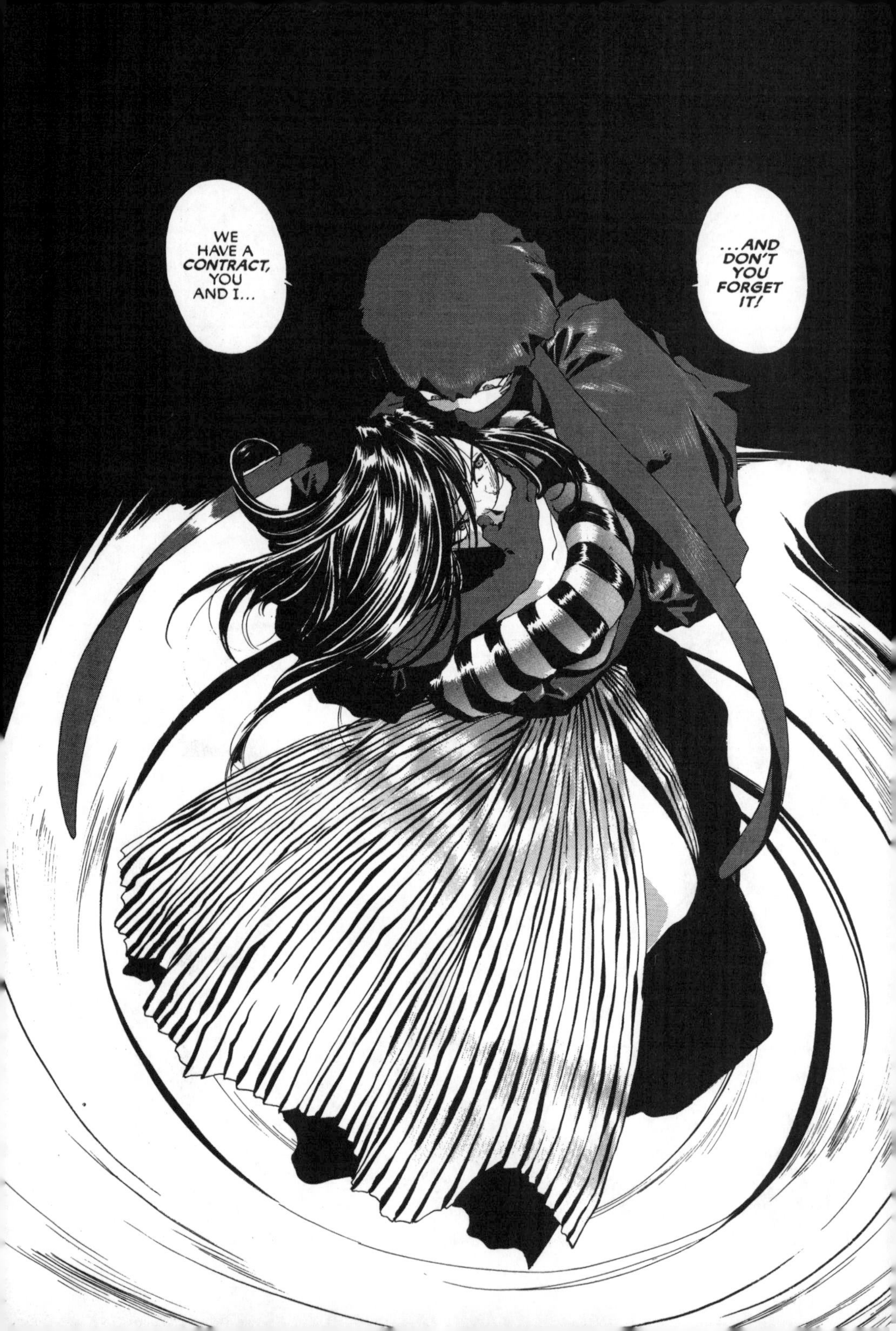
WE HAVE A CONTRACT, YOU AND I...
...AND DON'T YOU FORGET IT!

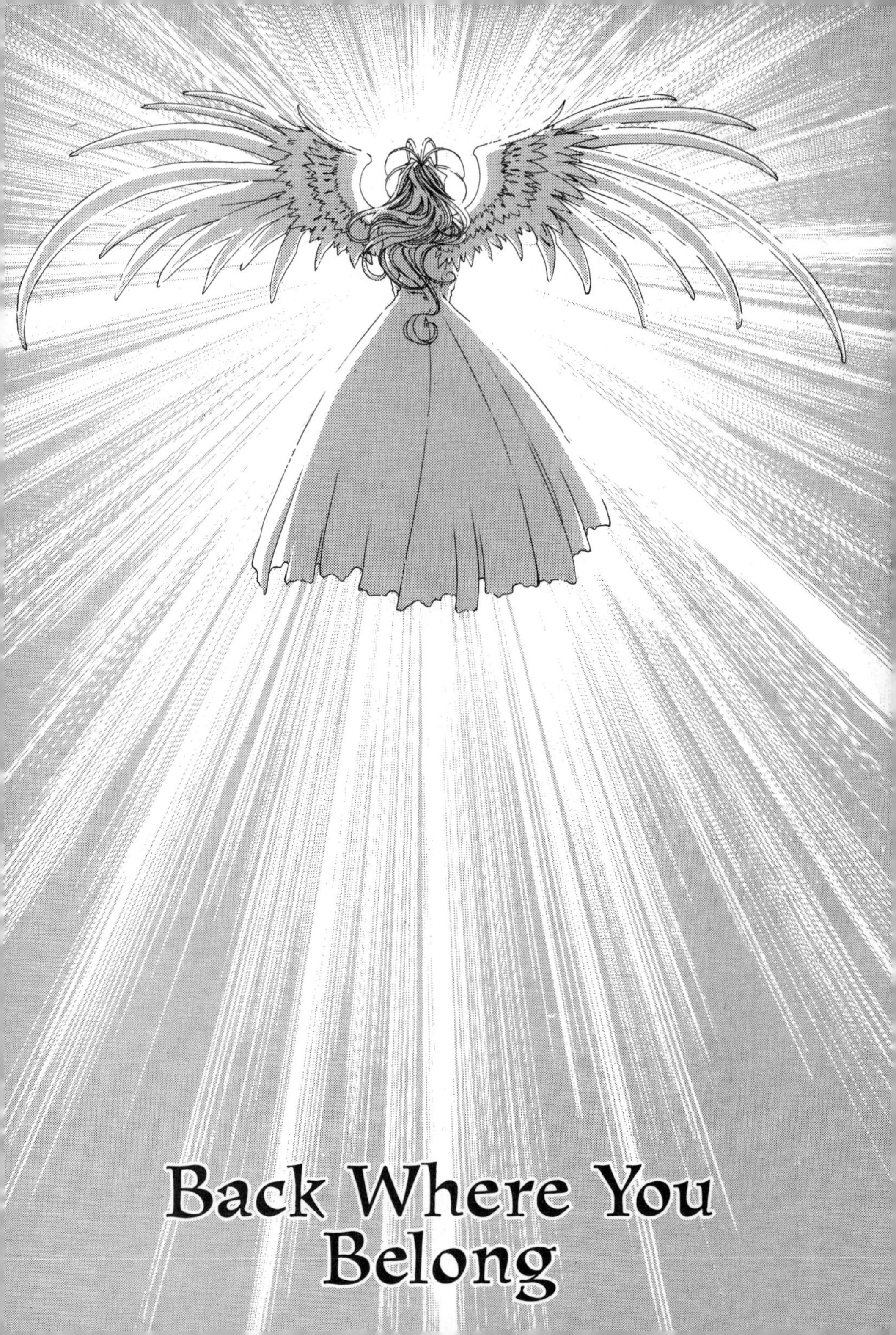
Back Where You
Belong

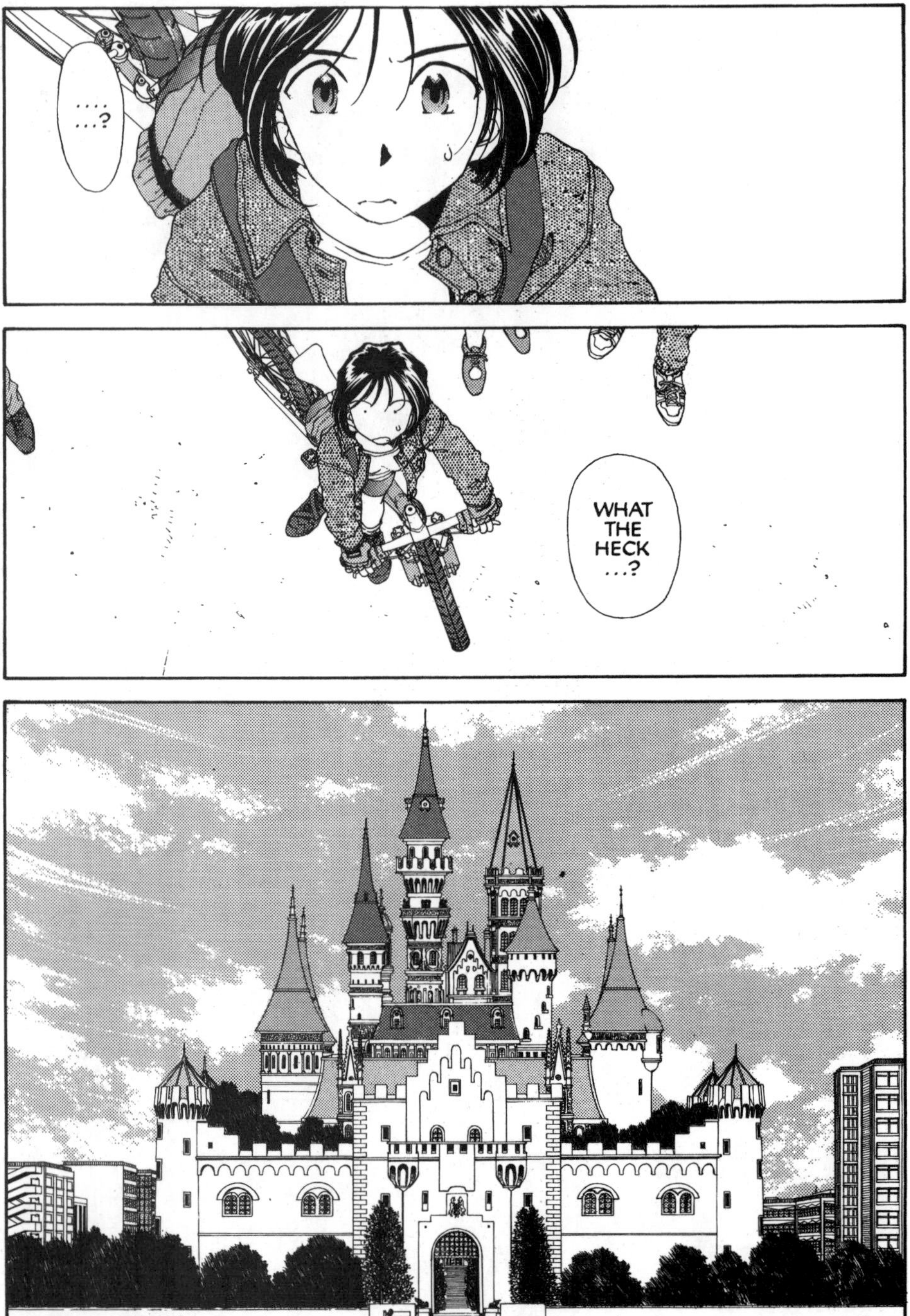
....
...?
WHAT THE HECK ...?

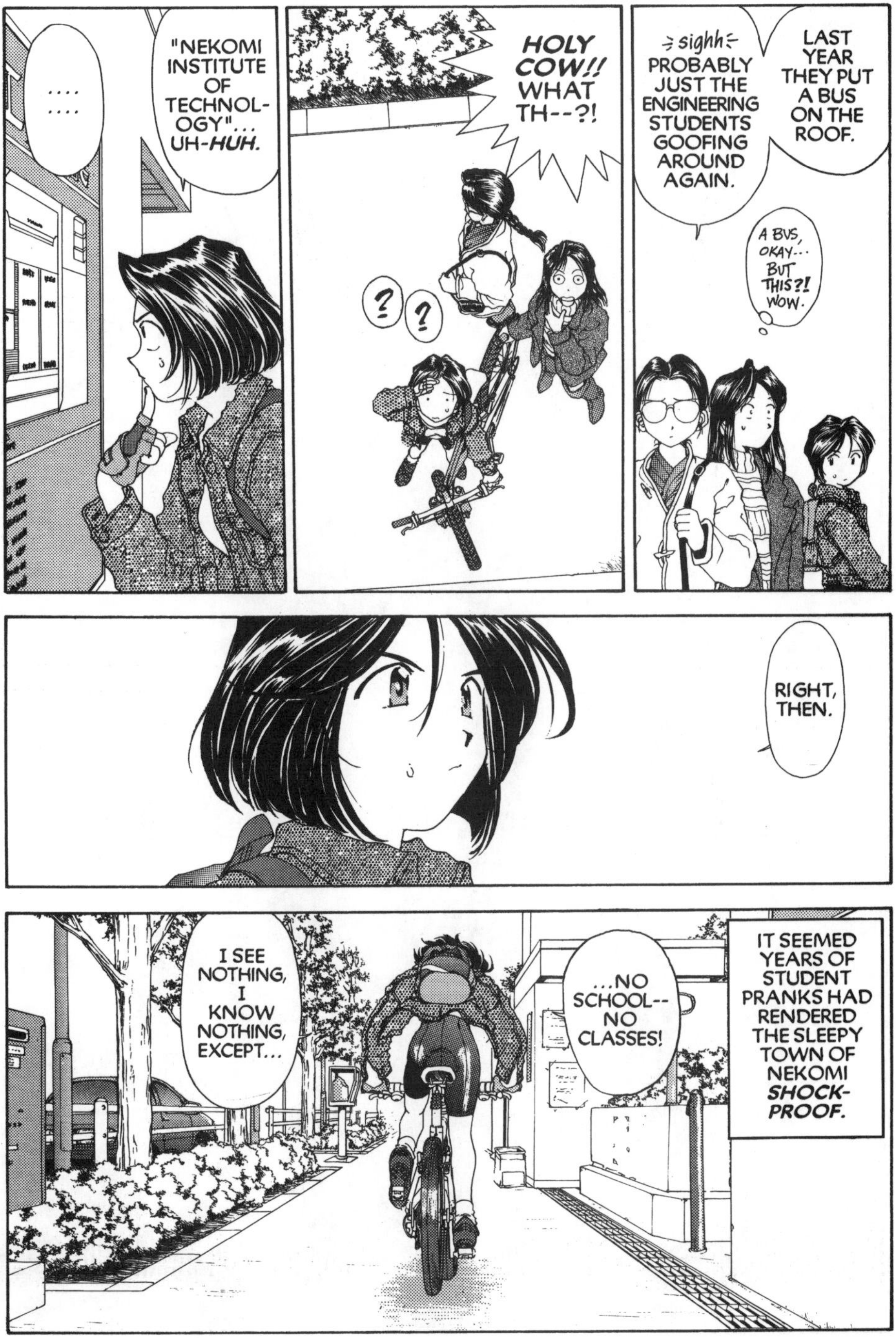
....
....
"NEKOMI INSTITUTE OF TECHNOLOGY"... UH-*HUH.*
HOLY COW!! WHAT TH--?!
?
?
sighh
PROBABLY JUST THE ENGINEERING STUDENTS GOOFING AROUND AGAIN.
LAST YEAR THEY PUT A BUS ON THE ROOF.
A BUS, OKAY... BUT THIS?! WOW.
RIGHT, THEN.
I SEE NOTHING, I KNOW NOTHING, EXCEPT...
...NO SCHOOL-- NO CLASSES!
IT SEEMED YEARS OF STUDENT PRANKS HAD RENDERED THE SLEEPY TOWN OF NEKOMI *SHOCK-PROOF.*

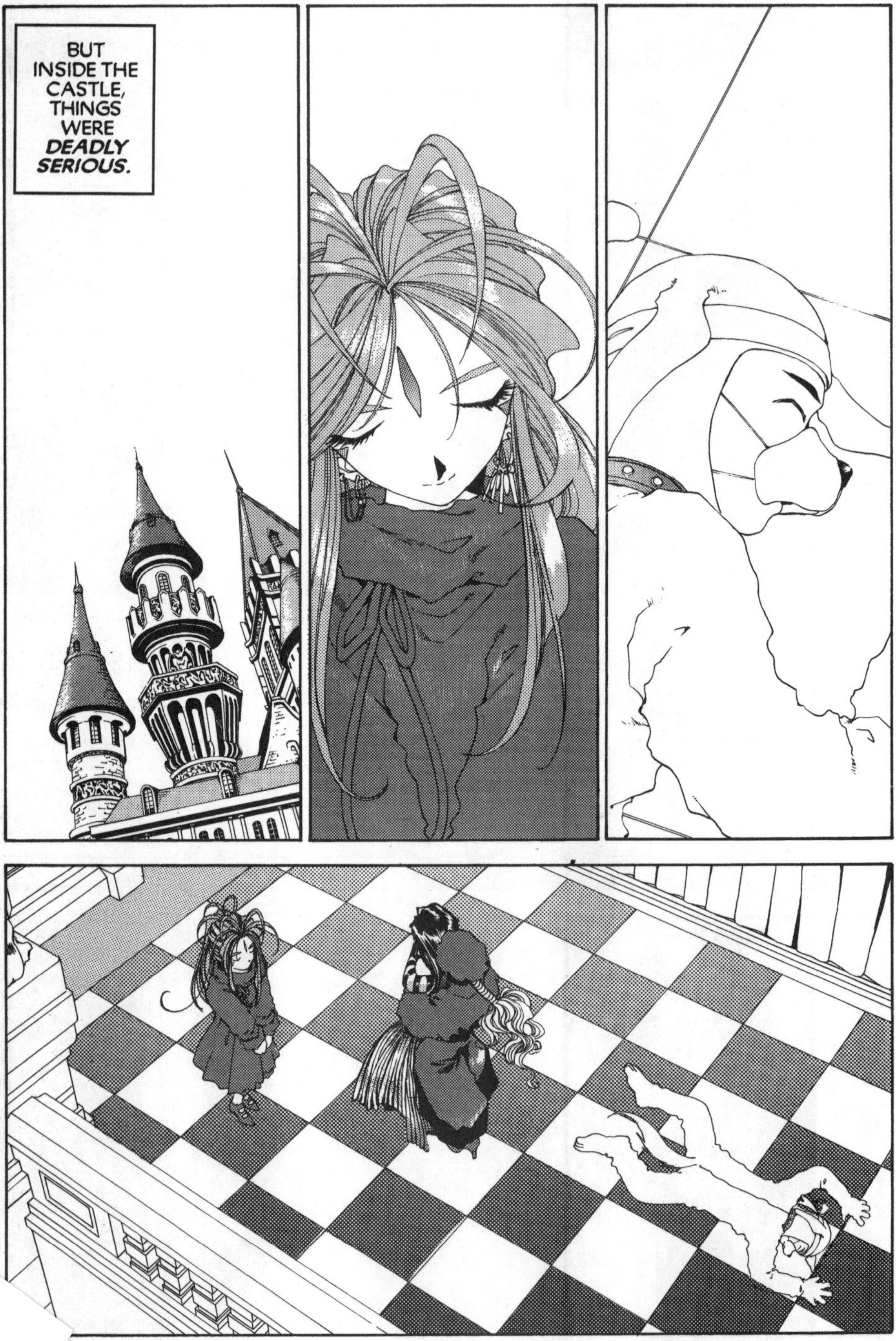
BUT INSIDE THE CASTLE, THINGS WERE ***DEADLY SERIOUS.***

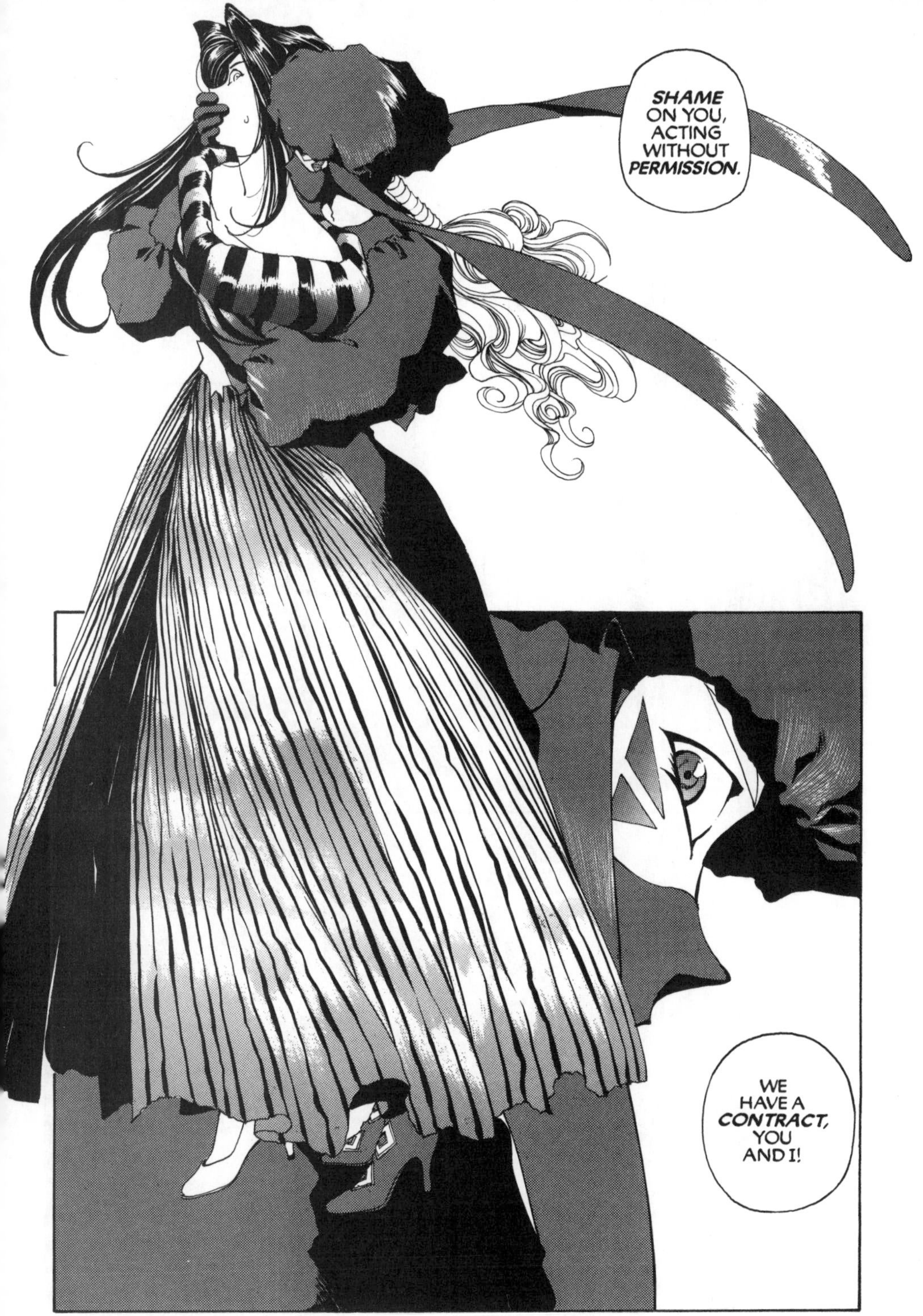
SHAME ON YOU, ACTING WITHOUT PERMISSION.
WE HAVE A CONTRACT, YOU AND I!

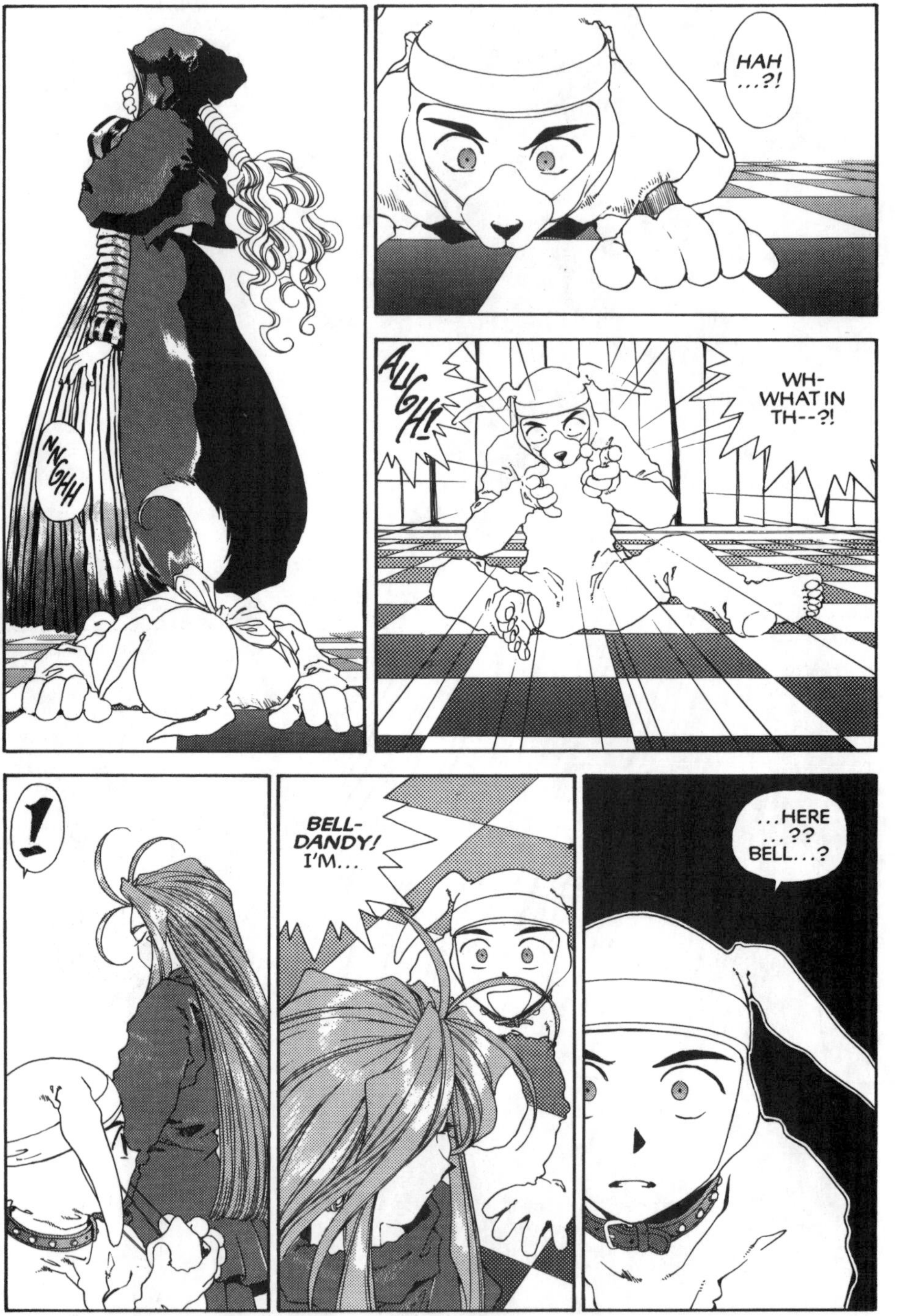
NNGHH
HAH ...?!
AUGH!
WH- WHAT IN TH--?!
!
BELL- DANDY! I'M...
...HERE ...?? BELL...?

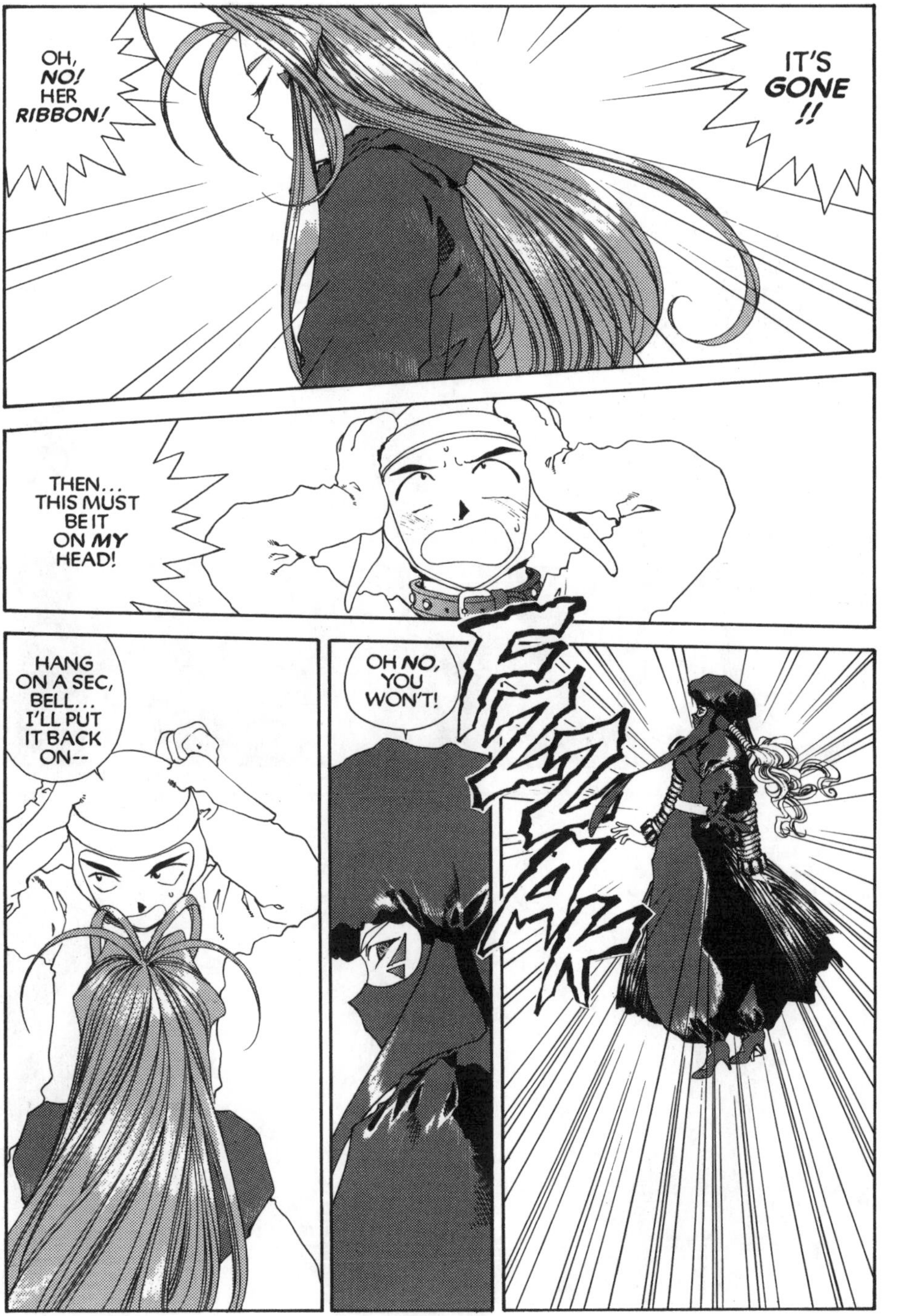

OH, NO! HER RIBBON!
IT'S GONE !!
THEN... THIS MUST BE IT ON MY HEAD!
HANG ON A SEC, BELL... I'LL PUT IT BACK ON--
OH NO, YOU WON'T!
FZZAK

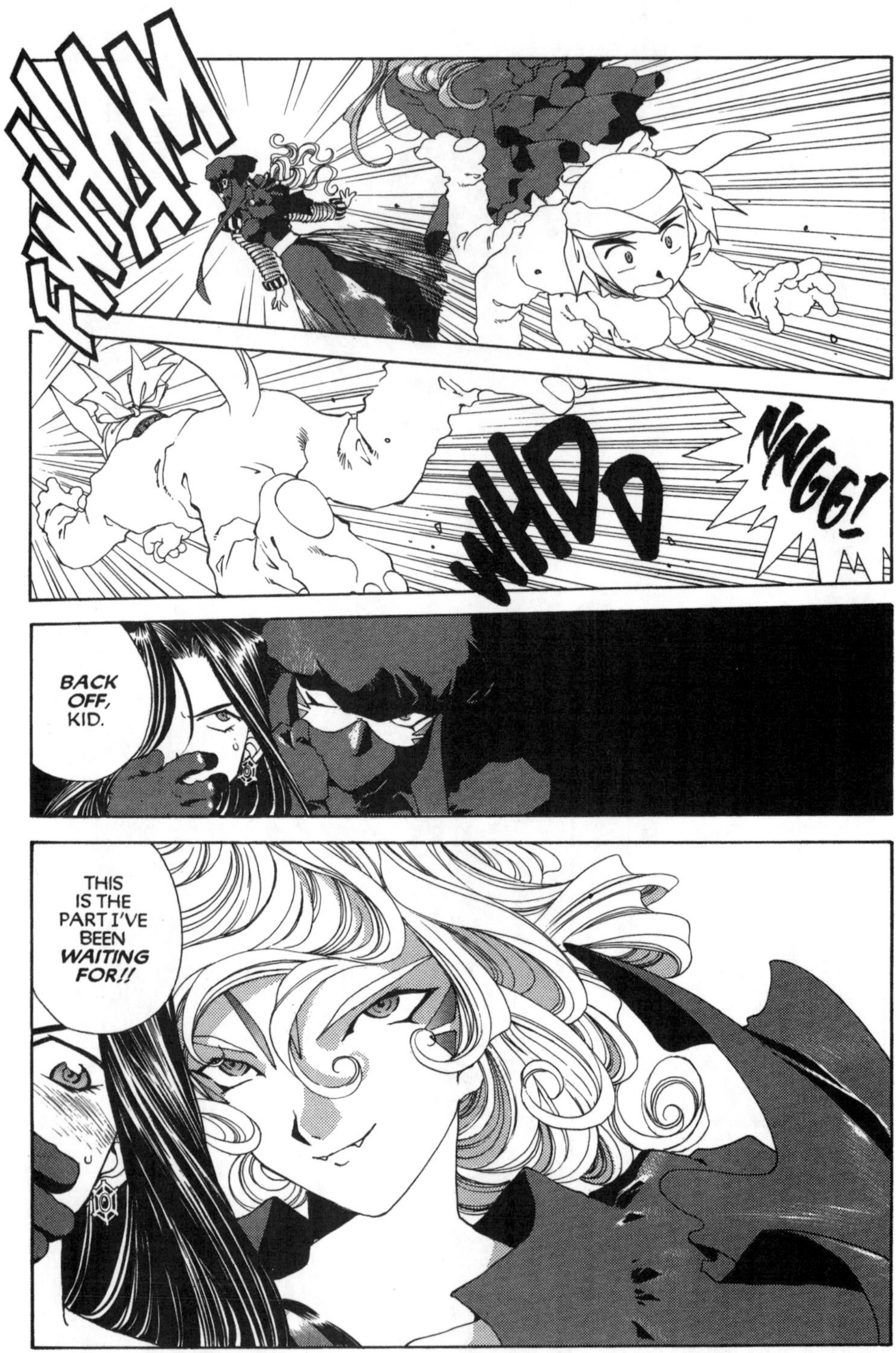
FWHAM
WHDD
NNGG!
BACK OFF, KID.
THIS IS THE PART I'VE BEEN *WAITING* FOR!!

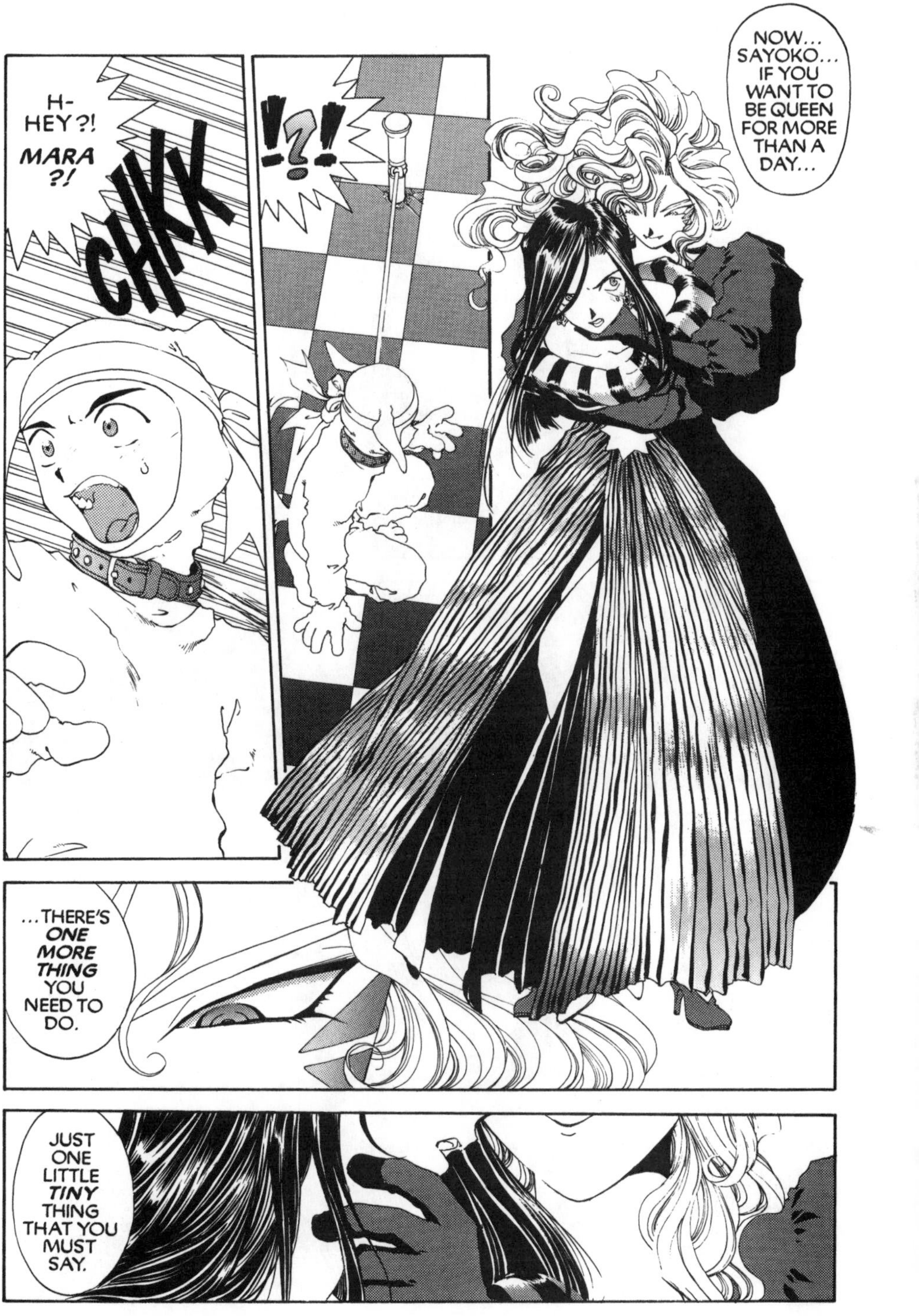
H- HEY?! MARA?!
CHKK
!?!
NOW... SAYOKO... IF YOU WANT TO BE QUEEN FOR MORE THAN A DAY...
...THERE'S ONE MORE THING YOU NEED TO DO.
JUST ONE LITTLE TINY THING THAT YOU MUST SAY.

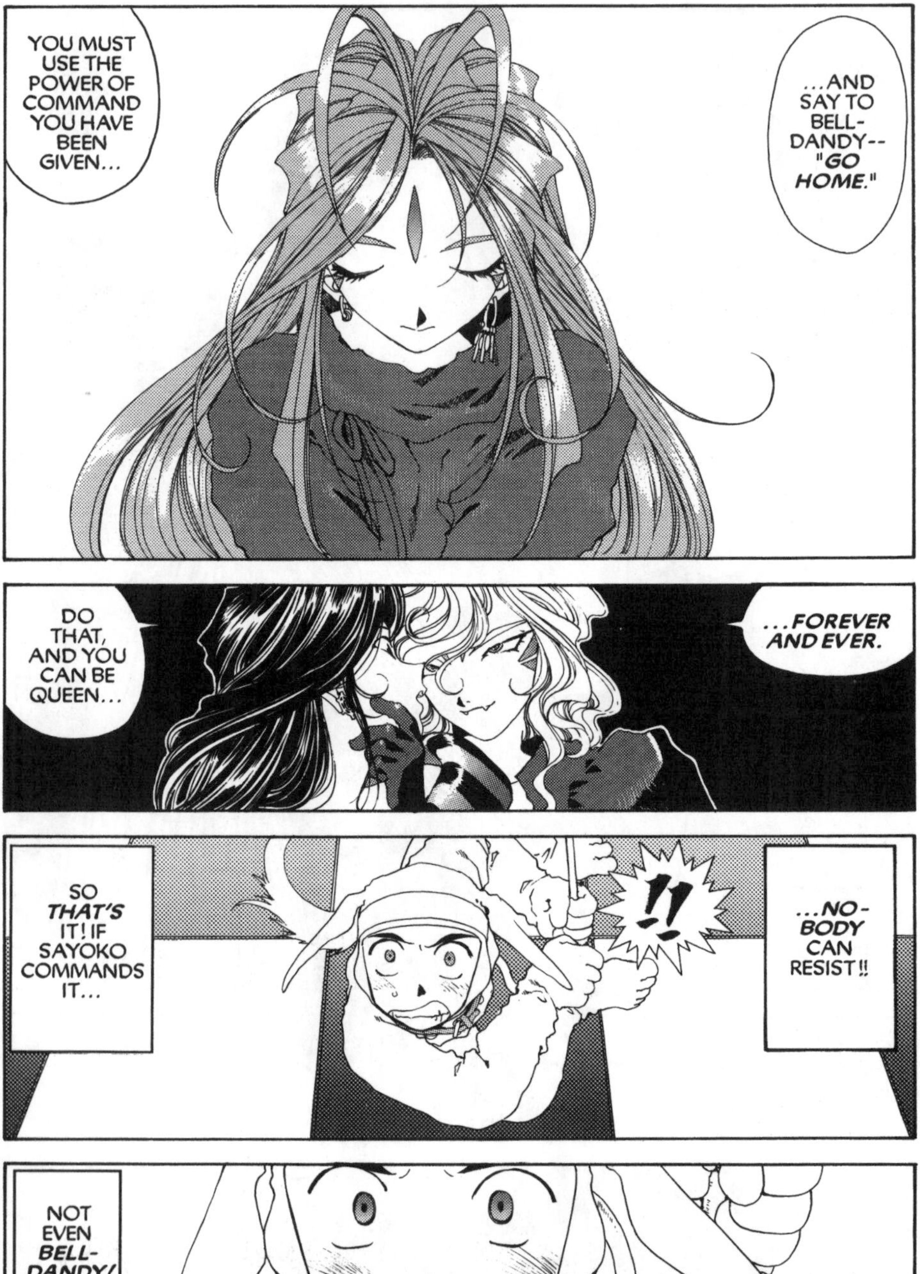
YOU MUST USE THE POWER OF COMMAND YOU HAVE BEEN GIVEN...
...AND SAY TO BELL-DANDY-- "*GO HOME.*"
DO THAT, AND YOU CAN BE QUEEN...
...FOREVER AND EVER.
SO *THAT'S* IT! IF SAYOKO COMMANDS IT...
!!
...NO-BODY CAN RESIST!!
NOT EVEN *BELL-DANDY!*

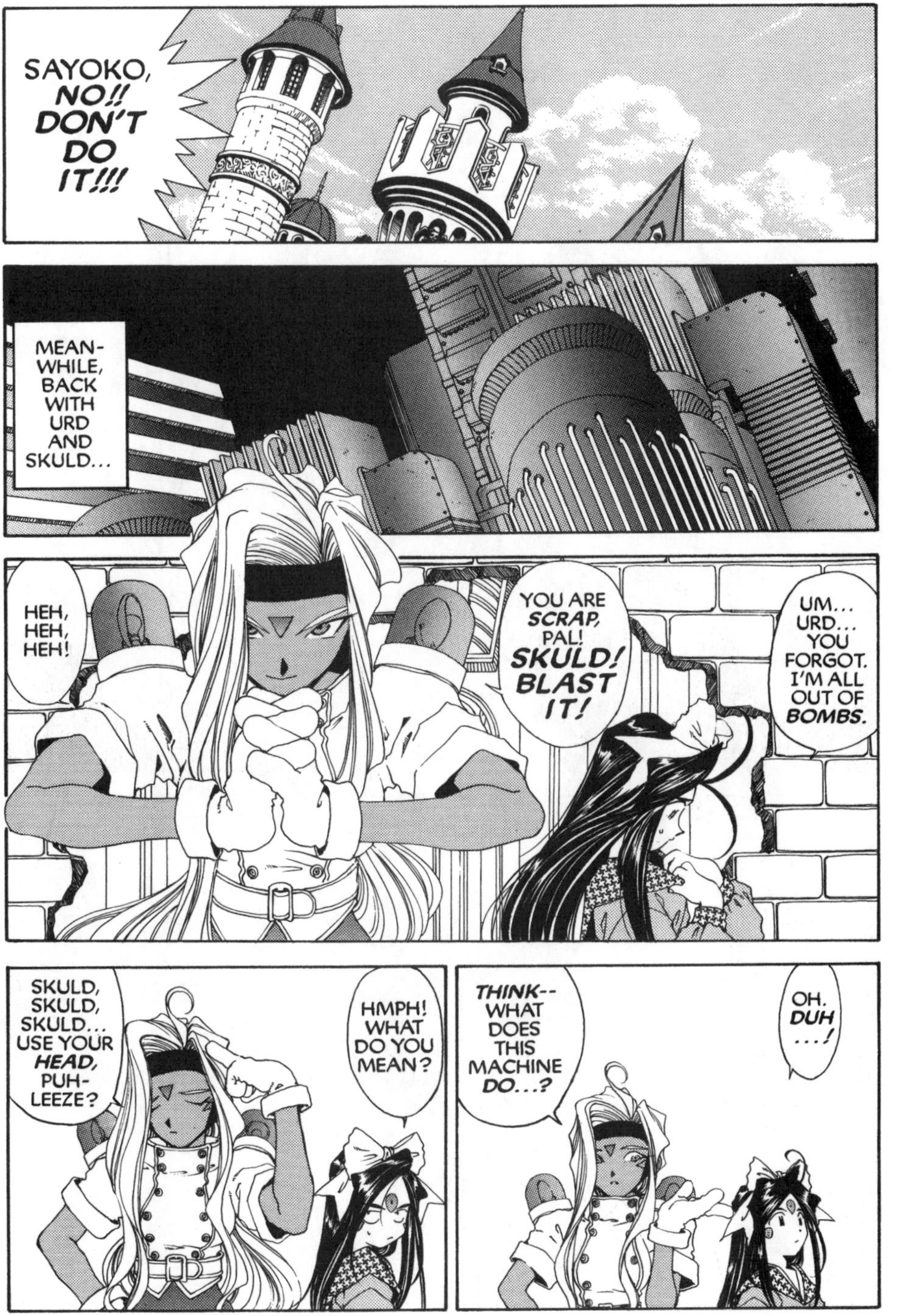
SAYOKO, ***NO!! DON'T DO IT!!!***
MEAN-WHILE, BACK WITH URD AND SKULD...
HEH, HEH, HEH!
YOU ARE *SCRAP,* PAL! ***SKULD! BLAST IT!***
UM... URD... YOU FORGOT. I'M ALL OUT OF ***BOMBS.***
SKULD, SKULD, SKULD... USE YOUR ***HEAD,*** PUH-LEEZE?
HMPH! WHAT DO YOU MEAN?
THINK-- WHAT DOES THIS MACHINE ***DO***...?
OH. ***DUH*** ...!

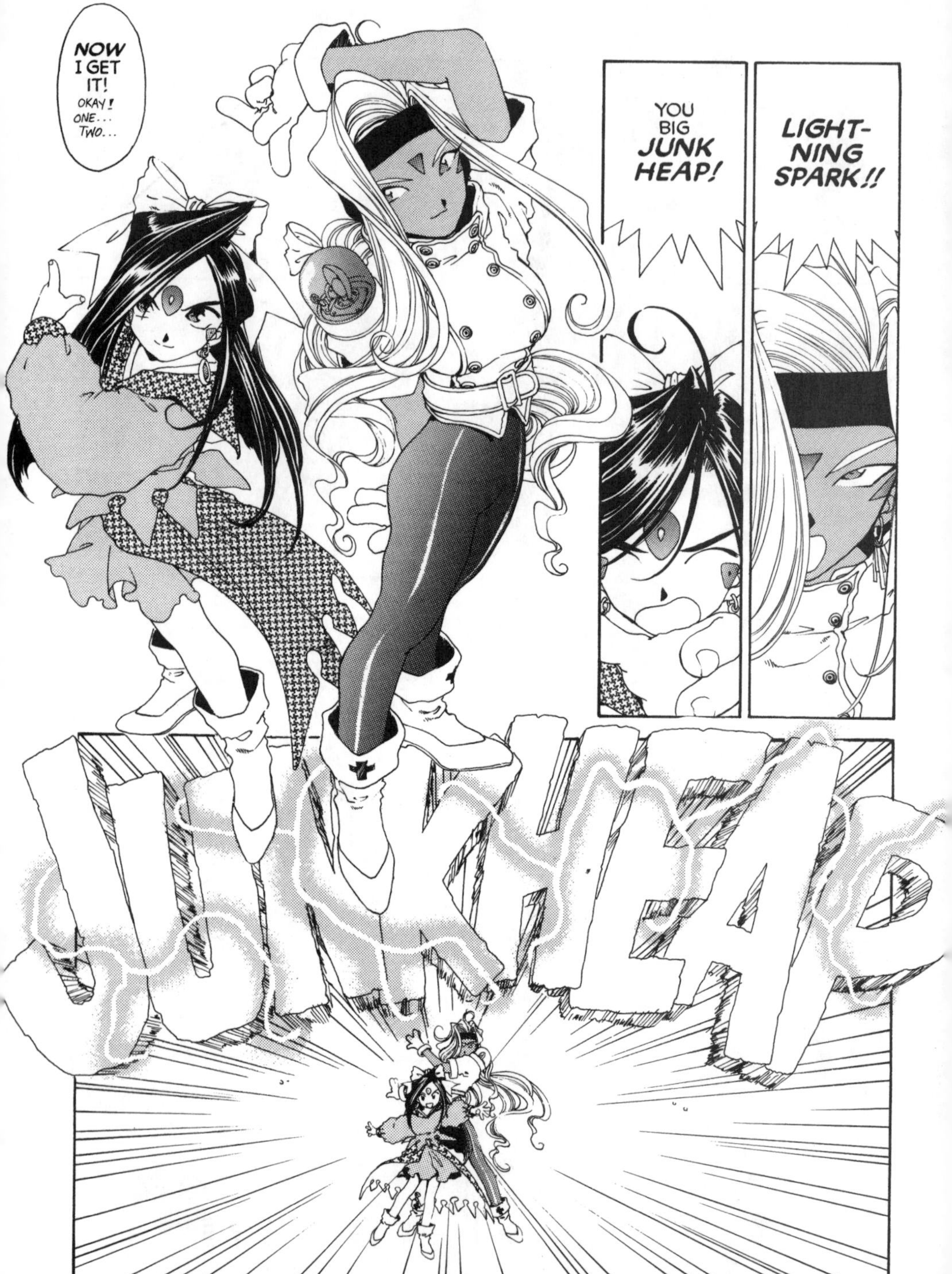
NOW I GET IT! OKAY! ONE... TWO...
YOU BIG JUNK HEAP!
LIGHT-NING SPARK!!

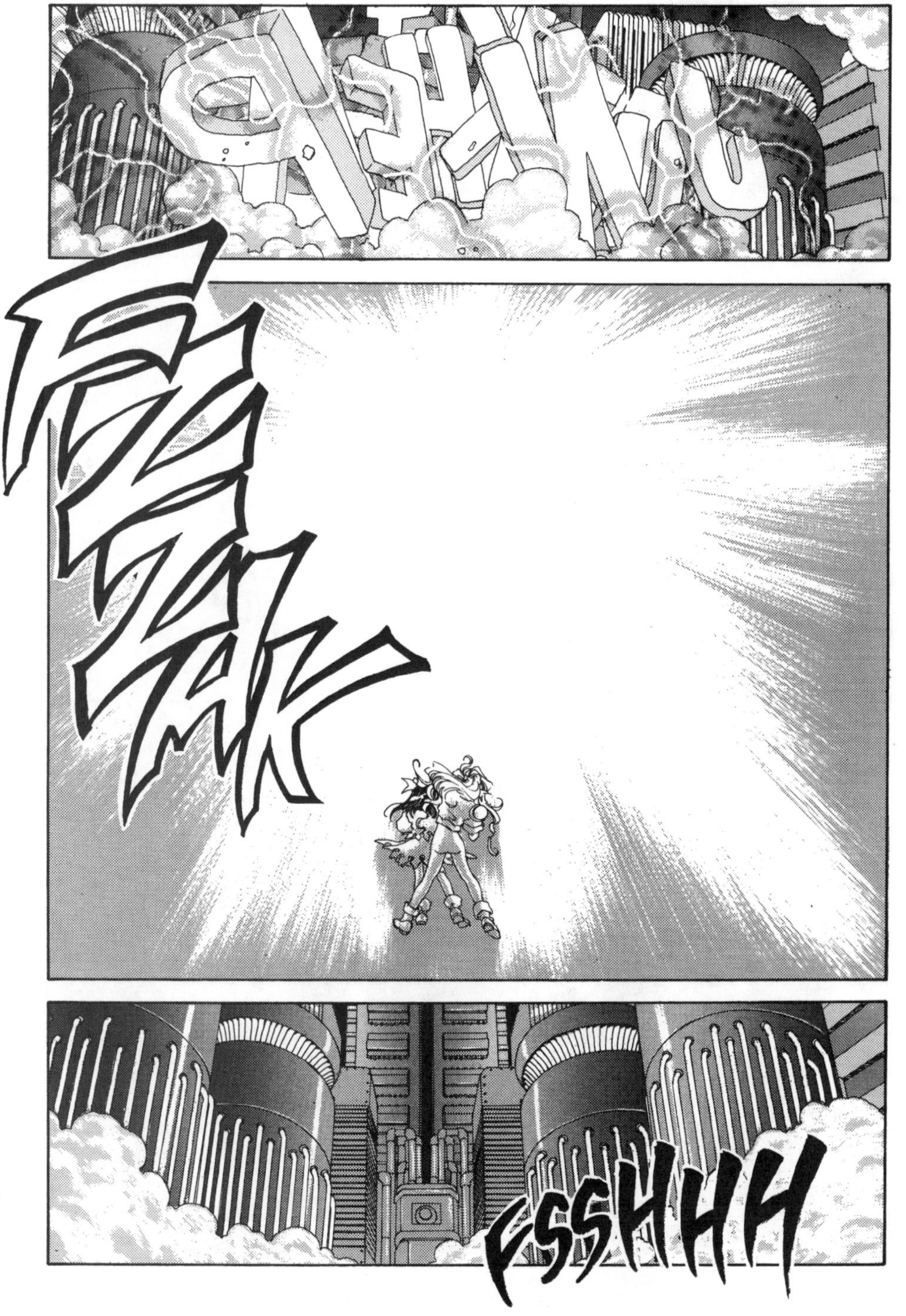
FZZZAK
FSSHHH

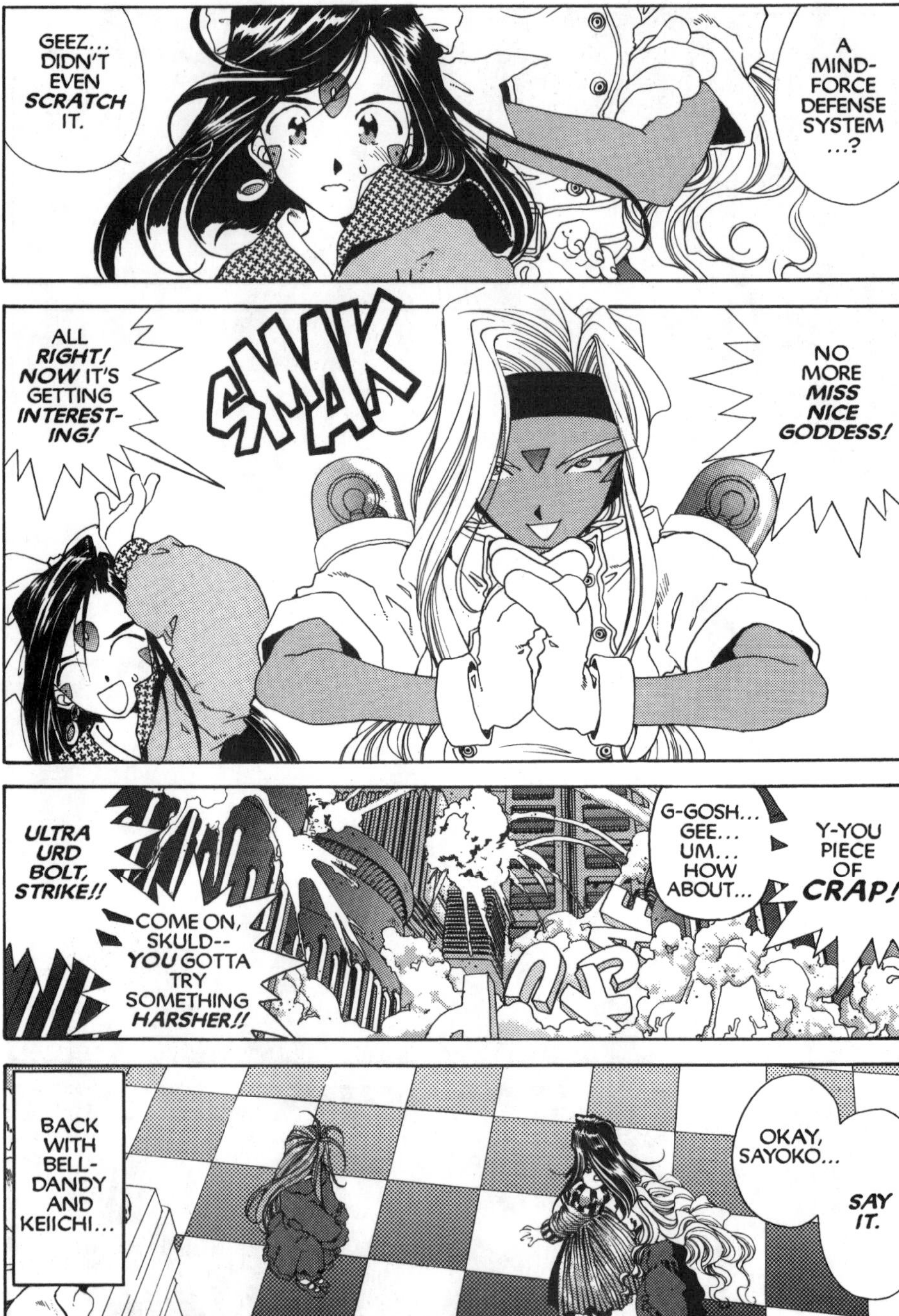
GEEZ... DIDN'T EVEN SCRATCH IT.
A MIND-FORCE DEFENSE SYSTEM ...?
ALL RIGHT! NOW IT'S GETTING INTERESTING!
SMAK
NO MORE MISS NICE GODDESS!
ULTRA URD BOLT, STRIKE!!
COME ON, SKULD-- YOU GOTTA TRY SOMETHING HARSHER!!
G-GOSH... GEE... UM... HOW ABOUT...
Y-YOU PIECE OF CRAP!
BACK WITH BELLDANDY AND KEIICHI...
OKAY, SAYOKO... SAY IT.

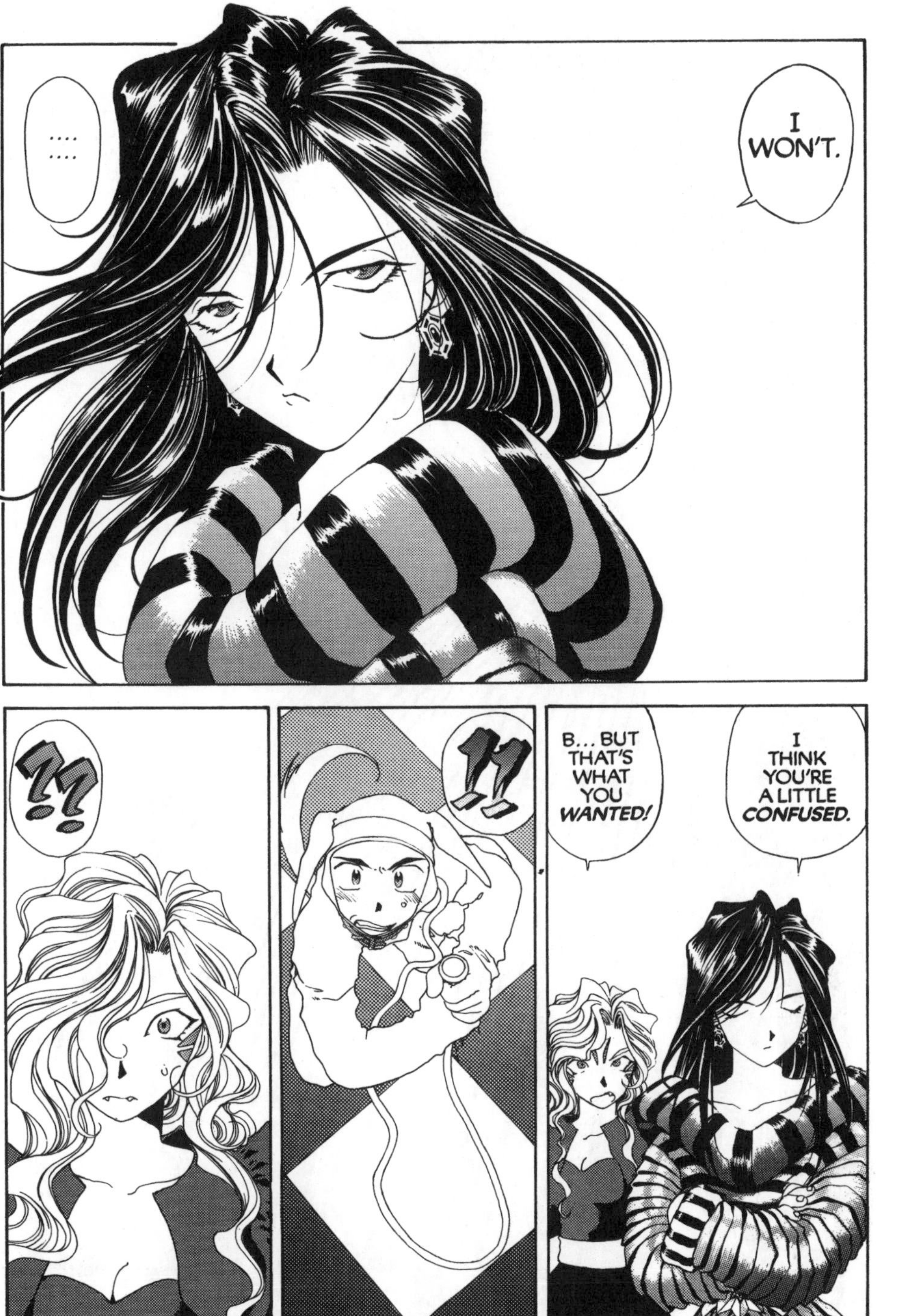

....
....
I WON'T.
B... BUT THAT'S WHAT YOU *WANTED!*
I THINK YOU'RE A LITTLE *CONFUSED.*

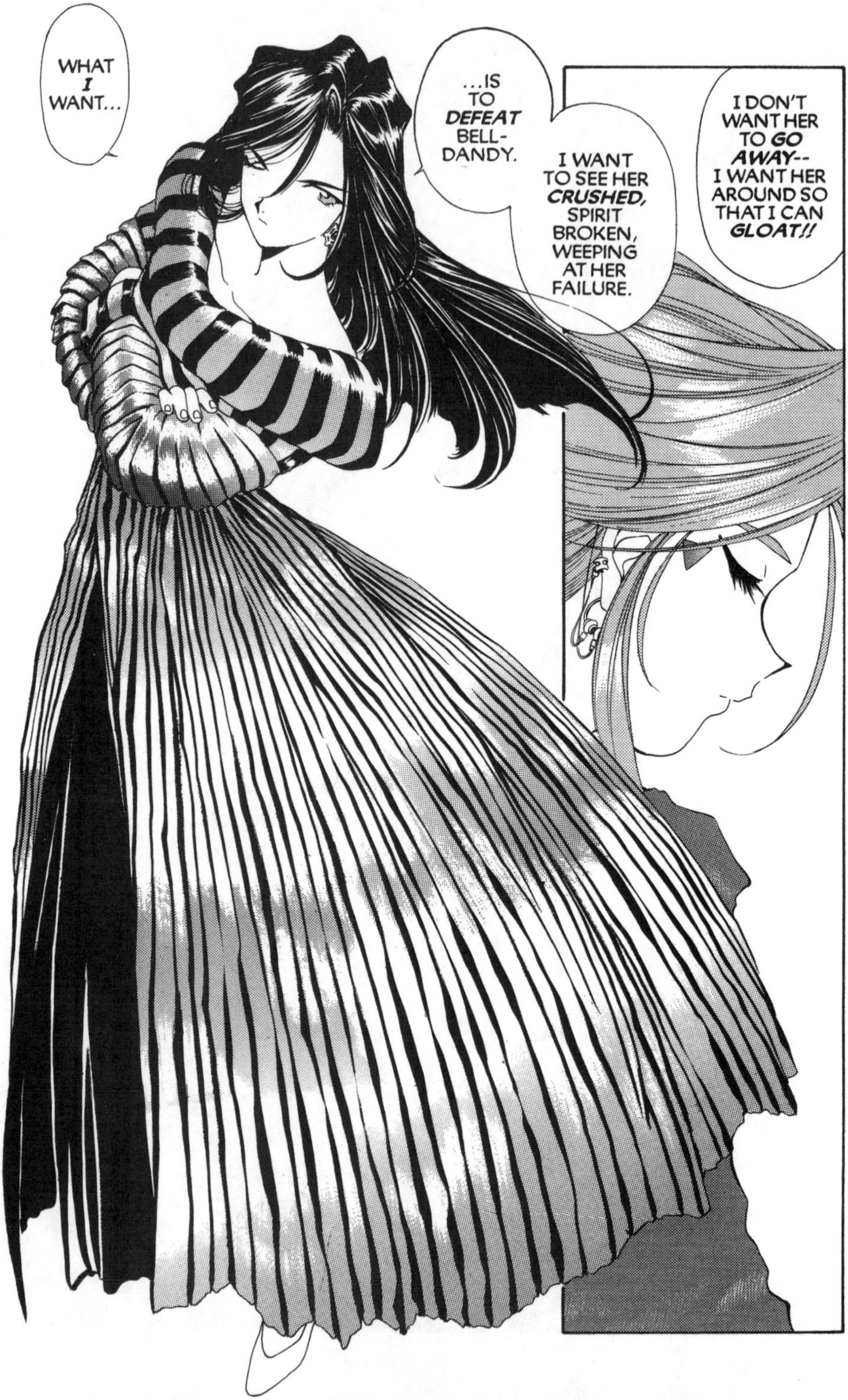
WHAT I WANT...
...IS TO DEFEAT BELL-DANDY.
I WANT TO SEE HER CRUSHED, SPIRIT BROKEN, WEEPING AT HER FAILURE.
I DON'T WANT HER TO GO AWAY-- I WANT HER AROUND SO THAT I CAN GLOAT!!

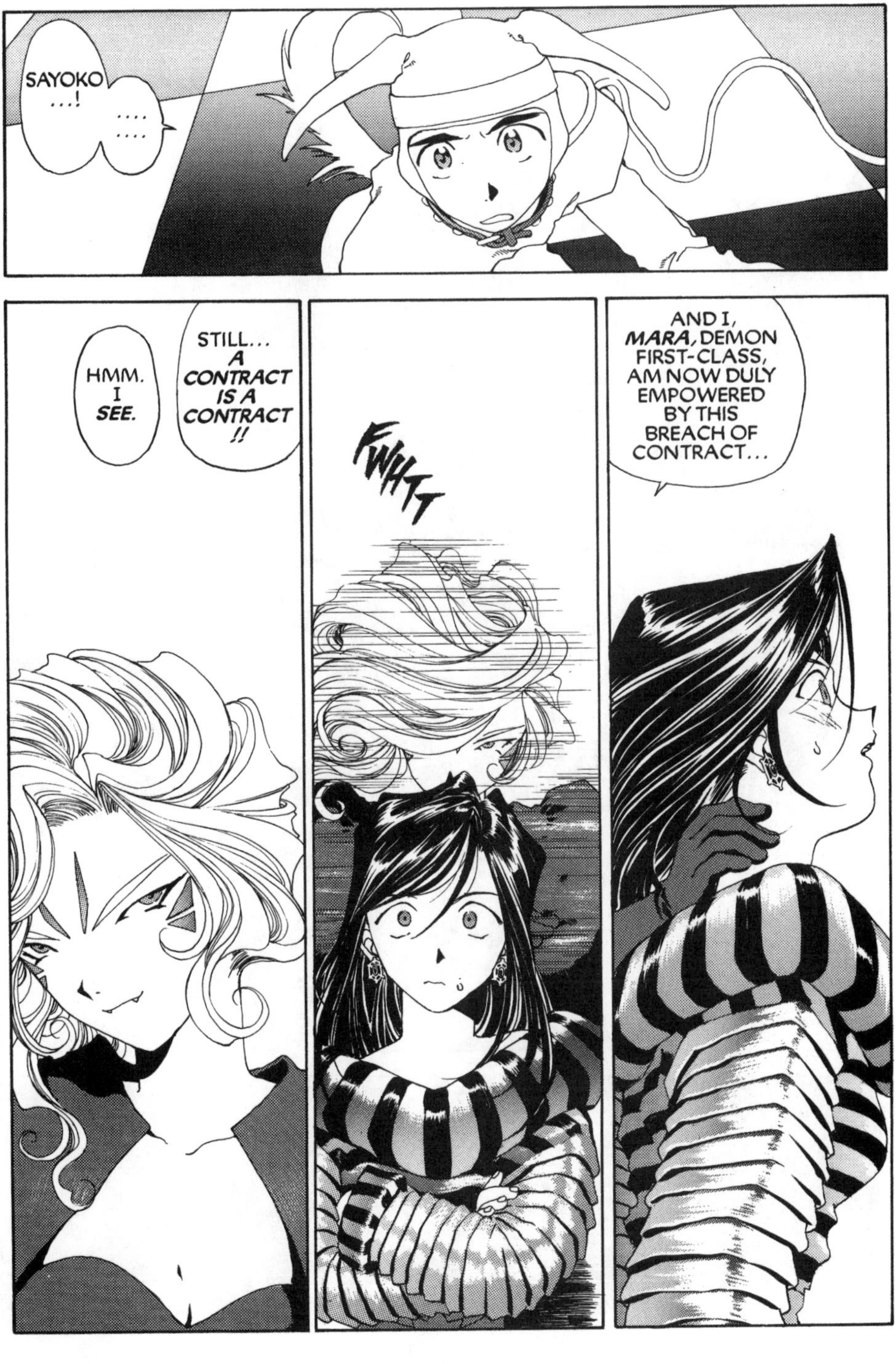
SAYOKO ...!
....
HMM. I SEE.
STILL... A CONTRACT IS A CONTRACT !!
FWHTT
AND I, MARA, DEMON FIRST-CLASS, AM NOW DULY EMPOWERED BY THIS BREACH OF CONTRACT...

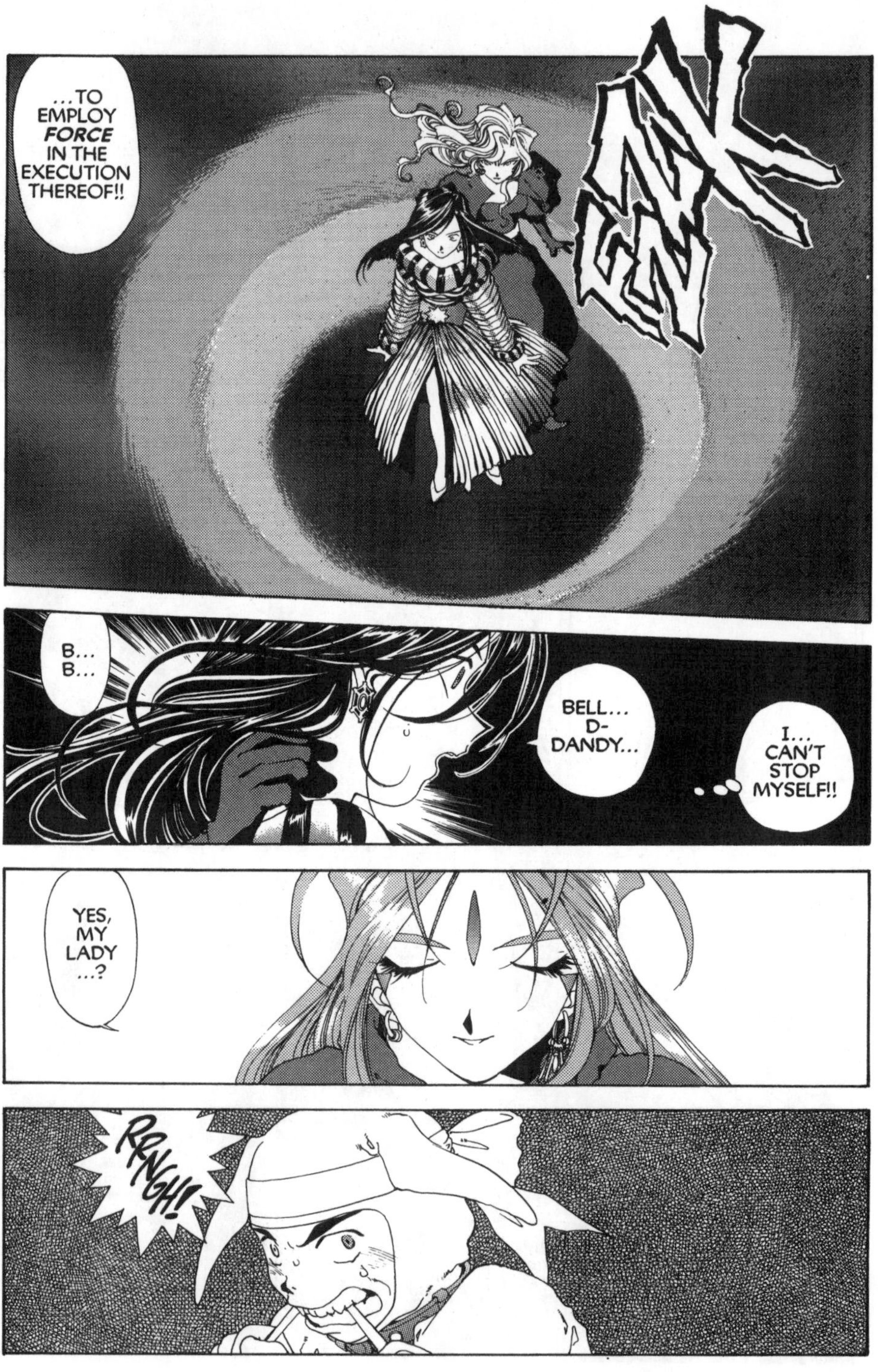
...TO EMPLOY FORCE IN THE EXECUTION THEREOF!!
B... B...
BELL... D-DANDY...
I... CAN'T STOP MYSELF!!
YES, MY LADY ...?
RRNGH!

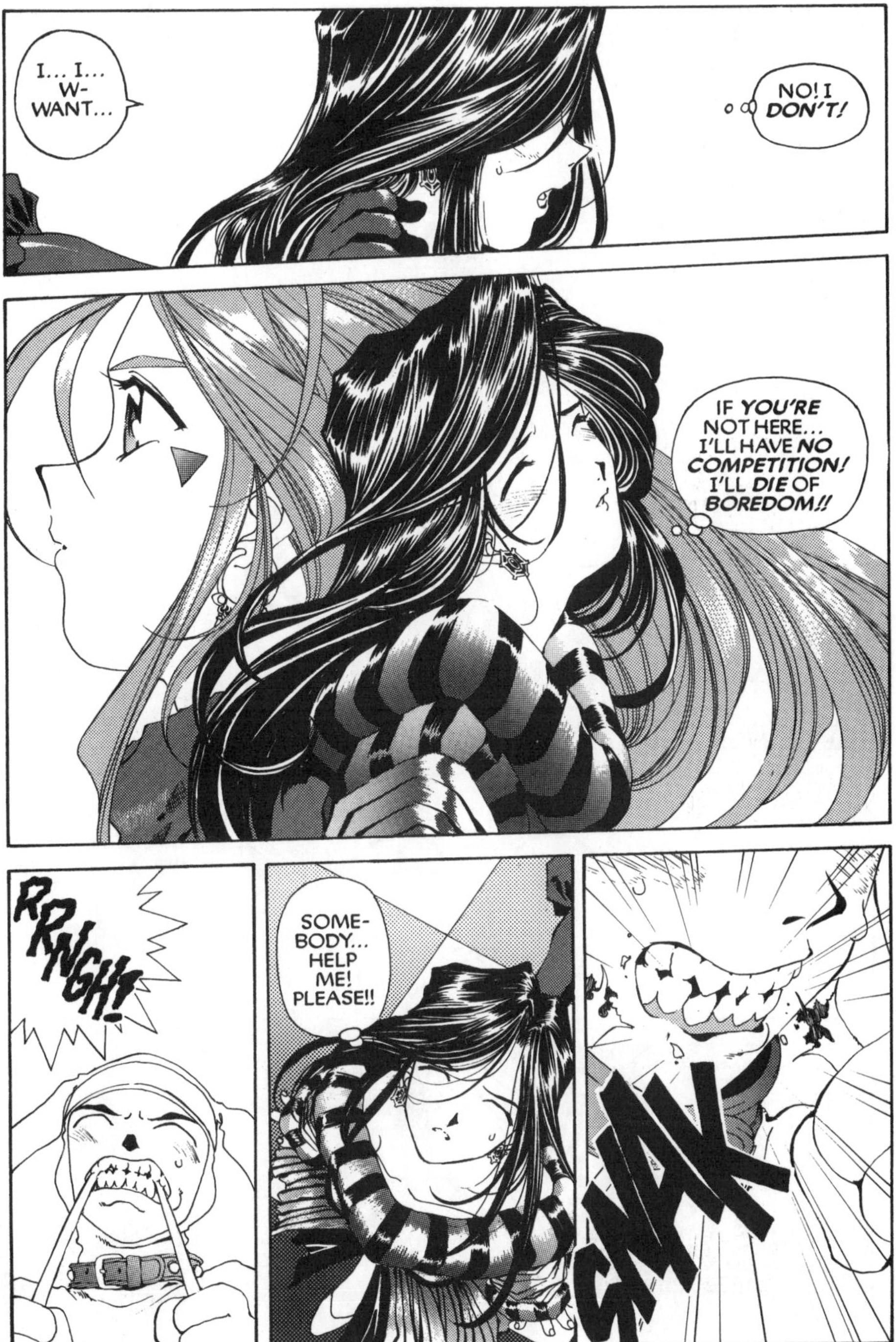
I... I... W-WANT...
NO! I DON'T!
IF YOU'RE NOT HERE... I'LL HAVE NO COMPETITION! I'LL DIE OF BOREDOM!!
RRNGH!
SOMEBODY... HELP ME! PLEASE!!
SMAK

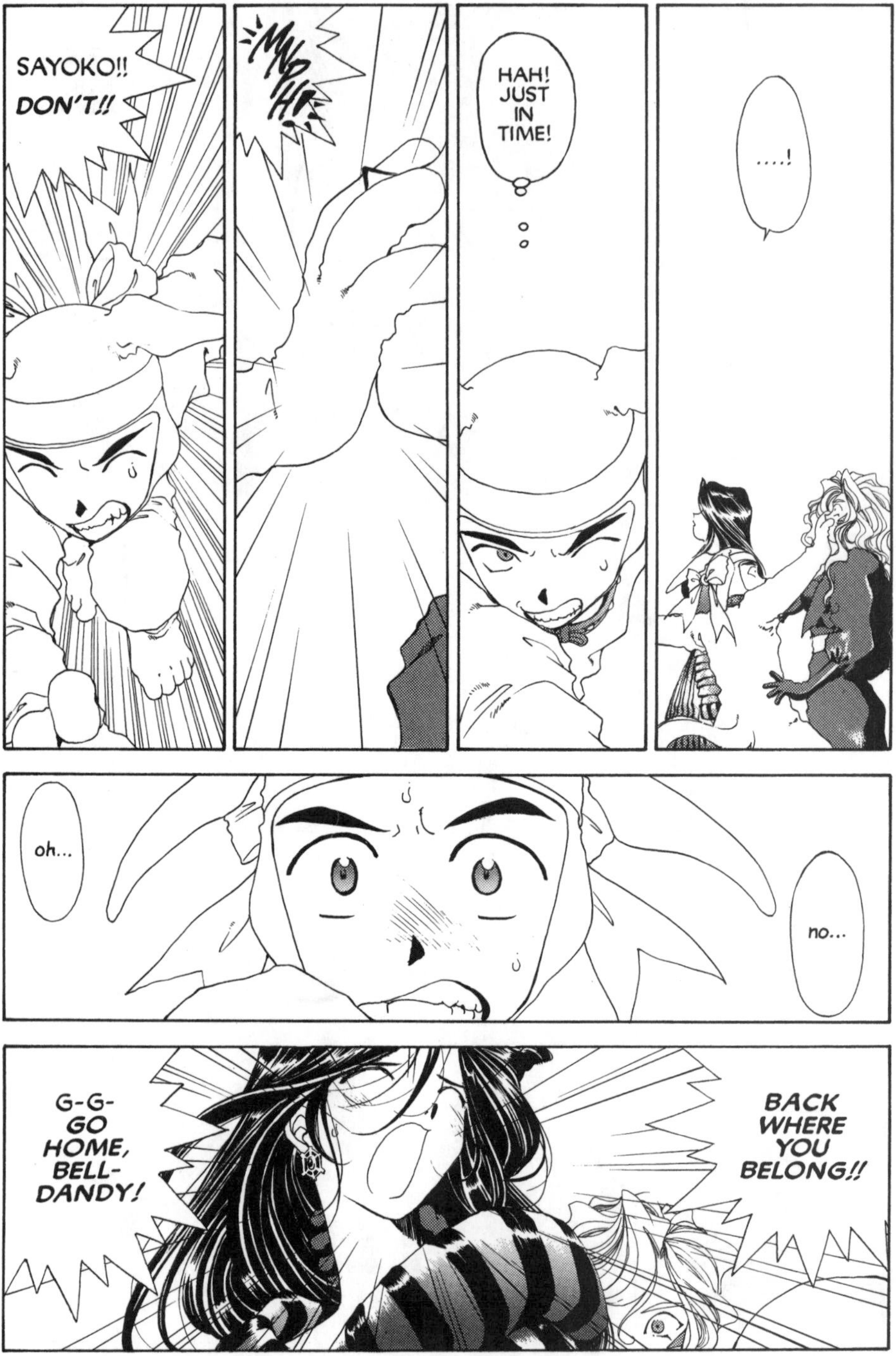
SAYOKO!! DON'T!!
MNGH!
HAH! JUST IN TIME!
....!
oh...
no...
G-G-GO HOME, BELL-DANDY!
BACK WHERE YOU BELONG!!

MY LADY!

AS YOU COMMAND!

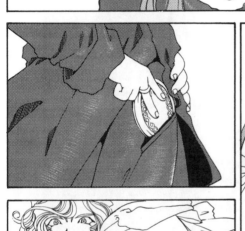

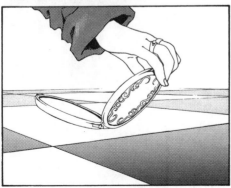

"WHEN THE TIME COMES, YOU'LL HELP ME-- RIGHT?"

DARN RIGHT! AND THERE'S STILL ONE CHANCE!!

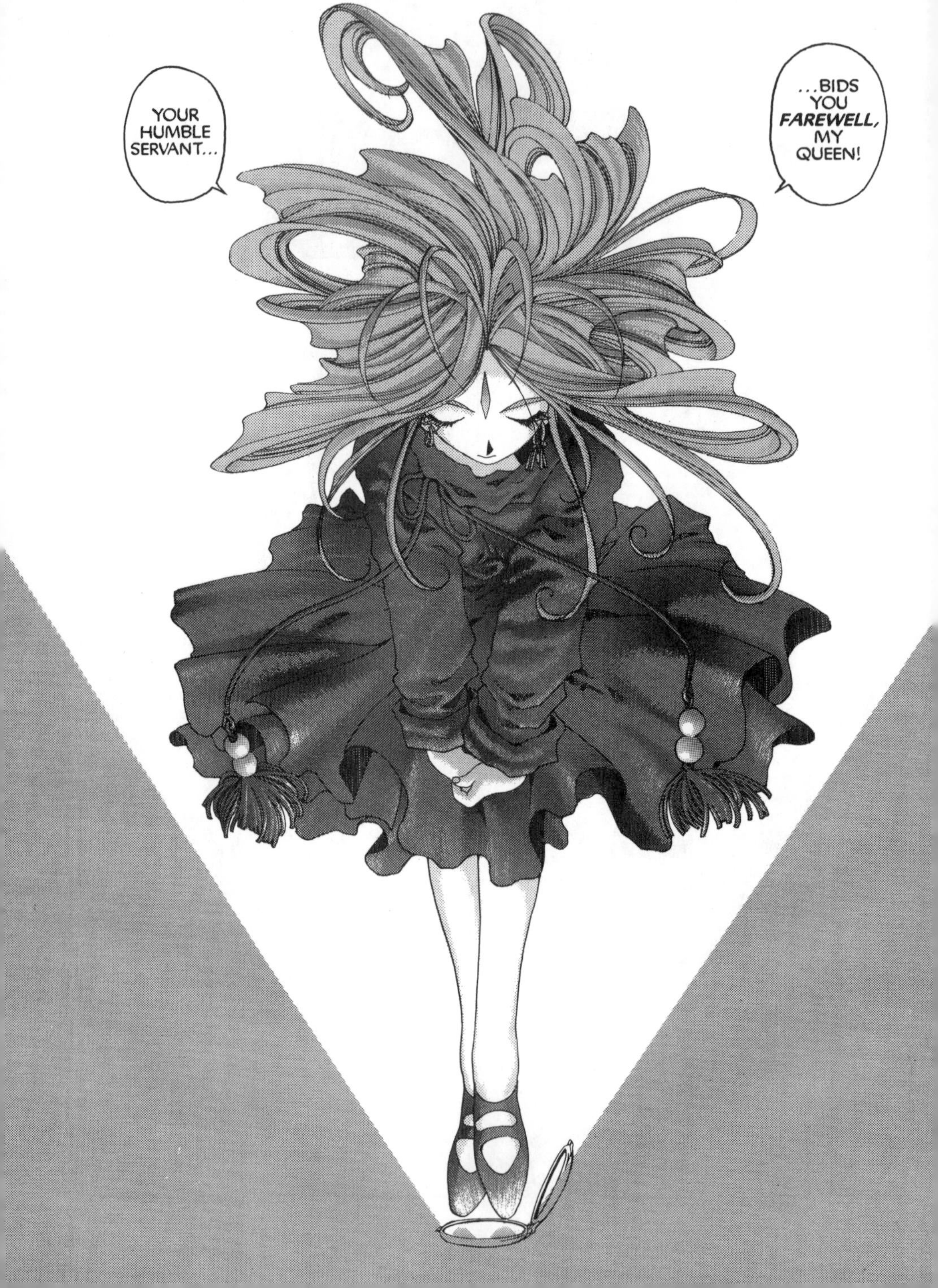
YOUR HUMBLE SERVANT...
...BIDS YOU *FAREWELL,* MY QUEEN!

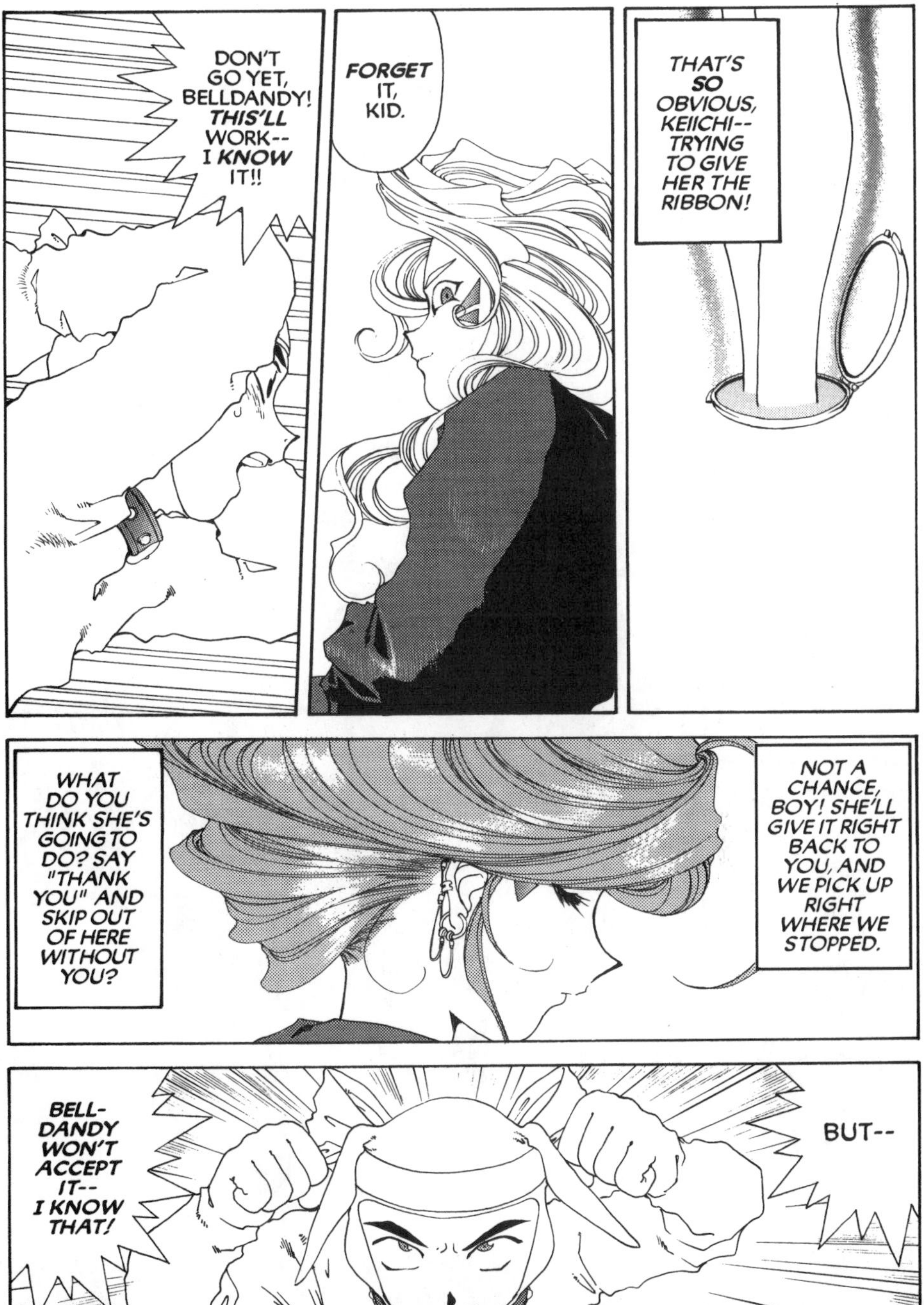
DON'T GO YET, BELLDANDY! THIS'LL WORK-- I KNOW IT!!
FORGET IT, KID.
THAT'S SO OBVIOUS, KEIICHI-- TRYING TO GIVE HER THE RIBBON!
WHAT DO YOU THINK SHE'S GOING TO DO? SAY "THANK YOU" AND SKIP OUT OF HERE WITHOUT YOU?
NOT A CHANCE, BOY! SHE'LL GIVE IT RIGHT BACK TO YOU, AND WE PICK UP RIGHT WHERE WE STOPPED.
BELL-DANDY WON'T ACCEPT IT-- I KNOW THAT!
BUT--

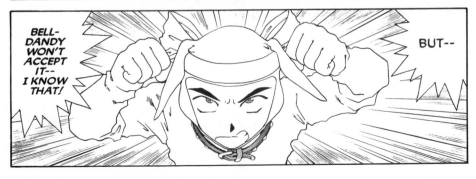

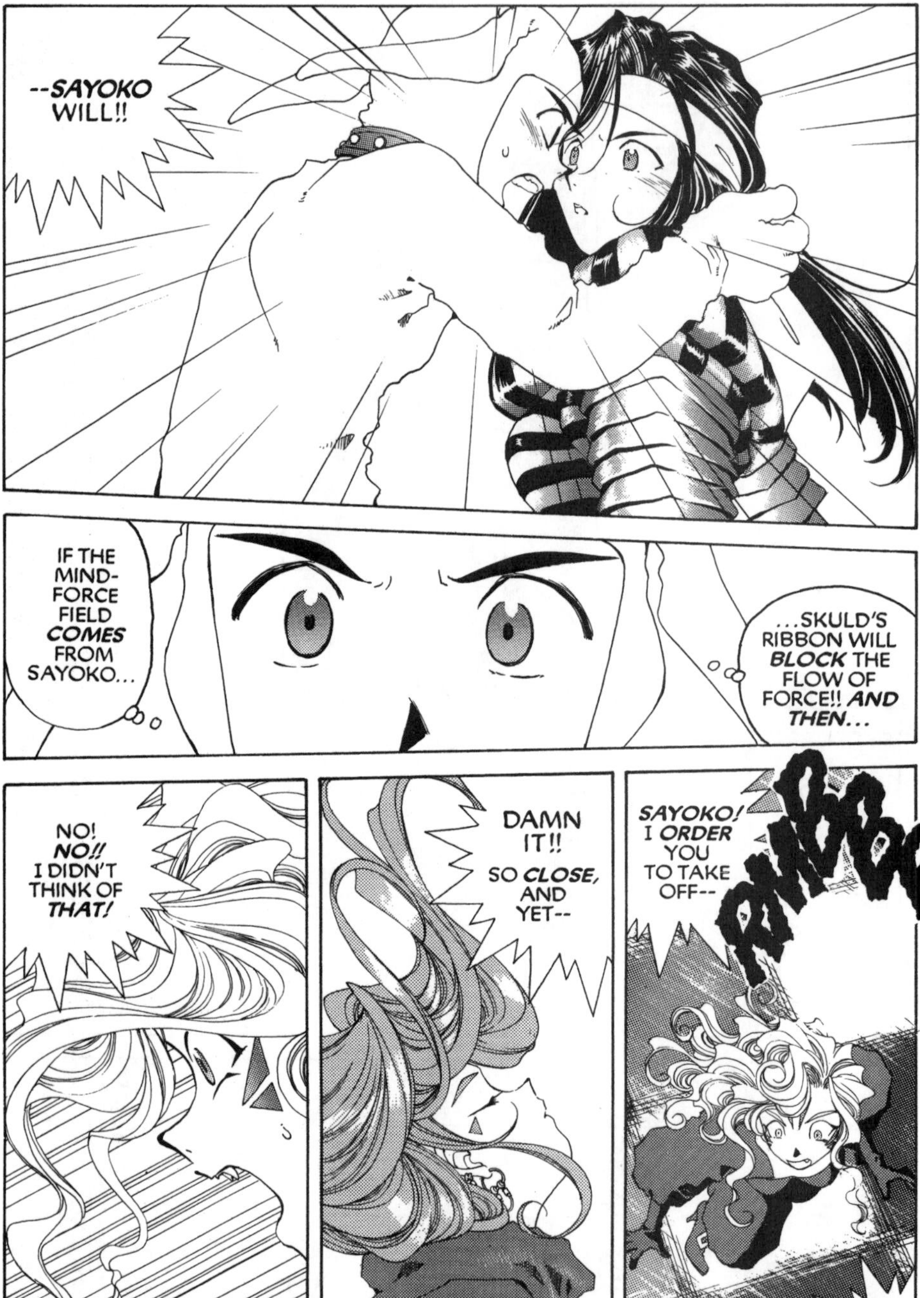
--SAYOKO WILL!!
IF THE MIND-FORCE FIELD COMES FROM SAYOKO...
...SKULD'S RIBBON WILL BLOCK THE FLOW OF FORCE!! AND THEN...
NO! NO!! I DIDN'T THINK OF THAT!
DAMN IT!! SO CLOSE, AND YET--
SAYOKO! I ORDER YOU TO TAKE OFF--
RRRBBB
??

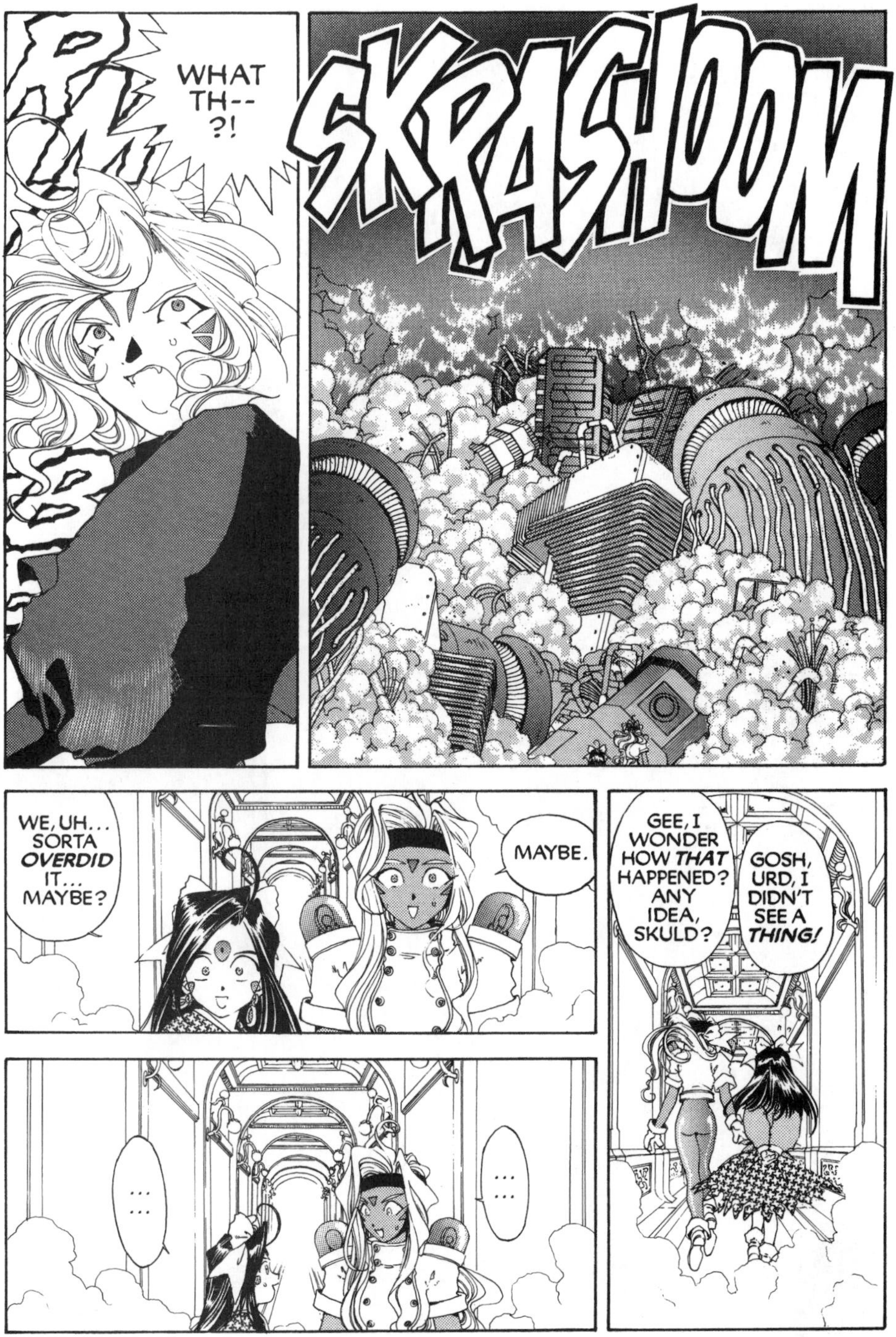
WHAT TH-- ?!
SKRASHOOM
WE, UH... SORTA *OVERDID* IT... MAYBE?
MAYBE.
... ...
... ...
GEE, I WONDER HOW *THAT* HAPPENED? ANY IDEA, SKULD?
GOSH, URD, I DIDN'T SEE A *THING!*

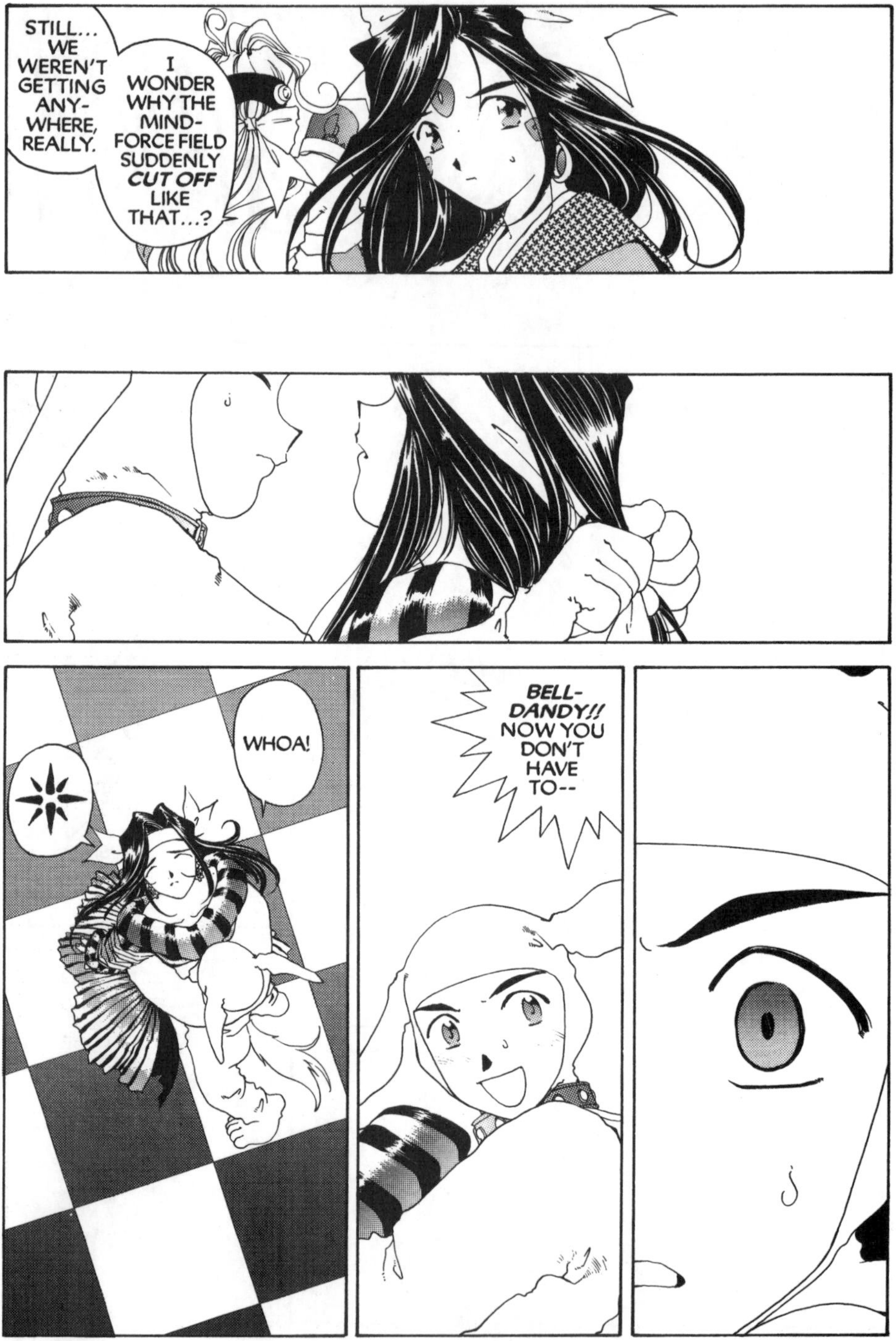
STILL... WE WEREN'T GETTING ANY-WHERE, REALLY.
I WONDER WHY THE MIND-FORCE FIELD SUDDENLY *CUT OFF* LIKE THAT...?
WHOA!
BELL-DANDY!! NOW YOU DON'T HAVE TO--

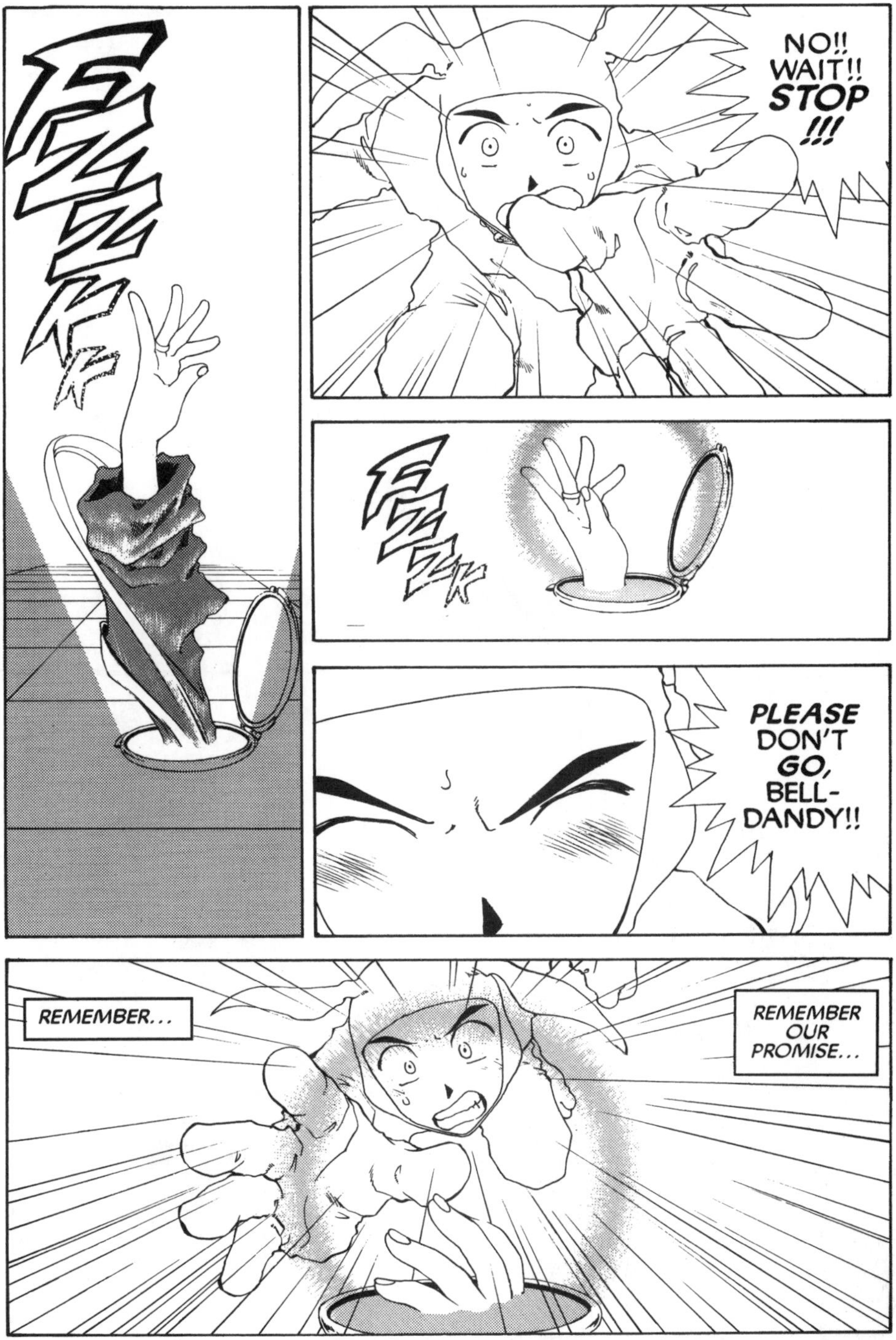
FZZZKK
NO!! WAIT!! STOP!!!
FZZK
PLEASE DON'T GO, BELL-DANDY!!
REMEMBER...
REMEMBER OUR PROMISE...

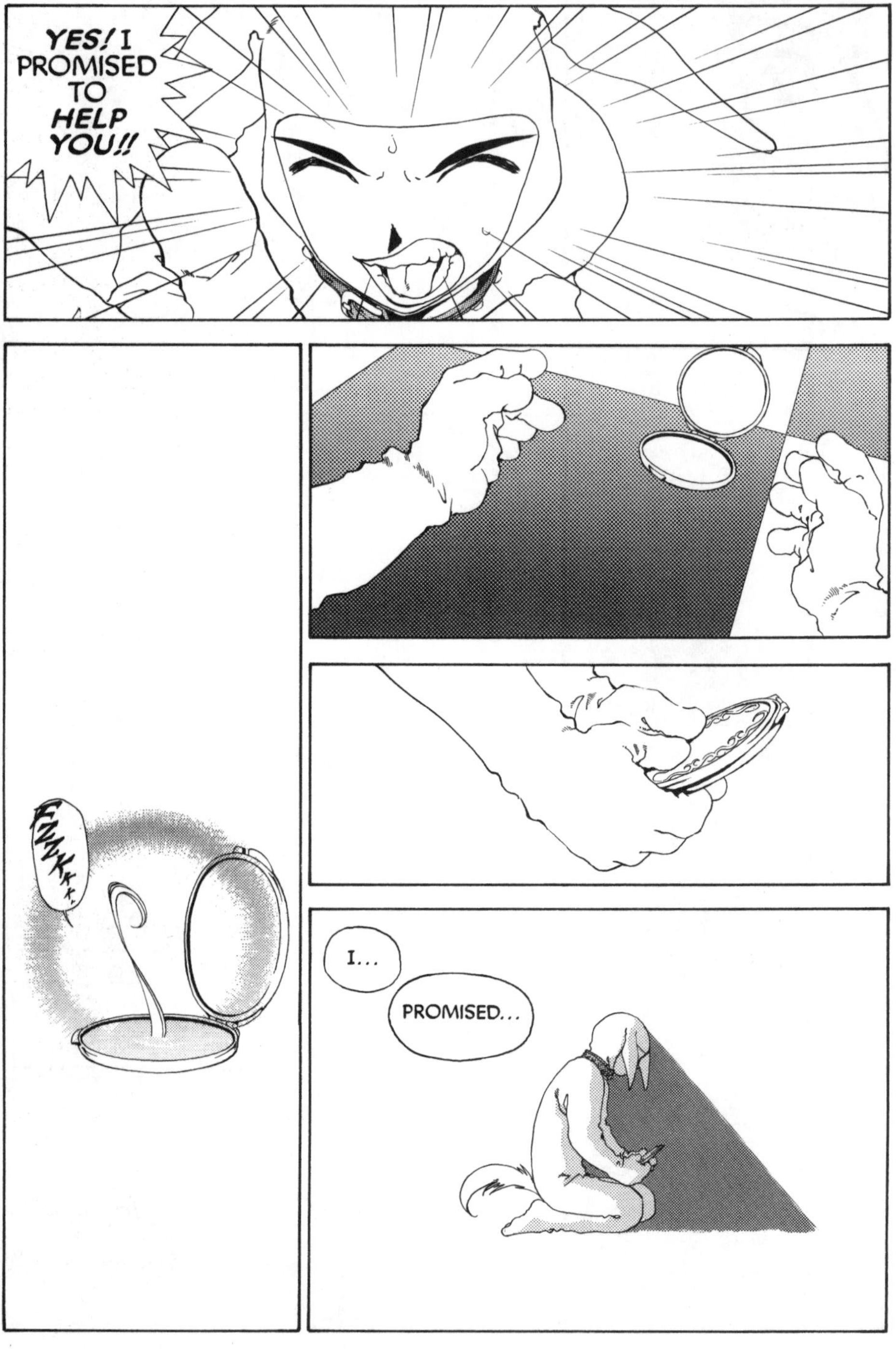
YES! I PROMISED TO HELP YOU!!
FZZKKK
I...
PROMISED...

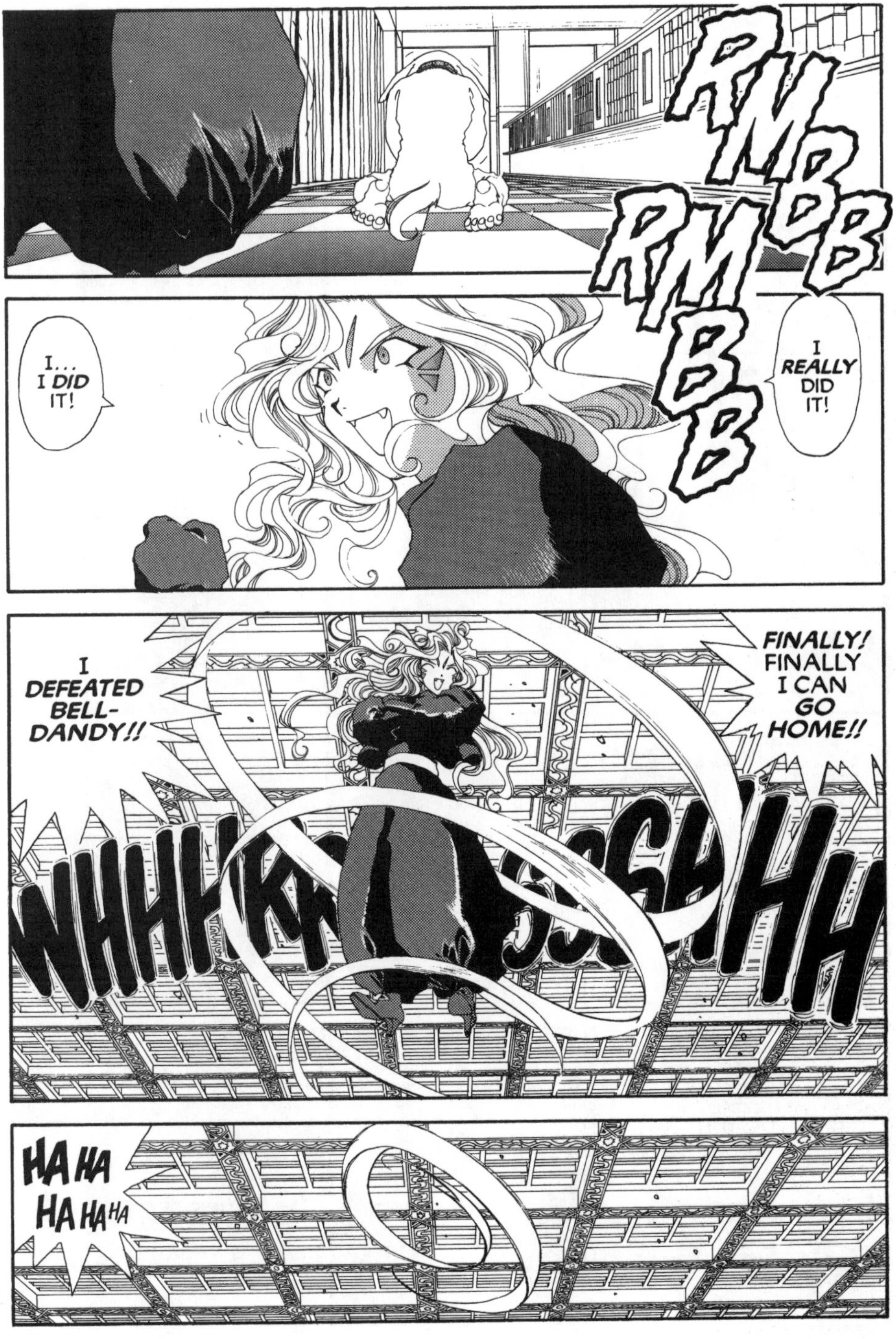
RMBB RMBBB
I... I DID IT!
I REALLY DID IT!
I DEFEATED BELL-DANDY!!
FINALLY! FINALLY I CAN GO HOME!!
WHHHRRRSSSCHHH
HA HA HA HA HA

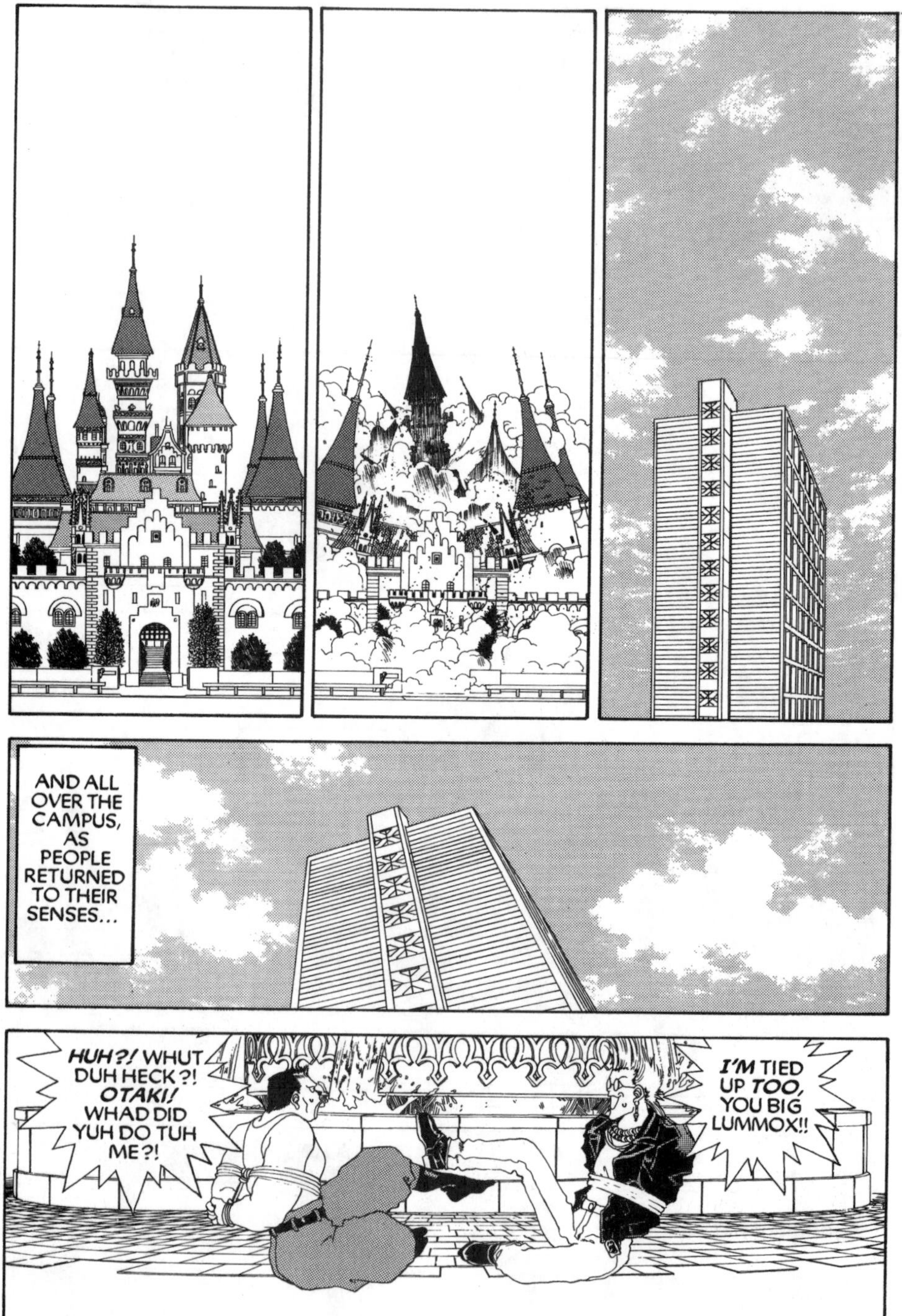
AND ALL OVER THE CAMPUS, AS PEOPLE RETURNED TO THEIR SENSES...
HUH?! WHUT DUH HECK?! OTAKI! WHAD DID YUH DO TUH ME?!
I'M TIED UP TOO, YOU BIG LUMMOX!!

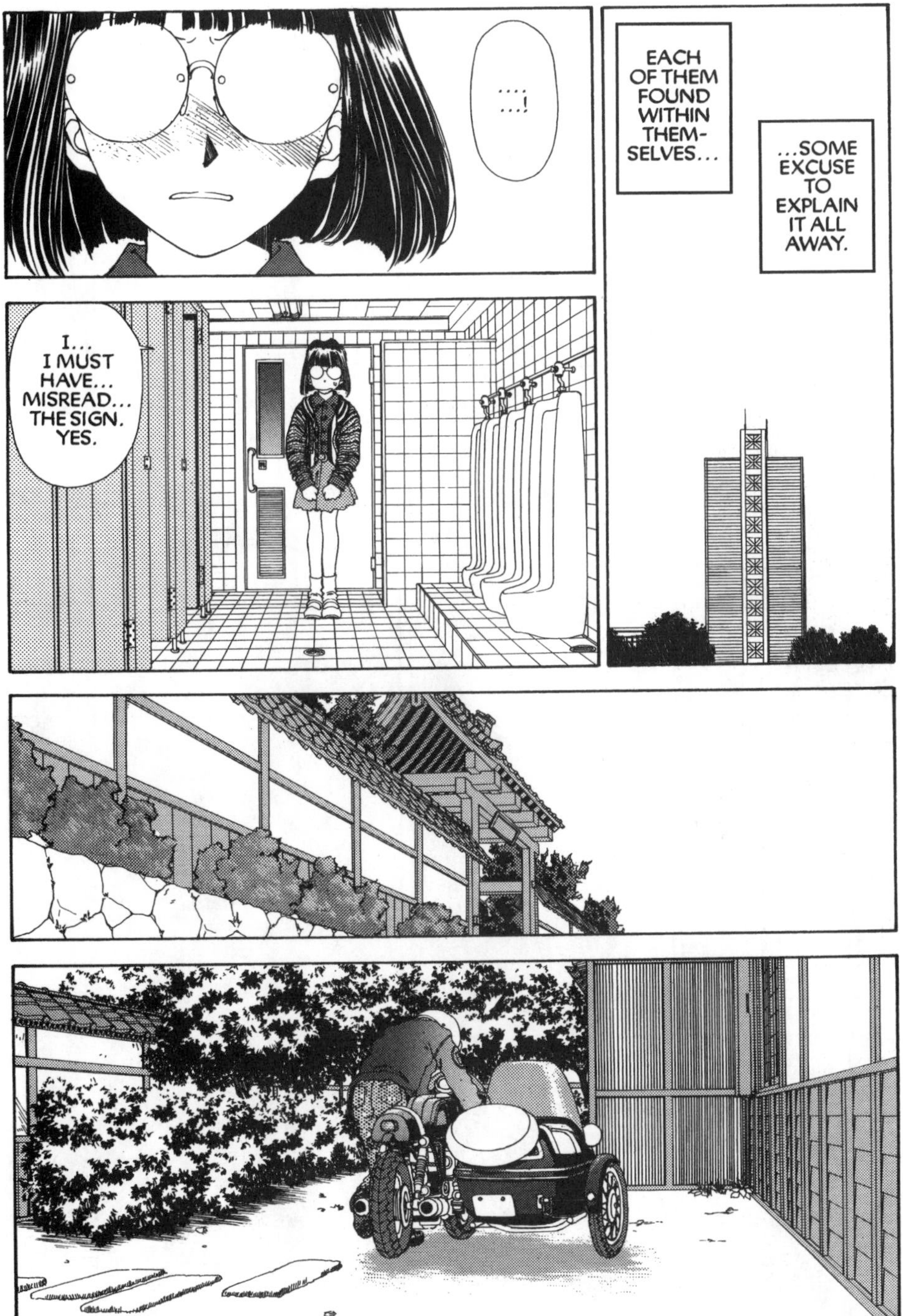
……!
I… I MUST HAVE… MISREAD… THE SIGN. YES.
EACH OF THEM FOUND WITHIN THEM-SELVES…
…SOME EXCUSE TO EXPLAIN IT ALL AWAY.

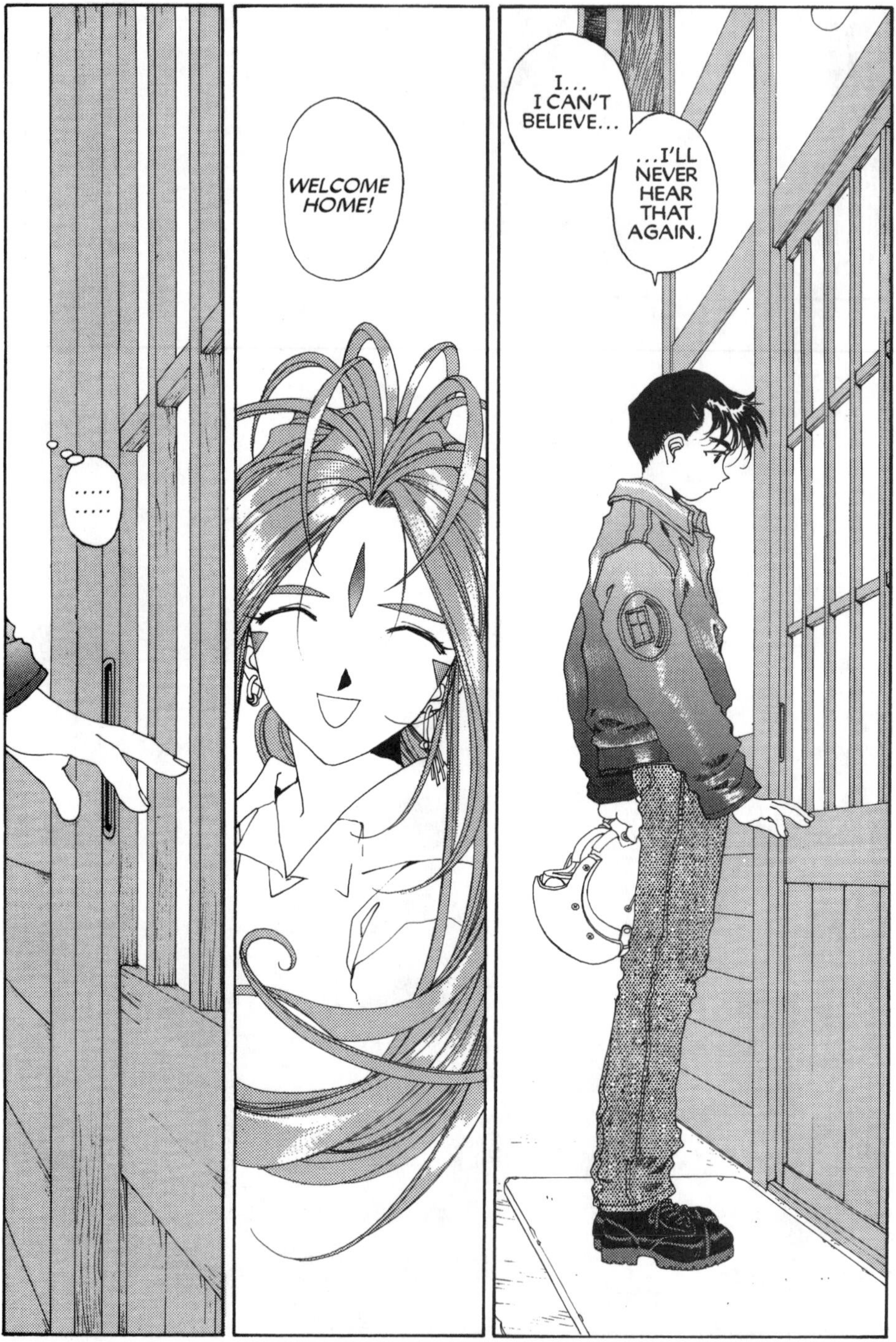
......
......
WELCOME HOME!
I... I CAN'T BELIEVE...
...I'LL NEVER HEAR THAT AGAIN.

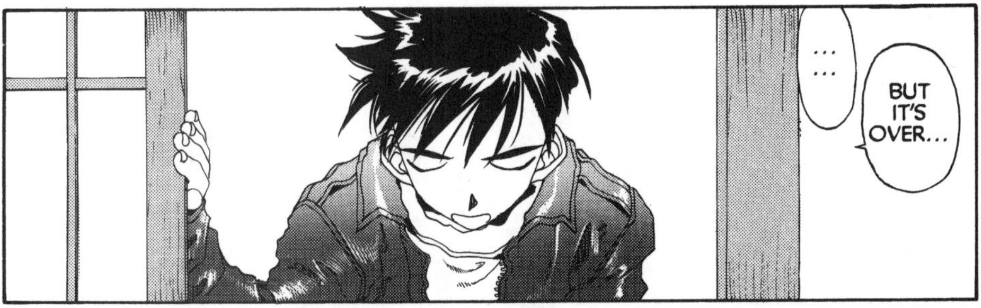
...
...
BUT IT'S OVER...

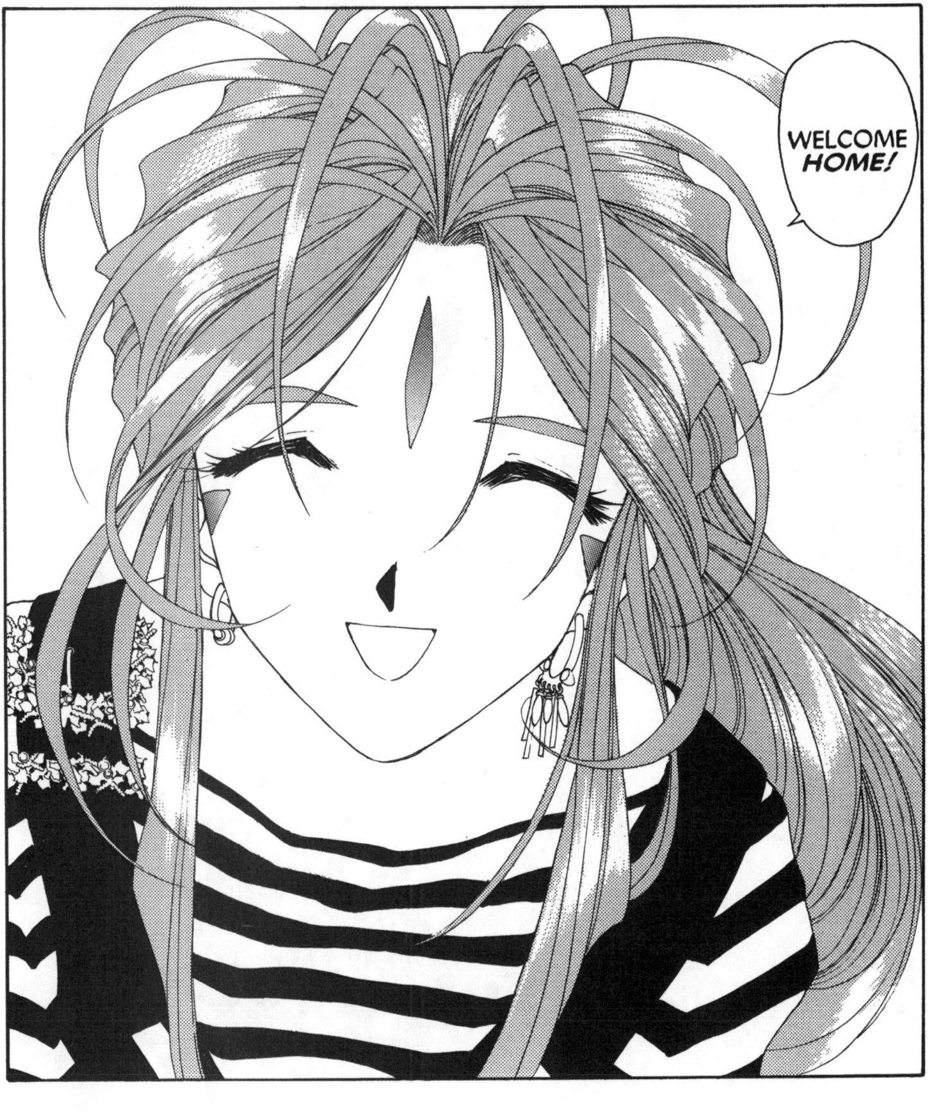
WELCOME HOME!

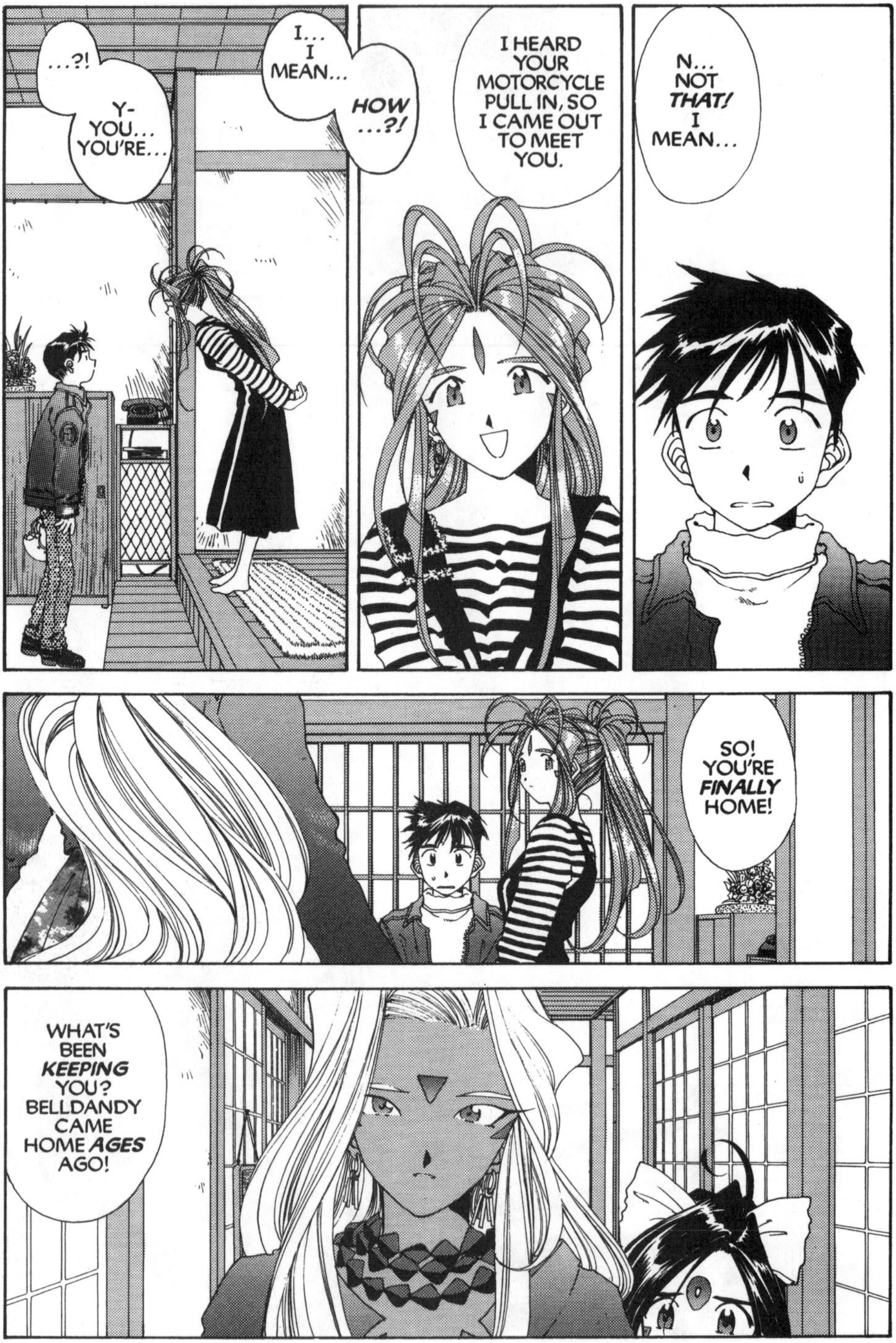
...?!
Y- YOU... YOU'RE...
I... I MEAN... *HOW* ...?!
I HEARD YOUR MOTORCYCLE PULL IN, SO I CAME OUT TO MEET YOU.
N... NOT *THAT!* I MEAN...
SO! YOU'RE *FINALLY* HOME!
WHAT'S BEEN *KEEPING* YOU? BELLDANDY CAME HOME *AGES* AGO!

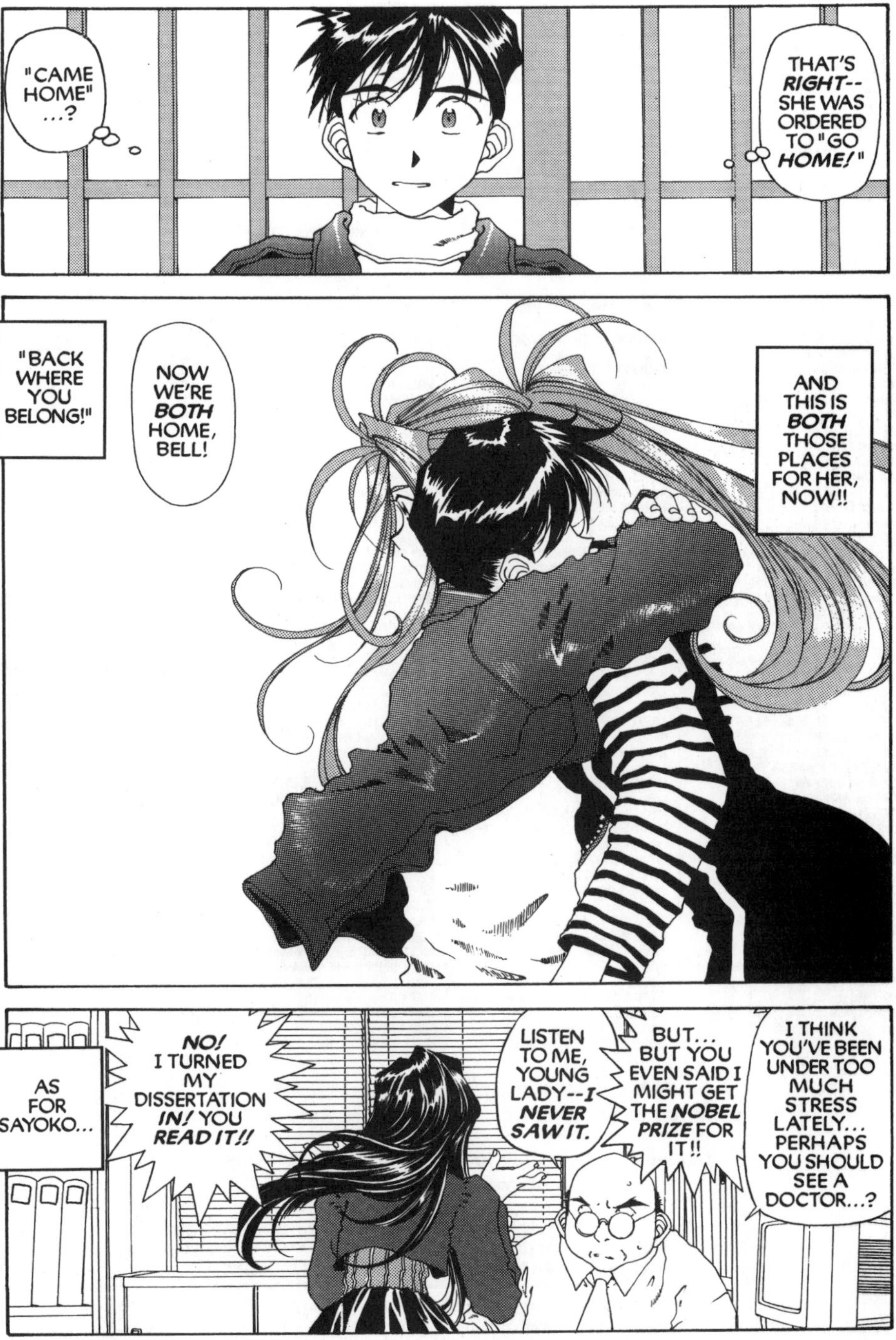
"CAME HOME" ...?
THAT'S RIGHT-- SHE WAS ORDERED TO "GO HOME!"
"BACK WHERE YOU BELONG!"
NOW WE'RE BOTH HOME, BELL!
AND THIS IS BOTH THOSE PLACES FOR HER, NOW!!
AS FOR SAYOKO...
NO! I TURNED MY DISSERTATION IN! YOU READ IT!!
LISTEN TO ME, YOUNG LADY--I NEVER SAW IT.
BUT... BUT YOU EVEN SAID I MIGHT GET THE NOBEL PRIZE FOR IT!!
I THINK YOU'VE BEEN UNDER TOO MUCH STRESS LATELY... PERHAPS YOU SHOULD SEE A DOCTOR...?